D1555377

THE BURDENS OF SURVIVAL

DAVID C. STAHL

THE BURDENS OF SURVIVAL

ŌOKA SHŌHEI'S WRITINGS ON THE PACIFIC WAR

UNIVERSITY OF HAWAI'I PRESS
HONOLULU

Printed in the United States of America
08 07 06 05 04 03 6 5 4 3 2 1

Library of Congress Cataloging-in-Publication Data
Stahl, David C.
The burdens of survival : Ooka Shohei's writings on the Pacific war / David C. Stahl.
p. cm.
Includes bibliographical references and index.
ISBN 0-8248-2540-3 (cloth: alk. paper)
1. Ōoka, Shōhei, 1909—Criticism and interpretation. 2. World War, 1939–1945—Literature and the war. I. Title.
PL835.O5 Z88 2003
895.6'35—dc21 2002012309

Cartography by Bradley Corr

University of Hawai'i Press books are printed on acid-free paper and meet the guidelines for permanence and durability of the Council on Library Resources.

Designed by Trina Stahl
Printed by The Maple-Vail Book Manufacturing Group

"Our memory repeats to us what we haven't yet come to terms with, what still haunts us."

Kai Erikson

~~~

"Man is the being who is capable of becoming guilty and is capable of illuminating his guilt."

Martin Buber

~~~

"Without a working-through of guilt, however belated, there [can] be no work of mourning."

Alexander and Margarete Mitscherlich

~~~

"And it's carrying through that responsibility [to the dead] via one's witness, that survivor mission, that enables one to be an integrated human being once more."

Robert Jay Lifton
~~~

Contents

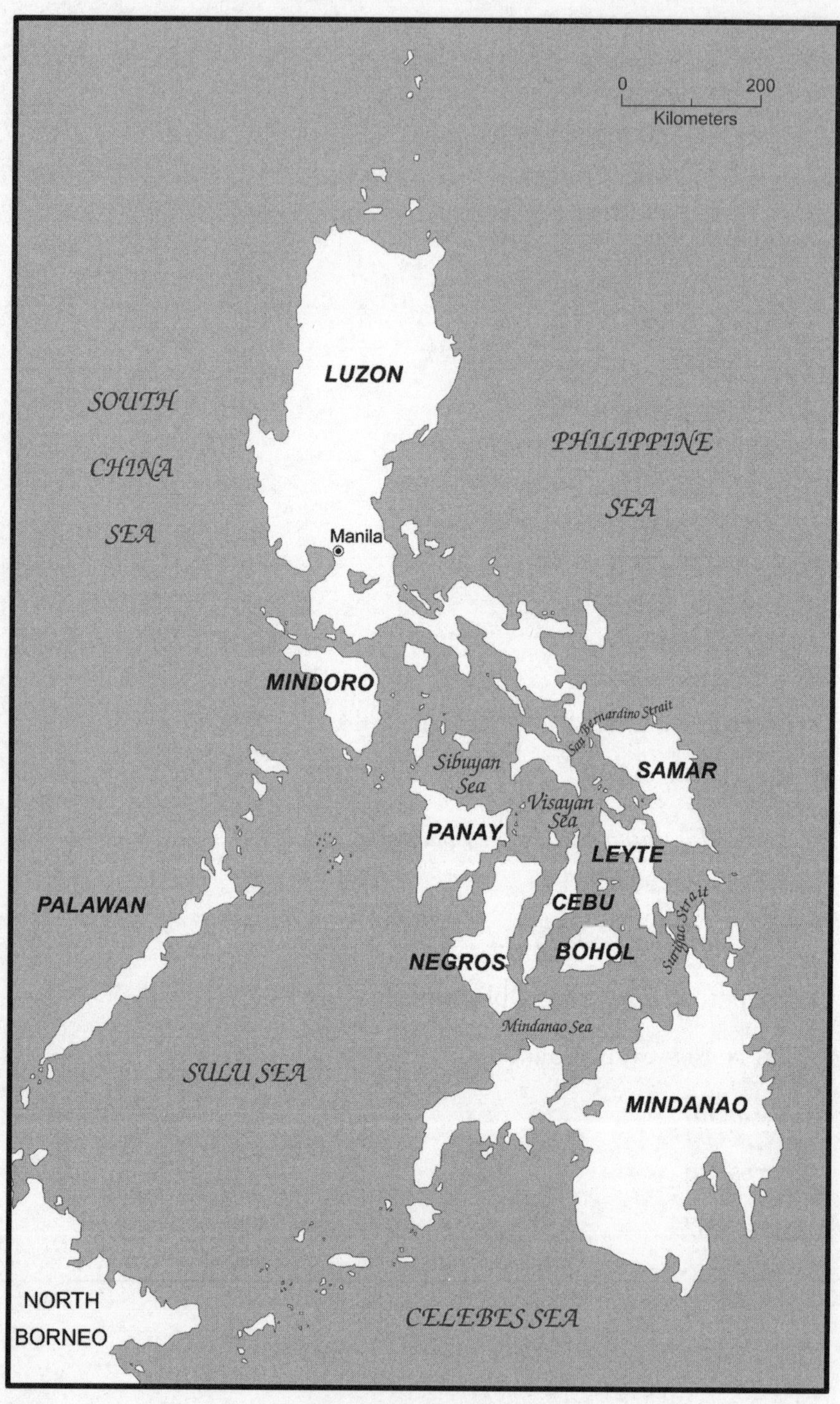

Map 1. The Philippines

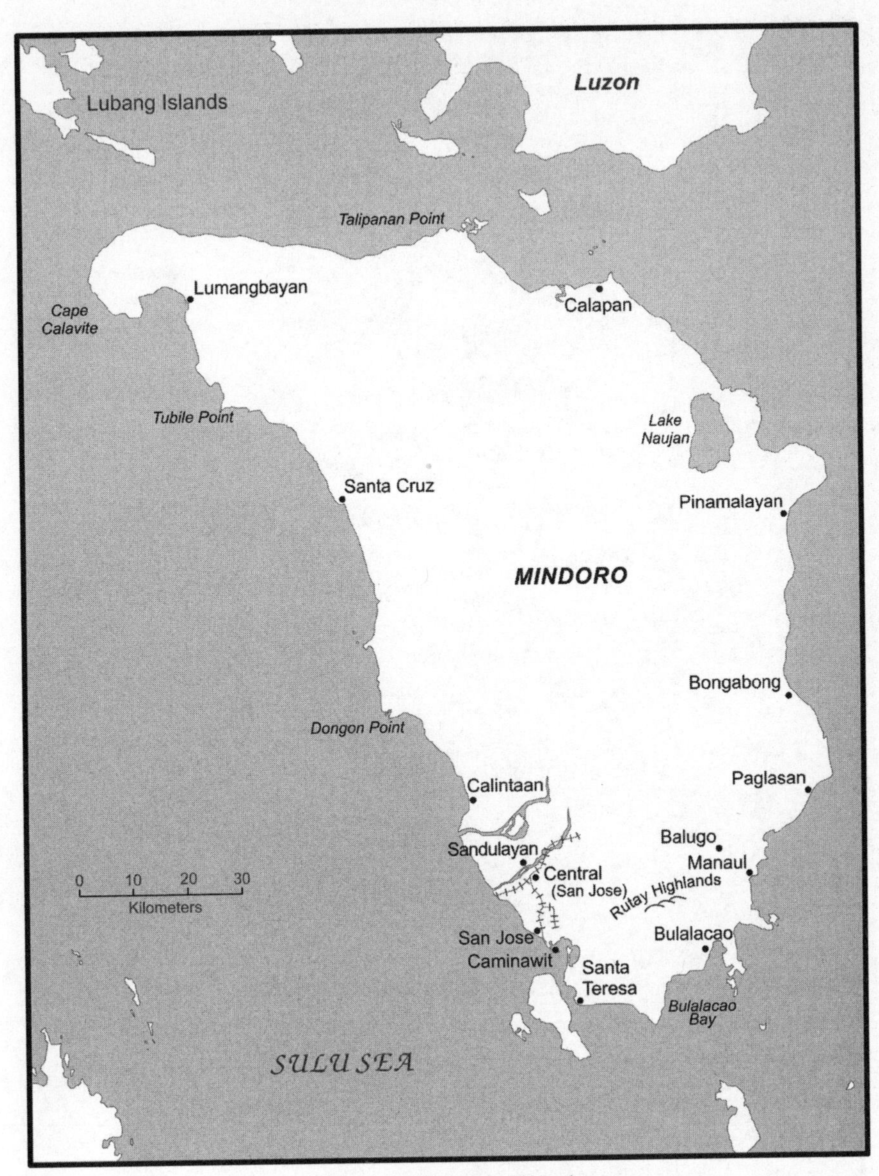

Map 2. Mindoro Island

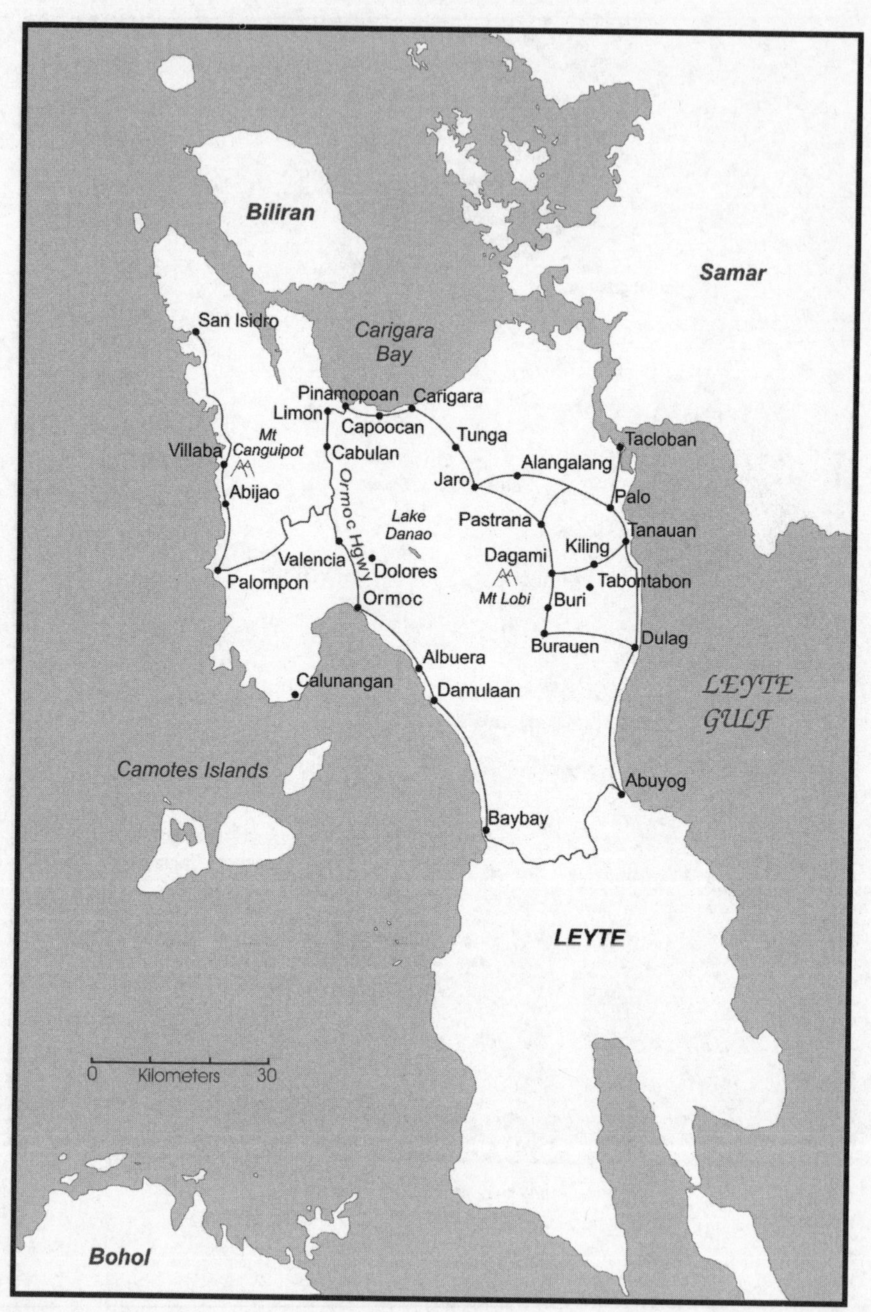

Map 3. Leyte Island

Introduction

The burdens of survival are many, varied, and overwhelming. This is particularly true of survival in war. Veterans tend to bear their burdens in silence. Some, however, are able to speak or write about their traumatic experience. A precious few make it their life's work.[1] The postwar Japanese writer Ōoka Shōhei (1909–1988) was one such man. While his frontline experience in the Philippines toward the end of World War II was extraordinary, his literature addresses issues universal to war, survivorship, and recovery. After a quarter century of literary struggle, Ōoka managed to come to terms with his own—and his nation's—troubled past, unburden himself, and enlighten his countrymen about the dynamics, miseries, and legacies of the Pacific War. This book tells the story of his long, convoluted journey of formulation that began in naked, guilt-ridden survival and ended with the fruitful completion of survivor mission.

Brief Critical Biography

Few in Japan would doubt Ōoka's place among the most important and influential postwar Japanese writers. While best known for his writings on the war, he also earned high acclaim for many other literary endeavors—translation, romance, mystery, travel and historical writing, critical biography, anthology, autobiography, literary criticism and debate, and social and political commentary. Ōe Kenzaburō, recipient of the Nobel Prize for Literature in 1994, suggests that Ōoka is to the postwar period what Natsume Sōseki (1867–1916) was to the early modern; both resolutely exposed and confronted the most pressing social and ethical problems of their day.[2] And in so doing, they served as the conscience of their society.

Looking back on his life, Ōoka recalled that he was "born in Meiji [1868–1912], raised in Taishō [1912–1926] and lived through Shōwa [1926–1989]."[3] During the eighty years of his life, he experienced Japan's rapid modernization and rise to prominence, its fateful turn toward militarism and expansionism, its defeat and rise from the ashes, and its period of high economic growth and resurgent nationalism. Born in Tokyo's Ushigome ward (present-day Shinjuku) on March 6, 1909, Ōoka spent a good part of his youth in and around the Shibuya area.[4] He entered the Methodist-run Aoyama Gakuin in 1921, where for a time he found religious conviction and aspired to be a minister. This adolescent spiritual faith and his innocent trust in his fellow man, however, were soon shattered by knowledge of biblical history, his teachers' immoral behavior, and the frightening egoism revealed in early modern Japanese novels such as Sōseki's *Kokoro.*

After matriculating to Seijō Higher School in 1925, Ōoka befriended Tominaga Jirō and came to know of the modernist poetry of his recently deceased older brother, Tarō. From this time, Ōoka was increasingly drawn to European—particularly French—literature and thought. This orientation was shared with other aspiring young writers of the time. As Paul Anderer observes, "By the mid-1920's French culture had been identified as the center of high European modernism and so an exemplary subject of study, at least for students of literature at elite universities."[5] In his last year at Seijō, Ōoka began studying French with Kobayashi Hideo, a recent graduate in French from Tokyo Imperial University who went on to become one of Japan's most original and highly respected literary critics. Soon after meeting Kobayashi, Ōoka read the works of Baudelaire and symbolist poets such as Rimbaud and Verlaine, and got to know such up-and-coming Japanese poets as Nakahara Chūya.

After graduation, Ōoka entered the French department of Kyoto Imperial University. While studying in the old capital he kept company with other important literary figures such as Yoshida Ken'ichi, Sakaguchi Ango, and Aoyama Jirō. Upon finishing his course of studies in 1932, Ōoka failed the entrance exam for the *Asahi Newspaper.* This marked the beginning of the decade-long period he later referred to as "domestic exile" (*kokunai bōmei*).[6] Indeed, Ōoka's shaky entry into society coincided with mounting oppression at home and armed aggression in China. As Kobayashi Hideo, Nakamura Mitsuo, Kawakami Tetsutarō, and others of his circle made names for themselves, Ōoka fell into relative obscurity. Although he wrote a number of articles on Stendhal and published translations of his literary works and book-length critical studies on him,[7] he eventually drifted away from Tokyo and the world of letters it represented. The year 1937 was decisive in this regard. Not only did full-scale hostilities break out in China, but Ōoka suffered the loss of both his father and Nakahara Chūya.

The following year, Ōoka took a job in the translation section of the Imperial Oxygen Company, a firm jointly operated by Japanese and French interests, and moved to Kobe. Soon thereafter, he married and started a family. He resigned when the Imperial Navy began to take over the company after the attack on Pearl Harbor. In 1943, Ōoka found employment in the materials division of Kawasaki Heavy Industries. He worked at the Kobe Shipyard until he was called to arms in the summer of 1944.

The literary critic Akiyama Shun has put forth a compelling argument concerning the process by which important young writers such as Tominaga, Kobayashi, Nakahara, and Ōoka began on their distinctive literary careers.[8] He begins by observing that each fervently aspired to break new intellectual and literary ground, and they prepared themselves by internalizing the work of prominent European writers. Akiyama suggests that before embarking on their respective literary paths as poet, critic, and novelist, each of these budding writers had to undergo twin *jiken,* or transformative experiences—the first symbolic and the second more direct and experiential. The initial *jiken* involved a destabilizing encounter with a particular foreign artist: for Tominaga, it was Baudelaire; for Kobayashi and Nakahara, Rimbaud; for Ōoka, Stendhal. In each case, the works they encountered "grabbed [them] by the throat," brought on a collapse of prior symbolic worlds, and sent them on a quest for a new language to express their experience and reconstruct their lives. Before their experiences could be "humanized" (*ningenka*) in this way, however, another, more immediate and physical *jiken* was necessary.

Whereas Tominaga, Kobayashi, and Nakahara experienced their second transformative experience relatively quickly after the first,[9] Ōoka did not encounter his until 1944: "In Ōoka's case, it took him wholly by surprise. And his was an actual, tangible *jiken*—war. This brutal force took him by the neck and suspended him before death. His second *jiken* was a direct encounter with a real force that shook his existence to its very foundations."[10] The nature of this transformative experience and how he came to "humanize" it in his writings are at the heart of this book. These important matters will be returned to after the major contours of his postwar literary career are outlined below.

Shortly after reuniting with Kobayashi Hideo in January, 1946, Ōoka produced the initial draft of his maiden work, "Before Capture" (Tsukamaru made, 1948, trans. 1967, 1996).[11] Although concerns over occupation censorship delayed publication until 1948, its importance was recognized immediately. In the same year, he completed translations of Stendhal's *On Love* and *The Charterhouse of Parma.*[12] In 1949, Ōoka joined the Potted Plant Group (Hachinoki kai), a gathering of prominent literary figures such as Nakamura Mitsuo, Yoshida Ken'ichi, Fukuda Tsuneari, and later, Mishima Yukio that published the influential magazine *Voice* (*Koe*). In 1950, Ōoka produced the best-selling novel *Lady Musashino* (*Musashino fujin*); two years later he put the finishing touches on his early masterpiece, *Fires on the Plain* (*Nobi,* 1952; trans. 1957). By the end of the Allied occupation of Japan, Ōoka's position as a representative writer of the Postwar Group (Sengoha) was firmly established.[13]

In many ways, 1953 was a watershed year for Ōoka. By year's end, he had finished writing his battlefield and prisoner-of-war memoirs, studied Edgar Allan Poe as a Rockefeller Scholar at Yale University, toured Europe, announced his intention of writing a factual account of the Battle for Leyte Island, and resettled in a new house in the coastal town of Ōiso. Higuchi Satoru has written that the period between his move to Ōiso and relocation to Setagaya (present-day Seijō) in 1969 was among the most fruitful and productive of his long career.[14] During this time, he anthologized the works of Nakahara Chūya, Masaoka Shiki, and Kobayashi Hideo, engaged in high-profile debates (*ronsō*) over the use of the historical record in fiction,[15] produced a series of short historical pieces and a novel on men who sacrificed themselves for lost causes about the time of the Meiji Restoration (1868),[16] published the highly regarded novella *In the Shadow of Cherry Blossoms* (*Kaei,* 1959; trans. 1998), and serialized his monumental narrative account of the failed campaign for the Philippines. Official recognition of these achievements soon followed. In 1971, he was invited (but declined) to join the prestigious Academy of Arts, and in 1976 he was given the Asahi Culture Award.

The two decades between Ōoka's move to Seijō and his death on Christmas Day 1988 have been described as his "evening years" (*bannen*), a period during which he "gathered in the harvest" of twenty-five years of incessant literary activity.[17] His health, never very good, began to decline markedly. While devoting much of his time to polishing or completing earlier works, he also penned prize-winning mysteries,[18] wrote a series of critical studies on Natsume Sōseki's fiction,[19] worked on a definitive anthology of Tominaga Tarō's writings, and researched and wrote his own account of the infamous Incident at Sakai.[20]

While serial publication of *The Battle for Leyte Island* (*Reite senki,* 1967–1969) and *Return to Mindoro Island* (*Mindorotō futatabi,* 1969) mark the culmination of his literary journey of survivor formulation, Ōoka continued to remind his countrymen of the origins, miseries, and consequences of the Pacific War and alert them to the dangers still facing them. Toward the end of his life, he emerged as one of the most valued social and political critics of his time. In newspapers on anniversaries of defeat; in lectures, a succession of interviews, dialogues, and roundtable discussions regularly appearing in literary magazines; and in a long, serially published "diary," *Tidings from Seijō* (*Seijō dayori,* 1980–1986),[21] he resolutely labored to keep memory of the war alive, teach the lessons of defeat, and suggest how they might be used to bring about a better, brighter future. In Ōe Kenzaburō's words, "From the defeat in the Pacific War through to the economic boom of the 1980's . . . Ōoka was the writer and intellectual who was most representative of the time, whose cultural criticism was most trusted. That Ōoka continued to write about Sōseki must surely have been because in the 1980's he found himself in a position similar to Sōseki's regarding his awareness that moral issues were being neglected while material desires were being stoked by the 'outside.'"[22] Ōoka's mature views were the ethical fruits of thoroughly confronting and working through his own and his comrades' terrible battlefield experience toward the end of the Pacific War. Crucial to full appreciation of this outstanding writer and his important contributions to postwar Japanese literature and society, then, is understanding of this personal and collective trauma and how he came to terms with it in literature.

Traumatic Battlefield Experience

Ōoka was thirty-five years old when he was finally drafted in the summer of 1944. After three months of basic training, he was sent to the Philippines. He served as communications man for Nishiya Company, an infantry unit attached to the 105th Division's Ōyabu Battalion. Like Ōoka himself, most of the soldiers in his company were middle-aged, inexperienced, and hastily trained. Upon laying eyes on them in Manila, staff officers abandoned plans of deploying them to defend the city and reassigned them to Mindoro, a minor island to the south. At the beginning of August, Nishiya Company and another infantry company began occupation of San Jose and several other coastal positions.[23]

With the exception of several casualties incurred during sporadic skirmishes with Filipino guerrillas and a fatal case of malaria, the first four and a half months were relatively uneventful. Toward the end of the year, however, Imperial Headquarters' last-ditch strategy of frustrating the American advance in an all-out attack at Leyte failed miserably, and because of its proximity and favorable airfields, Mindoro was chosen as the main staging area for the attack against Luzon. When an overwhelming American invasion force reached the island on December 15, the Japanese defenders could do little but abandon their coastal positions and withdraw into the interior.

For the next forty days, the men bivouacked in the Rutay Highlands, a mountainous region above the east coast town of Bulalacao. Since medics had forgotten to take the preventive malaria medicine, soldiers came down with the disease soon after arrival. During the fortnight prior to the American assault on their bivouac, three men died on average each day. Ōoka developed a life-threatening malarial fever on January 16, 1945. When the American attack commenced on January 24, he had barely recovered enough to stand and walk. Shortly after escaping the initial bombardment, he became separated from his comrades. During the day and night he spent alone, he had a life-altering encounter with an enemy soldier and attempted suicide. He was later discovered unconscious by two Americans and taken captive. Ōoka returned home toward the end of the year after spending the remainder of the war as a prisoner of war on Leyte Island.

Only some 60 of the 350 Japanese soldiers defending Mindoro Island survived; of the 180 men of Nishiya Company, all but about 20 died at the front. Ōoka came through his traumatic frontline experience without resisting the forces that all but annihilated his brothers-in-arms—he did not engage, wound, or kill a single enemy soldier. He survived, but did so as a man heavily burdened—burdened by protracted psychic and physical immersion in death, by what he did and failed to do to preserve his life, by the ruthless acts of survival egoism he witnessed, by the mass, seemingly pointless loss of his comrades and the indelible shame of being taken alive, burdened most of all, perhaps, by survival itself.

Analytical Approach

Writing was Ōoka's chosen means of unburdening himself and coming to terms with his traumatic battlefield experience. This raises an important question: how does one best approach the literature of a man who has undergone such extreme experience? Writing about the existence of a distinct "literature of trauma," Kali Tal argues that the writings of survivor-narrators should not be conflated with that of untraumatized authors: "To posit a literature of trauma one must assume that the identity of the author as author is inseparable from the identity of author as trauma survivor. This means that literature written about the trauma of others is qualitatively different from literature by trauma survivors."[24] According to Tal, extreme experience has the effect of shattering both "personal myth" and the "national myth" upon which it is based,[25] and the "process of storytelling" survivor-narrators engage in is a "personally reconstitutive act and expresses the hope that it will also be a socially reconstitutive act—changing the order of things as they are and working to prevent the enactment of similar horrors in the future."[26]

If the writings of trauma survivors differ in substantial ways from those of nontraumatized authors, it follows that special interpretive strategies are called for. As Tal writes, "Crucial, then, is the ability to consider the author as survivor, to bring to bear the tools of sociology, psychology, and psychiatry—an understanding of *trauma*—to the task of reading the literature of survivors."[27] Thorough appreciation of traumatic literature, in other words, necessitates a multidisciplinary approach and intimate knowledge of the experience and psychological effects of extremity.[28]

Through my own work, I have reached the conclusion that Ōoka is most profitably approached as a burdened battlefield survivor and that his war-related writings are best approached as a "literature of survival." And in this regard, I have found Robert Jay Lifton's work on survivor psychology and traumatic syndrome to be especially illuminating.[29] While there is much common ground in Tal and Lifton's general thinking about overwhelming experience, "storytelling," and recovery, the latter places greater emphasis on survivorship than on the traumatic experience itself. As he explains in a 1990 interview, "Focussing on survival, rather than on trauma, puts death back into the traumatic experience, because survival suggests that there has been death, and the survivor therefore has had a death encounter, and the death encounter is central to his or her psychological experience."[30] Foregrounding survival and the psychological effects of death immersion facilitates better understanding of the importance to the survivor-narrator of deep-seated feelings of death guilt, self-recrimination, and loss.

A number of prominent Japanese literary critics have adopted a similar approach to interpreting Ōoka's war-related writings. Kanno Akimasa, Nakano Kōji, and Ikeda Jun'ichi have all viewed Ōoka as a survivor (*seikansha, ikinokori*) who endeavored to recover from his traumatic battlefield experience by progressively confronting and working through it in literature.[31] Each of these distinguished scholars, moreover, has drawn special attention to the importance of "death guilt" (*zaiakukan, ushirometasa, tsumi no ishiki*) and Ōoka's evolving relationship to the war dead to full appreciation of his memoirs, fiction, and historical works on the war.[32] Before I turn to the contents and organization of the present book, it will be useful to set forth key elements of the particular paradigm that serves as its underlying structure.

The image is of fundamental importance to Lifton's work on survivor psychology and traumatic syndrome.[33] This is clear from the opening lines of *The Broken Connection: On Death and the Continuity of Life*: "WE LIVE ON IMAGES. As human beings we know our bodies and our minds only through what we can imagine. To grasp our humanity we need to structure these images into metaphors and models. Writers, artists, and visionaries have always known this—as have philosophers and scientists in other ways."[34] Mental images are the constituent elements of the "formative-symbolizing process":

> A key principle is that of the formative process: the continuous creation of psychic images and forms, so that every encounter with the environment is newly reconstructed according to prior and anticipated experience—according to what one "knows" and expects. Here I extend the classic psychoanalytic idea of a symbol as a relatively primitive, conscious substitution of one thing for another . . . to a more contemporary view of symbolization: the specifically human need to *construct* all experience as the only means of perceiving, knowing and feeling.[35]

While smooth operation of this fundamental psychic action generates and sustains connection, integrity, and vitality, its trauma-induced disruption results in their polar opposites—separation, disintegration, and deadness.[36]

Lifton defines a survivor as "one who has come into contact with death in some bodily or psychic fashion and has remained alive." The survivor's challenge is ultimately to formulate their traumatic death-encounter in such a way as to reestablish the symbolic connection, integrity, and vitality lost through the extreme experience. This comes to involve confrontation with, and working through a constellation of basic survivor "themes."[37] The themes and subthemes most pertinent to the present study are death imprints, psychic numbing, death guilt, bearing witness, impaired mourning, and formulation.[38]

Death imprints are the "basis for all survivor themes." By virtue of its "suddenness, its extreme or protracted nature, or its association with the terror of premature, unacceptable dying," extreme experience cannot be fully assimilated or integrated with prior or anticipated experience at the time of occurrence. Consequently, survivors are constantly engaged in ongoing struggles to master death immersion experiences that defy, or at least strongly resist, internalization.[39]

Psychic numbing is our natural defensive against overwhelming, unbearable experience. In extremity, emotions quickly become dissociated from knowledge or awareness of what is occurring in the external world. Such being the case, the capacity a survivor has for belated emotional response has significant bearing on his or her efforts to come to terms with the traumatic experience.[40] To facilitate recovery, survivors at some point need to experience and work through repressed or suppressed feelings of death guilt, self-recrimination, and loss.[41]

Death guilt is the natural and inevitable attendant of survival. Survivors simultaneously suffer from two types of guilt. The first, and most fundamental, has to do with "survival priority": "The survivor can never, inwardly, simply conclude that it was logical and right for him, and not others, to survive. Rather he is bound by an unconscious perception of organic balance which makes him feel that his survival was made possible by others' deaths: If they had not died, he would have had to; if he had not survived, someone else would have." Since survivors feel profound anxiety over survival itself, they continually feel a pressing need to justify themselves and their continued existence. Survivors, in short, must somehow resolve the self-accusatory question Why did I live while they died?[42]

The second kind of death guilt concerns the failure to behave or respond as one later feels one should have: "One feels responsible for what one has not done, for what one has not felt, and above all for the gap between that physical and psychic inactivation and what one felt called upon . . . to do and feel."[43] Lifton defines guilt in general as "an image-feeling of responsibility or blame for bringing about injury or disintegration, or other psychological equivalents of death."[44] Survivors, it seems, cannot help but feel personally responsible for their involvement in death and destruction.[45]

Two basic psychological patterns—static and animating—emerge in relation to death guilt. The former is characterized by a "series of maneuvers designed to avoid the experience of guilt feelings." The latter, in contrast, is positive and adaptive, and can help bring about recovery and renewal. Animating guilt is described in terms of the "anxiety of responsibility," as it is characterized by a continuous transformation of self-condemnation into the feeling that one must, should, and can act against the wrong and toward an alternative.[46] Such anxiety can, as it did Ōoka, spur survivors to take up survivor mission.

It bears repeating here that survivors' capacity for belated emotional response substantially shapes the outcome of their struggles to master their pasts, because "in severe traumatic experience, grief and loss tend to be too overwhelming in their suddenness and relationship to unacceptable death and death equivalents for them to be resolved. And many of the symptoms in the traumatic syndrome have to do precisely with impaired mourning, or what Mitscherlich has called 'the inability to mourn.'"[47]

The crucial survivor theme is formulation, "evolving new inner forms that include the traumatic event, which in turn requires that one find meaning or significance in it. . . . Formulation means establishing the [psychic] lifeline on a new basis." Coming to terms with extreme experience and survival is facilitated by working through a three-stage process of confrontation, reordering, and renewal. In the absence of "guilt-associated struggles around fidelity to the dead and the experience of deadness, and to oneself as a witness," however, "no such renewal or formulation is feasible."[48]

Contents and Organization

This book is structured as follows. Chapter 1 opens with introductory sections on Ōoka's psychological condition after returning from the Philippines and the specific circumstances that led to his postwar birth as a writer. Subsequent sections examine his battlefield and relevant prisoner-of-war memoirs (1948–1953) generally in terms of death immersion, psychic numbing, death guilt, bearing witness, and impaired formulation. This approach not only allows for thorough treatment of the war experience so integral to his fictional and historical writings, but also enables identification and articulation of the obstacles he faced as he struggled autobiographically to deal with the multifaceted burdens of survival. By the time Ōoka was composing the last of his war memoirs, he had not only become aware of but disgusted by the lengths he had gone to justify his battlefield conduct and rationalize survival. The fruits of his initial formulative breakthroughs are most conspicuous in his fictional treatments of his traumatic battlefield experience.

Chapter 2 examines Ōoka's major war novel, *Fires on the Plain.* Here, his creative reworking of his burdened past takes the form of a battlefield memoir composed in a Tokyo mental hospital by a deeply disturbed veteran of the Battle for Leyte Island. Creating an insane alter ego and exposing the defensive embellishments and omissions of his recollective account allowed Ōoka to gain perspective on, indirectly criticize, and ultimately transcend the limitations of his own autobiographical handling of his frontline trauma. In addition, he was able to give cathartic creative expression to the extraordinary experiences that haunted him, interrogate the survival egoism he was initially loath to acknowledge in his own frontline conduct, and begin to confront and work through deep-seated feelings of guilt, self-recrimination, and loss. And, by the end of the work, he seems to have realized that his subsequent literary efforts would have to begin where his protagonist's leave off—with the forgotten, the as yet unmourned and unmemorialized spirits of the war dead.

Chapter 3 retraces the difficult steps Ōoka took to move from anxious rejection and scapegoating of his fallen comrades to intimate identification, empathy, and mourning by comparing and contrasting an earlier and a later fictional work—*Lady Musashino* and *In the Shadow of Cherry Blossoms*—and discussing the intervening emotional turning-point experience that enabled this crucial formulative breakthrough. While both works concern the experiences of women who suffer psychological breakdowns and commit suicide, the difference in his attitude toward and treatments of their lives and deaths is an accurate measure of the progress he made toward coming to terms with his burdened past. Ōoka's newly developed capacity to empathize with people "fated" to die premature, unnatural, and seemingly pointless deaths enabled him to abandon his defensive scapegoating formulation and engage in more appropriate blaming. In so doing, he extended the concentric rings of responsibility outward from the individuals concerned to the macrocosmic social and historical forces that combined to bring about their tragic, untimely ends.

Six years after publishing *In the Shadow of Cherry Blossoms,* Ōoka joined a meeting of the Leyte Brotherhood (Reite dōseikai), a group of Japanese veterans from the Philippines. He left the gathering with the promise to write the battle account of the ill-fated Sixteenth Infantry Division, the corps that met the massive American invasion force when it reached Leyte Island in October 1944. This project evolved into a full-fledged survivor mission. Chapter 4 analyzes *The Battle for Leyte Island,* the seminal work in which Ōoka exposes the whole truth of the land, air, and sea battles that effectively sealed Japan's fate in the Pacific War. The completion of this work and *Return to Mindoro Island,* an intensely personal work about his experience of revisiting Leyte and Mindoro Island shortly after embarking on his mission of survivor illumination, brought Ōoka's formulative journey to a positive, vitalizing conclusion.[49] In the former, he fulfills his solemn obligations as a survivor to the living *and* the dead. He consoles the restless spirits of his fallen comrades by faithfully reproducing their frontline experience and revealing how bravely and effectively they fought. And at the same time, he also clarifies who and what was responsible for defeat and draws the redemptive lessons that can be learned from honest interrogation of the past. In so doing, Ōoka managed to give meaning to both his own survival and the tragic loss of some ninety thousand comrades in the Battle for Leyte Island.

In the epilogue of *The Battle for Leyte Island* and in *Return to Mindoro Island,* Ōoka considers the profound effect of the Pacific War on the Filipino and Japanese people. After describing its enduring, problematic legacies, he articulates the outstanding moral obligations of survivors to the war dead and suggests that these solemn debts can be repaid thorough collective confrontation, working through and coming to terms with the past, learning the lessons of defeat and using them to rectify lingering social evils, and recovering full national sovereignty and independence. Ōoka thus brings his survivor mission to a fitting and enlightening conclusion by describing the work that needs to be done to put the ghosts of Japan's war years to rest and move forward into the future with greater confidence, responsibility, and vitality. And to the end of his life in 1988, he continued to reflect meaningfully on the present in ethical terms of the past.

CHAPTER ONE

Memoirs of a Burdened Survivor

ON DECEMBER 10, 1945, Ōoka Shōhei was physically repatriated to Japan from the Philippines along with hundreds of other former prisoners of war and demobilized soldiers. Psychologically, however, he returned alone. Ōoka's traumatic frontline experience alienated him from the living and the dead. The difficult task before him was to reconstruct his identity in light of his extreme experience, repair his broken connections with his countrymen and with those who did not return from the Philippines, and find meaning in their deaths and his own survival. While he was able to reintegrate with the living relatively quickly, it took him a long time to work out his relationship with the war dead.

NAKED SURVIVAL

Ōoka disembarked at the northern Kyushu port town of Hakata. In "My Demobilization" (Waga fukuin, 1950), he records his thoughts as he waited for the train that would reunite him with his family: "Anyway, it was all over. Now that I was no longer a soldier or a prisoner of war, I was free to live each moment of my life as I saw fit. It was such an odd feeling. For a moment, I had the illusion that I could go anywhere I pleased. Of course, my destination had already been decided—I was returning home" (2:330).[1] The train left Hakata that evening and, after passing through the bombed-out ruins of Hiroshima and Okayama by night, arrived in Kobe the following day. After several false starts, Ōoka eventually reached the house in Okubo where his family and in-laws had been living since being evacuated from Kobe. He fainted upon seeing his wife's silhouette at the top of the stairs. Ōoka had been convinced all along that he would die at the front. Upon regaining consciousness, he blurted out, "I almost didn't make it back," and then excitedly explained how he had survived.

Shortly after returning home, Ōoka, his wife, Harue, and daughter ventured out into the foothills behind Okubo to gather firewood. When they reached the edge of the forest, Ōoka continued on alone until he found a secluded place to rest and reflect on survival:

> It was quiet. The winter sun penetrated the pine trees and illuminated the withered grass and underbrush. I tossed aside the saw I was holding and lay down on my back.
>
> The forest I had been in in the Philippines had been quiet too, and I had been alone as I was now. Then, however, I had been ill and awaiting death surrounded by lush greenery.
>
> Now I am in a withered, winter forest. And I am alive. While still alone, I intend to live out the rest of my allotted days. Distant sounds made by my wife and daughter reach me through the dry air. They are apparently moving about cautiously. I hear my daughter say "Mommy, let's search closer to the pond." She must be frightened by the stillness. My wife's comforting words reach my ears like whispers. I am alive. (2:362)

Ōoka spent his first month home recuperating. Since he had been well fed and cared for in the Leyte prisoner-of-war camp, he was in relatively good physical condition. What he needed was time to recovery psychologically. As he writes in "My Wife" (Tsuma, 1950), "I needed mental rest. Actually, more than rest, I needed time to adjust to being back in normal society. After two years of animalistic (*dōbutsuteki*) life as a soldier and prisoner of war, I had to become 'human' again" (2:351–352). The "animalistic" life he refers to was one in which war, the continual threat of death, psychic numbing, and survival egoism combined to undo human relations. Ōoka needed time to reconstruct broken connections. In "Mr. Nerves" (Shinkeisan, 1951) he writes about the difficulties he had thinking and communicating: "The mechanism that integrated my thoughts was probably frozen. During my two years of animalistic life as a soldier and POW, I felt no need to understand others or make myself understood to them" (2:412).

Emotional detachment was one of the enduring legacies of Ōoka's traumatic battlefield experience. While psychic numbing shielded him from the terrible suffering and loss of life he witnessed, it also inhibited recovery long after his return from the front. Ōoka's postwar psychological condition is palpable in his description of the illness and death of a young neighborhood woman:

> Our verandah faced the river. The back yard was barely two feet in width and ended abruptly in a slope that extended down to rice fields bordering the water. The yard was too narrow to warrant a fence, and neighbors used it as a shortcut.
>
> Since the yard faced east, it received good morning sun. A young woman often came into the narrow yard and crouched down out of view near our shutter boxes.
>
> She appeared to be about twenty-seven or twenty-eight. She wore a silk kimono that, although dirty, was rather colorful for this rural village. She had apparently economized on undergarments—the outline of her shoulders and hips was clearly visible through her clothes. She was tall, had a smallish head and nice figure, but she was extremely thin. One day when I tried to peer down at her from the verandah, she turned away as if to hide her pale face, rose quickly, and walked away.
>
> I asked my wife, "Who's that?"
>
> "A relative of the porcelain dealer. Looks like she's ill."
>
> The "porcelain dealer" was a local man who lived just down the street. . . . The woman in question was his wife's younger sister. During the war she had worked as a waitress in Osaka, but she had been living with her elder sister since she had taken ill not long before it ended.
>
> Since she suffered from tuberculosis, she was an unwelcome visitor. There were young children in the main house, and she was not allowed beyond the entryway. She lived in a shed with no electricity. She probably came to our yard because her sister's place did not have good sun exposure.
>
> Over the next several months—up to the day she died in the shed—I never heard her utter a word. A few days before she died, I saw her leaning against the shed door. Her face was puffed out like a balloon, and it looked dreadful. (2:416–417)

This description is remarkably matter-of-fact. Ōoka describes the young woman's plight without the slightest hint of emotional involvement. Given his psychically numbed condition, he can only regard this postwar tragedy of illness, quarantine, precipitous decline, and premature, grotesque death with what amounts to detached curiosity. Conspicuously absent are any expressions of sympathy, empathy, or compassion.

For quite some time after demobilization, Ōoka was indifferent to the hardship and suffering of his countrymen. He draws special attention to this condition in "Pleasant Company" (Yukai na renchū, 1951) a short piece he wrote about his January 1946 trip to visit literary friends in Tokyo. The train he takes from Kobe is crowded with newly demobilized soldiers and returnees with all their worldly possessions. Ōoka is oddly impressed by some delinquents who inconspicuously relieve their dispirited compatriots of their belongings. While contemptuous of the victims, he is thrilled by the youths who prey on them. Ōoka explains his attitude in terms of having become "accustomed to the battlefield, where 'necessity' crushe[d] all 'morality.'" He goes on to observe that "while [he] didn't feel like being immoral and flouting the law [himself], [he] did have the tendency to relish watching those who did."[2] The returnees realize what has happened soon after the gang departs. Their loss and disappointment, however, have no effect on Ōoka; indeed, he finds their confusion and quarreling amusing.

After reaching Tokyo, Ōoka regales some friends with stories about his battlefield experience and the absurdity of life as an overfed, underworked prisoner of war, then touches on his recent experience on the train. His friends' reaction to his final account makes the nature of his postwar condition clear:

> "They were terrible, but I hadn't seen such dignified faces since returning home. And to think they were nothing but common thieves. There must be something wrong with me."
>
> "That much, at least, is beyond doubt."
>
> "The returnees were particularly interesting. Over here a husband and wife were arguing, over there a parent and child. They kept it up all the way to Tokyo. I couldn't help but laugh."
>
> My friends smiled graciously at my boastful war and prisoner-of-war stories and the mistake I made with the hoodlums on the train. When it came to laughing at my unfortunate countrymen quarreling among themselves, however, they pulled a face. My friends who remained behind in Tokyo endured the war collectively, so they suffered more than I did as a frontline soldier—they still knew how to empathize with their fellow man.
>
> But my callousness was more than an attitude; it was virtually a

> "sensation." This feeling that alienated me from my friends was clearly produced by my battlefield experience. I returned from the war naked, with literally nothing intact but my physical body.
>
> That, however, was a long time ago.[3]

Ōoka published "Pleasant Company" some six years after the war. As implied in the final sentence, the callousness (*hijō*) that estranged him from his friends passed relatively quickly. As will be shown, however, his numbed attitude toward his dead comrades was not only more enduring, but also substantially impeded his initial autobiographical and fictional efforts to come to terms with his burdened past.

Traumatic Birth of a Writer

The trip Ōoka made to Tokyo shortly after his return from the front determined the future course of his life. After demobilization, Ōoka didn't know how he would support his family. His first thought was to see if he could reclaim his job with Kawasaki Heavy Industries. Within a week of his return, he made his way to the shipyard through the burned-out ruins of Kobe only to learn that there was no job awaiting him there. He was, however, given six months' severance pay. On his way home, he stopped by the Imperial Oxygen Company just long enough to confirm that he had no future there either.

When Ōoka found the doors to company employment barred, he began to think seriously about writing. In "My Wife" he describes his thoughts after making his unsuccessful trip: "At the time, a thousand yen was more than enough to support our life in the countryside for a month. It looked like I'd even have the margin to travel to Tokyo to visit my friends" (2:359). The friends Ōoka had in mind—Kawakami Tetsutarō, Nakamura Mitsuo, Kobayashi Hideo, and others—were all professional writers. In mid-January, Ōoka braved the crowded, sixteen-hour train trip to the capital to see if he could use his connections to launch his career as a writer.

The first man he visited was Kawakami, from whom he learned of Kobayashi's intention of asking him to write something for his new journal, *Sōgen* (Creative source). This was too good to be true:

> It was my good fortune to have kept company with outstanding writers such as [Kawakami] and [Kobayashi]. I never once had to go to a publisher manuscript in hand. While inwardly rejoicing over having Kobayashi waiting for me just when literature had become my last hope, I feigned nonchalance and said, "Well, I don't know. I'm not sure whether I could write that sort of thing or not. And besides, there's nothing universal about war experience."
>
> I thought secretly to myself, however, that were I to do so at all, this was what I would try to write about. (2:385–386)

When Ōoka met him in the resort town of Ito, Kobayashi wasted no time in making his request: "Ōoka, how about writing a war correspondent's piece (*jūgunki*) for me?" (2:396). Because Ōoka went to war as a soldier, he was initially taken aback by this request for a "correspondent's piece." After a moment's reflection, however, he realized that since he had had no will to fight, his position had been comparable to that of a correspondent. When he hesitated, Kobayashi asked him if he was averse to the idea. Ōoka explained his reluctance as follows: "It's not that. It's just that battlefield events are limited to that place [and time]. I'm not sure if they're even worth writing about. I could, however, write about my life as a prisoner of war. I could write three hundred pages on how decadent (*daraku*) men can become (2:397)." To this, Kobayashi replied, "Write whatever you want, just write. But three hundred pages is too long. Make it a hundred. And don't worry about the others—just write about your soul (*tamashii*)" (2:397).

In his conversations with both Kawakami and Kobayashi, Ōoka questioned the significance of his battlefield experience. At the time, his prisoner-of-war experience was not only fresher in his mind; it also overlay the traumatic frontline experience that preceded it. The work he eventually submitted to Kobayashi, however, involved a serious struggle to come to terms with his experience of war. "Before Capture" not only marked Ōoka's postwar birth as a writer, but also the beginning of his long, arduous journey of survivor formulation.

On the crowded, homebound train, Ōoka thought deeply about the project he had just agreed to undertake. After expressing a number of doubts and reservations, he comes to the heart of the matter:

> I simply must understand by writing. If I don't, chances are my war experience will continue to haunt me like a nightmare, and my present life will amount to little more than sleepwalking.
>
> To fully account for that past which is now an integral part of my present self, I will have to take on all the root causes that produced it, even those beyond the sphere of my own personal responsibility. Why must an untalented man like myself do such a thing? Is there no one else?
>
> On the crowded night train, surrounded by people asleep on their feet, I was overcome by sentimental tears. It felt good to cry. (2:405)

This can be read as Ōoka's survivor manifesto. What haunts him like a nightmare and demands understanding is his traumatic battlefield experience. Writing, moreover, will be his chosen means of confronting and working through this heavily burdened past. Thorough formulation will enable him not only to reach full consciousness, but also to recover his sense of interconnection, meaning, and vitality. From the outset of his journey of survivor formulation, Ōoka seemed to have realized that he would have to reconstitute himself in light of his extreme experience, and that this reconstitution, in turn, would necessitate a thorough consideration of responsibility. Finally, and perhaps most challenging of all, he knew at a deep level that at some point he would have to reconcile his relationship as a survivor to the war dead. Ōoka broaches this last and most painful issue when he asks, "Why must an untalented man like myself do such a thing? Is there no one else?"

Through this self-questioning, one catches an early glimpse of what Lifton refers to as the "anxiety of responsibility." Formulation of his war experience and fulfilling his obligations to the dead required Ōoka to move beyond the sphere of his own personal responsibility and exhaustively look into the root causes of his own and his comrades' horrible experience. The significance of his tears, moreover, must not be overlooked. Upon realizing that he is probably the only one capable of illuminating the dark past in this way, psychic numbing is momentarily broken through and he is able to express in small measure the profound grief he feels upon suddenly recalling his fallen comrades.

After completing "Before Capture," Ōoka alternately wrote battlefield and prisoner-of-war memoirs. Between 1946 and 1953, he published more than thirty such autobiographical works on his war experience. Well over half of these treat his experience between conscription and capture. They are the main subjects of this chapter.[4]

Death Immersion

On March 16, 1944, Ōoka received official notification that he was to begin three months' basic training in Tokyo in three days' time. This came as no great surprise.[5] Since the atmosphere on base was relaxed and the training was not too demanding, the trainees entertained hopes of remaining in country as reserves. When they began to receive instruction in ship evacuation and tropical hygiene, however, their hopes dimmed.

On the night of their second-to-last day before discharge, Ōoka and a friend were standing sentry duty when a senior officer returned to barracks. As he approached, Ōoka's comrade happily announced that this was their final night of guard duty. After an awkward silence, the officer replied, "What's that? I thought you were bound for the front" (2:2). This exchange marks the beginning of Ōoka's protracted psychic encounter with death: "It was as if an electric shock wave had passed through my body. This fear had been lurking behind the elation we were beginning to feel over imminent discharge. While not wholly unexpected, I was nonetheless struck dumb and my knees began to buckle under me" (2:3). From the moment he learned that he would be conscripted and sent to the front until he realized shortly after he was captured some seven months later that he had been saved, Ōoka was continually immersed in symbolic and physical death. And the psychological effects of this ongoing, traumatizing death encounter were profound, multifaceted, and far-reaching.

Ōoka's initial response to conscription is loss of hope, and his primary means of coping with imagined death is resignation. Viewing death as imminent and inescapable allows him for a time to forgo the struggle for survival: his primary task becomes one of passively awaiting death's inevitable arrival. After his hope-withering psychic death encounter, Ōoka also becomes increasingly distanced from others. This is conspicuous in his attitude toward his family. The new conscripts are informed that although they cannot leave base, they will be allowed a single day of meeting before heading for their embarkation point in southern Japan. Reasoning that "meeting them or not will do nothing to alter the reality of being sent off to die at the front as part of a defeated army" (2:7), Ōoka decides not to contact his wife. Instead, he writes his last will and testament and entrusts it to a friend in Tokyo:

> I intend to return alive, but chances are I will die. You're probably determined to raise the children by yourself, but that doesn't necessarily accord with my wishes. If you think you've found happiness, don't hesitate to act.
>
> Tell Tomoe . . . that since she's not gifted, she'll have to study hard and become clever or she won't be able to find a husband.
>
> Since Tei'ichi . . . is talented, he'll need to be watched carefully or he'll become a delinquent.
>
> To the children: Although Father may not come back, you must take good care of your mother and do well in life. A child who goes bad just because he loses his father will be no child of mine. (2:8)

Ōoka is subsequently persuaded to inform his wife of the meeting day. She and the children, however, fail to appear. The following morning, the men march from the base to Shinagawa Station. As the soldiers rest before boarding the train, Ōoka's wife finally arrives with one child strapped to her back and the other in tow. The trip—her first to Tokyo—has obviously been trying. Ōoka describes this reunion in terms of separation and death: "When I saw her, I thought I was seeing her as she would look upon [hearing of] my death. She later told me that she saw 'death' in my own completely transformed appearance" (2:17). Lifton reminds us that such physical separations are psychological "death equivalents."[6] At this crucial moment of parting neither harbors any hope of seeing the other again. After both break into tears, Harue timidly hands him the thousand-stitch belt (*senninbari*)[7] she contrived to make en route to Tokyo.

Ōoka's eleventh-hour reunion with his family has the temporary effect of rekindling marginal hope in survival: "Meeting with my wife brought a faint ray of light into my heart. Absurd thoughts came to mind. Being included among the forty percent of trainees conscripted was the rock bottom of my luck. From here on, my prospects just might improve. If I was fortunate enough to avoid enemy torpedoes and reach Manila, and my good luck kept up, I might even make it back home alive" (2:21). These comforting thoughts, however, do not last long. On the train to Moji, the draftees are each given a twenty-day ration of candy. Ōoka decides to mail all of the sweets to his children as his final parting gift: "As I worked on the parcel in the dark car surrounded by my slumbering comrades, I couldn't restrain sentimental tears. With my face pressed against the window, I freely shed the tears that had only begun to emerge when I parted with my wife" (2:23).

Ōoka and his comrades spend ten days in Moji awaiting formation of the transport convoy. Once on board, they must wait another five days before finally setting sail for the Philippines. During this extended period of idle waiting, Ōoka is repeatedly assailed by premonitions of death (*shi no yokan*) that disrupt his inner construction of experience and bring on a sense of stasis and despair: "It is difficult to describe what it felt like to experience these death premonitions. All I can say is that it was eviscerating, and produced a sense of oppressive listlessness. Most of the time, I was absorbed in my daily activities. In the midst of some menial task, however, I would suddenly think 'Ah, but I'll be dead before long'" (2:26).

At such times, Ōoka is confronted not only with symbolic death, but also with meaningless death. He was disillusioned with the Greater East Asia War (Dai tōa sensō) from the outset:

> I didn't believe Japan would win the war. While I loathed the military for dragging my homeland into such a hopeless conflict, I had risked nothing to stop them. I felt at this late date that I had no right to object to the fate that they had now chosen for me. While I was aware of the absurdity of pitting a powerless citizen against the organization that carried out the violence of the nation, I had to think of it in this way to avoid laughing at the sheer ludicrousness of being driven toward meaningless death.
>
> But in the evening, as I stood on the deck of our anchored transport ship and watched the red and green lights of the ferries moving like so many toys through the Kanmon Straits, the wretchedness of being shipped off to my death like a slave weighed heavily on me.
>
> Until the day I was sent to the front, I had lived easily with concepts such as "sharing the destiny of the nation" and had laughed at the rhetoric of opportunists and the futile pronouncements of defeatists alike. Once I was actually on board the transport ship, however, I was stunned when "Death" settled down in front of me and refused to budge. (1:7)

One of the important effects of Ōoka's psychic immersion in death, in short, is to render all abstractions—from sharing the fate of the nation to sacrificing himself for the so-called Divine Emperor—devoid of value and significance.

Ōoka's psychic immersion in death also causes him to lose his grip on reality. Even before setting sail for the South Seas, he has a deeply disturbing experience:

> I stared at the water. The image of a woman I had thought of as a mere plaything rose to the surface. She probably appeared to me like that because in the past we had swum together in the sea. She was a consummate coquette. Wearing a brightly colored swimsuit, she smiled alluringly as she twisted her body about on the waves.
>
> My meditations gradually began to take on the character of full-blown daydreams. Now, my daughter crawled toward me over the surface of the water. She slid forward with both arms held out before her like a toy horse moving around on a carousel. She passed below the place I stood at the stern of the ship, and I kept my eyes on her until she disappeared around the bow. My daughter had long since passed the crawling age. This hallucination probably arose when the surface of the water became a stage for my daydreaming.
>
> Following my wishes, the child reappeared at the stern and moved resolutely forward. (2:30–31)

While Ōoka describes these daydreams (*hakuchūmu*) as if he had a measure of control, they are clearly profoundly unsettling. His visions of his former lover and daughter can be understood as expressions of his subconscious desire to reunite with his loved ones. The forms his compensatory imagination takes, however—especially related to his daughter, who moves about as if frozen in time—are clearly more disturbing than comforting.

After having these hallucinations, Ōoka feels an urge to throw away his *senninbari.* He removes it from his duffel, casts it over the gunwale, and watches it unfurl on the water. Discarding this tangible link to his family is more than an act of despair; symbolically, it represents the severing of fundamental human bonds. And the grave implications of this behavior are not lost on his comrades. A groundswell of horrified disbelief, anger, and censure quickly rises around him. Ōoka hastily withdraws to the latrine. As he crouches amid the stench, his eyes begin to burn. This is the second-to-last time before capture that he describes himself weeping. By the time the nine transport ships finally depart for Manila on July 3, psychic numbing has already rendered such emotional responsiveness all but impossible.

Ōoka's ongoing psychic encounter with death not only produces listlessness, loss of meaning, and a shaky grasp on reality, but threatens ultimate concerns as well. In "Reunion" (Saikai, 1951), Ōoka describes an extraordinary experience he has on the shores of Dannoura Bay just before departing for the front. This experience haunted him long after survival. Indeed, it is part and parcel of his indelible imprint of death:

> I was thinking about the death that awaited me. A solitary rock near the shore protruded slightly above the water, and waves sported about on its exposed surface. As I gazed at the waves, I thought that after I died my body would disintegrate and turn into water like that before my eyes. While consciousness, which seemed to want to go on forever, would end upon my death, the water in my body would probably continue to exist eternally in the universe, in constant motion like the waves before me. The thought that my mortal remains would remain *in motion* after my death was consoling. (2:402–403)

Ōoka's primary concern here is with what will remain after his passing. Whatever symbolic immortality[8] he had theretofore consciously or unconsciously ascribed to has clearly begun to break down, and in desperation he struggles to imagine a substitute. The details of the makeshift symbolic system he comes up with have significant bearing on his attitude toward his comrades. Finding himself in a state of symbolic breakdown and deadness, Ōoka locates vitality and continuity in the dynamism of nature. Psychically confronted by death imagery, he seeks solace not in God or in his companions, but in the perpetual movements of the nonhuman world. And the symbolic immortality Ōoka envisions centers on the material body. Instead of the spirit continuing on in some fashion after the disintegration of the body, he imagines the cessation of consciousness and permanent, physical union with nature. While providing a measure of comfort and protection during his protracted immersion in death, this formulation later impairs mourning.

As the transport ships finally move into the open ocean on July 3, Ōoka comes into ever closer proximity to actual death. American submarines are his most immediate concern. It is very telling that when faced with real danger, Ōoka begins to take more active steps to further survival: he avoids the hold as much as possible and sleeps on deck. When he compares his intense death anxiety to the relative composure of his comrades, he concludes that his terror stems from his "overactive imagination." While his comrades have apparently found ways to avoid preoccupation with death, Ōoka can think of little else.

After about a week at sea, Ōoka sees columns of water rise up near one of the escort destroyers. Although he knows intellectually that the destroyer is dropping depth charges, he becomes obsessed with the thought that it is being attacked from below by an invisible enemy. And these fears are not groundless. Several days later, he notices smoke pouring forth from the stern of the transport following his. After falling behind, it abruptly sinks. From this point on, Ōoka takes no chances; when the transports pass Corregidor under the cover of night, he sleeps on deck in a life vest.

Two weeks after reaching Manila, Nishiya Company takes up their assigned coastal positions on Mindoro Island. For the next four and a half months, guerrillas pose the only significant threat. From the beginning of their occupation of San Jose until the American landing on December 15, there are only two relatively minor clashes, and these result in only a handful of casualties. As the only communications man in the company, Ōoka is exempt from fatigue duty, maneuvers, and patrols.[9] He passes his days encoding and decoding messages, chatting with army meteorologists stationed in the same town, and studying Tagalog with local villagers.

The psychological effects of Ōoka's ongoing psychic immersion in death, however, continue to be manifest. After training a back-up communications man, he too must periodically do fatigue duty, stand guard, and go out on maneuvers. An experience he has while on sentry duty graphically conveys his extraordinary state of mind during the relatively quiet days preceding the American invasion. After detailing the view from the front of the barracks—the open, marshy fields, the tree-lined roads to the right and left, the distant forests and saw-toothed peaks looming in the background—Ōoka describes how repeatedly scanning the landscape becomes tedious and eventually puts him in a contemplative frame of mind: "Time and again, my eyes would come to rest on a particular object. I remember a fallen tree in the middle of the marshy field. One by one, I would count the exposed roots, which the elements had bleached bone white. To this day, I can recall their ominous shapes—evocative of suffering and agony—so clearly that I could reproduce them accurately" (2:170). Kamei Hideo has interpreted this experience in terms of objectification (*taishōka*).[10] When Ōoka enters this altered state of consciousness, elements from his inner psychology are objectified, or projected into the external environment. In this case, the fallen tree becomes the physical embodiment of his innermost fears—painful, solitary death without proper burial or memorialization.

It is fitting that Ōoka describes his psychological state at such times in terms of melancholy (*yū'utsu*). After writing about the ill-omened tree, he turns to the sunsets he watched while standing guard duty. It was his custom to recite Nakahara Chūya's "Afterglow" as he gazed at the dimming landscape:

> *The hills*
> *withdraw,*
> *with arms folded.*
>
> *The setting sun—*
> *golden,*
> *the hue of benevolence.* (2:171–172)

Ōoka read this poem as an aestheticized expression of despair and resignation.[11] As he absentmindedly watched the scenery darken and recede from view, he felt that his life, too, was rapidly drawing toward a predetermined end, that he could do little but await its arrival with folded arms.

The resignation and despair Ōoka experienced in San Jose is also poignantly reflected in the diary he kept at the time. He began looking back on his life when "'Death' settled in front of [him] and refused to budge." He continued to do so during the monotonous days of occupation:

> Since death was imminent, I had good reason to try to figure out just what kind of a person I had been. I reflected on my life as I lay in the dark after lights out, and then briefly recorded my thoughts the following day. After examining each moment of my life from youth to conscription, I came to realize that I was a nobody. Eventually, I reached the conviction that I wouldn't be missed when I died pointlessly on this isolated, unknown island in the South Seas. I thereupon stopped fearing death. Following Stendhal, I chose my own epitaph—"Forlorn and Crestfallen"—and recorded it at the end of my notes. (1:246)

The Americans arrived in force on December 15, 1944. By 0600 hours, the first shells of the naval bombardment reached the Japanese barracks in San Jose. The men were immediately ordered to pack, fill their mess tins with rice, and muster at the edge of the woods. After regrouping, the men—sixty-one soldiers and officers from Nishiya Company, eight army meteorologists, four Japanese nationals, and about ten sailors and pilots who had made emergency landings on Mindoro—begin an arduous, three-day trek through the central mountains. As the soldiers ascended the grassy foothills, they saw smoke rise up from the top of a hill ahead of them. Although they worried that the column of smoke was a signal fire (*rōka*) set by guerrillas, they had no choice but to press on. As they marched forward, similar fires continued to rise in their path. In the end, they never saw who set them. Toward dusk, the men finally arrived at some huts, where they passed their first night.

As the trail steepened and became increasingly difficult, they decided to abandon the heavy wireless radio.[12] It fell upon Ōoka to compose and send the last message to battalion headquarters on Luzon Island: "Yesterday, the fifteenth at 0600 hours, the enemy landed at Sandulayan, four kilometers west of San Jose, with a force of sixty warships.[13] Will march toward Bulalacao, rendezvous in three days with the Tanaka Platoon, and then determine our next course of action. Present position: ten kilometers north of San Jose. Morale is high. We vow to annihilate the enemy" (2:193).

Upon transmitting this final message, Ōoka cannot restrain his tears. The next time he records expressing such emotion is after capture when he learns of Japan's unconditional surrender. Ōoka cries at times of actual or symbolic separation: before leaving his wife at Shinagawa Station, as he boxed his parting gift for his children, after discarding the *senninbari,* and sending this message to Batangas. With each separation, Ōoka becomes increasingly distant from others and at the same time moves ever closer toward actual death.

After two and a half more days of marching, the men pass over the crest of the central mountain range and successfully rendezvous with the Tanaka Platoon that withdrew to the Rutay Highlands from Bulalacao. Although well-supplied, the men quickly fall victim to and begin to die from malaria. Ōoka's proximity to physical death and dying coupled with his ongoing symbolic immersion in death produce ever more serious psychological effects. One day while on sentry duty, he has a profoundly disturbing experience reminiscent of the one he had just before departing for the front. As when he was on lookout duty in San Jose, his scanning eyes come to rest on a lone tree, and he enters an altered state of consciousness. As he gazes at the tree, he becomes preoccupied with the shadow of death (*shisō*), an image that has been haunting him ever since a comrade who was a Buddhist monk in civilian life informed him that he sensed it in him:

> The tree before me . . . cast a shadow on the grass. It looked like a pleasant place to sit and rest, and I imagined my wife and children sitting there in the shade.
>
> My wife smiled happily as she watched the children play at her feet. Having no way of knowing that I would die there, they played innocently before my eyes. . . . They would probably continue to do so interminably, even after my death. . . .
>
> I freely created this vision to stave off the tedium of sentry duty. . . . Although these daydreams were the unadulterated products of my imagination and emotions, from time to time something exceedingly strange would happen—the images would take on lives of their own.
>
> A child too old to crawl slides without moving either arms or legs over the surface of the Moji waters like a toy horse moving around on a carousel. Now, without being led to do so by my imagination, my son playing under the tree runs out into the sun, turns and smiles back at his mother, who calls for him to stop.
>
> These caprices of imagination were clearly produced by my extraordinary emotional state, itself the product of my death premonitions. If my condition deteriorated any further, I would surely go insane. (2:246–247)

Faced with impending violent and meaningless death in the remote mountains of a foreign land, Ōoka conjures up visions of those nearest to his heart. Just as the surface of the ocean became the stage for his daydreams of his former lover and daughter and the fallen tree an embodiment of his innermost fears, the shaded area beneath the tree serves as a screen onto which he projects desperately needed imagery. In a sense, these visions of his wife and children provide a momentary haven from the death that plagues him internally and presses in on him externally. As he himself realizes, however, these compensatory maneuvers involve serious risks of their own. While hallucinating in this way, he not only loses touch with reality, but also control of the very images in which he seeks consolation. Entering too deeply into this beckoning refuge threatens to usher him into another from which return might have been impossible—madness.

Ōoka subsequently joins a detachment ordered to descend to Bulalacao to rendezvous with reinforcements reportedly being dispatched from Batangas. All they see upon reaching the coastal town, however, are the bloated, dog-eaten corpses of the Japanese naval men who left their highland position ten days earlier. The men spend a fitful night on the coast waiting for troops who never arrive. While on lookout duty, Ōoka has an utterly baffling experience:

> From the direction of the ocean, I suddenly heard the sound of a woman singing. It was a Spanish love song . . . and it had a doleful melody common to popular Filipino tunes. I had often heard Filipina women singing it in San Jose as they washed clothes.
>
> I watched through the palms as a dark, spindle-shaped object slowly passed by over the moonlit surface of the water. The song seemed to emanate from the object. I simply couldn't fathom what was happening.
>
> The object—I had finally recognized it as a small boat—disappeared into the shadows of the houses on my left. At that instant, the song suddenly became a long, drawn-out scream. It is extremely difficult to put the sound of that scream into words; it was something like "oh wa, a, a, a, aa—." Actually, it sounded more like the howling of a beast than a human being. After a moment, the scream trailed off.
>
> Then I heard a gunshot. The spindle-shaped object again passed before me, this time moving much faster in the opposite direction. (2:227)

At such moments, Ōoka is in a state of severe desymbolization. As with a heap of corpses he failed to notice the first time he passed through the central plaza, the events transpiring before his eyes are so unexpected, and bear so little resemblance to any prior experience, that he can only stare in dumb amazement. It was simply too incongruous to hear the lovely voice of a woman singing a love song out on the ocean on a moonlit night as he sits fearing imminent attack on the fringes of a deserted, war-ravaged, corpse-strewn village. Ōoka later learns that there had been a young couple on the boat. When they came ashore, they were immediately confronted by his comrades. The man was captured, but his partner escaped after being shot at. When the special attack force fails to materialize the next day, the men return to their highland encampment.

As the days and weeks pass, virtually every soldier is stricken with malaria. About a week before the American assault on their position, Ōoka begins to run a high fever. By the second day he is virtually incapacitated, and by the third he can no longer speak. His squad mates die one after another, and the shadow of death literally falls upon him as their bodies are carried away over him. As his condition continues to deteriorate, he becomes convinced that death is at hand. At this crucial juncture, he "sees" his loved ones once again: "I dreamed frequently. In addition to my wife and children, all the other people I loved visited me by turns in my dreams. Although these were just dreams, it was extraordinary that each and every person dear to me appeared in them. I took this as an unmistakable sign that I was dying. The only hope I retained was that all the people from my past had come to me in this way because I thought I was going to die" (2:273).

After a week, however, Ōoka's fever breaks, and he improves to the point where he can stand and begin to eat again.[14] Just as he starts to recover, three American ships are spotted entering Bulalacao Bay. Ōoka finds it exceedingly strange when nothing has changed by the following day: "I recall gazing in disbelief upon waking the next morning as dawn broke around the huts and nothing was amiss. I had vaguely thought that the Americans would come at daybreak" (1:12). When reports come in on January 24 that a patrol has been attacked, the walking ill and noncombatants are ordered to prepare to withdraw to a position some fifteen kilometers away toward San Jose. In the end, Ōoka is told to stay behind with three of his stricken comrades. Given no special orders, the men remaining behind ready themselves for combat and wait for the attack to commence. Before long, they hear three dull discharges followed by three clear explosions nearby. This shelling marks the beginning of a chain of traumatic events that comprise the core of Ōoka's most traumatizing frontline experience.

After abandoning his feeble efforts to transfer water from a mess tin into his empty canteen, Ōoka hobbles off toward company headquarters ahead of his comrades, who linger on in the hut to gather their belongings:

> To travel light, I took a minimum of equipment. I exited the hut with little but my loaded rifle. At the time, I felt that my life would be over before I could empty the thirty rounds in the only cartridge belt I took.

> The other three were still moving about in the hut. I wasn't sure if I'd be able to walk the hundred yards separating our hut from company headquarters. Saying I'd go on ahead, I started to walk up the hill.
>
> K objected: "But aren't we going together?" I turned and said, "I don't know whether I'll be able to walk or not, so I'm going on ahead by myself. I'll probably be waiting for you along the way," and then started climbing the narrow, zigzagging path using my rifle for support. That was the last I ever saw of them. None of my three comrades who remained in the hut escaped that ravine, which took the brunt of the American bombardment. (1:16–17)

When Ōoka reaches the top of the hill, he sees his comrades running around frantically in groups of twos and threes amid the explosions. He enters a hut occupied by sick soldiers, but just as he sits down, the area is rocked by an explosion and he dives out onto the ground. After hearing someone shout "Forward!" he watches a shell shatter the femur of a man ten yards to the rear. Ōoka crawls forward but stops when the bombardment intensifies. He then recalls seeing Commander Nishiya stride forth bareheaded, smile, quip "Nice and lively now, eh?!" and then walk off toward the incoming shells. After a pause, shouts of "The commander's been hit!" "Medic!" echo through the air. The second-in-command orders the sick and wounded to descend into the opposite valley and immediately begins to retreat himself.

When Ōoka comes to the valley floor, he notices several men collapsed and presumably dead by the side of the trail and sees about thirty others milling about in a clearing. Although the senior officer tells everyone to await orders, Ōoka mechanically follows a corporal who says he will lead them to safety. As they climb up the opposing slope, Ōoka becomes exhausted and lags behind. Before long, the group returns, passes him, and rushes off in another direction. At this point, Ōoka gives up hope: "I absentmindedly watched them as they marched away. I had used up all of my energy just to climb to where I was. I thought of following them and about whether I'd be able to keep up, but in the end, I just plopped down where I was" (1:19). When he sees a young soldier he was fond of fleeing with another group, he forces himself up and attempts to follow. By the time he returns to the valley floor, however, he realizes it's useless: "Other than my fallen comrades, there were no other people in the clearing. The forest was trailless. The voices of the retreating men echoed all around me. They receded, hushed to whispers, and then became inaudible" (1:19).

Ōoka sits down under an oak tree and prepares to kill himself. Although he's on the verge of taking his life, the instinct for survival comes to the fore:

> I felt nothing. I had already thought enough about death. There was no way to escape the fate that had been determined before I even left Moji for the front. I had simply arrived at the final point of that preordained course. Muttering, "After a last drink of water," I raised my canteen. It was empty.
>
> I recalled throwing away the mess tin of water when I left the hut. I never imagined at the time that I'd have the margin to drink at my leisure. It looked like I'd been too hasty yet again. I forced a smile. Then, I was assailed by a terrible thirst. (1:20)

As will be discussed in the following section on psychic numbing, the emergence of this primal, inner drive for water is indicative of intrapsychic dissociation. His emotions have already long since been divorced from cognition and perception. Now, the instinct for self-preservation is separated from, and progressively comes into conflict with, his conscious thought processes. Psychologically speaking, Ōoka is disintegrating.

Ōoka's mounting biological needs spur him to struggle to his feet and look for water. As he mechanically follows a trail along a dry riverbed punctuated with dark, stagnant pools, his thirst becomes unbearable. He tries some water from one of the pools, but it is undrinkable. He continues along the trail, which moves away from the streambed, enters the forest, and begins to climb. When he can go no further, he collapses under a tree at the edge of a clearing. This is the site of his pivotal *jiken,* or transformative experience.

As Ōoka lies on the ground, he imagines an American soldier appearing in the clearing. Reasoning that killing a lone enemy would alter neither his fate nor that of his comrades, he resolves not to shoot. Rather than surrendering, however—an act almost unthinkable for an Imperial soldier enjoined not to suffer the humiliation of being taken alive—he intends to expose himself, raise his rifle as if to shoot, and then allow himself to be shot and killed. Before long, Ōoka is abruptly brought back to awareness by the sound of voices and the rustling of approaching men, and an

American soldier emerges into the clearing much as he had envisioned. He feels no urge to shoot, but as the enemy closes in on him, he automatically raises his rifle, releases the safety lock, and prepares to engage the enemy. The American continues to press in, but just before the moment of truth, machine-gun fire erupts from the vicinity of Nishiya Company's hilltop emplacement, and after a brief but interminable pause, his enemy walks off toward it.

When Ōoka subsequently conducts a thorough analysis of his psychology during these decisive moments, he discovers that crucial elements are missing from memory:

> A comrade of his on the other side of the ravine shouted something and the American responded. His face turned toward the voice. At that instant, I clearly saw the rosy color of his cheek.
>
> He must have faced forward again and continued toward me. For some reason, the image of him at this moment is absent from memory.
>
> The next image I retain is one of the American cocking his head in the direction of the gunfire that erupted from the hilltop; this time his other cheek was facing me. Because of a feeling that still lingers in my memory, I am certain that I suffered a disruption of consciousness between observations of these two profiles of his face.
>
> Apparently, it was during this time that I lifted my gun and released the safety lock. Or did I shift my gaze down to my hands to do so? The image of the rifle I held in my hands, too, is missing from memory.
>
> The next recollection I have following this blank is of the sound of gunfire. (1:29)

The threat embodied in the approaching enemy soldier is overwhelming. Ōoka's only remaining psychic defense is to blank out and bar the unbearable image from consciousness. Awareness returns only when the extreme danger diminishes.

Ōoka is deeply disturbed by his lapse of memory. In "Before Capture," he interrogates himself as follows: "Did I forget because I didn't really want to remember? Or, in the same way women forget the agony of childbirth, did nature remove the memory of these moments from my mind because they were simply too painful to bear?" (1:34). With his second question, Ōoka approaches the psychological crux of his traumatic experience. Instead of nature erasing memory too painful to bear, however, it might be more accurate to say that these images of overwhelming threat could not be fully absorbed and integrated with prior experience in the first place. Even the images he does retain remain beyond the full grasp of his conscious mind. They are, in Lifton's terms, indelible death imprints inseparably bound up with the traumatic experience of having touched death and survived.[15]

Machine-gun fire continues sporadically for a time after the American soldier departs, but it subsides after a while. Ōoka is again left to face death alone. When he contemplates suicide his unbearable thirst returns with a vengeance, and he decides to kill himself after finding water. When the moon rises enough to illuminate his quest, he attempts to struggle to his feet, but collapses after taking just a few steps. As he rests in hopes of regaining his strength, he begins to suffer aural hallucinations in which a gentle but insistent voice warns him that if he doesn't immediately get up and look for water, his internal organs will go on strike. When the voice finally quiets down, he is assailed by excruciating chest pains.

With the coming of dawn, Ōoka discovers that he can walk again. As he gets under way, however, he hears shots ring out in front of him. Assuming that he's surrounded, he resigns himself to death without water. He carefully removes his grenade from his belt and prepares for the end: "I tried to conjure up the faces of all the people I loved, but none of them appeared clearly before my mind's eye. Feeling sorry for the people who milled about in confusion in the lower reaches of my consciousness, I smiled, bid them farewell, and struck the pin of the grenade against a rock. The pin flew off, but the grenade failed to explode" (1:43–44).

Ōoka happened to be carrying a dud. His subsequent attempt to kill himself with his rifle also fails: just as he gets his big toe on the trigger and the barrel to his forehead, he loses balance and falls to one side. Incapable of imagining a more stable arrangement that will ensure death rather than maiming, he sets his rifle aside and lies down. He describes his capture as follows:

> Although I was probably suffering from thirst, I have no memory of it.
>
> It's also unclear whether I fell asleep or lapsed into unconsciousness. As I slowly regained awareness, I became aware of repeated blows to my lower back. Just as it dawned on me that I was being kicked, I was grabbed firmly by one arm, and I fully returned to myself.
>
> While one American soldier held me by the right arm, the other

> pointed a rifle at me at close range. The one holding the rifle said, "Don't move. You're my prisoner." (1:46)

Even after capture, Ōoka is convinced that he will be killed after interrogation. After questioning, however, he is informed that he will be given food, water, and medical treatment and that he will be able to return home after the war. The next morning two soldiers help him walk down from the mountains toward Bulalacao. After reaching the foothills, he is carried the last ten kilometers by a group of Filipinos. It is only at this juncture that it dawns on him that he has escaped death: "All that reached my eyes as I lay on the stretcher carried on the Filipinos' shoulders were the bright sky and the branches of the trees along the path. Watching the beautiful greenery flow by above me, I finally had the margin to realize that I had been 'saved,' that my life would now continue on indefinitely into the future. At the same time, I realized how strange it had been to have lived for so long in constant anticipation of death" (1:53). By this time, Ōoka had been constantly immersed psychically and physically in death for nearly seven months. En route to Bulalacao, death finally recedes enough for him to know that he would live. There was no way for him to know at the time, however, that this same moment also marked the beginning of an even longer struggle with the burdens of survival. From the moment Ōoka realized he would live, his struggle changed from one against death to one with life as a heavily burdened battlefield survivor.

Psychic Numbing

Psychic numbing, a person's primary defense against overwhelming experience, was one of the most enduring psychological effects of Ōoka's traumatic frontline experience. His numbing began from the moment he learned that he would be conscripted, continued throughout the time he was at the front, and persisted for many years after survival. Indeed, to a significant extent, it frustrated his early literary efforts to come to terms with his traumatic battlefield experience and survival. Psychic numbing played an important role in three important areas of his war experience: his relationship with his comrades, extraordinary experience, and sense of self.

Impaired Mourning

From the moment his psychic immersion in death began, Ōoka became emotionally distanced from others. En route to Manila, for instance, he watched the sinking of another transport ship in the convoy with remarkable detachment:

> The squall passed quickly, barely moistening the soldiers' uniforms. The *Nichiranmaru* continued to fall behind. I thought, "It must be an accidental fire. If it had been hit by a torpedo, it would have sunk by now." After thoroughly searching the surface of the water for signs of approaching torpedoes, I casually looked back again.
>
> When I did, I noticed the dark, vibrant clouds that lingered on after the squall had passed. The *Nichiranmaru* was up against this vibrant backdrop, its prow raised high above the water. The ship was now so distant that its silhouette—half of which was concealed by the horizon—was hazy and indistinct. This shadow picture disappeared smoothly, as if being slowly pulled down from below. (2:50)

This description is suffused with a strange, surrealistic beauty. Ōoka gazes upon the unfolding disaster as if he were watching a shadow play being performed on a remote stage. The physical distance separating him from the sinking ship is equaled, perhaps even exceeded, by emotional distance. Before even reaching the Philippines, Ōoka's feelings had been dissociated almost completely from his perceptions and cognition of the tragic events taking place around him.

Psychic numbing is especially pronounced in his experience related to the corpses he encountered in Bulalacao. When his detachment first entered the village, they expected to be attacked at any moment. As Ōoka and his comrades moved through the streets, they saw dogs in the distance rise up from unidentifiable objects. They passed through the village square, and as they proceeded along a fence-lined residential street, Ōoka noticed a twisted expression cross the face of the young soldier immediately behind him. While knowing intuitively that he had seen a gruesome sight in one of the yards, Ōoka was preoccupied at the time with detecting the enemy. When they reached the outskirts of town, they realized that it was deserted. As they returned to the central square, Ōoka had the margin to glance back into the yard in question:

> There was a single corpse. It lay on its stomach, its face turned away. Its bloated, bare-skinned upper torso was reddish-brown, and the army fatigues beneath were smeared with death juices. It was clearly one of the navy men who had been attacked ten days before.
>
> The dead man had apparently either been shot where he was after fleeing into the yard from the square or had collapsed there when his strength ran out. The slightly bent arms were extended out beyond the head, and only the leg on one side was bent at a right angle. The position of the body suggested that his last intention had been to circle around behind the house. Perhaps it was simply the result of death throes.
>
> When I looked away, I saw another corpse in the yard on the opposite side of the street. A large ax had been thrown down next to the head. The profile of the immobile face was that of one sunk deeply in thought. (2:221–222)

Ōoka is conspicuously detached and matter-of-fact in his description of this scene of carnage. Although in close physical proximity, Ōoka nonetheless maintains a safe emotional distance from these grotesque embodiments of the violent, premature death he so dreads. As with the deaths of his comrades in San Jose, he is unaffected by the sight of these slaughtered, unburied bodies.

Ōoka is stunned, however, upon realizing that the yard is not the only place containing such corpses:

> A stench filled the air. That odor must have constantly been in our nostrils from the time we reached the square; I simply hadn't had the margin to notice. . . .
>
> When I returned to the square, I was stunned by my carelessness. There were several more bodies piled haphazardly one atop the other. Covered as they were in filth, the skin and clothes were hardly distinguishable from the surrounding earth. How could I have missed these enormous images? Was it because they resembled nothing in my prior experience, or had my eyes been solely concerned with detecting the enemy?
>
> The buttocks of one corpse was visible. The flesh was missing, exposing blackened vertebra. When we first saw the dogs they appeared to have been standing up on something; now I knew what their front legs had been resting on.
>
> There were flocks of carrion crows perched on the tops of the palms. They appeared to be waiting for us to move away from their food. (2:221–222)

Under the circumstances, all that warranted attention were the things that posed direct and immediate threats to life and limb. Bloated corpses, like carts or flower boxes, are inherently harmless.

Psychic numbing is also conspicuous in Ōoka's reaction to the loss of Private Kobayashi, the first Nishiya man to die on Mindoro Island. Ōoka had been on good terms with this young medic. In mid-November, Kobayashi was fatally wounded during a guerrilla ambush as he and several others were en route to the nearby coastal village of Caminawit. Ōoka describes his reaction to this loss in "Attack" (Shūgeki, 1950):

> Medic Kobayashi's body was brought back to barracks on a special car of the gasoline-powered train. I had just begun guard duty at the time. As his remains were carried past, the guards formed a line and raised their rifles. The dirty sheet didn't cover his body completely, and his pale, death-hardened face was exposed to one side.
>
> Don't think I was moved, however: after I became a soldier, I was unaffected by the loss of men who died as a result of the same cause that would take my own life. (2:154)

This last statement becomes Ōoka's defensive mantra.[16] He repeats it—with slight variations—in four separate places in his war memoirs. Ōoka sought to justify his callousness in terms of the conviction that he, too, would not return from the front. His seeming indifference, however, was clearly a defense against unbearable loss. The nature—violent, grotesque, premature, and pointless—and scale of death was simply too overwhelming and unacceptable for him to retain his normal capacity for emotional response.

Another of his compatriots dies—this time of malaria—just before the American landing. Once again, Ōoka is literally and figuratively on guard duty when he learns of the loss:

> I was on guard duty that day, and when the patient breathed his last at 10:00 A.M., I was standing in front of the barracks gate. I heard wailing voices from the sickroom. The patient was a distant relative of the company commander, and the laments of an NCO seeking to work his way into his good graces were especially audible.
>
> I was unmoved by the deaths of my comrades at the front. Once I decided that I too would die there, I lost all sympathy for the men who lost

> their lives as a result of the same cause that would take my own life. I have no idea whether others were like me in this regard or not.
>
> The local doctor who had attended the patient's last moments emerged from the sick ward. His eyes were red from weeping. Upon noticing me, he self-consciously said, "Japanese are sensitive," and walked away. (2:83)

Once again, Ōoka explains his lack of responsiveness in terms of the inevitability of his own death. His comment that he was unsure if others were as callous as he was is very telling. Even if one man's response was exaggerated, the expressions of lamentation emanating from the sickroom provide incontrovertible evidence that at least some of his comrades retained their capacity for emotional response. The doctor's bloodshot eyes and parting remark also serve to emphasize Ōoka's insensitivity.

Ōoka was not only incapable of responding emotionally to the deaths of his comrades while at the front, but steadfastly refused to mourn their loss as well. He writes as follows, for instance, after noting that he was unaffected by Private Kobayashi's passing:

> Using guard duty as my excuse, I attended neither funeral services nor wake.
>
> The corpse was burned that night behind our barracks. The young soldiers with farming experience worked hard to split the complex-grained tropical trees and amass enough wood for the fire. Despite their best efforts, one part of the corpse was only partially consumed by the flames. In the end, it was buried as was.
>
> The deceased was posthumously promoted to Private E-2, and a plain wood tablet about three feet high with "Private Kobayashi's Grave" written on it was set up in one corner of the area behind barracks. A path was cut to the grave, and we visited it together on the one-month anniversary. That, however, was our first and last chance. Before the next observance, the Americans had landed, and we had to abandon our barracks. (2:154–155)

Ōoka avoided participation in death-related rites of passage during the war. To defend against unbearable present and anticipated future losses, he initially had to reject the dead and dying. His attitude and behavior toward his fallen comrades are clearly indicative of an inability to mourn.

As previously mentioned, psychic numbing and impaired mourning persisted long after survival and demobilization. An experience he has on the repatriation ship is revealing in this regard. "Homecoming" (Kikan, 1950) ends with an unattended funeral and unmourned deaths:

> Two of the three sick men from Mindanao who boarded our ship died. I heard there would be a burial at sea, and an announcement was eventually made for all interested parties to gather on the aft deck.
>
> The men who died three days from their homeland were certainly unfortunate. Their misfortune, however, was no different from that of the men who died in combat. I damn near died myself. I returned home just as calloused as I had been at the front: I felt no sympathy for those who died from the same cause that virtually took my own life.
>
> I hadn't felt any desire to participate in funerals up to this point, so it wasn't right for me to attend one held at sea. Although vulgar curiosity made me want to witness this once-in-a-lifetime spectacle, based on a certain feeling at the bottom of my heart that had been driven by the realities of war to feel no pity for the dead, I knew that it wasn't right. I did what I thought to be most proper at the time, and stayed down in the hold. (1:472–473)

Extraordinary Experience

The effects of psychic numbing were not limited to callousness and impaired mourning, but included extraordinary experiences as well. These were of basically three kinds: those involving intimate identification with specific natural elements, near-ecstatic responses to natural beauty, and surrealistic death-in-life experiences. Ōoka experiences the first when he reacts to nature in human terms. The second arise when psychic numbing is momentarily broken through and he is affected by the beauty and grandeur of his physical surroundings. And the third were brought on by psychic disintegration and symbolic breakdown. These experiences, which ultimately stemmed from ongoing psychic and physical immersion in death, left indelible death imprints. Ōoka repeatedly notes in his memoirs that he was "haunted" by his extraordinary frontline experience long after his return home. As mentioned earlier, they linger on in memory as disturbing reminders both of having touched death and of survival itself.

As Ōoka grew emotionally distanced from others, he increasingly found himself in psychological isolation. Since this condition itself was unbearable, he compensated by identifying with selected natural objects. Ōoka had his first strange (*kikai*) experience on the shores of Dannoura Bay. He was also strongly drawn to trees. As with the constantly shifting ocean waters, trees such as the one he gazed at while on sentry duty in San Jose were intimately linked with death imagery. Like the water he gazed down on from the transport ship, moreover, trees were also closely associated with thoughts of his family. And at times, trees served as surrogate companions. The way Ōoka writes about palm trees shows the extent to which he relates to natural objects in human terms:

> I was seeing palm trees and the ocean for the first time in two weeks. I hadn't seen them since leaving San Jose. Of all the trees I saw at the front, I loved the palm the most. To me, the fronds that extended out fully in all directions were the ultimate image of tropical growth. When on night patrol in San Jose, I would frequently linger beneath them and eagerly listen to the metallic rustling sounds of their fronds. It was the absence of palms that made me most forlorn once we abandoned the coast. Now, after crossing through the mountains from San Jose, I was once again reunited with palm and ocean. (2:226)

Ōoka writes about the palm as if it were a lover: "she" is the one he is most attached to, the embodiment of tropical vitality, the one he seeks out at night to listen to, pines for, and is finally reunited with in Bulalacao. Relating to natural objects in this way is not only compensatory, but also safe in that trees demand nothing in return.

While searching for water after becoming separated from his comrades, Ōoka has an even more striking experience of communing with nature. This time he doesn't just relate to a natural object as if it were human, but literally perceives it as such:

> There was a huge pool, and four or five water buffalo were soaking in it. They were the ones we had loaded and brought with us from San Jose.
>
> They regarded me suspiciously. One of them gazed directly at me, and we looked into each other's eyes. The more I stared, the more *human* the face became. I experienced a strange sense of confusion. The water buffalo looked away in apparent embarrassment, let out a bellow, and emerged from the pool. Water drained noisily from its enormous body. (1:22)

Psychically and physically immersed as he was in death and cut off physically and emotionally from his company, Ōoka was in desperate need of companionship. Under the circumstances, however, his identification with nature, like the daydream he had of his wife and children, threatens to spin out of control. Ōoka's perception of the water buffalo as human and his strange sense of confusion result from psychological breakdown; by this point his ability to internally construct and interpret his unfolding experience is severely compromised.

In addition to identifying intimately with natural objects, Ōoka also has a number of ecstatic or peak experiences. These occur when extreme threats to life and limb momentary abate. At these times, Ōoka has the psychological margin to experience emotions that have theretofore been repressed or dissociated from consciousness. It is very telling, moreover, that he responds not to his comrades, but to the surrounding physical environment. His relief is palpable, for instance, upon safe ocean passage to the Philippines, and his reaction to the natural beauties of Manila borders on ecstasy: "I was enraptured by the primary colors of the palm and flame trees and by the Philippine sunrises and sunsets. While seeing the shadow of death everywhere, I feasted my eyes on the tropical scenes of plant life overwhelming animal life. I thanked the fate that enabled me to see such an abundance of life before I died. . . . I felt that the ever-intensifying sensation of joy I experienced while cradled in the bosom of nature was a sure sign that my final moments were drawing near" (1:8). Ōoka's heightened awareness of and sensitivity to his natural surroundings are inseparable from psychic immersion in death, and his intense sense of beauty stems from gazing through the eyes of the dying (*matsugo no me*).[17] While psychic numbing had the effect of dulling perception and removing reality from the external world, the momentary reintegration of emotion, perception, and cognition made things appear superreal.

If the experiences he has after reaching Manila can, to reverse Lifton's phrase, be described as life-in-death, those he has en route to the Philippines and while retreating through the central mountains can be characterized as death-in-life. The first of these occurs on the transport ship: "The diesel engine droned on and on as the ship moved over the dull, monotonous waters. Scattered, flat-bottomed clouds reminiscent of pounded rice cake offerings floated in the sky at fixed heights above the water and at a fixed distance from the ship. As the ship proceeded forward, the clouds, pivoting on one point above the horizon, rotated outward like an opening fan. My dizziness persisted even after I looked away. The water, too, continued to spin before my eyes" (2:43). Ōoka conveys the surrealness of the scene in terms of monotony (*tanchō*) and dizziness (*memai*), which are suggestive of disruptions to his sense of time and space. The constancy of the droning engine and surface of the water combine to give the feeling that time has come to a standstill. Ōoka's sense of spatial relationship, too, is affected. He feels stuck in a scene that is paradoxically dynamic and static at the same time. As with the roots of the fallen tree, the deadness he perceives in the external world is a projection of his internal state.

Ōoka has another haunting experience after he and his comrades withdraw from the coast. As the men work their way up through the foothills, the smoke and flames from signal fires rise before them. The men never, however, see the people they know to be setting the fires:

> I felt neither fear nor uneasiness. I simply walked forward while indifferently gazing at the smoke.
>
> Smoke rose from the grass-covered slopes in front of us. Fanned as it was by the wind, it suddenly increased in volume and swirled in ever-expanding patterns. We, however, had to press on toward it.
>
> The path followed the rises and falls of the grass-covered hills. When we dropped down into a hollow, all we could see was the wind dispersing the smoke that rose just above the slope in front of us. Upon reaching the crest of the rise, I could see the fire line approaching as smoke enveloped and obscured the lower grassland in the distance.
>
> The flames straddled the path. By the time I reached it, the fire line had already moved on, and nothing remained but low-lying smoke crawling over blackened grass. The flames fled downwind to the right as if chased away. (2:190–191)

Ōoka feels nothing as he walks toward the fires and smoke and gazes at them distractedly. As a result of Ōoka's death immersion and advanced psychic numbing, the scene takes on an eerie, dreamlike quality, and the smoke and flames appear to have lives of their own. Ōoka was clearly transfixed by these fires and the smoke they produced. Indeed, they left indelible imprints of death, which combined incomprehensibility, thralldom, and impending annihilation.

Ōoka has a closely related experience as he and his comrades press on toward the Rutay Highlands. Once they leave the fires behind and pass over the crest of the central mountain range, Ōoka has a peak experience reminiscent of those he had after safe arrival in Manila:

> We descended the ridge. The wind was blowing. The grasses swayed from side to side, and the voices of the men talking in front and behind me were swept away before I could make out what they were saying. Before me as far as the eye could see were layers upon layers of convoluted mountains with complex summits. Everything was covered with a soft green hue. . . . The sensation of descending the gentle slope, the dreamy verdure flowing this way and that with the wind—this was undoubtedly one of the most beautiful moments of my life. I secretly thought that after seeing this exceptionally beautiful landscape, it was all right to die. (2:206)

Here again, Ōoka's brief emotional responsiveness is solely concerned with nature. Like their muffled voices, Ōoka's comrades do not enter into consciousness with anything near the intensity and immediacy of the expansive vistas in the distance. Rather than being superreal, as were his experiences in Manila, however, this experience was surreal. Under the circumstances, only marginal reintegration of emotion, perception, and cognition was possible, and the external world was perceived as if in a dream.

Ōoka has another, more unsettling experience just prior to capture. At this point, sensory perception is virtually all that remains of awareness:

> The passing shower came to an end. I twisted my head around and looked windward in the direction of our machine-gun emplacement. By the light of the misty moon I could make out a familiar stand of trees beyond the upper reaches of the gentle, grass-covered slopes. The emplacement was unexpectedly near.
>
> The grove was enveloped in mist. Sound returned to the area, the wind brushed my cheeks, and rain fell from the depths of the sky. . . . The clouds parted directly above me, and a misshapen moon came into view. The moonlight penetrating my eyes was unbearably bright. The rain stopped.
>
> How long could it have been until dawn? . . .
>
> The moon gradually moved behind the branches of the huge trees on the other side of the valley, where it seemed to linger on for a time. At some point, the shadows receded and the moonlit area was infused with the milky-white light of dawn. Then, all of a sudden, it was daylight. (1:41)

Ōoka recalls and records these extraordinary experiences because they are imagistic reminders of the protracted period during which he psychologically passed over into and dwelled in the realm of death. This made these experiences both haunting and unforgettable. His memories of touching death, or, put differently, of psychic death, result in what Lifton has called a permanent encounter with death. Even after survival, the traumatic intrusion of death into life can never quite be fully purged from memory.

The Nature of Self

Ōoka suffered from advanced psychic disintegration during the twenty-four-hour period between separation from his company and capture. As previously mentioned, psychic numbing caused emotion to be dissociated from cognition and perception long before this time. As circumstances worsened, another basic component of self—the survival instinct—not only became separated from, but also increasingly came to be at odds with consciousness. In addition to such intrapsychic dissociation, uncontrollable events transpiring in the external world also played a significant role in his extreme experience. Ōoka's traumatic battlefield experience—particularly his transformative encounter with the young American soldier—ultimately forced him to radically reconsider the very nature of self.

Ōoka describes the initial emergence and psychological effects of survival instinct as follows:

> [W]hen our escape route was finally cut off and I saw my comrades dying one after another all around me, a strange transformation occurred within me. I suddenly began to believe in the possibility of survival. In this way, the certainty of my death was brushed aside, and I suddenly felt like pursuing the fanciful thread of hope I began to imagine. I felt that at the very least I had to do everything I could to realize it.
>
> This was clearly a physical reaction to the shadow of death darkening around me. During extremity such as this, while the things our bodies make us do are practical in the extreme, the thoughts that accompany them are invariably absurd. (1:8–9)

Ōoka approaches his extreme experience partially in terms of a strange internal transformation. When his body kicks into survival mode, he can no longer sit on his hands and passively await death. And once his body begins to act on its own in the interest of self-perpetuation, his conscious mind is effectively co-opted into its service.

The first biological demand is that Ōoka believe in the possibility of survival. This instinctually mandated hopefulness can be seen in the fanciful escape plans he and "S" come up with. Both assume that they will be attacked and routed. Once the assault begins, they plan to slip through enemy lines, make their way to the coast, appropriate a sailboat, and follow the trade winds to Borneo. If they cannot get a boat, they intend to return to the mountains and live off the land like Robinson Crusoe until the end of the war. Conceiving of escape spurs Ōoka into taking more positive steps to extend his life:

> These were pipe dreams, but we were convinced that they could actually be realized. We went over our plans again and again. As three of our comrades died around us every day, we were as cheerful as grave diggers (we actually did dig graves). We also thought of what to do in the event that we were attacked by our most immediate enemy—malaria—and did everything we could to build up the strength that was our only defense against it. We ate the rice gruel left by the sick and scrounged for grains that had fallen to the ground. (1:10)

After Ōoka becomes separated from his comrades, his biological drives assert themselves ever more forcefully. When he begins to seriously consider suicide, he is assailed by a thirst so intense and insistent that attending to it immediately takes priority over everything else. Keiko McDonald has rightly suggested that Ōoka's search for water was inseparable from his quest for life.[18] He rationalizes this paradoxical quest in terms of providing himself *matsugo no mizu,* (the last drink of water for the dead and dying). During his traumatic encounter with the enemy, moreover, instinctual self-preservation takes over almost completely, forcing him to act contrary to the dictates of "free will." Despite resolving not to shoot, he mechanically prepares to defend himself when the young American soldier actually appears before him: "I picked up my rifle and released the safety. Was I not, after all, intent on shooting? Or was I preparing to protect myself, reacting instinctually in the same way I would close my eyes just before an insect landed on my face?" (1:34).

As important as Ōoka's multifaceted intrapsychic dissociation was to his actions and experience in extremity, however, the significance of events taking place in the external world at the time was undeniable. Through his detailed analysis of his *jiken* in "Before Capture," Ōoka not only came to realize the extent to which he was reacting to the enemy who approached him, but also that the critical factor in his encounter was the eruption of machine-gun fire: "I remember the natural movement of my hand as it reached for, and then released the rifle's safety lock. In light of this fact, I can only say with *certainty* that the sole reason I was able to actualize my decision [not to shoot] was due to the sudden eruption of gunfire that caused the American to walk away. This was nothing more than chance (*gūzen*)" (1:28).

Accompanying Ōoka's recognition of the importance of chance was the realization that prior notions about the nature of self were wholly inadequate to account for his extreme experience. As he writes in "The Rains of Tacloban" (Takuroban no ame, 1948):

> I, however, have been presuming all along that in terms of chronological continuity, my restraint resulted from my earlier decision. Can I really be so sure of this? There is nothing in my *psychology* from the time to support it.
>
> Up to this point in my analysis, I seem to have been ruminating continuously on my resolve. This, however, did not necessarily extend beyond the bounds of vague daydreaming; there is no reason to believe that it was still viable when the American actually appeared before me, that I was continually determined not to shoot. I was unexpectedly brought back to awareness by the voices that reached me from the other side of the valley. I was *shocked*. The psychological state that then began to unfold within me in conjunction with a new sense of *anticipation* need not have had any connection whatsoever to my earlier daydreaming. (1:30–31)

Ōoka eventually comes to the following conclusion: "Despite the commonly held view that takes human will as the foundation of consciousness, the more I reflect on my inner psychology of the time, the weaker its influence becomes" (1:105).

In the end, in-depth analysis of his traumatic encounter enabled Ōoka to realize not only that the self is constructed, but also the extent to which it is inextricably intertwined with and contingent upon the external world. Ōoka was one of the first postwar writers to expose, stress, and pursue the ramifications of the complex, multidimensionality of identity.[19] As Kamei Hideo observes, his experience led him to reject the basic assumption that psychological continuity (*renzokusei*) or integrity was the ground of selfhood and, in so doing, challenge the commonly held view of modern Japanese literary figures that simplistically conflates inner psychology with identity. In other words, Ōoka realized that to be holistically grasped and articulated, the self had to be seen as a complicated, multifaceted construct inextricably embedded in physical (and sociopolitical) context. As Ikeda Jun'ichi so suggestively intimates, the meaning of individual existence emerges only in relation to others.[20]

Ōoka's condition of advanced psychic disintegration persisted beyond his transformative encounter with the enemy soldier. After the American departs, Ōoka is again left to face death in isolation. When he removes his equipment, takes off his puttees, and lies down, however, he is again assailed by unbearable thirst. Once again, moreover, his mind works to rationalize his biological demand: "I tried to convince myself that by ending my life then and there, I could kill my thirst as well. My thirst, however, did not agree. My throat wanted me to end my life only after I had first slaked its burning thirst. This seemed to be a reasonable enough demand. I liked the theme of the 'suicide who wants to kill himself after drinking water,' and I came to accept my bodily desires" (1:36).

Subsequently denied access to water and having no means of knowing how long the enemy would remain in the area, Ōoka eventually despairs and attempts suicide:

> I unclipped the grenade from my belt, placed it on the ground in front of me, and stared at it. It was a Model 99—a small, hexagonal steel cylinder painted reddish-brown and crisscrossed with deep grooves. It was designed so that the one-centimeter-square pieces formed by the indentations would be blown in every direction when the gunpowder ignited.
>
> I tried to remove the safety wire inserted through the pin. It was wrapped around it tightly, and I couldn't free it by hand. As I attempted to dislodge it with the tip of my bayonet, it suddenly occurred to me that if I couldn't remove it, I probably wouldn't be able to die. One part of me seemed to feel that it would be fine if I failed. My hands, however, continued to work resolutely on the wire and eventually succeeded in removing it against what could be called my wishes.
>
> I won't go into the reasons my suicide attempt ended in failure. Even the psychology of a person who succeeds in killing himself is of little interest. All the more so for one who fails. Success or failure hinges on the outcome of the struggle between a considerably strong will seeking to carry out a fundamentally unnatural act and the sound instinctual forces that oppose it. And what ultimately determines the final result is a variety of totally random, external conditions. It was pure chance that I survived: the grenade I carried happened to have been a dud. (1:42–43)

Death Guilt

Lifton asserts that "no survival experience . . . can occur without severe guilt" and that the way survivors deal with deep-seated guilt feelings has a significant effect on the outcome of their formulative struggles. Ōoka's battlefield memoirs and early, war-related fictional works such as *Lady Musashino* and *Fires on the Plain* are marked by "numbed guilt," which is characterized by "a series of maneuvers designed to avoid the experience of guilt feelings."[21] The first part of this section will consider the psychological tactics Ōoka employed to ward off feelings of guilt and self-recrimination and will highlight several key instances when the sudden return of the repressed momentarily breached his psychological defenses.

Interspersed with Ōoka's rationalization, self-justification, and scapegoating of his comrades are implicit and explicit admissions of personal failings. The guarded confessions (*kokuhaku*) that will be taken up in the second part of this section are closely linked to incipient struggles to come to terms with death guilt and personal responsibility and expose the countervailing desire to confront, reflect, and pass judgment on survival. While partial in the sense that there are crucial aspects of his traumatic experience Ōoka could not bring himself to fully acknowledge and work through in his memoirs, the revelations he does manage to make facilitated progress on his journey of survivor formulation.

Anxious Rationalization

Ōoka accounts for his survival—and explains away the deaths of his comrades—primarily in terms of luck (*un*) and chance (*gūzen*). While containing a measure of truth, these formulations aim to avoid the painful emotional issues that are integral to survival. The exclusive focus on luck, chance, and fate not only implies survivor passivity, but also preempts thorough consideration of what one actually did or failed to do in the interest of self-preservation. Rationalizing survival in terms of luck and chance was Ōoka's initial means of fending off guilt feelings, absolving himself of responsibility, and dodging the crucial matter of indebtedness to those who "died in his place."

In "Departure for the Front" (Shussei, 1950), Ōoka writes as follows about survival: "In the end, I arrived at Manila safely. I survived to write this account because of a chain of fortuitous events. After reaching Manila, however, I had to squeeze through innumerable narrow passageways of chance—my survival certainly wasn't a simple matter of ever-improving fortune" (2:22). If he survived because of a complex chain of good luck, then his comrades must have died when their luck ran out. Ōoka approaches Nakano's death precisely in these terms. After avoiding malaria and slipping unharmed through enemy lines after the January 24 attack, he and a small group of companions were detected and chased by Filipinos: "Being agile, he started out at the front of the fleeing group, but tripped on something and fell to the ground. With no margin to pause and help him up, the others surged by and disappeared into the underbrush. While they escaped unharmed, this was the last that was seen of Nakano. . . . His decisive misfortune was the single act of tripping in those Philippine mountains" (2:314). Undeniably, it was a decisive misfortune for Nakano to have fallen when and where he did. Ōoka seems reluctant, however, to consider his other, equally decisive misfortune of being abandoned by his brothers-in-arms: had someone stopped to help him up, his luck may well have changed.

The Nishiya squad stationed in Caminawit, too, was woefully unfortunate:

> The men who happened to be away on lookout when the Americans landed were just unlucky. Although we didn't lose a single man during our withdrawal, two men disappeared from their squad during their retreat. Many of their men wore out their boots on the march and had to wrap their bare feet in rags. How miserable! Some among us had extra pairs of boots, but no matter how good-hearted, not a single man thought to give a pair to those in need.
>
> We all bore the fate of being routed soldiers with no idea what the next day would bring. Under these circumstances, even when a man has the emotional margin to feel compassion for another, there is absolutely nothing to make him act on his feelings. (2:233–234)

Even as he maneuvers to account for the deaths of an entire squad in terms of chance and bad luck, Ōoka can't help but acknowledge the human factors that also conditioned their fate. Like the men who abandoned Nakano, the men in the Rutay Highlands had thoughts only for themselves. Too exhausted upon reaching the encampment to build adequate shelter, the men from the Caminawit squad fell ill and died long before the others. None of their comrades—most of whom were still healthy and strong—lifted a finger to help them. While Ōoka subsequently accounts for their behavior in terms of military "sectionalism," his underlying anxiety is discernable in his acknowledgment of his comrades' survival egoism. Their luck, too, might have changed had they received timely assistance.

Because Ōoka was extremely uneasy over survival in the face of the deaths of so many of his comrades, his rationalizations about luck and chance could only partially shield him from deep-seated feelings of guilt and self-blame. While effective during his traumatic ordeal, defensive formulations such as these became extremely problematic after survival. This is noticeable in the following passage describing his departure from San Jose after being taken prisoner:

> We passed by our former barracks. All the windows were shut tight and the building was silent. The sandbag fortifications and the water tank we had used were still there just as they had been, as if somehow forgotten amid the vast changes wrought upon the area by the Americans. Now, virtually every man I had lived with in those barracks for those six months was dead. As we drove toward the airfield, I continued to look at our former barracks until they disappeared from view; my heart, however, was all but indifferent.
>
> They died; I lived. There is no other way to view this incontrovertible reality. Every survivor conceals this kind of egoism behind mournful masks that seem to bid tearful farewell to the dead. This is not an emotional matter. It is the the product of reality. (1:71)

Ōoka feels virtually nothing as he leaves San Jose—no sadness, grief, anger, remorse, or even nostalgia. If anything, he feels joy over survival—a feeling that, under the circumstances, is natural, but wholly unacceptable.[22] Here, Ōoka attempts to dismiss the entire experience with a formulation even more basic than luck or chance: "They died, I lived." While accurate and undeniable, this fails to adequately address crucial psychological issues related to death guilt, to how and why he came through the ordeal when so many of his comrades did not.

Toward the end of the passage, Ōoka expresses his ambivalence over survival. While he explains the joy he feels over having come through alive as the result of reality, at a deeper level he clearly feels that his inner celebration of personal survival is not only unseemly, but also morally wrong.

Even while indirectly expressing self-recrimination, he seeks to rationalize his lack of grief. His elation over survival seems to preclude, or at least render insincere, any belated expression of emotion for the war dead. And despite Ōoka's insistence to the contrary, these kinds of survivor responses are inseparable from emotional issues.

Despite Ōoka's best efforts, repressed feelings of death guilt periodically break through into consciousness. This initially occurs soon after capture. After interrogation, the American commander informs him that he'll "probably be able to go home after the war" (1:51). Ōoka recalls listening to him "absentmindedly." He adds that at the time, his "heart didn't have the resiliency to respond" to this wholly unforeseen development. He does, however, react spontaneously to the sight of a physical reminder of a dead comrade:

> [A] soldier put the papers into a Japanese duffel. The owner's name sewn on the cover seared into my eyes. It was the Taishō critic's son who had stayed behind with me in the sick hut to the bitter end. When I left ahead of the others, he had been the one who protested, "But aren't we going together?" This was a terrible blow. I looked away and shouted, "Someone kill me, shoot me right now! I can't go on living when all my comrades are dead!" I heard someone say, "He's all mine." I turned around to see a soldier aiming a machine gun at me. I presented my chest and said "Go ahead," but my face twisted when I saw the mischievous look in his eyes. (1:51)

The impassioned words that pour forth at this moment are a rare but highly significant and sincere expression of deep-seated feelings of death guilt and self-recrimination. Emotionally speaking, it is unacceptable to go on living when "all" his comrades have died.

Ōoka's feelings of survivor guilt find expression again the following day as he is being transported by ship from Bulalacao to San Jose:

> As I looked at the shadow-filled coastal mountains and the sparkling sea, I reflected anew on the reality of having been saved. At the same time, my chest tightened painfully at the thought that I was now a prisoner of war.
>
> Despite the teachings of the Japanese military, I hadn't thought that it was all that shameful to be captured. In this day and age when advancements in weaponry had drastically reduced the role manpower played in determining the outcome of battle, I thought the commander was to blame if a gross disparity in fighting strength arose on the battlefield, and that it was every

> soldiers' right to forgo useless resistance. Now that I had actually become a prisoner of war, however, I realized how strange and unworthy it was to be calmly enjoying life among the enemy while my comrades continued to put their lives on the line.
>
> I was suddenly assailed by an urge to kill myself by jumping into the sea right then and there. As when I yelled "Kill me!" the day before upon seeing my dead comrade's duffel in the hands of the enemy after interrogation, however, this was a false impulse lacking any foundation in the truth of my existence. There were no nearby Americans on guard at the time, but I didn't move a muscle.
>
> This urge eventually passed, leaving only profound sadness in its wake. I felt sorry for myself for having to experience such false impulses. (1:59)

There is great disparity between Ōoka's thoughts and feelings after he realizes he has survived. While he thinks that there is no real shame in a soldier's being taken alive, his chest tightens painfully and he feels unworthy when it actually happens to him. Although he clearly thinks that he is fortunate to have come through alive, he feels it to be so terribly wrong and unacceptable that he is again overcome by a powerful impulse to kill himself. It is also significant that Ōoka expresses a range of powerful emotions—relief, joy, shame, self-pity, and, perhaps most significant of all, grief—in this passage. This period of emotional responsiveness, however, is of short duration. Ōoka quickly maneuvers to stave off the feelings underlying his spontaneous expression and urges by dismissing them as false impulses. While insisting that his desire to end his life has absolutely no foundation in the truth of his existence, he assumes that the natural but unacceptable happiness he experiences over survival does. In his early autobiographical writings, Ōoka was clearly more concerned with survival egoism than death guilt.

Guarded Confessions

Ōoka usually referred to the relatively short, autobiographical pieces he wrote on his war experience as ***kiroku*** (memoirs). From time to time, however, he described them as his ***kokuhaku*** (confessions).[23] The Japanese term "***kokuhaku***" has two related meanings. In the context of early modern Japanese literary history, it is used to designate the nonreligious, personal, self-revelatory autobiographical writings of *shishōsetsuka,* or "I-novelists" such as Shiga Naoya. As in the West, moreover, the term can also be used for painful admissions of moral or ethical transgression. Ōoka used the term primarily in this latter sense. In 1953, after he had for the most part finished writing his battlefield and prisoner-of-war memoirs, he reflected as follows in "Those I Can't Forget" (Wasureenu hitobito): "What had *my* attitude been like during the war? Out of my personal need to confess (*kokuhaku*), I've written hundreds of pages on my battlefield experience. Reading back through what I've written today, I'm disgusted by the lengths I went to to justify myself. How did I look to a more objective eye while I was at the front? . . . Just once I'd like to ask one of my comrades how I appeared to them at the time" (2:302).

One of Ōoka's deep motivations for writing about his war experience was to divulge his own inferior frontline attitude and conduct. Even as he sought to do so, however, he couldn't help but engage in defensive self-justification. Ōoka's literary confessions are consequently not only guarded, but also ambivalent. For these reasons, they must, like Mishima Yukio's cagey postwar autobiographical work *Confessions of a Mask* (Kamen no kokuhaku, 1949), be engaged with caution and awareness of the psychological and emotional conflicts of traumatized authors. As the death camp survivor-narrator Aharon Appelfeld warns us, "While the survivor recounts and reveals, at the very same time he also conceals."[24] When approached with these matters in mind, Ōoka's *kokuhaku* provide a relatively accurate picture of what he did and failed to do in the name of self-perpetuation and enable us to appreciate the extreme difficulty of coming to terms with the complex burdens of survival.

Ōoka's confessions are of two types: those concerning his own inferior attitude and conduct as an Imperial soldier and those directly related to survival egoism and his callous, occasionally antagonistic relations with his comrades. Ōoka openly admits that throughout his tenure as a soldier he was preoccupied with himself and thoughts of his impending death. Thus, one of his central revelations has to do with the extent to which psychic numbing and immersion in death negatively conditioned his frontline attitude and conduct.

From conscription to capture, Ōoka maintained a resigned, defeatist attitude toward Japan's "holy war" (*seisen*). In contrast to his younger, idealistic comrades, Ōoka could find no meaning or value in the Greater East Asia War. While his disillusion stemmed from in-depth studies of the

Napoleonic wars and World War I and his detailed knowledge of Japan's severely limited production capabilities, Ōoka couldn't help but be aware of—and admit—that he lacked something fundamental. And while his attitude may have seemed justifiable during the war, in retrospect he came to feel that it was wrong, unseemly, and reprehensible.

In "Departure for the Front," Ōoka records the thoughts that came to him just before being shipped off to war:

> As I idly passed the time gazing at the ocean, the wretchedness of my situation gradually settled to the pit of my stomach. For all I knew, the ship would pull anchor the next day. Death had now pressed in until it was right before my eyes. I had resigned myself to dying, but how pointless it would be.
>
> I thought this hopeless war was started because of the desperation of poor Japanese capitalists and the vanity of old-headed militarists. It was ludicrous for me to be sacrificed as a result, but it was unavoidable since I had been powerless to stop them. In the depths of my despair, I felt that my homeland wouldn't be worth living in after defeat anyway.
>
> When meaningless death pressed in on me, however, I realized for the first time that *I would be killed.* I reflected on whether, since I was to die in any event, I shouldn't have risked my life to resist the capitalists and military men who were now killing me. (2:27–28)

For Ōoka, the war—be it in China, Southeast Asia, or the Pacific—was little more than the product of Japan's economic difficulties and anachronistic, martial hubris. As such, it was inherently stupid and meaningless, and his death at the front could be nothing else. Toward the end of the passage, Ōoka broaches the issue of nonresistance. As a man who came of age in the 1930s witnessing the most important and influential Japanese intellectuals and artists undergo apostasies (*tenkō*), however, he was well aware of the extraordinary coercive powers of the state (2:28). He first considered resistance when he changed jobs six months before being drafted. In the end, however, he decided to pursue the path that offered the best chances of survival: "In short, instead of actively opposing the military, which at the time would *certainly* have gotten me killed, I thought that if I laid low, I wouldn't necessarily be conscripted; if conscripted, I wouldn't necessarily be sent to the front; if sent to the front, I wouldn't necessarily be killed" (2:28).

Ōoka briefly reconsidered resistance as he awaited departure for the front, but he quickly realized that it would be little but a symbolic, self-destructive gesture. After explaining his capitulation in this way, Ōoka makes an important confession: "I was painfully aware of my stupidity, but since it was the inevitable outcome of a life devoid of ideals, there was nothing I could do about it. And nothing's really changed—I'm still a man lacking ideals" (2:29). Ōoka openly acknowledges that before, during, and even after the war he had absolutely no sense of higher purpose or ultimate value to guide his conduct. Without such ideals and beliefs, it was virtually impossible for him to find meaning in, rely on, or invest in anything but himself.

Communications would seem to have been the only area in which Ōoka fulfilled his military duties. In several places, he asserts that he performed his job seriously and conscientiously. Even his relatively positive self-depictions, however, are not free of self-criticism. In "Journey of the Routed" (Haisō kikō, 1950), he portrays himself as follows: "I was constantly preoccupied with how I would die. I nonetheless flattered myself by thinking that the communications work I did meant life or death for our sixty-man defensive force in San Jose. I carried out my duties to the best of my abilities during the six months of our occupation" (2:194). Even while acknowledging his exemplary performance, Ōoka feels compelled to draw attention to his self-absorption, preoccupation with death, and inflated sense of self-worth.

The complex interweaving of self-justification and confession that characterizes much of Ōoka's autobiographical writing on his war experience is especially apparent in two rifle-related incidents. The first concerns abandoning his weapon during the retreat from San Jose, the second, his failure to engage the enemy. Ōoka was particularly troubled by the latter incident, which he wrote about at length in his first *kokuhaku,* "Before Capture."

Ōoka was forced to carry a useless rifle during the long march to the Rutay Highlands. In "Journey of the Routed," he explains the circumstances leading to this state of affairs: "My rifle lacked the metal plate needed for securing the ammunition clip. Since the supply sergeant . . . neglected to follow the necessary procedures for retiring it, someone had to keep carrying it. Exempt as I was from guard duty and patrols, that honor fell to me" (2:185). Ōoka was just recovering from his first bout with malaria when the Americans landed at Mindoro. Given his weakened physical condition, he was understandably upset over having a useless weapon foisted on him. When he asked his squad leader if he could discard the rifle if it proved too much for him, the squad leader looked away and mumbled a vague affirmation. This is the context for Ōoka's next confession:

> While I don't think it was particularly devilish of me to gleefully smile to myself for getting my way, I clearly wasn't a very good soldier; I had already arbitrarily predicted defeat and thought exclusively about my own death. Even if I was ill at the time, however, I shouldn't have so readily accepted this NCO's pragmatism.
>
> As an expedient for easing my conscience, I told myself I'd only get rid of the rifle when I was physically incapable of carrying it any further. In actuality, however, I abandoned it well before this point. "Expedient" placations of conscience are impotent before the desire for rest. One is not at liberty to senselessly postpone realization of the rest they imagine. (2:186)

Ōoka manages to carry his rifle for two days. On the second night, however, he decides to dispose of it first thing in the morning. He describes his subsequent actions with brevity and concision: "And so, I abandoned my rifle. I waited until the line of marching men thinned out, slipped into the woods, and carefully hid the useless weapon under the thick grass at the base of a tree" (2:200). Ōoka certainly had ample justification for abandoning his weapon. While logically defensible, however, the action was unacceptable ethically and emotionally. Regardless of the circumstances, Ōoka cannot help feeling that he committed a grave social transgression. In retrospect, Ōoka felt that his behavior exposed a fundamental aspect of his character: in extremity he was a man who would think and act only in his own personal interest.

At the time, Ōoka obviously didn't think of the potentially grave consequences of his conduct (abandoning one's weapon on the battlefield was an offense punishable by death). When he emerges from the thicket, his comrades immediately see that he is unarmed. Before long, he attracts the attention of his company commander, who demands an explanation. After admitting what he has done, he is ordered to retrieve the rifle and give a full accounting of himself at day's end. In the end, Commander Nishiya overlooks his transgression. Neither rationalization nor official leniency, however, can ease his burning shame (*haji*). During this experience, and the one to be discussed below, he is a man divided: while logic and survival instinct spur him to act in the interest of self-preservation, conscience reminds him of the serious ethical ramifications of his behavior.

After Ōoka recovers his rifle, an NCO comes up to him, briefly studies his gait, judges him recovered from his illness, and orders him to carry the rifle of a stricken comrade in addition to his own. This ironic development leads in to Ōoka's next confession:

> Why did I agree to do such an unreasonable thing? Whether officially pardoned or not, a soldier in the army who abandons his rifle is plagued by guilty conscience (*ushirometai mono*). My position in the group was now extremely insecure; although no one mentioned it, my comrades all knew what I had done.
>
> I undoubtedly pushed my fever-wracked body to carry the stricken man's rifle out of a secret desire to regain my former position in the group. I wanted as many of my comrades as possible to see me with two rifles.
>
> Thinking, "Dammit! the line's thinned out too much—the next guy's still forty yards away—no one'll notice my beautiful act," I rested in the grass. (2:209–210)

Ōoka's most difficult *kokuhaku* concerns the details surrounding his failure to engage the enemy. Consequently, his treatment of this experience is obscured by rationalization, self-justification, and omission. After outlining his traumatic encounter in general, Ōoka writes, "Since that time, I have often reflected on my conduct during those moments" (1:26). These reflections (*hansei*) are both stimulated and inhibited by deep-seated feelings of death guilt and self-recrimination.

Until his traumatic encounter, Ōoka had assumed all along that he would fight. This is clear from an incident that occurred before the American landing. Immediately upon being informed that Private Kobayashi and his comrades had been ambushed, Commander Nishiya leads a punitive force to the scene. Ōoka and nine others are ordered to stay behind and guard company headquarters. A local farmer subsequently tells them that a 150-man guerrilla force is closing in on them. Taking this report at face value (it turned out to be false), the soldiers hurriedly prepare for combat. At the time, Ōoka was determined to fulfill his patriotic duty: "I set my rifle on the ground at the edge of the trench. I intended to shoot the instant the enemy appeared" (2:145). He goes on to note that although he "didn't despise the enemy," he had no doubts that he was capable of "hating them with a passion if they killed his comrades" (2:145). By the time Ōoka had his fateful encounter with the young American, the enemy—both Filipino and American—had done just that. Yet when the lone soldier appeared before him, he felt neither hatred nor an urge to shoot. The burning question he struggles to formulate a viable answer for is Why not?

Ōoka writes that as he lay at the edge of the clearing, he resolved not to shoot. His decision is premised on the assumption that he and every man in his company is predestined to die. Thinking of things in this way works to relieve him of personal responsibility: since death is inevitable, nothing he does or fails to do can have any significant effect on the final outcome.

In the scene Ōoka envisions to himself before the encounter, when the enemy appears, Ōoka stands and exposes himself, raises his rifle as if to shoot, and then allows himself to be shot and killed. This scene, however, bears little resemblance to what actually occurs:

> I heard a voice from the high ground on the other side of the valley. Another voice answered "Yes,——" in a Filipino accent. The voices echoed through the still air of the forest. There was a strange vividness to this, my first direct contact with the violent forces we had opposed from a distance for so long. I got up quickly.
>
> I heard no more voices, just the rustling sound of men walking through the underbrush. I felt compelled to keep my eyes on the clearing before me. Just as I imagined, a lone American soldier was coming into view.
>
> As anticipated, I felt no urge to shoot.
>
> He was young—about twenty years old—and tall. His rosy cheeks were conspicuous beneath the outline of his deep combat helmet. He approached with his rifle held diagonally before him. He kept his body upright and walked with the slow, methodical gait of a mountaineer.
>
> I was shocked by his lack of caution. He appeared not to have the slightest idea that a Japanese soldier might lie directly in his path. A soldier on the other side of the valley shouted something. The soldier before me responded briefly. The exchange went something like "How is it over there?" "A-Okay." The soldier slowly closed in on me.
>
> I experienced a peculiar shortness of breath. I, too, was a soldier. Although I was virtually incapacitated, I had been strangely confident in my marksmanship ever since I had scored well with live rounds during shooting practice at school. No matter how debilitated, I would not miss a fully exposed opponent I detected first. My right hand moved instinctively and released the rifle's safety catch.

> The soldier covered half the distance initially separating us. Machine-gun fire then erupted from the area of our company's emplacement on the hilltop to my right. The American faced the direction of the disturbance, which continued for a time. He then came to a stop, and, after briefly assessing the sounds, calmly changed direction and began to walk away toward them. He gradually picked up speed, and, in the blink of an eye, disappeared from view.
>
> I breathed a sigh of relief, forced a smile, and muttered, "Well, now, I deserve the gratitude of a mother somewhere in America for that." (1:24–25)

It is revealing that Ōoka's first thoughts after the encounter are of the thanks he deserves from the enemy's mother for "saving" her son. He is much more reluctant to consider the implication of his actions to his comrades. Eventually, however, he brings himself to briefly reflect on this disturbing matter as well:

> Anyway, the American soldier walked off without noticing me, and I was left alone to drink the heady brew of my "beautiful act" of "saving" the youth. This liquor, however, had a bitter aftertaste. It suddenly occurred to me that the soldier I just allowed to escape would now add to the heavy burden borne by my comrades by immediately joining the battle taking place near our machine-gun emplacement.
>
> This reflection was hard to bear. Outnumbered as we were, however, my comrades would all die anyway. I, myself, *probably wouldn't live much longer.* This notion, as always, was my universal excuse. (1:35)

Ōoka opens and closes his detailed treatment of this encounter in "Before Capture" with overt references to serious, ethical reflection on his conduct. The *hansei* he engages in after the encounter comes to a bloodless end, however, is bitter and guilt ridden. Ōoka immediately maneuvers, however, to stave off rising feelings of guilt and self-recrimination by invoking his universal excuse (*bannō no kōjitsu*). While this may have been effective at the time, after survival he cannot help but admit that it was little more than a defensive rationalization. And once survival undermines his primary means of justification, Ōoka finds himself in the position of having to belatedly come up with something to replace it or more fully confront the excruciating truth of his traumatic experience. In his memoirs, he attempts to do both.

In "Before Capture," Ōoka seeks to explain his failure to carry out his soldierly duty in terms of his preencounter resolve not to shoot, his humanism, an animal aversion to spilling blood, hesitation, paternal feelings, fear, chance, and, in another memoir to be turned to below, divine intervention. In the end, however, none of these factors—either in isolation or in combination—adequately accounts for his conduct. Ōoka cannot formulate an explanation he can live comfortably with. The closest he comes are the paternal feelings he imagines he might have experienced when the enemy soldier momentarily stopped advancing toward him:

> I don't believe that my decision not to shoot came from my love of humanity. When I *saw* that young American, however, I loved him for personal reasons. I believe that this was the reason I didn't feel like shooting him.
>
> Because my initial decision left no trace in the chain of elements that make up my psychology from the time, it is difficult to view it as the guiding force of my thoughts and actions. However, I have no choice but to believe in the proposition that my sensibilities as a father prevented me from shooting. Although I have no memory of actually feeling that way at the time, I can't help but believe it because it *explains* certain subtleties related to the images that remain in my mind and the thoughts that came to me immediately after he walked away. (1:33)

In a desperate attempt to find a satisfactory explanation for his problematic conduct, Ōoka grasps for emotions he cannot remember having. Given psychic numbing, death immersion, and his deteriorated physical condition, it is extremely unlikely that he could have been experiencing anything other than primal terror.[25] It is all but impossible to imagine that a man incapable of responding emotionally to his comrades suddenly is able to do so toward an armed enemy during a hostile encounter.

In "The Rains of Tacloban," a prisoner-of-war memoir published about six months after "Before Capture," Ōoka divulges the lengths he was willing to go to in search of a comforting explanation. The following thoughts occurred to him in the Leyte POW hospital:

> In that clearing in the woods, I wanted nothing more than to convey my goodwill to the man who would kill me. Alive in my sick bed, I could now call upon God to be my witness.
>
> If God approved of my pitiful goodwill, then I can think that he watched over me from Heaven to see if I would actually carry through with

> my resolve. If so, there is nothing to prevent me from thinking that once I had succumbed to my animal instincts—and it was doubtful whether I would do so—the Almighty caused gunfire to erupt in the distance and removed my tempter from before me.
>
> The easiest way to explain the miracle of suddenly abandoning the will to shoot the enemy that had gone unquestioned until that moment is that God sent the silent message "Do not shoot" to me through the void. He probably granted me this privilege because he loved me. (1:105–106)

Ōoka felt such a pressing need to assuage his guilt feelings and absolve himself of personal responsibility for his actions that he was willing to entertain thoughts of divine intervention. In the end, however, conscience would not allow him to deceive himself with self-serving rationalizations of being God's Chosen One:

> Now, of course, I cannot approve of this kind of egocentric thinking. For a time, however, the myth of God as my witness provided solace to me as a sick, prostrate prisoner of war. While I was dangerously close to believing in God, I was held back by the self-love implicit in the view that God would intervene solely on my behalf. While it accorded conveniently with the circumstances of my personal experience, this theology had nothing whatsoever to do with the events continually taking place on other battlefields. No matter how fitting an explanation may be to one's own situation, I think it's repulsive to overrate oneself. (1:106)

Ōoka subtly acknowledges that there were thousands of men—many more deserving than he—who were not so blessed by divine intervention. Struggle as he might, he cannot bring himself to forget his fallen comrades completely; in the end, he somehow had to reconcile his survival with his comrades' deaths.

Because of his reluctance to thoroughly examine all the possibilities, Ōoka was unable to come up with an adequate explanation for his conduct in his early memoirs. Survival egoism is the critical factor Ōoka gingerly approached, but quickly pulled away from.[26] As he considers that his conduct may have resulted from an aversion to spilling blood, he realizes that "the aversion implied in the statement 'I don't want to kill others,' is most likely none other than an inversion of our own desire not to be killed ourselves" (1:27). Toward the end of "Before Capture," Ōoka comes close to seeing survival egoism as the ground of his behavior:

> When I revive the full intensity of the inner tension [fear] I experienced during those moments, I know that I cannot be proud of myself.
>
> Now the object I admired for its youth and beauty was closing in on me, increasing my anticipation of the impending, decisive moment. It is difficult to determine the extent to which the *severity* I noticed when I first caught sight of him was intensified as he approached me. Despite [the beauty of] his red cheeks and white skin, I cannot be absolutely sure that his face didn't look *terrifying* to me at that moment. And if I still didn't feel like shooting, that image must have been all the more unbearable.
>
> I picked up my rifle and released the safety. Was I not, after all, intent on shooting? Or was I preparing to protect myself, reacting instinctually in the same way I would close my eyes just before an insect landed on my face? (1:34)

Ōoka stops at anxious self-inquiry in his early autobiographical writings. He leaves off with such questions because he is loath to face the most viable answer or its unacceptable implications. Ōoka *was* reacting instinctually to save himself, and he was obviously prepared to do whatever was necessary to extend his life even for a few more seconds. Since he was outnumbered, not shooting initially offered the best chance of survival: if he stayed put, the enemy might pass without noticing him. As the soldier pressed in on him, however, shooting first increasingly became his only means of preserving his life. His hesitation paid off when chance intervened. While unharmed physically, Ōoka did not come through the experience psychologically unscathed—and the psychological wounds incurred through this traumatic experience were long in healing.

As will be made clear in a subsequent section on bearing witness, Ōoka was able to readily acknowledge and condemn the egoistical behavior of others. Although he found it difficult to subject himself to the same scrutiny and judgment, he eventually did so, to some extent. Ōoka relates several telling incidents that clearly weighed heavily on his conscience.

From the time the Americans arrived at Mindoro, Ōoka was constantly surrounded by comrades in dire need; because of psychic numbing and preoccupation with his own death, however, he rarely, if ever, did much to help them. While retreating from San Jose, he notices in passing a despairing, prostrate comrade: "At the time, there were five of us, including myself, who suffered from malarial fever. One was collapsed by the side of the road. He sat in a dry drainage ditch, head pitched forward, elbows supported by the dirt banks on either side. In time, I'd surely find myself in the same condition" (2:184). Ōoka does not pause to encourage or assist his desperate brother-in-arms. All he can see in the man's crumpled figure is a reflection of his own inevitable fate. This, of course, is a variation on his universal excuse.

Ōoka also draws attention to his antagonistic behavior toward another stricken comrade during their forced march. Among the group of sick soldiers he walked with was "Fujimoto," an "extremely weak-willed" man obsessed with water. After exhausting his own supply, he badgers comrades for more. During a rest stop, he importunes Ōoka, who instead of refusing verbally, raises his canteen and drains it. When a sergeant who notices him quaffing his water scolds him for not conserving it, Ōoka tells him that he did it so he wouldn't have to share any with Fujimoto. Ōoka's assessment of his behavior is brutally honest: "I spoke the truth, but the fact of the matter was that I took great pleasure in using my comrade as a pretext for drinking my fill. The figure I cut as a calculating soldier must have been self-evident" (2:303).

Ōoka also admits to "stealing" a pair of new army boots while encamped in the Rutay Highlands. Although from another squad, Matsumoto was one of Ōoka's closest friends. During transport to the Philippines, Matsumoto mentions the episode in *All Quiet on the Western Front* concerning the disposition of Kemmerich's leather knee-boots. The episode later takes on significance when he dies. Shortly after reaching the Rutay Highlands, Matsumoto is bedridden with malaria. One day while on sentry duty, Ōoka watches as he struggles to crawl out from his hut to relieve himself. When an NCO takes notice and orders someone to lend a hand, Ōoka goes to his side. He quickly sees that Matsumoto is incontinent and on the verge of death. After helping him back to bed, Ōoka spots a new pair of boots next to his friend's pillow and recalls their earlier discussion. Ōoka's next important confession begins as follows: "Unlike Kemmerich's long boots, which were personal property, these boots were government issue, and soldiers only had the privilege of using them. It wouldn't do any good to ask Matsumoto to leave them to me, because upon his death they'd simply be returned to the supply sergeant. I'm not sure if he knew what I had in mind. His clipped responses to my ministrations were perhaps best viewed as the ill-humor common to the terminally ill" (2:253).

When Ōoka learns of Matsumoto's death the next day, he is clearly more preoccupied with the boots than with thoughts of their "owner." When he goes to see what became of them, he happens to arrive at the hut when Matsumoto's squad mates are out digging his grave. "As if in a dream," the boots are in front of the hut along with Matsumoto's personal effects. "I couldn't resist taking them. Even though they were only made of sharkskin, the feel and smell of those new boots was far from unpleasant. There wasn't a soul around. My heart was pounding in my chest" (2:254). Just as Ōoka is about to grab the boots, an NCO he was on good terms with happens by, notices them, and tells Ōoka to take them. Ōoka snatches up the coveted footwear and hurries back to his hut, his "heart filled with a kind of evil pleasure" (2:254).

Eventually, the men from Matsumoto's squad find out who took the boots and come to demand their return. By this time, Ōoka himself is bedridden with malaria, and the boots are now beside his pillow. He feigns sleep during the ensuing argument. In the end, his squad leader sends the men away empty-handed. At this point in his guarded confession, however, Ōoka takes a significant step in the direction of extending the concentric rings of responsibility outward from himself and his immediate company: "After all is said and done, only the boots were 'real.' The only 'reality' was the weakness of a nation that forced its soldiers to fight on with such lousy footwear. While this reality didn't necessarily operate in a soldier's psychology to make him think or feel in a particular way, it did fundamentally condition his behavior" (2:256).

The final example involves not only a confession of Ōoka's hatred of and mean-spirited behavior toward one of his less fortunate comrades, but also an indirect expression of his disgust and self-contempt concerning the lengths he was willing to go to justify himself both at the time and in his memoirs. Ōoka's feelings about Yasuda are clear in a description of his physical features: "Private Yasuda was a restless soldier. While just twenty-two, the oversized face that hung over his flat chest was covered with the wrinkles befitting an old man. His eyes were large, and while his nose was straight, it was absurdly elongated. Beneath it was an ill-formed, lopsided mouth. He was short, and had a bad complexion" (2:264). Yasuda was one of the weakest and most incompetent soldiers in Nishiya Company. Consequently, he was frequently subjected to verbal and physical abuse.

During basic training and occupation he sought to compensate by flattering his superiors. After the men retreated into the mountains, he played the sycophant to their squad leader. The men lying nearby were subjected nightly to their irritating duet of flattery and smugness.

When Ōoka fell ill, he was, like other malaria patients, prohibited from drinking any water. Since he couldn't walk, he clandestinely asked soldiers from other squads to fill his canteen. One day when Yasuda noticed Ōoka drinking, he reported him to the squad leader, who immediately made Ōoka pour out his water. Prevented from obtaining water from others, Ōoka struggles to reach the nearby spring on his own. As he staggers back from tree to tree, he sees Yasuda standing in front of the hut glowering at him. Knowing he won't be helped, and unsure whether he can walk between the nearest tree and the hut, Ōoka must crawl back under Yasuda's hateful gaze.

Ōoka begins to recover about the time reports reach them that three American warships have entered Bulalacao Bay. Yasuda chooses this crucial moment on the eve of attack to confess his illegitimacy. Under the circumstances, his personal revelation about how he learned the truth of his parentage, sought out and was coldly rejected by his biological mother, and ran away from home attracts the undivided attention and sympathy of his squad mates. Ōoka's reaction, however, is strikingly different:

> I listened in silence. Deep in my heart I felt a mounting irritation. Ever since reading Strindberg, I had been sick and tired of such confessions of "illegitimacy." Since heaven didn't make people higher and lower, the womb one emerged from should have made absolutely no difference at all. Behind confessions of "illegitimacy" was the lowly scheme of justifying oneself by blaming one's inferiority on their environment.
>
> While seemingly relevant, there was actually no connection between Yasuda's toadying character and his illegitimate origins. I felt this was obvious from his tone and the complete change in his attitude while making his confession from habitual timidity to petulance. Legitimate children, too, go bad and become brownnosers. (2: 276–277)

Instead of feeling sympathy, Ōoka is enraged by the lengths Yasuda goes to to avoid taking personal responsibility for his inferiority. He is so disgusted, in fact, that he seeks him out later with the expressed intention of rebuking him. Although Ōoka cannot recall his exact words, he imagines saying something like this: "You boasted earlier of being illegitimate. Should the spawn of a housemaid really be so full of himself? Couldn't die without getting it off your chest, could you? But let's face it—illegitimate or not, you're nothing but a small-fry. You're just a punk kid gone bad" (2:277–278). Although memory of what immediately followed was repressed for a time, after capture Ōoka is able to recollect that Yasuda stabbed him so violently in the side with a pencil that bits of lead and splintered wood had to be surgically removed in the POW hospital.

Something about Yasuda's eleventh-hour confession broke through Ōoka's psychic numbing and brought on unbridled anger. Ōoka expresses more animus toward this petty flatterer than toward anyone or anything else prior to capture. What about Yasuda's behavior upset Ōoka so much at this critical moment? There is clearly much more to his reaction than the grudge he understandably held against Yasuda for mistreating him when he suffered from malaria. Ōoka's emotional response is psychologically complex and revealing. In a sense, Yasuda served as Ōoka's alter ego: he was an offensive reflection of Ōoka's own inferiority and reprehensibility. In striking out at Yasuda, Ōoka was simultaneously attacking what he most hated in himself. From the moment he learned he would be sent to the front, he admittedly behaved in a weak-willed, self-absorbed, cowardly manner. While Yasuda maneuvered to compensate for his deficiencies by fawning on his superiors, Ōoka did so through preoccupation with himself and his impending death. He, too, watched indifferently a comrade feebly crawl about before his eyes. And, as previously noted, after thoroughly reflecting on his life, Ōoka concluded that he himself was a nobody. Most important, perhaps, in his own mind during the war and in the literary confessions he made after survival, Ōoka too engaged in "lowly scheme[s] to justify [himself] by blaming [his] inferiority on [his] environment." In Ōoka's case, the key environmental factor was not illegitimate birth, but inevitable defeat and death. These revealing psychological parallels, moreover, are punctuated by a seamless shift from critical assessments of Yasuda's behavior to despairing judgments of himself:

> I had already examined my own past during the free time I had during occupation and discovered that there was no connection whatsoever between it and my present self.
>
> Now that the enemy pressed in on us, I tore up the diary in which I had

> recorded the results of my examinations. Even though it was written in a language incomprehensible to the local inhabitants of these mountains, I didn't like the idea of the written records of my misrepresented egoism outlasting me.
>
> I wasn't satisfied with tearing my diary to pieces. I asked Yasuda, who happened to be cooking rice outside the hut at the time, to burn them for me. Since he tossed the pieces haphazardly under the suspended mess tins, some of the pieces of white paper were scattered about on the surrounding ground. (2:277)

While Ōoka may have been further along the path of painful self-awareness than Yasuda, his attitude and behavior toward his comrades at the front involved a disregard and egoism that differed little from the characteristics of the man he despised. As one of the few men of his company to survive, Ōoka found it extremely difficult to fully acknowledge the survival egoism that greatly conditioned his own frontline attitude and conduct. As the incident with Yasuda makes clear, Ōoka initially found it easier to recognize and condemn the egoistical conduct of others. It should be kept in mind, however, that the harsh criticism and condemnation he directs toward his comrades is ultimately inseparable from self-criticism and self-condemnation.

Bearing Witness

In his memoirs, Ōoka bears witness to the frontline attitudes, conduct, suffering, and tragic deaths of his comrades. Making a detailed record of his battlefield experience was integral to his project of coming to terms with his burdened past. As Lifton declares, "Without guilt-associated struggles around fidelity to the dead and the experience of deadness, and *to oneself as a witness,* no . . . renewal or formulation is feasible."[27] Providing testimony—both positive and negative—on the attitudes and conduct of his comrades facilitated consideration of dimensions of war and survival that, while inseparable from personal experience and responsibility, nonetheless transcended it. Writing about the battlefield attitudes and behavior of his fellow soldiers enabled treatment of his traumatic war experience at one level of remove from himself. Temporarily relieved of the pressing need to rationalize and justify his own conduct and survival, he could more freely and critically address some of the difficult survivor issues that frustrated his initial formulative efforts.[28]

Ōoka testifies at length about the middle-class and survival egoism displayed by his older, more highly educated counterparts in Nishiya Company. In "Cherry and Gingko" (Sakura to ichū, 1972), Ōoka writes about the profound effect the things he witnessed at the front had on him: "My experience in the Philippines taught me many things. I was deeply wounded by the egoism (*egoisumu*) my comrades exhibited on the threshold of life and death" (16:190). Not all his comrades, however, comported themselves in such a way: Ōoka also highlights the outstanding attitude and conduct of a few good men. These rare individuals continued to be positive, sympathetic, and helpful despite rapidly deteriorating circumstances, overcame the pull of survival egoism, and selflessly fulfilled their soldierly duties. For the most part, these superior men were in their late teens and early twenties. Ōoka's handling of these exemplary young men borders on elegy and provides an early indication of the kind of writing he subsequently engaged in wholeheartedly upon taking up his survivor mission in 1967.

Survival Egoism

Although Ōoka praises his younger comrades, he does so mainly to expose the egoism of older soldiers like himself by negative comparison. While conscience would not allow Ōoka to ignore them completely, dwelling too long on the idealism, patriotism, and self-sacrifice of his younger compatriots—none of whom survived—might have pushed him toward confrontation with unresolved emotional issues related to death guilt and indebtedness. Stressing the flagrant egoism of the majority amounted to a kind of scapegoating.

Establishing the unworthiness of his comrades en masse allowed him to feel justified in summarily dismissing them from further consideration. This defensive maneuver is readily apparent in the ironically titled "Brothers-in-arms" (Senyū, 1949). After painstakingly detailing the deplorable, self-serving conduct of the small number of Nishiya soldiers taken captive, Ōoka writes that the incorrigible egoism of the men in his company precluded any meaningful bonding:

> Of the 180 men from our company charged with defending half of Mindoro Island, 17 came to the Leyte POW camp. The men in our company were sent to the front at the beginning of 1944 after receiving just three months' basic training. We were an "over-the-hill unit" and we could scarcely have been called real soldiers. While our fates on Mindoro, which the Americans chose to take after Leyte, were miserable, what happened there wasn't worthy of the name "combat"—it wasn't enough to shatter our middle-class egoism. We never were brothers-in-arms. (1:233)

Ōoka refers repeatedly to the middle-class egoism (*shōshiminteki egoizumu*) he felt to be characteristic of his older counterparts. Several representative examples of this form of selfishness will be considered before I turn to discuss the more egregious acts of survival egoism manifest after withdrawal into the mountains.

The older soldiers' negative character traits are first exposed during basic training. Assuming it to be the most efficient and effective approach, the commander of Konoe Regiment decided to train the educated middle-class recruits separately from the farmers and laborers. Since he "neglected to consider the moral corruption (*dōtokuteki fuhai*) of the educated" (2:9), however, this approach failed miserably. As when they were in school, the older trainees were concerned with getting through their basic training with minimum effort and investment (2:9). From the outset, the older men thought of little but themselves.

The deep-seated egocentrism of the middle-aged trainees is tempered somewhat after conscription. After noting this positive development, however, Ōoka quickly adds a parenthetical comment on its short-lived and circumstantial nature:

> The attitude of these corrupt, educated recruits changed markedly once it was decided that we would be sent to the front. Our students' cunning was suspended, and for a time it seemed that we were united by genuine concern for one another. Our cunning, which had theretofore been aimed at foisting unpleasant work onto others as much as possible, was abruptly replaced by a spirit of mutual assistance, and men took on onerous tasks on their own initiative. (This communal spirit, however, was fleeting, and seemed to have been based solely on the fact that we shared the common misfortune of being conscripted. Before long, the necessities of everyday existence in the army during transport and occupation returned us to our habitual egoism,

which then remained intact even after we were routed when the Americans landed.) (2:10)

In addition to criticizing his older comrades for their extreme selfishness, Ōoka takes them to task for their lack of patriotic spirit and sense of obligation. In "Seasons" (Kisetsu, 1949), after reiterating that he became tired of the middle-class egoism exhibited by his comrades at the front, Ōoka excoriates them for their inability to acknowledge, let alone accept and fulfill, the duties attendant on citizenship: "It was thoughtless of them not to have considered the obligations enjoined on them by peaceful social life. Even at the front, all they thought about was how to deploy their work-a-day cunning to get through their predicament in a 'routine' way. Nothing could have been more pointless at a time when the great violence of nations was erupting on the battlefield" (1:239).

Ōoka was the only communications man in his company. As the days and weeks passed in San Jose, he thought of training someone to replace him in case he fell ill or was killed. While knowing that this was best for the group, self-interest for a time kept him from doing anything to jeopardize his special status. Training a substitute went against one of the fundamental lessons he had learned in the business world: "One of the rules of thumb of company employees was that they could advance themselves by creating work that only they themselves could do" (2:111). As circumstances worsened, however, Ōoka resolved to abandon his self-serving philosophy and act more altruistically.

Ōoka chose Nakayama, an older, university-educated man like himself. Nakayama was overjoyed, since receiving such instruction would exempt him from fatigue duty. His middle-class egoism, however, quickly came to the fore. Nakayama was determined to take full advantage of this fortuitous turn of events. He subsequently gained promotion by bribing his squad leader and the paymaster. And his rise ultimately came at Ōoka's expense. When his training was complete, some officers disgruntled with Ōoka's exemption from maneuvers and guard and fatigue duty and envious of the access he had to confidential messages regarding promotions, forced him to alternate shifts. Thus, when Nakayama was on duty, Ōoka had to perform the onerous tasks he had theretofore avoided. Nakayama's crooked promotion gave him rank over Ōoka, and his attitude changed markedly. He sported an ostentatious mustache, refused to grant Ōoka a single point during discussions, and actively excluded him from conversations with the officers he had theretofore been on good terms with. Ōoka summarizes the miserable result of his rare attempt at altruism as follows: "In this way, what I feared most when I made the decision to train a replacement came to pass. It was terribly ironic that I had to suffer because I chose a man hell-bent on taking full advantage of the company employee's wisdom I had rejected myself. Since I decided to do so from idealism, I suppose I had no real grounds for complaint. Nevertheless, it was disappointing" (2:119).

Nakayama was not alone in acting shamelessly to further himself during occupation. Whereas he was willing to use any means to rise in the hierarchy, Ikeda, another middle-aged recruit, was determined to eat better than others. Ōoka prepares the ground for his description of Ikeda's gluttony by contrasting the behavior of younger and older soldiers:

> Our company guarded a remote area in the Philippines, and for a while after we arrived we weren't getting enough rations because of the inexperience of the NCO quartermaster. Instead of bearing their hunger with relative composure during this time as the "sentimental," "impulsive" younger soldiers did, the "stoic," "reasonable" older soldiers exhibited the utterly disgraceful behavior of famished little devils. It was the middle-aged soldiers, for instance, who went as far as to help themselves to the food intended for the Filipino prisoners as they carried it to them from the mess. (2:158)

Among these gluttonous older men, Ikeda's behavior was extreme. His gluttony seemed to know no bounds: "When it came to food, it was as if he became a different person. He was shameless and ruthless in baldly satisfying his cravings" (2:159). Ikeda constantly loitered around the mess in hopes of picking up some extra scraps. When it was his turn to dish out food, conflicts inevitably arose because "he couldn't resist the temptation to short others soup and rice and thereby increase his own portion" (2:161).

If Ōoka was disgusted by Ikeda's undisguised egoism, he was repulsed by Yasuda's self-serving behavior. After withdrawal to the Rutay Highlands, Yasuda sought to ingratiate himself with the cooks, who comprised a distinct privileged class in the company. In the end, his groveling and toadying paid off. After a regular cook fell ill, Yasuda was allowed to take his place. Like Nakayama, his attitude and behavior changed markedly once he gained his new position:

> From that point on he acted with an air of unrestrained self-importance. With the alacrity of a veteran cook, he began to rain abuse on the men who, as always, loitered about the mess. While he gave us, his squad mates, slightly better servings than the others, he did so in an oddly patronizing manner. He gorged himself on the delicacies the cooks prepared exclusively for themselves, and his stomach began to protrude conspicuously from his otherwise slight frame. He carefully wrapped this paunch with a stomach band, and as a sign of the privilege afforded to cooks who worked around fire, he sauntered around shirtless. The figure he cut at such times was utterly detestable. (2:266)

There can be little doubt that Ōoka was repulsed by the shameless behavior exhibited by Nakayama, Ikeda, and Yasuda during occupation of San Jose. Each in his own way was motivated primarily by self-interest and furthered himself at his comrades' expense. Each was doing what he felt was necessary to get by in the army: Nakayama took advantage of Ōoka's altruism to get out of maneuvers and guard and fatigue duty; Ikeda equated food with life itself; and Yasuda acted as he did to avoid physical and psychological abuse. Nakayama and Yasuda, moreover, sought to get ahead through flattery, and none of the three, upon gaining the slightest advantage, could resist the temptation to abuse his newly gained position.[29]

While Ōoka was repulsed by the middle-class egoism displayed by his comrades during the relatively peaceful months in San Jose, he was appalled by the individual and collective acts of survival egoism he witnessed once the men withdrew from the coast. One of the most disturbing examples of group egoism Ōoka bears witness to concerns the callous treatment of the unfortunate squad assigned to Caminawit:

> The eight soldiers . . . who struggled on their own through the mountains were in terrible shape when they arrived at our encampment. Since they had marched for two days more than the rest of us, they were utterly exhausted and lacked even the strength to build adequate shelter for themselves. They entered the dense woods near the lookout post, wove reeds through tree branches, and slept directly on the damp ground below. After twenty days, they were all dead.

> People will probably wonder why a work detail wasn't formed to construct huts for them. The old Imperial Army, however, was organized such that each squad was an independent unit expected to provide for itself and overcome hardships on its own; it simply wasn't something the men from other squads needed to be concerned with. (2:233–234)

Ōoka accounts for the neglect that contributed substantially to the deaths of these comrades in terms of military sectionalism, but given the circumstances, the indifference of these men can also be understood in terms of collective egoism. The late arrivals were left to their own devices because at the time, everything—emotion, energy, food, clothing—was being strictly conserved in the interest of survival. Ōoka acknowledges as much in a subsequent passage: "We all bore the fate of being routed soldiers with no idea what the next day would bring. Under circumstances such as these, even if a person has the emotional margin to feel compassion for another, there is absolutely nothing to make him act on his feelings" (2:233–234).

In addition to bearing witness to collective acts of survival egoism, Ōoka also testifies about egregious individual behavior. He devotes the greatest attention to the conduct of his squad leader, a man who goes unnamed because he survived. For convenience' sake, he will henceforth be referred to as "Butaichō," the Japanese term for squad leader. Butaichō was a cunning, middle-aged man Ōoka characterizes as egoism incarnate (*egoizumu no gonge*). An NCO sergeant, Butaichō was a veteran of the Japan-China war. During basic training and occupation, he was a model instructor and officer. He was not only loved by his men, but also enjoyed the full confidence and respect of Commander Nishiya. In addition, he reportedly acted courageously during a guerilla surprise attack. After the American invasion, however, Butaichō underwent a striking transformation. Ōoka comments on this change specifically in terms of survival egoism: "In short, as soon as we were routed, this NCO who has been kind to his men during occupation and well thought of by senior officers instantly became an egoist (*egoisuto*) who thought solely of [preserving] his own life" (1:128).

Butaichō's extreme selfishness is initially exhibited during the forced march through the mountains. On the first day, the medic collapses under a heavy load of medical supplies, which are then divided up among squad leaders. Few, however, are ever recovered. Butaichō was the worst offender:

he stuffed his allotment into a large leather briefcase purchased with army funds and then hoarded it for his own personal use. When the men in his squad began to fall ill with malaria, Butaichō wouldn't have anything to do with them for fear of contagion. He resolutely refused to attend vigils held for the dead men under him, although he insisted on taking immediate possession of their personal effects, which he added to his briefcase. Even when company medical supplies ran out and men were in dire need, he would not part with a single item—not even for his own squad mates.

Despite being in good health, Butaichō feigned illness to evade patrol and reconnaissance missions. When the Americans attacked their encampment, however, he jumped to his feet and joined—but refused to lead—the group of walking ill ordered to withdraw toward San Jose. After telling Ōoka to stay behind, he forced Yasuda, who was already weighed down with his own belongings, to carry his duffel and bulging briefcase. All he carried himself was his rifle and a small handbag, which he subsequently foisted off on another stricken soldier. While in the Leyte POW camp, Ōoka heard detailed testimony about Butaichō's later behavior. After slipping through American lines, he flew out (*tobu yō ni*) ahead of his debilitated comrades. This was particularly upsetting because Ōoka's friend "S" was among them: "This in effect meant that he abandoned my buddy S. In the main, I don't condemn soldiers for the egoism they exhibited in life-and-death circumstances. I am, however, free to loathe Butaichō as an individual for abandoning my dear friend" (1:133). When they rested, he devoured twice as much food as anyone else. After weeks of aimless wandering, he was taken prisoner with his unused grenade at his side. And even though he made no attempt to end his life before being taken prisoner or to resist his captors, he did halfheartedly try to hang himself with his belt in plain view on the ship taking them to the Leyte POW camp. According to one eyewitness, his act was motivated not by shame, but by gastrointestinal discomfort. Upon meeting Ōoka in the POW hospital, the first thing to pass his lips was, "They've taken away everything!" Even after capture, he thought only of his precious briefcase.

After thoroughly detailing Butaichō's reprehensible battlefield conduct, Ōoka feels compelled to reconsider his seemingly praiseworthy conduct during the surprise guerrilla attack. In the end, he concludes that his behavior at that time, too, was best understood in terms of egoism:

> Since the other NCOs who remained inside [the school building] were, like him, all veterans of the China Incident, their ability to assess the situation must have differed little from his. They, however, were not as concerned as he was with saving their own skins. This was probably the only difference between them. This is borne out by the fact that once we entered the mountains, they couldn't bring themselves to abandon their men as easily as our squad leader.
>
> That this sergeant was able to do what the other NCOs could not can be understood in terms of opportunism. Doing so explains subtle matters related to his conduct: he braved the bullets and jumped out of the window only after anticipating the moment when there would be a break in enemy fire. Here one must acknowledge his talent for combining openheartedness toward his men (a form of social opportunism) with the wisdom of a drill instructor. As a farmer from an outlying area of Tokyo, he probably developed this talent during the war. This, however, was not what made him jump out the window once he judged the time to be right.
>
> It's regrettable for all concerned that he was motivated not by patriotism, but by attachment to his own life. (1:136–137)

Ōoka's squad leader may not have been as educated as his middle-aged counterparts, but he clearly had a full measure of their characteristic cunning. Like his older brothers-in-arms, moreover, he failed to live up to his patriotic duties and obligations. Ōoka observes that life as an NCO was probably preferable to working as a small-plot farmer under an oppressive patriarch and that, as oldest son, he probably volunteered for service during the Japan-China war with the intention of inheriting after his father's death. This part of his scheme was realized in 1942. "What didn't enter into his calculations," however, "was being called back into service toward the end of the Pacific War and finding himself in charge of inexperienced soldiers in an army going down to defeat. Thereupon, he simply abandoned responsibility" (1:137). In the end, self-perpetuation was the only value Butaichō held to be absolute. His conduct—both during the war and after—was the unadulterated product of circumstance and radical egoism: "His frankness as a squad leader, his daring in battle—everything he displayed was probably produced by his environment. I have little doubt that he is prospering to this day as a cunning, countryside black marketeer, baking bread or some such thing" (1:138).

Although Ōoka writes that in general he doesn't blame soldiers for the egoism they displayed in life-and-death situations, he does condemn, in the strongest terms, men who acted in radically egoistical ways before circumstances reached desperation. Ōoka takes special pains to document the abominable conduct Sergeant Kurokawa exhibited after the Americans overran their highland position. Like Butaichō, Kurokawa was a seasoned veteran of the Japan-China war who had been called back into service. Ōoka learned of his conduct from a comrade named Watari, who entered the POW camp along with Kurokawa and four others. According to Watari, twenty men managed to slip through American lines. In time, they joined forces with another group of fifty who, anticipating attack, had fled northward with hopes of escaping Mindoro and crossing to Luzon. After marching together for some two weeks, the soldiers were discovered and attacked by guerrillas as they rested by a river. While some went downstream and others forded the river, Kurokawa, Watari, and eighteen others fled upstream. After summarizing their collective experience, Ōoka turns to Kurokawa's scandalous behavior:

> The group's experience between February 8 and March 26 was similar to that undergone by routed soldiers throughout the Pacific—long, forced marches with nothing to eat but roots and nuts, descents to coastal areas in search of food, and flights back into the mountains upon detection by Filipinos. About the time they reached the mountains behind Calapan . . . Sergeant Kurokawa proposed finding, killing, and eating a Filipino the next time they ventured to the coast. Watari said that he initially thought Kurokawa was joking and let it go. When Kurokawa kept repeating the proposition, however, he looked at his face, saw the crazed look in his eyes, and felt a chill run down his spine. (1:220)

After following a drainage down toward the coast, the men came upon a farmer walking on the far side of a corn field. The soldier carrying the only gun, who entered the POW camp with the others, told Ōoka that he was feeling frustrated and desperate at the time. Upon seeing the Filipino, he suddenly felt like shooting him. Without a word of warning to his companions, he raised the rifle and squeezed the trigger. The bullet missed its mark, and the man ran away calling for help. Before long, the men began to hear drums. As they attempted to retreat into the mountains, they were surrounded and captured by thirty well-armed Filipinos.

Ōoka is deeply disturbed by Kurokawa's advocacy of cannibalism. After hearing this firsthand account, he severs all relations with him. What

Ōoka finds so appalling and unforgivable is that Kurokawa—the senior officer in the group—made this atrocious proposal at a time when others could still believe he was only joking. In the end, Ōoka castigates men such as Kurokawa for their utter disregard for others, be they comrades, enemies, or noncombatants:

> While the tragedy that occurred on the Medusa raft is beyond reproach, I can't help but condemn the Japanese officers who dined on the flesh of prisoners of war. I don't condemn them simply because what they did went against international agreements regarding the [humane] treatment of POWs, but because it is inhuman to cannibalize in extravagance. Their criminal acts resulted from their perverted hatred of the enemy and their frontline gormandism. Kurokawa's thought of eating a Filipino was no different. He came up with the idea before his men, who were themselves hungry, because of the "by any means" convention he had internalized as a brutal soldier during the Japan-China war and based on his thinking as an oppressor that the people in the areas he occupied were subhuman. If these battlefield conventions had developed to the point of obliterating his humanity, then he was nothing but a monster (*kaibutsu*). (1:221–222)

Ōoka's treatments of the attitudes and conduct of his comrades' frontline behavior clearly indicate conflicting intentions and emotions. On the one hand, writing detailed accounts of his comrades enabled him to bear witness, an act integral to fruitful formulation of his traumatic war experience. On the other, focusing almost exclusively on their egoism gave him the justification he needed to dismiss them, en masse, as unworthy of further consideration. This is readily apparent in "Brothers-in-arms": "Writing [about my comrades] in this way, I cannot but regretfully acknowledge that the officers and enlisted men on Mindoro Island were not only inferior soldiers, but also detestable human beings. Moreover, if it was wholly because of their deficiency in fighting spirit that the disgracefulness of these worldly, middle-aged men reached such extremes on the extraordinary stage of the battlefield, it is a source of regret both for the nation and for the men themselves that they were ever sent to the front in the first place" (1:214).

While reluctant to openly acknowledge survival egoism in his own battlefield conduct, Ōoka was more than willing to identify it as the wellspring of the shameful, abhorrent behavior of his Nishiya Company comrades. For Ōoka, this egoism was at the very core of all that was most repulsive and abominable in the frontline behavior he witnessed. He expresses his most scathing condemnation, moreover, toward fellow survivors. The observation made at the close of the section on death guilt bears repeating here: Ōoka's negative treatment of his comrades' attitude and conduct was ultimately inseparable from self-criticism. In the face of so many agonized, premature, grotesque, and seemingly pointless deaths, not only what men did in the name of self-preservation, but also survival in and of itself were felt to be repugnant and unconscionable.

The Good Die Young

There was a handful of men in Nishiya Company whose attitude and conduct were so beyond reproach that Ōoka could not in good conscience ignore or dismiss them entirely. While his attention was primarily focused on describing and condemning the egoistical frontline behavior of the majority, he could not help but acknowledge the few good men who willingly accepted and fulfilled their duties and retained their capacity to care for and respond to others even in extremity. As might be expected, none of these predominantely young men survived. As a guilt-ridden survivor, Ōoka was burdened by the memory of these superior soldiers and human beings. In fact, they serve as unforgettable reminders that the war could not summarily be dismissed as "stupid" or "meaningless." Indeed, in a number of places in his battlefield memoirs Ōoka takes his first tentative steps in the direction not only of engaging in more appropriate blaming, but embracing, mourning, and memorializing his dead comrades as well.

In contrast to their middle-aged counterparts, the younger, working-class recruits in Nishiya Company were naïve, idealistic, and eager to do their part. In "Before Capture," Ōoka recalls them as "kind and generous. They worked hard and took good care of us calculating, indolent, middle-aged soldiers. Because they didn't know how to conserve their energy, they died quickly after falling ill" (1:51). While these wholesome youths may have lacked basic survival skills, they were richly endowed with a clear sense of purpose, duty, and obligation. Although the following passage specifically describes the young, active-duty soldiers Ōoka met during basic training, at the front, and in the POW camp, it applies equally well to the young men in his company: "[they] were, of course, extremely ignorant, but they were conscious of their patriotic obligations and knew that they were working as hard as machines to carry them out. Consequently, many were bright, cheerful, and carefree. When they weren't directly involved in their soldierly duties, they were open and generous. While it was regrettable that they had been deceived by corrupt militarists, this had no adverse effect on their hearts or behavior because they were unaware" (1:239–240).

Ōoka writes very positively about his relatively young (twenty-seven years old) company commander, First Lieutenant Nishiya Masao. Nishiya was a veteran of the disastrous Japanese conflict with Russia at Nomonhan. Unlike many other Japanese army and navy officers, he saw to it that face slapping (*pinta*) and more severe martial punishments were minimized in his company. Realizing the hopelessness of their position, he did everything in his power to lessen his men's suffering and give them a fighting chance to survive—all the while carrying out the spirit of all battalion orders. It was his policy during the occupation of San Jose not to engage guerrillas unless attacked. After Nishiya Company withdrew into the mountains, he not only allowed the local guides to return home, but gave them provisions as well.

First Lieutenant Nishiya was not only considerate of but cared deeply for the men under his command. On several occasions, he noticed Ōoka deciphering messages late at night and ordered him to rest and finish up in the morning. When Ōoka abandoned his rifle during the retreat, he let him off with a verbal reprimand. And when his men began to fall ill to and die from malaria, he looked in on them regularly and with genuine concern: "Every morning, Commander Nishiya visited all the squads. After gazing in on the huts filled with sick men, he would linger on in silence at the entrance" (1:5).

Commander Nishiya himself was a burdened battlefield survivor. Ōoka describes him as "somber and taciturn. He didn't look a day under thirty. Although he never spoke of what he saw or did in Nomonhan, it lingered about his face and eyes. The scent of his dead comrades still seemed to cling to his body" (1:6). Like the author who recalls him fondly, Commander Nishiya was profoundly uneasy over survival. His look and scent were that of a man continually immersed in death. This was the basis of the special bond Ōoka felt with him: "Out of a kind of sympathy, I secretly loved this young officer. In my own way and for quite different reasons, I too lived with my eyes firmly fixed on Death" (1:7). Unlike Ōoka, however, Commander Nishiya viewed death in combat as an act of atonement. The death he personally longed for was inseparable from that of the soldiers who had died—and continued to die—on the battlefield. He had somehow managed to survive Nomonhan, but he was determined not to return from the Philippines:

> He all but sought out death. During the occupation of San Jose, he always led patrols and fought at the head of his men without seeking cover. He was a kindhearted leader: he accepted the demands of war as absolute and took personal responsibility for what he asked of his men. There is only one way for commanders like this to justify what they demand of those under them—by dying themselves.
>
> When the Americans finally attacked our highland position, he strode off alone directly toward the incoming shells and took a direct hit. This, most likely, was the fulfillment of a long-cherished desire. (1:6–7)

Ōoka praises his company commander for his genuine compassion and concern for his men, his acceptance and fulfillment of his military duties, his competence and sense of personal responsibility, and his willingness to do himself what he had to ask of his men. In short, Commander Nishiya was wholly untainted by survival egoism. Shortly after capture, Ōoka heard that the body of a Japanese officer who had committed seppuku had been discovered near their former encampment. He was certain that this must have been the body of his beloved company commander.

It goes without saying that to Ōoka, First Lieutenant Nishiya was not only a fine commander, but also an outstanding human being. As Ōoka recalled and wrote about him after survival, moreover, he surely couldn't help but have been painfully aware of the glaring contrast between Commander Nishiya's attitude and conduct and that of himself and his older counterparts. The following passage effectively conveys the irresponsibility and survival egoism exhibited by other officers soon after the attack began:

> Someone called out "The commander's been hit!" and shouts of "Medic!" followed. . . . The ranking sergeant appeared and immediately ordered all sick to descend to the valley. . . . Everyone—even those sound of body—abandoned their hilltop positions. The senior sergeant marched directly in front

> of me. Again, we heard someone yell, "The commander's been hit!" I watched the sergeant's back as he pressed forward without the slightest sign of hesitation with the sense of beholding some kind of unfamiliar beast. I said, "Sergeant, it's being reported that the commander's been hit." Without turning around, he said "Really? . . . I doubt it," and pushed on.
>
> When we reached the valley, we came upon another sergeant sitting on the ground. The senior sergeant walked up to him and said, "I hear the commander's been hit, but I doubt it." The other responded in kind, "Hmm, I doubt it, too." I couldn't bear listening to any more of their conversation. (1:18)

Commander Nishiya is not the only man Ōoka finds praiseworthy. He also draws special attention to Private Kobayashi. Kobayashi, a twenty-two-year-old medic assigned to Nishiya Company after just two months of basic training at the army hospital in Tokyo, was a kind and considerate young man who conscientiously carried out his medical duties. He augmented the company's inadequate medical supplies by trading with a local doctor and convinced the quartermaster to give the men more rations. His selfless devotion to his medical duties led to his death in mid-November. Hearing that the naval air base in Caminawit had an abundance of medical supplies, he joined a small group of soldiers heading there to make contact with their squad stationed at the base. Their gasoline-powered train was ambushed by guerrillas when they stopped to change tracks. Kobayashi took two slugs to the chest as he struggled to escape out the train widow. His comrades deserted him, except Private Shibamoto, who stayed behind, returned fire, and drove off their attackers.

When Shibamoto came to Kobayashi's side, he found the medic on his back writhing in pain. Shibamoto gave emergency aid according to Kobayashi's instruction. At one point, tears began to pour from Kobayashi's eyes and he repeatedly said, "I'm sorry. I'm sorry. Mom, Dad I'm so sorry!" (2:150). When he became incontinent, he realized that his wounds were fatal. After Shibamoto cleaned him and did all he could to make him comfortable, Kobayashi looked him in the eye and said, "'I shit myself. I'm done for. It's unpardonable to die without fulfilling my duties. Be my witness. I'm going to recite Long Live the Emperor.' Thereupon, he said Tennō Heika Banzai three times in a frail voice" (2:151). Ōoka comments as follows on Private Kobayashi's final act:

> What followed "Be my witness" was a kind of performance, but it was no less authentic for being so—some truths must be enacted.
>
> [The practice of saying] Tennō Heika Banzai originated in education centered on the Imperial portrait. When politics come into education it's invariably falsified. People, however, are not so easily deceived. Because Kobayashi adhered to a special ethical code of filial piety and diligence that demanded the highest expression, political deception became truth in him. Since Japanese don't have God, such expression probably had to take the form of emperor worship.
>
> Politics is nothing but lies. The truths that emerge from them, however, accumulate to make life and history. (2:151–152)

Ōoka is unreserved in his praise of Kobayashi. The wellspring of his exemplary attitude and conduct was not indoctrination, but an internalized, personal ethic based on hard work, selflessness, obedience, and dutifulness. After realizing the seriousness of his wounds, Kobayashi first apologizes to his parents for dying before fulfilling his obligation to them as their son. And just before dying, he enacts a ritual giving expression to his heartfelt desire for the emperor, the "father" of the nation, to live on and prosper. Ōoka holds this young man in such high esteem because he not only held but also acted in accordance with absolute, inviolable values. Political falsehood and deception were distilled in the pure heart and mind of this youth and integrated with traditional morality such that when they were expressed in word and deed, they were truth itself.

Ōoka also ultimately assesses Ikeda and Konoshita, two older soldiers he initially found fault with because of their obsession with food, in positive terms. After withdrawing to the Rutay Highlands, Ikeda took part in the first reconnaissance mission to monitor American activities in San Jose. He fell ill while out on assignment and died five days after his return. Even while gravely ill himself, Ikeda continued to do all he could for his debilitated comrades:

> After developing a fever, he lost his appetite and his obsession with food was replaced by an irrepressible craving for warm water. He would come all the way down to the ravine we cooked in laden with canteens (the water was warmed by placing them next to the fire). Despite pneumonia and a fever over 39 degrees Celsius, he brought the canteens of all of the men in his squad. He continued to do so virtually until the day he died. When there was no shortage, he was kind and considerate toward others. I still recall the way

> he looked as he squatted down by the fire—water bottles hanging from his shoulders, legs splayed out to either side like an octopus. (2:164)

Ōoka remembers his platoon leader, Second Lieutenant Konoshita, in similar terms. He, too, is initially introduced as an incorrigible glutton. Ōoka is shocked, however, to see that even after they withdraw into the mountains, he maintains the same composure he exhibited during the occupation of San Jose. Under the pretext of making inspections, he visited every squad hut each afternoon to be treated to fried bananas. Ōoka is surprised, however, when he continues to make these daily rounds even after the men can no longer provide for him in this way. Like Ikeda, Ōoka respects and praises Konoshita for the kindness and concern he shows the ill and dying even in extremity: "I can no longer recall the words he used to console the sick, but I do remember the genuine sympathy conveyed by his tone of voice. There was no trace of hollow military encouragement or perfunctoriness. His voice contained the civility and considerateness common to peacetime society. Under the circumstances, this was nothing short of extraordinary" (2:165). In the end, Ōoka is compelled to reconsider this man whose behavior he at first found fault with:

> The truth of his humanity was overlaid by a thick veil of cunning.
>
> The day the American attack force landed [in Bulalacao] he went out on a scouting mission with an NCO and two soldiers and never returned. I have no doubt that he died in an honorable manner befitting a military man—fighting on to death with his pistol. Since their idea of patriotism was unsullied by military cynicism, enlisted men were frequently more soldierly on the battlefield than their professional counterparts.
>
> I cannot help but think that like Ikeda, this weak officer's extraordinary concern with food not only underlay his composed attitude, but also left him no room to think of the dark future pressing in on us. (2:166)

During occupation, Konoshita's humanity was hidden behind a veil of cunning. As circumstances worsened, this veil was removed to reveal the beautiful truth of his character. Ōoka is confident that Second Lieutenant Konoshita, like Commander Nishiya, fulfilled his martial obligations by dying honorably in combat. Ōoka clearly valued most highly in these few good men what was lacking in himself. He reserves his highest respect and praise for the men whose unwavering sense of duty and responsibility, firm code of ethics, and fundamental humanity enabled them to transcend the drives of survival egoism.

Ōoka also reversed his opinion about the group of men who gave false names after capture. In "The Rains of Tacloban," Ōoka notes that numerous Japanese prisoners concealed their true identities. And when the war ended, this practice had unforeseen consequences. The Americans, who had drawn up lists of soldiers suspected of war crimes, continued to detain all those with matching names. Ōoka had been convinced that he would be killed after interrogation, and he readily provided his real name in hopes that his family might eventually learn the details of his death. He admits to taking pride in his honesty and to openly expressing disapproval of those whose repatriation was delayed because of their dishonesty. Upon hearing him hold forth in this way, a man who had given a false name but was not detained angrily explained that having suffered the shame of capture, many men concealed their identities out of consideration for their families back home. This explanation not only sheds valuable light on their conduct and Ōoka's own self-centeredness in this regard, but also enables him to realize the importance of not forgetting the soldiers who truly did display selfless, self-sacrificing behavior:

> Their conduct not only involved thoughts of their family's honor, but also consideration of the money their loved ones would be denied if it became known that they hadn't died in battle. In any case, these soldiers themselves were not the immediate beneficiaries. The quick thoughtfulness of those who gave false names [for these reasons] was far better than the calculated conceit that led me to want to leave my own trace. This self-sacrificing spirit, unlike that of kamikaze pilots, was clearly not the product of indoctrination.
>
> Today, such Japanese responses to the realities of war are simply thought of as "stupid." Nothing makes one into more of a fool, however, than denying the truths of one's past. (1: 91)

Formulation

Formulation is integral to recovery and renewal. Lifton defines it as "evolving new inner forms that include the traumatic event, which in turn requires that one find meaning or significance in it so that the rest of one's life need not be devoid of meaning and significance. Formulation means establishing the lifeline on a new basis."[30] By the time random machine-gun fire erupted on that remote hilltop in the Philippines, Ōoka's psychic "lifeline"—his inner symbolization of identity, meaning, human connection, relationship to the external world, and immortality—was already gravely frayed. It would take many years of struggle before he was able to reconstitute his traumatic past in such a way as to recover connection, integration, and vitality.

Ōoka's transformative encounter with the young American soldier was at the heart of a constellation of survivor issues he struggled to come to terms with in his memoirs, fiction, and historical writings on the war. As shown in this chapter, he was initially reluctant to thoroughly face and work through his frontline trauma autobiographically. While he wrote honestly about his experience of deadness and desymbolization and testified at length about what he witnessed at the front, his literary endeavors to make sense of his burdened past were frustrated by ongoing psychic numbing, repressed feelings of guilt and self-recrimination, and impaired mourning. While he occasionally struggled with death guilt, his pressing need to justify himself and reject the war dead continued to cause difficulties. There are, however, sporadic indications in his memoirs of his potential for making crucial breakthroughs. Scattered in his recollective accounts are expressions of the anxiety of responsibility that ultimately facilitated movement from static to animating guilt.

Impaired Formulation, Impaired Mourning

As seen at the beginning of this chapter, Ōoka's initial autobiographical attempts to formulate his battlefield experience were partially inhibited by the death imprints that continued to haunt him long after survival. This is most conspicuous in his treatment of his encounter with the young American. Ōoka's minute reconstruction and analysis of this *jiken* in "Before Capture" leaves off as follows: "Gunfire resounds. Just as it echoed then, and blew away my tension and the impending moment of decision, so it reverberates in my ears even now and *forces an end to all thought*" (1:35; emphasis added). In Lifton's terms, such traumatic experiences are comparable to death imprints; they defy full assimilation and integration with prior and anticipated experience and consequently present serious formulative challenges. Ōoka never was able to completely purge his death-immersion experience from memory. As shown in the following passage from *Return to Mindoro Island,* it continued to haunt him some twenty-five years after survival:

> The American forces finally reached our encampment. I was stricken with malaria, and could barely walk. In the end, I was isolated in the forest. At that time, I . . . crossed over into a world from which there was no return.
>
> No one can know what I saw, thought, and did during those twenty-four hours. I survived as a result of a series of miraculous, chance occurrences. I wrote in various ways about that other world. I wrote about the voices of enemy soldiers that suddenly echoed around me in the empty forest and the rosy cheeks of the young American soldier. I described the misshapen moon that appeared directly overhead through a break in the rain clouds, and the water buffalo that looked at me intimately and then walked away in the milky light of dawn.
>
> I wrote about the ways a man is affected when existence loses all meaning. I wrote accounts that, like the experiences of kamikaze pilots, can normally not be told. As punishment, I live constantly with death. I live in a perpetual state in which existence is apt, at any moment, to be emptied of meaning. At such times, a strangely desolate world progressively infuses and replaces the everyday objects before my eyes. (2:445–446)

Indelible death imprints were but one integral element of Ōoka's frontline trauma that raised formulative difficulties. Ōoka was also preoccupied with matters of meaning, or perhaps more accurately, meaninglessness. This can be seen in his deep concern with *gūzen.* In the end, the most important factor in his encounter was a random eruption of machine-gun fire. And this incidental occurrence that not only caused his enemy to walk away but also "brought an end to all thought," was just one essential link in a chain of chance events that enabled survival.[31] The crux of Ōoka's formulative difficulties surrounding chance can be expressed as follows: to the extent that it depends on random, chance events, survival in and of itself is meaningless.[32] As a burdened survivor, Ōoka faced the daunting task of formulating his traumatic battlefield experience in such a way as to find significance and value in seemingly pointless survival.

An intimately related element of Ōoka's encounter that served to obstruct formulation was the trauma-induced undoing of character. His extreme experience forced him to fundamentally reconsider the nature of self. His actions during the encounter and the disruptions in consciousness he discovered through writing about his experience pushed him toward confrontation with the fact that the ultimate ground of being was not character-based integrity, but perception, instinct, and chance. In his autobiographical writings, Ōoka was reluctant to fully acknowledge the role of egoism in his survival or allow for the necessary degree of dissolution of his positive, pretrauma self-image. Instead, he maneuvered elaborately to justify his conduct and recoup his fragile symbolic world. Part of the formative challenge Ōoka faced was wholly accepting the new basis on which his posttrauma identity would have to be reconstituted.

Ōoka was reluctant to confront the central role egoism played in his own survival not only because doing so threatened to open the floodgates of repressed emotion, but also because of its deeply unsettling implications to human relationships. To openly acknowledge the primacy of the instinct for self-preservation in extremity is to deny the viability of human bonds. In Ōoka's case, this would have entailed confronting the fact that the ultimate price of personal survival in human terms may well have been the lives of one or more of his comrades. He was probably even less eager to consider the psychological corollary of this—that he was deeply indebted and obligated to those who died in his place.

Ōoka's literary journey of survivor formulation was also substantially impeded by deep-seated feelings of death guilt and self-recrimination. Such repressed anxiety over survival lay not only behind his defensive rationalizations concerning luck and chance, but also behind his pressing need to shift blame onto and scapegoat his comrades. Ōoka's primary justification for his own defeatism, passivity, and self-centered conduct was the presumption of the inevitable battlefield deaths of himself and every last man in Nishiya Company. In the end, however, some few survived; and it would be many years before Ōoka was as psychologically willing to face and work through the emotional issues that were part of survival as he was instinctually and physically prepared to deal with the enemy who pressed in on him in that remote mountain clearing on Mindoro Island.

It was the inability to mourn, however, that most inhibited Ōoka's formulation and recovery. At the heart of this condition was psychic numbing and his uneasy relationship as a guilt-ridden survivor to the dead. It is thus highly significant that "Homecoming" leaves off with an unattended funeral. Just as Ōoka evaded taking part in funeral and memorial services for Private Kobayashi—the first of his Nishiya Company comrades to die—so he avoided attending the last rites for the two comrades who died virtually within sight of home. In the end, Ōoka could not properly attend to the war dead until he reached the point of being able to belatedly experience and work through the emotions he could not afford at the time.[33] Impaired mourning was the enduring legacy of the psychic numbing that functioned to protect him during his protracted immersion in death. Until he could open himself up emotionally to guilt, pain, grief, and sadness—particularly in relation to his fallen comrades—he could not do the work of mourning necessary for more fruitful formulation of his traumatic war experience.

Anxiety of Responsibility

While clearly marked by impaired formulation and impaired mourning, Ōoka's memoirs do contain a number of significant expressions of the anxiety of responsibility, the "transformation of self-condemnation into the feeling that one must, should, and can act against the wrong and toward an alternative." Lifton writes as follows about the important link between formulative progress and "appropriate blaming": "To break out . . . in the direction of formulation, the survivor must find a balance between appropriate blaming (which may indeed include considerable anger toward those who bear some responsibility for the traumatic events) and scapegoating (total concentration on the target for anger in a way that continues to literalize and inhibits assimilation of the experience)."[34] Productively harnessing the anxiety of responsibility to convert static to more animating forms of guilt required Ōoka to abandon his scapegoating formulation and begin to extend the concentric rings of responsibility outward from himself and his immediate company toward the more distant forces that conditioned their experience of war.

In "Before Capture," Ōoka initially moved to take personal responsibility for the predicament he suddenly found himself in. While expressing anger at the army for "drawing [his] homeland into such a hopeless conflict," he quickly shifted the target of blame toward himself because theretofore he had done nothing to resist. Significantly, from the outset, Ōoka refuses to treat his (or his comrades') battlefield experience in terms of victimization. In his autobiographical writings he is preoccupied with personal responsibility, first his own, and then increasingly that of those around him. There are, however, several highly significant instances in which he begins to cast the net of accountability more widely. This movement toward more appropriate blaming can be seen toward the end of his confession of stealing Matsumoto's boots: "After all is said and done, only the boots were 'real.' The only 'reality' was the weakness of a nation that forced its soldiers to fight on with such lousy footwear. While this basic reality didn't necessarily operate in a soldier's psychology to make him think or feel a particular way, it did fundamentally condition his behavior" (2:256). Bearing witness to the few good men in his company, too, brought Ōoka to a more inclusive consideration of responsibility. This is most conspicuous in his treatment of Private Kobayashi. The death of this ethically and spiritually pure young man—wholly unsullied by the egoism that enabled Ōoka to condemn and summarily dismiss his older comrades—raised issues of accountability that clearly extended well beyond immediate circumstances.

Ōoka's potential to transcend the individual level in formulating responsibility is most strikingly revealed in "The Rains of Tacloban" when he steps back to consider the macrocosmic context of his traumatic encounter with the enemy:

> Japanese capitalists wanted to solve their financial crisis by means of aggression. The reckless military agreed, and as a result, I was sent to the Philippines with a Model 38 rifle and a grenade. Because of Roosevelt's determination to maintain world democracy by military force, that innocent young American appeared before me with an automatic rifle. We had no personal reason to kill one another, but we had to. While it was national policy, it was not one we chose ourselves.
>
> The situation in which two soldiers come face to face in the remote jungles of the Philippines is so meaningless it is doubtful whether it even deserves to be called a "battle" of modern war. Even in the grandest engagements, when foot soldiers—members of that most lowly and scorned branch of the army—encounter one another, this kind of meaninglessness inevitably emerges. Why is it necessary for worthless soldiers to kill each other meaninglessly? Because it's kill or be killed. This is the consequence of our carrying deadly weapons. These weapons, however, were not taken up by us of our own free will.
>
> Before the American actually appeared, the will to refuse to use this deadly weapon came to me. Because I was a solitary, routed soldier, I could choose my own actions. Although I have embellished my psychology at that

> time with humanism, instincts, and God, just as they are not part of the consciousness of a soldier the instant he kills his enemy, so they were ultimately unimportant in determining my actions as well.
>
> In actuality, my conduct was nothing more than the instantaneous reality (*isshun no jijitsu*) of abandoning the shooting of an "enemy" forced on me by my country. What determined my behavior at that moment was the fact that from the very beginning he was not an enemy I had chosen myself. All this was decided before I even departed for the front.
>
> The man who approached me at that time was not my enemy; my enemies are elsewhere. (1:107–108)

Conspicuous here is the emphasis on the overarching political and military forces that fundamentally shape the actions and experiences of individual soldiers on the battlefield. The last statement concerning the identity of the enemy is of particular importance. The pivotal insight that his enemies were elsewhere led toward a more inclusive moral perspective that in time enabled him to become a "collector of justice."[35]

Another poignant example of Ōoka's potential for converting static to animating guilt appears in the prisoner-of-war memoir "August Tenth" (Hachigatsu tōka, 1950). In this work, Ōoka describes his visceral reaction to news of the atomic bombing of Hiroshima: "The *Stars and Stripes* article was somewhat exaggerated. It reported that ten square miles had been completely and instantaneously destroyed, and that the entire area would not support life for at least twenty years. I shuddered when I thought of vast numbers of my countrymen being exposed to radiation and dying after profound and varied suffering. This marked the first time since I had become a prisoner of war that I was genuinely affected by the misfortune of my homeland" (1:354). Ōoka is baffled by the intensity and persistence of his emotional reaction to news of this unprecedented catastrophe. Up until this point, psychic numbing and repression had effectively shielded him from painful thoughts of his proximate comrades and distant compatriots who continued to suffer and die while he enjoyed a safe and comfortable life in the POW camp. When there is no word of Japan's surrender several days after the decimation of Hiroshima, Ōoka's agitation reaches the boiling point. Finally, theretofore suppressed feelings of anger and indignation not only find expression, but are also directed toward more fitting targets: "I just could not sit still. I realized that not surrendering was the 'height of folly.' I suppose the lunatics directing the war felt that they had to press on to the bitter end. Chances were that in the safety of their underground bunkers, they would continue to savor dreams of Okehazama no matter how many atomic bombs the people were subjected to" (1:356).[36]

As Ōoka struggles to account for his unexpected and persistent emotional response, he summarily discounts sympathy or empathy: "Many of those who died gladly accepted the benefits of the nation's preparations for and waging of the war. Strictly speaking, those who lost their lives simply reaped what they sowed. As with myself, the people of Hiroshima had it coming. After becoming a soldier, I lost all sympathy for those who died from the same cause that nearly took my own life." (1:358). Ōoka accepted personal responsibility not only for nonresistance, but for personally profiting from the war as well; and here he demands that the people of Hiroshima, and by extension all his countrymen, do the same. He will not allow these grave matters to be obscured by victim consciousness. Ōoka's treatment of his reaction to the abominable events that signalled the end of the disastrous Pacific War contain a clear expression of the anxiety of responsibility he was subsequently able to use for his survivor mission:

> Ultimately, I must seek the origins of my anxiety and restlessness in the effect on my psychology of imagining tens of thousands of fellow humans killed instantaneously. That an urbanite like me, so lacking in any social emotions, could be moved this much by the "masses" was surely due to some basic instinct related to collective living. My feelings were purely biological.
>
> From these biological emotions, I genuinely hated the military authorities. The military leaders were experts who knew only too well that the war was lost. They were also probably well aware that modern wars could not be won even with the honorable deaths of a hundred million. They probably put off surrender even after learning of the destructive power of the atomic bomb because they didn't want to be executed as war criminals themselves. I realize that they started the war for a variety of reasons, and that many things didn't go their way. Only their biological instinct for self-preservation, however, could have led them to sit idly by for days at such a critical moment. I therefore have every right to despise them for biological reasons. (1:358–359)

These emotional reactions well up from the deepest core of Ōoka's being. While still unable to embrace or grieve for his comrades or the men and women who died on the home front, he strongly reacts against what he perceives as a serious threat to humankind as a whole. Once again, Ōoka finds more appropriate targets for his "biological" outrage in Japan's wartime leadership. It is important to note, moreover, that his formulation of his intense and lasting emotional response is inseparable from his awareness of the survival egoism of those who had the power and ability to end the war sooner. As he wrote upon learning that Nagasaki had suffered nuclear attack and that the Russians had entered the war against Japan,

> I was enraged. I was incensed both for the soldiers in Manchuria forced to die pointlessly and for my compatriots whose houses were being destroyed meaninglessly under the pretext of [preserving] the national polity (*kokutai*). My reactions, once again, were biological.
>
> I claim no knowledge of lofty matters such as the "economic foundation of the emperor system" or the "smile of the human emperor." Based on the biological emotions of a prisoner of war, however, the existence of the emperor between August 11 and 14 was clearly a bane to the spirits of those who had to die meaninglessly. (1:374)

The fundamental barriers to and potential for fruitful formulation of his traumatic battlefield experience coexist in "August Tenth." It is important to bear in mind that while for the most part repressed, the anxiety of responsibility was an ever-present current flowing just beneath the surface of Ōoka's—and his early protagonists'—callousness, anxious self-justification, and defensive rationalization.

In "Those I Can't Forget," one catches an important glimpse of the progress Ōoka made after struggling with the burdens of survival in memoir and fiction for eight years. He opens this memoir—one of his last—as follows: "Heretofore, I have done a number of prose portraits of the comrades I knew at the front. What they all had in common was [premature] death" (2:298). After testifying about the attitudes and conduct of a number of men he had theretofore neglected to write about, he reveals a significant change in his overall attitude toward his fallen comrades: "As I wrote earlier, all of my comrades (*senyū*) died: death was the one thing they all had in common. Death clearly alters the relationship between people. It was undoubtedly through death that these men became precious (*kichō*) to me" (2:315). Ōoka doesn't elaborate on how or when he came to value his fallen comrades. As shown in this chapter, in his memoirs he testified voluminously on their reprehensible acts of middle-class and survival egoism, claimed that they never were brothers-in-arms, and dismissed them en masse as inferior soldiers and detestable human beings. By 1953, however, these same comrades had become precious. Examination of the fictional works he wrote based on his war experience and intervening events in his personal life during the decade following the publication of his first battlefield memoir in 1948 enables retracing of this crucial leg of his arduous formative journey. This is the main subject of the next two chapters of this study.

CHAPTER TWO

Fires on the Plain

FIRES ON THE PLAIN, the tortured memoir (*shuki*) Tamura composes as a patient in a Tokyo mental hospital, is one of the most important, highly acclaimed, and popular novels about Japanese Pacific War battlefield experience.[1] Ōoka Shōhei's fictional treatment of his frontline experience endures because of the compelling nature of Tamura's harrowing story of battlefield survival, the extent to which Ōoka enables his readership to identify and empathize with his "insane" protagonist and know the horrors of war, and the realism, power, and beauty of the descriptive language.[2] Readers—Japanese readers in particular—are drawn to Tamura by his seeming innocence and sensitivity and his serious existential struggles with cannibalism and the existence of God. Tamura presents himself as a deeply troubled veteran who deserves sympathy and compassion.[3] Despite guarded confessions of engaging in atrocities—killing a noncombatant, fratricide, and cannibalism—he comes across as a burdened survivor whose suffering continues long after the war ends.

While *Fires on the Plain* is usually read as a sincere account of traumatic battlefield experience, Tamura's memoir is actually an unstable combination of confession, dissembling, omission, and concealment. This important aspect of Ōoka's imaginative working through of his personal war experience has yet to be sufficiently appreciated. Although clearly a work of fiction, *Fires on the Plain* is substantially based on Ōoka's frontline experience and the testimony of Japanese survivors of the Battle for Leyte Island he met in the POW camp.[4] Tamura offers up his memoir as an honest account of his frontline trauma, but there are significant intimations that important elements of his story have been wholly fabricated. Full appreciation of this complex, multidimensional work challenges one not only to come to grips with the thorny issue of truth and fiction, but also to articulate its relationship to Ōoka's ongoing literary endeavor to come to terms with his traumatic battlefield experience.

Ōoka began writing the "Diary of a Madman" section of *Fires on the Plain* in May 1946, immediately after finishing the initial draft of "Before Capture." Because of concerns about occupation censorship, serialization of the work in *Tembō* was not completed until late 1951. And when the novel finally appeared as a book the following year, it had been substantially revised and rewritten.[5] Ōoka produced the bulk of his own battlefield (and prisoner-of-war) memoirs during the five-year period in which he wrote and reworked the novel, and Ikeda Jun'ichi has enumerated the many significant parallels between Ōoka's autobiographical and fictional treatments of his war experience.[6]

There can be little doubt that Private Tamura is Ōoka's alter ego.[7] In "My Intentions in *Fires on the Plain*" (*Nobi* no ito, 1953), Ōoka comments on the close connection between his maiden work and his first war novel: "I conceived of *Fires on the Plain* as a supplement to 'Before Capture.' The amnesia the protagonist suffers in the novel, for instance, is a magnification of the memory loss . . . I discovered I suffered during my encounter with the American soldier. I felt, moreover, like approaching cannibalism as an extreme form of a routed soldier's egoism" (15:415). Ōoka comments in the same piece on another important reason for fictionalizing his war experience:

> In "Before Capture," I made every effort to understand my battlefield experience rationally. . . . There were aspects, however, that I could not get at fully with this method. In short, using the logical approach I employed in "Before Capture," I couldn't adequately convey the mental and emotional confusion I experienced as a routed soldier.
>
> I made the protagonist insane to express this confusion. . . . It was a means of presenting confusion directly, just as I experienced it. (15:411)

Even more explicit in this regard is a June 27, 1946, entry appearing in his "Evacuee's Diary" (Sokai nikki, 1953): "My mind is filled with thoughts and feelings I want to confess (*kokuhakushitai omoi*). This is because I have begun writing 'Diary of a Madman'" (15:23). In *Fires on the Plain,* Ōoka subtly exposes the fictionality of a survivor-narrator's literary reconstruction of his battlefield experience. Indeed, he was as concerned in the novel with the crucial matter of Tamura's reliability as he was with giving unrestrained expression to his extraordinary frontline experience.

In his own battlefield memoirs, Ōoka concerned himself almost exclusively with reproducing and examining his wartime experience. While maintaining fidelity to his past experience in this way, he avoided dealing with his postwar thoughts and feelings about it. Creating an alter ego enabled Ōoka to more productively confront, express, and work through deep-seated feelings of death guilt, self-recrimination, and loss. Tamura repeatedly describes himself experiencing deep emotion, partially to elicit the reader's sympathy and to present himself in a more positive, human light. And at a number of crucial junctures, he engages in authentic, present-tense struggles with the overwhelming return of repressed memories. As indicated in the previous quotation, moreover, Ōoka also continues to wrestle with survival egoism. And toward the end of the work, he is able to begin to face the all-but-forgotten spirits of the war dead.

Truth and Fiction in *Fires on the Plain*

Tamura's memoir can be divided into three sections. The first, and longest, consists of his recollected account of his battlefield experience from the time he was driven from his company by illness until he suffered a ten-day memory loss before capture. In the second, narrative time and space abruptly shift from Leyte Island to Japan. "Diary of a Madman" opens as follows: "I am writing this [memoir] in a room of a mental hospital on the outskirts of Tokyo" (3:397). The year is 1951, and nearly six years have passed since Tamura's frontline ordeal. In the second section, Tamura comments on his postwar experience and psychological condition, explains how he came to be a patient in a mental institution, and relates the circumstances surrounding the writing of his battlefield memoir. In the third and final section, Tamura progressively recovers and records memories from his extended period of amnesia. Thus, in chronological terms, his memoir begins in the wartime past, abruptly shifts to the contemporary present, and then returns to the past—or, more accurately, the repressed past returns to occupy the present.

The problematic nature of Tamura's account is most clearly exposed in the third section. After leading a relatively normal life in Japan for five years after the war, Tamura suddenly reverts to his immediate postcapture habit of bowing to his food. This peculiar habit first developed when he was in the POW hospital on Leyte Island. Tamura describes and explains this compulsive behavior as follows:

> I was told that when I was first admitted to the prisoner of war hospital, I attracted the attention of my fellow inmates by performing a sort of ritual before the trays of food I received. People assumed I was crazy. At the time—even now for that matter—I made it my policy to feel no shame over things I couldn't help doing. Since I am moved to act by an external force, there is nothing I can do about it.
>
> Although I must eat to sustain myself, before I consume food consisting of organic matter, I apologize to the animals it was taken from. I myself am at a loss as to how others can eat without feeling any self-reproach whatsoever. (3:398)

Tamura's denial of control over, and thus responsibility for, his actions is conspicuous here, as is his justification for them. Although he writes that he has "made it [his] policy to feel no shame over doing the things [he] couldn't help doing," his compulsive behavior is a physical expression of repressed death guilt. And Tamura doesn't feel guilt simply over survival itself, but also over what he did and failed to do at the front to perpetuate his life. There can be little doubt that his compulsive rite is inseparable from past acts of eating human flesh. Reluctant to acknowledge or confront the unbearable truth at the heart of his eccentric behavior, he maneuvers to justify it in spiritual terms.

Tamura, however, quickly senses the danger of physically expressing himself in this way: "I abruptly stopped performing my ritual one day when I realized that whether I expressed it or not I would still feel the same way. I subsequently came to take interest in concealing my heart (*kokoro*) from others" (3:398). This statement is applicable to Tamura's memoir as a whole. Close reading reveals that much of the account shows evidence of his efforts to conceal his heart from others. Tamura's immediate motivations are readily understandable: "Since I was afraid that I might be taken as a war criminal for killing the Filipina, I didn't tell anyone about my experience after separating from my unit. I also didn't know what my fellow prisoners would think about my killing a comrade, even if he had been a cannibal" (3:398–399).

Tamura's memories of traumatic battlefield experience, however, cannot be repressed completely. The timing of the return of repressed material signaled by the reemergence of his compulsive habit, moreover, is significant. The revival of this practice, and its eventual transformation into a total denial of food, coincide with the buildup of tensions on the Korean Peninsula. Rumors of war in Japan in the summer of 1950 symbolically reactivate Tamura's battlefield trauma.[8] And the progressive return of repressed war memories has the effect of rendering his present life meaningless, alienating him from his family and society and making him long for isolation. When he sees that the mental hospital is surrounded by trees reminiscent of those he saw in the Philippines, he thinks, "Yes, in all the world this is the place for me. If I had only known about this place sooner" (3:400).

In the second part of his account, Tamura explains how he came to take up his pen: "I originally began writing this memoir at the urging of my doctor. He seemed to be of the opinion that it was appropriate for me to write about my past as an extension of free-association therapy. Relying on his professional obligation to maintain doctor-patient confidentiality, I decided to relate the experience I had theretofore kept strictly to myself. Since I figured that the doctors probably already knew some of my secrets from Amytal interviews, I found it convenient to fill in the details myself" (3:403). Tamura openly admits to having secrets (*himitsu*) related to his wartime past. Aware that he had already divulged some of them during drug therapy, he in his own words found it convenient (*tsugō ga ii*) to explain things more fully himself. Composing his own account gave Tamura an opportunity to contextualize and explain the atrocities he was involved in. To this end, he was more than willing to dissemble.[9]

Tamura's motives are not lost on his physicians. In fact, in a conversation he has with his doctor after the latter has read through the first part of the former's account, Tamura admits to fabricating an important element of his memoir. One can only lament Ivan Morris' decision to remove this crucial passage from his English translation of the novel:[10]

"You were able to craft this with great skill, weren't you? It reads just like a novel."

"I described my experience exactly as it was."

"Ha, ha, ha. That's it. That's the source of the problem. The distinctive characteristic of your memoir is that in the very places you believe you were recording things exactly as they happened, you were actually maneuvering to obscure the truth. This psychology, too, is common to novelists."

"Recollection is inevitably accompanied by reordering and rationalization."

"How self-conscious we are. You, however, are making things up."

"Don't even popular commentaries acknowledge that recollection in some ways resembles imagination? What can I do other than compose my account according to present thoughts and feelings?"

"Look, what we're most interested in is your image of God. Your complex—we usually refer to it as a messiah complex—usually develops in compensation for guilt feelings. Do you still believe you're an [avenging] angel?"

"No, I'm not sure. You know, you may be right. I probably came up with that and worked it in as I was writing. For a messiah complex, my concept of God is pretty half-baked."

"Your symptoms are relatively mild, so there's really no need to be too concerned. There are times, however, when the things people write while insane unexpectedly contain profound human truths. It's too bad your concussion caused you to forget the last part of your experience. We think the root cause of your condition may well be there." (3:404–405)

Tamura's psychiatrists are aware of the contrived nature of his writings. When confronted with this in connection with his self-image as an avenging angel, Tamura confesses that it was not originally part of his battlefield experience, but something he "came up with and worked in *as [he] was writing.*"[11] Through this exchange, Ōoka subtly alerts the reader to the problematic nature of Tamura's memoir: it is, in substantial ways, a fabrication written in the interest of self-justification. Fatal truths do, however, slip out from behind his carefully crafted veil of fiction. Close examination of Tamura's handling of five key scenes of atrocity not only facilitates separation of truth from lies, but also articulates why Tamura ultimately fails to accomplish the explicit aim of his memoir—formulating his traumatic battlefield experience in such a way as to bring about recovery and renewal.[12]

The extreme nature of Tamura's battlefield experience made it impossible for him to completely conceal the truth of his past while composing his memoir.[13] The basic psychological conflict he struggled with as he composed his account is vividly conveyed through a dream. While wandering through remote mountains, Tamura stumbles upon an abandoned hilltop farm. After resting for several days and eating his fill of sweet potatoes (*kamote*), he explores the surrounding area and eventually notices a peculiar object protruding above the trees down by the coast. The night after he finally recognizes it as a cross, he dreams of descending to the coastal village and entering the church, where a funeral service is in progress. When he approaches the casket next to the altar, he is shocked to find his own name on it. After removing the lid and regarding his own gaunt face for a time, he notices that his hands are pressed together in prayer, thinks he looks like a martyr, and concludes that he is being honored by the villagers as a saint. This comforting thought, however, is short-lived:

> I was suddenly assailed by a disturbing thought. Did I really deserve to be revered in such a way? Had my soul really been so pious?
>
> I looked at my face again. Wait! I was still alive! My lips were bright red, as if covered with crimson lipstick, and my closed eyelids quivered. I was awake. I was feigning death, so I couldn't open my eyes. That familiar, derisive smile slowly took shape on my lips.
>
> Those lips suddenly called out "De Profundis!"
>
> "Out of the depths I have called to thee, O Lord. De Profundis Clamavi!" The fact that these words emerged from my mouth made it clear that I actually was in the depths; they were proof that I wasn't a saint. (3:290–291)

The divided self-image conveyed through this dream—one that recurs in various forms throughout the work—vividly reveals the psychological tension at the heart of his literary struggle to come to terms with his burdened past. Even as he labors to construct a positive self-image—in this instance, that of himself as a martyr and saint—the conflicting image he is so loath to confront—that of himself as an egoistical survivor willing to do whatever it takes to extend his life—threatens to displace it.

Tamura doesn't just struggle to stave off negative self-images; he also contends, with varying degrees of effectiveness, with deep-seated feelings of guilt, self-recrimination, and loss. This is initially apparent in his description of his fatal encounter with a young, noncombatant village woman. Before turning to his treatment of this first scene of atrocity—one he surely divulged to his doctors during drug therapy—it is useful to consider his contextualization of it. Like the notion of being an avenging angel, the reasons Tamura gives for descending to the coastal village are probably more related to contemporary imagination than to past experience.

The experience Ōoka relates in "The Rains of Tacloban" is particularly illuminating in this regard. As introduced in the first chapter of this study, while struggling after capture to understand why he failed to engage the enemy, Ōoka came up with the notion of divine intervention. This has bearing on Tamura's memoir in two distinct ways. First, and perhaps most important, this thought was not integral to his battlefield experience, but came to mind as he tried to make sense of it after the fact. Second, Ōoka later rejected this explanation that God would intervene solely on his behalf while letting so many others die as conceit. In *Fires on the Plain,* however, he created a protagonist who not only embraced the notion of being God's Chosen One, but also worked it into his memoir.

As he wrote about killing the young Filipina, Tamura was primarily concerned with contextualizing and explaining his war crime in such a way as to garner maximum sympathy while minimizing personal responsibility. As with his compulsive food ritual, he sought to do so in religious terms. According to Tamura, seeing the cross brought on a spiritual crisis. After spending an entire night thinking about this familiar Christian symbol, recalling his innocence, his adolescent belief in God, and having his disturbing dream, Tamura decides that by visiting the church he will be able to resolve the issue of whether it had been a serious mistake to abandon his religious orientation and embrace modern rationalism and hedonism. It is, of course, extremely unlikely that a lone, routed Japanese soldier would venture into the village of his enemies for such a purpose. A far more likely motivation was obtaining sorely needed supplies. This is borne out by subsequent events.

When Tamura reaches the village square, he finds it abandoned and strewn with the rotting corpses of his slaughtered countrymen. He must walk past a heap of bodies to enter the church. As when he caught sight of the cross as he came to the village, none of the religious images he sees retain any meaning or significance. In a multipaneled painting of the

Passion, he sees nothing but poor workmanship and a profusion of blood that smacks of medieval barbarism. When he looks at a wax image of the Crucifixion, he only notices the pull of gravity on Christ's physical body:

> In these images, which were the objects of these villagers' devotion and which had actually been the focal points of my own youthful longing, I saw nothing but a bloody corpse. . . .
>
> I lay on the dusty floor and wept. Why was I, who in all piousness was drawn down from the mountains to the cross, forced to see nothing but the twisted corpses of my comrades and unskilled religious representations of Jesus undergoing his death sentence on the cross? . . .
>
> "De Profundis!"
>
> The words I had heard from my own lips in my dream the night before echoed through the church. As the voice seemed to have come from the choir seats above and behind me, I turned to look in that direction.
>
> Even as my eyes searched for the origin of that voice, I knew that it had been an aural hallucination. Although the voice was familiar, at the time I couldn't place it.
>
> I know now. It was the sound of my own voice when I am agitated. If I am insane, my condition began the instant I heard my own voice in the church.
>
> "Out of the depths I have called to thee, O Lord. Lord hear my cry."
>
> The Old Testament verses I had memorized in my youth were revived. My eyes, which searched along the ceiling and throughout the inside of the shabby Filipino church, however, could find nothing whatsoever to answer my pleas.
>
> "I turn toward the mountains and raise my eyes; whence cometh my salvation?"
>
> At that moment, I became aware that the connection between myself and the external world had abruptly been severed completely. In all the world there was nothing to answer my pleas. This, I decided, was a reality I had to resign myself to. (3:308–309)

Thus does Tamura elaborately prepare the stage for his first act of atrocity. One has the strong impression that rather than describing his experience exactly as it was, Tamura was embellishing in order to present the image of himself on the brink of insanity, forsaken by God and sobbing in despair. Tamura was clearly willing to go to extreme lengths to portray himself in the most pitiable, understanding, and sympathetic light.

Tamura enters the presbytery after leaving the church. After searching in vain for matches and a magnifying glass, he sits down on a rattan chair and dozes off. He is subsequently awakened by the sound of a popular romantic song a young Filipina sings to her boyfriend as she rows him ashore. He grinds his teeth every time he hears their laughter. When the couple enter the presbytery and begin to search for something in the adjoining room, Tamura confronts them:

> I intentionally made some noise, and their conversation abruptly stopped. I stood, pushed the door open with the barrel of my rifle, and emerged before them.
>
> They stood there side by side. The flame from their palm-oil lamp was reflected in their wide-open eyes.
>
> I told them in the local dialect to give me matches.
>
> The woman screamed. . . . There was nothing human in that voice, it was the primal cry of an animal. . . .
>
> Her face remained riveted on me and contorted grotesquely as she continued to scream intermittently in a shrill voice. I reacted with rage.
>
> I shot. The bullet apparently hit her in the chest. A blood stain spread rapidly on her sky-blue silk dress. She clutched her breast with her right hand, rotated oddly, and fell forward. (3:312)

After chasing the young woman's companion, who manages to escape in the boat, Tamura returns to the presbytery and observes the young woman's final moments with detachment. After her death, he notices the cache of salt she and her companion had come for and fills his haversack.

When Tamura initially reflects on his conduct, he feels personally responsible for her death. He writes that regardless of the circumstances, he had to admit that he was "nothing but a brutal soldier" (3:313). Immediately afterward, however, he alternates between expressions of grief and remorse and defensive rationalization:

> Sadness possessed my heart. The details of the body of the woman I killed lingered persistently before my eyes—its position, the wide-open eyes, the sharp nose, the way her arm was thrown out to the side as if she had passed out during a moment of ecstasy.
>
> I had no regrets. Killing was a common, everyday event on the battlefield. It was chance that I had become a killer. She died because she entered the house I happened to have been hiding in.

> But why did I shoot? Because she screamed. This, however, was just the precipitating event; it was not the root cause of my conduct. Moreover, since I didn't really take aim, it was pure chance that the bullet struck a vital spot. It was an accident. If so, why do I feel so sad? (3:314)

Tamura initially writes that he was assailed by sadness, a clear sign that he felt personally accountable for his actions. In the second paragraph, however, he maneuvers to transfer blame to war and chance. The third, and for the present purposes most important paragraph, contains the first indication of the loss of emotional distance and narrative control that characterizes his subsequent treatments of atrocity. Even as Tamura seeks to evade responsibility by rationalizing the woman's death as an accident (*jiko*), deep-seated feelings of guilt and loss begin to intrude into the narrative present and compel him to ask "Why do I feel so sad?" (*naze watashi ga konna ni kanashii no ka*). In Tamura's treatment of this experience, one notices an internal division of self similar to that reflected in his dream. Even as he consciously seeks to construct an interpretation of past events that absolves him of or at least minimizes his responsibility, the conflicting emotional truth of his experience surfaces to underscore that responsibility.

While repressed emotions break through Tamura's psychological defenses enough to make him ask why he feels so sad, he does not seek to answer the question. Rather than moving in the direction of atoning for and coming to terms with his burdened past, he again engages in shifting blame:

> I suddenly realized that everything that had happened depended on this rifle. Despite my impulsive descent from the mountains and the woman's lack of caution when she entered the village, the whole incident would probably have ended in her being startled and running away had I not still held this rifle in my hands at the moment of our encounter.
>
> This rifle was forced on me by my country. Because of this weapon, I was as useful to my country as I was dangerous to my enemies. The root cause of that innocent woman's death was my continuing to carry this deadly weapon even after I became a lone, routed soldier deemed to be of no further use to his country.
>
> I thereupon threw it into the stream. (3:315–316)

Tamura can discard his rifle with relative ease; he cannot so readily purge the image of the woman he killed from memory or conscience. He is subsequently haunted by her both in the past and the present.[14]

The second scene of atrocity involves cannibalism. As with the first, his contextualization of the incident is dubious at best. Tamura describes himself chancing upon an insane Japanese officer propped up against a tree on top of a hill. He suggests that he probably climbed the hill to get a better view of the sunset. It is highly questionable, however, that such aesthetic interests would guide the behavior of a lone, traumatized soldier. A much more likely possibility is that this discovery was the result of an intentional search for food. This reading, too, is borne out by subsequent events.

Tamura sits down next to the madman and patiently awaits his death. In a moment of clarity that comes to him just before he expires, the officer reportedly tells Tamura that he can eat him when he dies.[15] After he breathes his last, Tamura drags his body to a secluded area and attempts to carry out his radical plan for survival. He recounts the second scene of atrocity as follows:

> I checked to make sure no one was watching.
>
> A peculiar thing then happened. My left hand grabbed the wrist of my right, which was holding the bayonet. . . . Although I have become accustomed to such behavior, and don't find it the least bit strange now, I was shocked when it first occurred. I felt that the animated left hand that grasped and restrained my right wrist from above belonged to someone else.
>
> . . .
>
> As I held this odd position, I again had the feeling of being watched. I felt that I had to maintain this posture until those eyes were no longer on me.
>
> "Do not let your left hand know what your right is doing."
>
> I heard a voice, but I was not particularly surprised. Since I was already being observed by somebody, there was nothing so strange about being talked to.
>
> It was not the sultry, animal-like voice of the woman I had killed. It was the same magnified voice that had called out to me from on high in the village church.
>
> The voice commanded me: "Rise, rise this instant!"
>
> I stood up. This was the first time someone had ever forced me to move like this.
>
> I walked away from the corpse. With each step, one finger of my left

> hand released its hold on my right. The middle finger, ring finger, and little finger came free. The index finger and thumb released simultaneously. (3:364–366)

Tamura would have the reader believe that even though he was starving to death next to a fresh body, he was not only able to physically restrain himself, but also have God intervene on his behalf. Surely, it was fantastic, finely crafted passages such as this that led Tamura's psychiatrists to conclude that he was making things up. The crucial question here, however, is *why?* As will become increasingly clear, he dissembles in an effort to avoid facing the unbearable truths of his heavily burdened past.

Tamura describes himself having a fantastic, animistic vision after walking away from the officer's corpse. During this extended hallucination, he more clearly envisions the transcendental being he increasingly comes to rely on to justify his atrocious behavior. When at the height of his vision a female flower raises itself above the grass and offers itself to him to eat, he has an insight that because they must be killed, it is worse to eat plants and animals than dead human beings. At this point, Tamura's hands again begin to work at cross purposes; he becomes conscious of starvation and returns to the officer's corpse, only to find that it has putrefied in his absence.

It is hard to believe that a starving man would abandon a fresh corpse and then return to it only after it has spoiled to the point of inedibility. It is precisely at this moment, moreover, that Tamura suffers the first of four distinct memory losses, each more severe and extended than the last.[16] Memory loss under such circumstances is indicative of overwhelming experience. Amnesia, or radical repression of memory, is Tamura's last line of defense against unbearable battlefield reality.[17] And the nature of the memories that are lost during Tamura's first three amnesiac episodes can be surmised from the immediate circumstances precipitating them: in each case, memory cuts off when he is starving by a corpse.

After he describes his return to the officer's body, Tamura loses emotional distance from and control of his narrative almost completely. His carefully constructed account cannot contain the overwhelming return of the repressed. As traumatic memories flood back to him, he seems to unself-consciously record genuine, current emotional struggles with his traumatic past. In the following extended passage, Tamura details the appearance of the officer's corpse, suffers his first major memory loss, and then begins to narrate the horrifying experience that unfolds from the time he returns to his senses. As he recalls, relives, and records some of his most horrifying battlefield experiences, distinctions between past and present, the Philippines and Japan, and his internal and external worlds break down. These changes are clearly marked by an abrupt shift from past to present tense. What follows is one of the experiences Tamura probably did describe exactly as it was:

> He had become enormous. He lay there on his back. Light green tattoo-like patterns ran along his swollen, reddish-brown limbs. Here and there his flesh had split open, exposing a dirty green substance. His body swelled in two great spheres on either side of his cartridge belt. He was inedible.
>
> God had changed him before I came back. God loved this man. I, too, was probably . . . [18]
>
> But if I am loved by God, why would I be here? Why must I lie in this shadeless riverbed exposed to the sun? . . .
>
> Why are there so many flies? They buzz around me, land on my desiccated cheeks, and crawl about. Eyes, nostrils, mouth, ears—they peck at the soft parts of my body with their enormous beaks.
>
> Why does neither my left nor right hand move to drive them away? My body *feels* languid. Since I resolved to stop eating other living things, I must now know what it feels like to be eaten. That, I *think,* is why my hands do not move to brush away the insects that gorge themselves on my mucus.
>
> Please spare my eyes. At least leave me the pleasure of sight. What could that be lying over there on the sand, shimmering in the sun like a flower?
>
> It's a foot. It has five dried-out toes and looks just like a chicken's foot. It's been severed just above the ankle. The bone protruding from the center shines whitely, like the pistil of a flower.
>
> The skin covering the flesh is jet black. Wait, that bulging black surface is moving, like ripples on the surface of the water. It's a writhing mass of flies.
>
> It looks like a human foot. But why would there be a human foot here before me in this dry riverbed? I didn't cut it off. That's not *his* foot. He was bloated and putrid. This foot before me is still fresh.
>
> This place, too, is different. He was in that concealed area near the hilltop. Why did I come here? Who cut off this foot? Why on earth would a solitary human foot be lying like a fish out of water in this dazzling riverbed?
>
> I certainly didn't come here to eat it. I was just about to feed myself to the flies.
>
> Why, then, does it approach me—swaying, shimmering, laughing as it closes in?

> I know this feeling. It's the feeling I had when crawling as an infant. I can't recall the sensation of my arms and legs, but I do remember my mother's smiling face, which appeared to move and sway from side to side as I moved toward her.
>
> I must be crawling toward that severed foot. The stench, one that seems to emerge from my own body, grows stronger. (3:370–372)

In this unforgettable passage, Tamura's provisional thought of being God's Chosen One is rudely swept away by the horrible reality he confronts, and he begins to interrogate himself in earnest. Here again, Tamura wrestles with irreconcilable self-images. While he initially thinks that he is doing penance by allowing himself to be consumed by insects, he finally realizes to his horror that far from passively sacrificing himself, he is actually moving toward the severed appendage. This brings forth strong denial: "I didn't cut it off. That's not *his* foot. . . . I certainly didn't come here to eat it." Denying any conscious desire to cannibalize is Tamura's defensive mantra. Although he readily admits to killing the Filipina and his comrade Nagamatsu, he repeatedly insists in his memoir that he never killed with the intention of eating. Anxious, repeated denial, however, expresses that most feared to be true. And the circumstances under which he suffers memory loss serve to augment his profound doubt and fear. While Tamura is more than willing to fill in many details in his account, he does not dare to speculate on his conduct between the time he stood next to the officer's corpse and the time he returned to consciousness in the dry riverbed.

As he approaches the severed foot, Tamura again has the feeling of being watched. This time, it is neither the ghost of the woman he killed nor God, but his comrade-turned-cannibal Nagamatsu. Tamura recalls seeing three eyes in the bushes; the third, it turns out, was the barrel of the rifle being aimed at him. When Nagamatsu recognizes the figure rolling about in the dry riverbed, he lays down his weapon and comes to his side.

Tamura's handling of his relationship with Yasuda and Nagamatsu shows signs of defensive manipulation. In fact, the contrived nature of Tamura's memoir becomes ever more apparent when his treatments of these comrades and his interactions with them are scrutinized. Tamura describes being with Yasuda and Nagamatsu on three occasions. The first is outside the field hospital. After recounting how this cunning, middle-aged veteran formed a surrogate father-son relationship with his young, unworldly counterpart, Tamura foreshadows a pivotal scene of atrocity:

> In this way, I came to know how this young, weak, illegitimate son of a maid was adopted by a cynical man who had an illegitimate child by a café hostess. I found it incredible that there could still be the margin for this kind of drama to be enacted among the superfluous remnants of a bestial army, and I was curious to know what would become of this hastily formed father and son duo as circumstances steadily worsened. By strange coincidence, I bore witness to their fate. Just what kind of denouement, however, was it to be? (3:266)

Like a skilled novelist, Tamura is concerned with producing a good story. Here, he builds suspense by suggestively preparing for future developments. Since he is not only narrator but central actor as well, however, much more is at stake here for Tamura than there would be for the ordinary creative writer. And Tamura prepares ahead in more ways than one: long before coming to the shocking incident in question, he characterizes himself as the passive witness of his comrades' fate.

Tamura encounters Yasuda and Nagamatsu again during the long death march toward the muster point at Palompon. This time, he notes an important change in their relationship. When Tamura meets them for the second time, Yasuda has increasingly come to rely on Nagamatsu, who is now conspicuously more confident and outspoken. When he joins them for the third and final time, their original roles have been reversed: by this time Nagamatsu is obviously in control and Yasuda is wholly dependent on him for survival. This dramatic role reversal helps make it more plausible that Nagamatsu was the main actor in the pivotal, fourth scene of atrocity.

After coming to Tamura's side, Nagamatsu gives him water and then puts something resembling a black cracker in his mouth. The third scene of atrocity is presented as follows:

> All I remember of that moment is the taste of dry cardboard. After eating a number of the same objects, however, it dawned on me that it was meat. It was dry and hard, but the taste of fat, a taste I had not known during the several months I had been away from my unit, spread throughout my mouth.
>
> An indescribable sadness pierced my heart. Had my resolve and restraint

> up to that point been nothing but an illusion? I met a comrade and because of his goodwill I was now eating without any soul-searching whatsoever. Even worse, I was eating animal flesh—the very food I had most strictly forbidden myself from consuming.
>
> It was delicious. As I chewed on the solid pieces with my terribly weakened teeth, it seemed that something was added to me, and, at the same time, something else was lost. Satisfied, the left and right sides of my body came back together.
>
> In response to my searching eyes, Nagamatsu looked away and said, "It's monkey meat." (3:374–375)

Upon realizing that he is eating meat, Tamura describes himself being overcome by profound sadness (*kanashimi*). Significantly, the Japanese term used here connotes both sadness and grieving. In fact, each of the experiences Tamura treats in terms of sadness—seeing himself in the casket in his dream, killing the young woman in the presbytery, watching a comrade get gunned down by a Filipina guerrilla as he attempted to surrender, and eating the dried "monkey meat"—is directly or indirectly connected with death and dying. As I will subsequently show, Tamura's *kanashimi* is linked not only to unresolved feelings of guilt and self-recrimination, but to impaired mourning as well.

Tamura portrays himself as innocent, naive, and passive in his relationship with Yasuda and Nagamatsu. Despite seeing the severed foot, realizing that the third eye was the barrel of the rifle Nagamatsu pointed at him, anxiously asking whether Nagamatsu mistook him for a monkey and what had become of Yasuda, he acts as if he doesn't know the true source of the meat. Similarly, he describes himself being at a loss as to why Nagamatsu and Yasuda no longer sleep in the same place. This treatment is consistent with his earlier foreshadowing of events, where he presents himself as passive witness to their fate.

Thus, despite Nagamatsu's stern warnings, Tamura inadvertently lets Yasuda take possession of his grenade. His request for it to be returned is met with a drawn bayonet. Just at this tense moment, the men hear gunshots in the distance. Tamura avoids confrontation by running off to see whether Nagamatsu has succeeded in getting a monkey. He arrives in time to see him chasing after a fleeing comrade. After another tense standoff and confirmation of the nature of the "monkey meat," Tamura tells Nagamatsu that Yasuda has his grenade. Nagamatsu knows that Yasuda will try to use it on them, and Tamura goes along with Nagamatsu's cunning plan to outwit Yasuda.

The plan works, but Yasuda manages to escape. After that, they patiently wait for him to expose himself by the only spring in the area. When thirst finally drives Yasuda out of hiding, Nagamatsu purportedly shoots him, drops his rifle, runs down to the body, and begins to butcher it. Tamura describes his reaction to the first act of the fourth, and most gruesome, scene of atrocity as follows:

> I vomited before the steaming, cherry-colored flesh. . . .
>
> If at that time God had already transformed me, glory be to God!
>
> I was enraged. If it was natural and inevitable for human beings to eat one another during extremes of starvation, then this world was no more than a remnant of God's wrath.
>
> If I could vomit and feel rage at that moment, I was no longer human. I was an instrument of God, and it was now up to me to manifest His wrath. (3:395–396)

At this crucial juncture, Tamura embellishes his memoir with the idea he later confessed was not a part of his original experience. As he first did before the officer's corpse, he calls upon God as his guardian and witness. This time, however, he depicts himself as an extension of the very God he imagines, as divinely authorized to punish others for their evil. Such defensive rationalization not only brings Tamura to transfigure himself into a messiah, but also provides him with a compelling justification for killing.

The interlinked atrocity Tamura describes next shatters the image of passivity he had taken such pains to construct. After barely beating Nagamatsu in a desperate race back to the rifle, Tamura picks it up and turns it on Nagamatsu. As before the officer's corpse, however, Tamura experiences amnesia at this crucial moment. Memory breaks off just as he is aiming the rifle at Nagamatsu at point-blank range, and he doesn't return to his senses until he is at a safe physical remove from the unbearable site of fratricide and cannibalism:

> I have no memory of shooting him. One thing, however, is certain: I did not eat him. I certainly would remember if I had.
>
> The next image I retain is of a distant view of the forest we had been in. It was dark, like a stand of Japanese cedars. Now nature appeared lifeless and heartless to me, and I hated it.

> Rain began to fall gently, and, like water running down a sheet of stained glass, the forest was gradually cut off from view.
>
> I gazed down at the weapon in my hands. It was a Model 38 rifle that had been repossessed from schools as the shortage of weapons worsened. The chrysanthemum seal on the stock had a large X carved over it. I took out a towel and wiped the raindrops from the breechblock.
>
> This is the last thing I can recall. . . .[19] (3:396–397)

As with his experience in the dry riverbed, Tamura is once again in denial. He states categorically that while he may have killed Nagamatsu, he surely did not eat him. Since this is precisely the kind of wholly unacceptable experience that could be barred from consciousness, his reasoning that he would certainly remember if he had is far from convincing. Such denial is the surest sign of profound self-doubt. This doubt is exacerbated by the ten-day period of amnesia that commenced at the time he wiped raindrops off his rifle and ended when the excruciating pain of having his fractured skull reset after capture jarred him back into awareness.

In the third and final section of his memoir, Tamura describes himself in a surrealistic land of the dead. At one point, he makes the following shocking confession: "People approach me through the grass. . . . They too have become denizens of my world. They are the people I have killed—the Filipina, Nagamatsu, and Yasuda" (3:412). Toward the end of his memoir a fatal truth slips out from behind Tamura's carefully woven veil of deception. The revelation of having killed Yasuda calls his reliability as a survivor-narrator, and thus his memoir itself, into serious question. If Tamura fabricated this part of his story, what of the rest? Here again, however, the fact that he fictionalized parts of his past is less important than his reasons for doing so. These eventually emerge through his treatment of one of his most atrocious frontline experiences.

The fifth and final scene of atrocity concerns Tamura's conduct during his extended period of amnesia. After much difficulty, Tamura finally gains access to his most thoroughly repressed battlefield memories.[20] Images of the fires on the plain, or *nobi,* of the book's title are the keys that open the floodgates of memory. Hypothesizing that after shooting Nagamatsu he probably walked down to the coast with the rifle in hand, Tamura imagines seeing the smoke from a fire on the plain. This image eventually ushers the past into the present:

> Deep within my ears, or deep within my heart, I think I hear the low sound of pounding drums.[21] Just as did the images of *nobi* that appeared before me as I walked on the plains of the Philippines, these incessant reverberations infuse the shadows of the red pines that extend across the plain before my eyes.
>
> I sense innumerable, invisible *nobi* rising up from the periphery of the Musashino Plain surrounding the mental hospital.
>
> I feel the ashen period of my memory loss being filled in with images of *nobi,* which appear here and there like bubbles forming in a void. Only the images of *nobi* are real; they are unaccompanied by any thoughts or feelings.
>
> I returned to my room. I continued to hear the drums while eating dinner and after going to bed. Eventually, I was able to recall everything from my period of amnesia—well, not everything—perhaps I will remember more as I write. (3:407)

Tamura recalls moving from *nobi* to *nobi.* Eventually the image of his walking figure rises before his mind's eye. And at this point, he loses emotional distance from and narrative control of his memoir for the last time. This transition is again marked by an abrupt shift from past to present-tense narration:[22] "It's my own figure walking between fields and hills with my rifle on my shoulder. My green military uniform has faded to brown and the sleeves and shoulders are torn. I'm barefoot. It's clearly me, Private Tamura; I can tell by the hollow in the emaciated neck of the figure walking several steps ahead of me. If so, who then is looking at me? It, too, must be me. Who the hell decided that I can't be two people?" (3:409). As in his dream when battling himself before the officer's corpse and in his experience in the dry riverbed, Tamura is internally divided. In each of these instances, the division stems from his inability to reconcile contradictions between the positive self-image he labors to construct and the negative self-image he cannot bring himself to fully face. Once again, moreover, the return of the repressed serves to clarify which is the more authentic. In the following passage, Tamura wavers between self-justification and genuine, contemporary emotional struggles with his burdened past:

> I, an arrogant man driven by dark desires, walk across this eternity. Rifle on my shoulder, I move with confident strides suggesting nothing of starvation. I go somewhere.
>
> Facing the *nobi,* I approach the place where the Filipinos are. I go to chastise all those who hurt God by moving horizontally across an earth on which everything is arranged to face Him directly.

> But if I am an avenging angel, why do I feel so sad? Why am I, who by now should have no more ties to the people of this earth, so filled with fear and misgivings? If I truly am an angel, I'll be all right.
>
> The smoke from a single *nobi* was rising from the top of a hill. Swaying from side to side like seaweed, it stretched up higher and higher toward the fathomless sky.
>
> Where is the sun? Like God it must be high in the sky, far above the waters filling the space in between. . . .
>
> There. A person. I shoot. I miss. He ran down the slope, and once out of range, confidently straightened up and briskly walked into the woods. (3:409–410)

At the end of his memoir, Tamura is finally able to begin to confront one of the most excruciating truths of his traumatic battlefield experience. The guarded confession he makes—that instead of approaching the Filipinos to chastise them as an agent of God, he was most likely hunting them with the intention of killing and eating them—is inserted between anxious denial of responsibility for his frontline conduct and a last-ditch effort to grasp at the straw of divine intervention:

> There are no people in the field. Just as it did when I was still alive, the grass swirls about me in eternal patterns. A black sun shines like obsidian, radiating a darkness even blacker than the dim sky that surrounds it. It's too late.
>
> People approach me through the grass. . . . They too have become denizens of my world. They are the people I have killed—the Filipina, Nagamatsu, and Yasuda.
>
> The dead smile. If this is what is called a heavenly smile, it certainly is terrifying.
>
> An excruciating pleasure-pain enters my head through the temple. It gradually penetrates the top part of my head, and, like a five-inch nail driven into my skull, extends to the base of my brain.
>
> I remember. They smile because I did not eat them. I killed them but I didn't eat them. I killed them because of war, God, chance—some force outside myself—but I did not eat them according to my will. That's why I find myself with them in this land of the dead illuminated by dark sunshine.
>
> In that other world, I carried a gun as a fallen angel. I intended to chastise those people, but I probably wanted to eat them too. Driven by this secret desire, I probably saw, and then approached them.
>
> If due to my arrogance I was struck on the head by an unknown attacker when I was on the verge of committing a sin . . . [23]

> If God prepared that blow for me because he loved me . . .
>
> If I was struck by the enormous man who offered me his flesh when I was starving on the top of that hill at sunset . . .
>
> If he was a transfiguration of Christ . . .
>
> If he was sent all the way to the fields of the Philippines for me and me alone . . .
>
> Then, glory be to God. (3:411–413)

Like Ōoka's battlefield memoirs, *Fires on the Plain* is most fruitfully approached in terms of impaired formulation. Because of Tamura's reluctance to thoroughly confront and work through the agonizing truths of his battlefield experience, his refusal to take personal responsibility for his conduct, his inability to adequately account for survival, and his failure to find any meaning or value in postwar existence, his memoir ends without resolution, recovery, or renewal. Tamura is simply too defensive, too arrogant in survival to allow for the necessary degree of dissolution of his positive pretrauma self-image, and the stress and strain of his untenable literary efforts to retain integrity and shore up his collapsing symbolic world only serve to bind him ever more tightly and pathologically to his unmastered past.

Ōoka was able to make substantial progress on his journey of survivor formulation by writing *Fires on the Plain*. As will be shown in the next three sections, he was not only able to give creative and cathartic expression to the "mental and emotional confusion [he] experienced as a routed soldier" (15:411) but also able to make headway toward reconciling his relationship as a survivor to his dead comrades.

Expressing Deadness and Desymbolization

In writing about the things that can facilitate fruitful formulation, Lifton stresses that "without guilt-associated struggles around fidelity to the dead and *the experience of deadness,* and to oneself as a witness, no . . . renewal or formulation is feasible."[24] While descriptions of extraordinary experience appear in Ōoka's autobiographical writings on the war, they are not given any particular emphasis or consideration. Ikeda Jun'ichi has suggested that because Ōoka's primary aim was to produce a comprehensive, factual record of his war experience, he purposely kept such descriptions to a minimum in his memoirs.[25] Fictionalizing the memoir of a psychologically destabilized veteran provided him with an effective means of exorcising the frontline experiences that haunted him by giving unrestrained, imaginative expression to them.

Ikeda has established that many of the extraordinary experiences described in *Fires on the Plain* are founded on Ōoka's personal experience.[26] In the novel, Ōoka not only transferred these experiences to Tamura, but also shifted the venue from Mindoro to Leyte Island. Another significant change has to do with his comrades. In his fictional reworking of his frontline trauma, Ōoka literalizes the psychic and emotional distance he felt by excluding others from a good part of the story. Thus, while Tamura's wanderings on Leyte parallel Nishiya Company's movements on Mindoro, Tamura is mostly alone. He has his most bizarre experiences when separated from his comrades.

The psychological effects of Tamura's psychic immersion in death appear soon after conscription. His first incident of experiential confusion takes place en route to Manila:

> As I was absentmindedly gazing at the water as the transport ship proceeded through the South Seas in June, I abruptly had the sensation that I was in an orderly, dreamlike scene.
>
> I was in the middle of the cobalt-blue sea. The distant horizon formed a perfect circle around me and seemed to pull the water slightly upward at the extremities. Layered clouds with perfectly flat bottoms like traditional rice-cake offerings floated at fixed heights above the ocean surface. The distance between them was unchanging. As the ship moved forward at a steady speed, the clouds moved with it. Pivoting on fixed points, they rotated open like fans. The monotonous vibration of the diesel engine merged with the uniform sound of the waves that marched in rows past the sides of the ship. At that time, this orderly scene struck me as extremely odd. (3:238–239)

This description is clearly based on the experience Ōoka describes in "On the Seas" (Kaijō nite, 1949).[27] While seemingly mentioned in passing in the former, Ōoka treats it at length in *Fires on the Plain.* This, as with many of the examples to be considered in this section, is comparable to what Lifton refers to as death-in-life experience. Tamura's psychic numbing and symbolic immersion in death disrupt the fundamental psychic process that assimilates and integrates new and prior experience. This results in a pervasive sense of unreality, confusion, and stasis described in terms of oddness (*kikai*). Indeed, the most vivid impression left by this ostensibly dynamic scene is one of deadness. Tamura feels as if he is stuck in a landscape that, while containing activity, is so orderly, uniform, and unvarying in its movements that it appears to be frozen in time.

Ōoka also incorporates the haunting experience he had on the shores of Dannoura Bay. Tamura, however, has his experience beside a river:

> Formerly a concept, death had by now been transformed into a concrete image that closed in on me. I imagined blowing myself up with my grenade by the side of the stream. My body would eventually decompose into its basic elements. Since humans are two-thirds water, most of my physical being would merge and flow along with the stream.
>
> I gazed again at the water before my eyes. It moved by making that whispering sound so familiar to me from my youth. It continually flowed down from above, moving over and around the rocks in its path. It appeared to me like perpetual motion.
>
> I heaved a heavy sigh. Although consciousness would surely come to an end upon my death, my body would combine with the cosmos. In this way, I would go on living forever.
>
> It was surely the water's *movement* that gave me this illusion. (3:273–274)

This is actually a composite of three of Ōoka's wartime experiences. The foundation experience was mentioned above. The second occurred on the transport ship when "'Death' settled down before [him] and refused to budge" (1:7). The third, of course, was his failed suicide attempt.

Tamura describes himself considering suicide on only two occasions—here, and once again several days later after collapsing under some palm trees at the confluence of two streams. Starving and in despair, he thinks to end his life while he still has the presence of mind to choose his actions. As he gazes into the night sky, however, he experiences a familiar sense of yearning that he at first associates with a desire for life. Try though he might, he cannot recall when he felt this way in the past. Before long, he has a disturbing hallucination:

> At that moment, I noticed the transformation of the surrounding palm trees.
>
> They came to look like the women I had loved in various ways at dif-

> ferent times in the past. The smaller palm that had its fronds held up like a dancer was the young woman who had departed without accepting my love. The tree in the dark shadows with heavy fronds hanging down like hair was the older woman who fell into unhappiness because of her love for me. The one with fronds radiating out proudly in all directions was the proud woman who loved me but had left me because she couldn't bring herself to admit her true feelings. I felt that they had all appeared to me in this way to attend my final moments. (3:275)

This is clearly a variation on Ōoka's experience of having each of his loved ones appear to him in his dreams. Here again, however, Ōoka not only transposes and imaginatively reworks, but also combines and concentrates his extraordinary death-immersion experience. As I pointed out in chapter 1, to the extent that Ōoka felt psychologically and emotionally alienated from his comrades, he felt intimacy toward natural objects. He identified most closely with water, water buffalo, and palm trees. It is thus fitting that palms would become the medium for expressing his death-saturated inner world.

After this hallucination passes, Tamura struggles in vain to remember the moments of pleasure he shared with his former lovers, but he can only recollect the yearning preceding sensual pleasure. These efforts, however, eventually lead him to the realization that his longing for the distant, moonlit sky resembles the way he felt toward the woman who left him. And the conclusion he finally comes to is significant: "I initially thought that it was because I was still *alive* that I yearned for life. However, was it not because I was already *dead* that I longed for it so? This paradoxical conclusion consoled me, and I smiled to myself. Since I was already no longer of this world, there was no need to kill myself" (3:276). Here, the thought of death makes the act itself unnecessary.

In a subsequent description of perceptual and emotional confusion, Tamura confronts more tangible images of death. The description of the objects he belatedly recognizes as corpses is clearly based on Ōoka's experience in Bulalacao. By fictionalizing this experience, however, he was able to provide fuller, more detailed descriptions of the bodies he bore traumatized witness to. In "Nishiya Company's Resolute Fight" (Nishiyatai funsen, 1949), Ōoka explains why he avoided writing exhaustively about this experience in his memoirs:

> Being totally unfamiliar with this kind of thing, most readers will probably think I should describe the appearance of the corpses in greater detail. I will refrain, however, from doing so. It is not easy for people to look at these kinds of things. I remember repeatedly looking away and then back again. In all, I probably looked at this miserable scene for no more than half a minute. I could fill a page with minute details, but is it not wrong to occupy reader attention for minutes with images that could be countenanced for no more than thirty seconds? (2:222)

Whether wrong or not, Ōoka still felt a pressing need to more thoroughly externalize the spectacle of death that was imprinted so indelibly in his mind's eye. Describing his experience in *Fires on the Plain* enabled him to record every chilling detail of these embodiments of the premature, violent, grotesque death that haunted memory long after survival:

> They had been there for some time, and their bodies had lost all resemblance to their former selves. Only their fatigues retained any hint of the time when they were still alive. Discolored as they were with mud and death juices, however, even these had lost the appearance of human clothing and had become virtually indistinguishable from the surrounding earth.
>
> As I attempt to describe them now, I realize that I could barely *look at* them at all. It wasn't just that I was initially unable to make out what they were; my eyes simply couldn't take in the details. After I recognized them as corpses, my eyes scanned over them in anticipation of finding familiar human shapes. This expectation, however, was continually betrayed.
>
> They had swollen to a size wholly incompatible with that of human bodies, and the shiny, bronze-colored skin on their exposed arms and backs had bulged out to the breaking point. Thumb-sized intestines protruded and hung down from the sides of some of the bodies. While probably extruded from bullet wounds, there were no signs of the holes, and the pressure produced by the encircling flesh squeezed the exposed intestines out like sausage ends.
>
> Their heads were swollen as if stung repeatedly by hornets. Their hair, plastered against their scalps as if glued in place by the liquid that had oozed out during decomposition, had flowed down toward and merged with their foreheads. I can no longer look at the indistinct hairlines of the mannequins displayed in city shop windows without recalling this detail.
>
> Their cheeks were puffed out, their mouths closed and puckered. If pressed to, I'd have to say that their frozen facial expressions were like that of a "thinking cat."
>
> Some had their heads resting on others' legs; others embraced the shoulders of those next to them. The seat of the pants of one body that was face

> forward had been torn away, exposing the tailbone. Now I knew why there were so many dogs and carrion crows in this abandoned village. (3:305–306)

One of the most disturbing and unacceptable aspects of Ōoka's experience in Bulalacao must have been his lack of emotional response. In retro-spect, survivors feel that their reactions (or lack thereof) were wholly inappropriate to the circumstances. An important part of the recovery process involves belatedly experiencing and working through the emotions—grief, death guilt, anger, loss—one could not afford at the time. Before this can be done, however, survivors must first honestly recall the experience as it was. This was one of the important tasks Ōoka accomplished in *Fires on the Plain.*

One of Tamura's early experiences of desymbolization and deadness occurs as he walks alone through the woods on the way back to the field hospital after being rejected by his company. While there is no corresponding experience mentioned in his battlefield memoirs, Ikeda Jun'ichi suggests that Ōoka did not treat his extraordinary frontline experience exhaustively in his autobiographical writings.[28] Be that as it may, the following experience has the feel of something Ōoka may himself have undergone on Mindoro Island.[29]

> It was dark in the woods and the path was narrow. Every space between the huge, towering trees that resembled oaks and elms was filled with lower, unfamiliar trees entwined by ivy and vines. The trail was buried under the decomposing leaves of tropical trees that dropped [their leaves] continually without regard to season, and I sensed their softness as I walked over them. Just as they did on paths I had taken through forests on the Musashino Plain, the freshly fallen leaves made rustling sounds as I walked through the silent forest. I proceeded while looking down at the ground.
>
> Suddenly, I was assailed by an odd thought: *"I am walking on this path for the first time in my life, but I will probably never walk on it again."* I stopped and looked around.
>
> Everything was the same. There was nothing but silent, deciduous trees I couldn't name that resembled—straight trunks, open branches, hanging leaves—those I knew from home. The trees had been there long before I came, would have been there whether I passed through or not, and would probably continue to be there just as they were into the future.
>
> Nothing could have been more commonplace. And it was also natural that since I would die soon, I would not again pass through these unfamiliar

> Philippine woods. My sense of oddness came from my awareness of the contradiction between my proximity to certain death and the reality of walking through this forest for the first time in my life. (3:238)

Tamura's extraordinary experience in the forest is characterized by perceptual-spatial and conceptual-temporal confusion. This confusion follows in the wake of a déjà vu experience. He subsequently realizes that this "odd" experience was brought on by a premonition of death.[30] When Tamura is symbolically confronted with mortality, or to put it differently, with *futurelessness,* he is unable to comprehend the paradoxical fact that he is simultaneously experiencing something for the first and last time. Because of his trauma-induced breakdown, Tamura cannot assimilate and integrate his perceptions with prior or anticipated experience, and consequently he is unable to process and interpret his unfolding experience in normal ways.

Desymbolization is most clearly at work in his treatment of his experience at the church. The extraordinary experience he had in the forest has its parallel in his frustrated struggle to find—or, more accurately, reconstitute—meaning and significance in the Christian symbol he sees. Through his depiction of Tamura's experience in the deserted village, Ōoka succeeds in conveying symbolic breakdown:

> The church was at a slight remove from the road, and one of its narrow chalky sides rose up above the row of houses to my left.
>
> As in my dream, the cross that towered above the wall before me was illuminated by the sun and glowed with a faint golden hue.
>
> My heart aches even now when I recall my impression upon seeing that longed-for symbol. The cross shimmered with a cold, barren indifference devoid of any emotional content. There was absolutely no distinction between it and the other sundry objects within my field of vision. (3:300)

Tamura has a related experience upon entering the church. As with the cross on top, the religious symbols he encounters inside appear to him as little more than insignificant material objects. Indeed, it is precisely this kind of desymbolization experience that is linked to "insanity." After hearing his own voice call out to him, Tamura gets to the root of his perceptual and emotional confusion: "At that moment, I became aware that the connection between myself and the external world had been severed completely" (3:309).

Tamura's haunting experience of deadness and desymbolization is conspicuous in his treatment of *nobi.* Ōoka himself was clearly enthralled with these fires and the odd-shaped pillars of smoke they emitted. Indeed, he describes them at length in five separate places in *Fires on the Plain.*[31] There can be little doubt that these images were linked closely in Ōoka's mind to his own traumatic death-immersion experience. As with his experience during transport and in Bulalacao, he sought to exorcise these haunting images by giving them fuller, more sustained and imaginative expression.

Tamura first sees *nobi* shortly after having his unsettling experience in the forest. These fires are ambiguous symbols. As Tamura elaborates in connection with his first sighting, they were set by farmers to burn off chaff after harvest or by guerrillas to communicate with one another. Under the circumstances, however, all Filipinos, combatant or noncombatant, are potential enemies. In this sense, *nobi* are incontrovertible danger signs. What makes them particularly enigmatic is that the people setting them are never in view. *Nobi* thus stand as symbols of invisible threat.

After leaving the plain, passing through some woods, and encountering a villager (who easily manages to escape by promising to go get him some food), Tamura sees more fires on the plain:

> I came to the end of the forest and saw the same *nobi* across the river I had seen before. At some point, however, a second fire had been set. Another line of smoke now rose from the top of an isolated hill in the distance that had the shape of a man facing away in a crouching position.
>
> The smoke from the *nobi* at the base of the cliff was thick and rose straight up, but that rising from the top of the hill ascended only slightly before the winds coursing at higher altitudes bent it over to the side and tattered its extreme end into the shape of a broom head. While the smoke at the base of the cliff surged upward as if struggling with the heavy air, that from the top of the hill was tall and thin and rose proudly, swinging and swaying as if sporting with sky and wind. It gave me a peculiar sensation to be part of the same scene as these odd-shaped pillars of smoke that defied the laws of meteorology.
>
> The smoke rising from the top of the hill was probably produced by the fire of burning fodder, and it closely resembled what we call a beacon fire. What kind of signal, however, could it be? (3:246–247)

Tamura's experience with the *nobi* again involves perceptual and conceptual confusion, which is conveyed in terms of oddness, dreaminess, and unreality. His depictions of the columns of smoke, moreover, are anthropomorphic—while one appears to struggle with the heavy air above it, the other ascends proudly and sports with the surrounding elements. The relatively mild sense of confusion Tamura describes in the final sentence intensifies substantially after he passes through another wooded area, comes to an open plain, and sees a broad swath of flames sweeping across it:

> I stopped and gazed at the smoke.
>
> It simply wasn't possible that my movements caused the *nobi* to rise progressively before me. This much was clear from a comparison of my position as a lone soldier with the collective act of setting these fires. The random course I had taken as a solitary traveler just happened to enable me to see them in the order they were lit.
>
> The uneasiness I felt was related to the odd perceptual confusion I had been experiencing since leaving home. The only actual basis for this feeling was that wherever there were *nobi,* there were Filipinos. Since there were no people on the plain, however, this causal connection did not adequately account for my uneasiness. It stemmed, rather, from the *number* and *sequence* of fires I observed. . . .
>
> I couldn't take my eyes off the smoke. The sun was low on the horizon, and at some point the wind had risen. The smoke crawled over the ground and engulfed the grass. From time to time some of it broke loose and flew off toward the woods bordering the river like pieces of cotton.
>
> There was no sign of anyone on the open plain. Who could have set this fire? This, as before, was a question that could not be answered based on the scene before my eyes. (3:247–249)

Tamura's preoccupation with and confusion over the *nobi*—both on the battlefield and after survival—is effectively conveyed through an experience he has just before falling asleep after rejoining his comrades by the field hospital. The following description reveals Tamura's thralldom:

> As I began to fall asleep, I recalled the various events of this trying day. The thick lips of the squad leader who slapped me, the narrow eyes of the supply sergeant, and the looks of fear in the eyes of my comrades as I left the encampment came to mind and receded one after another. They were pure images that were unaccompanied by emotion of any kind. As far as I know, this is probably the most appropriate way of regarding things on the battlefield.
>
> After a time, images of *nobi* appeared. The patterns of light projected by my optic nerves against the insides of my dark eyelids were freely transformed

> according to the whims of my half-slumbering brain. Against the backdrop of a dry-aired sky reminiscent of artificial stage scenery, the smoke of the *nobi* on the other side of the river rose up intermittently like puffs of steam emitted from an old locomotive laboring to leave the station. The smoke from the *nobi* rising from the hill was folded over at the top like the head of a bent nail, and its compass-like point shifted incessantly from side to side. I, of course, was not afraid. (3:267)

The images that appear to Tamura's mind's eye as he hovers between consciousness and unconsciousness are pure in the sense that they are unaccompanied by any feeling. The final images to appear are of the two eerie fires so indelibly imprinted in memory. To a certain extent, Tamura is able to control and creatively manipulate these images. And in a way, this is what Ōoka was doing. And each time he did so, he allowed himself ever greater freedom and poetic license.[32]

In the second part of his memoir, Tamura asserts that "no one can force [him] again to die on the battlefield" (3:401). While Ōoka didn't explicitly treat his own frontline experience in such terms in his autobiographical writings, he clearly experienced psychic death at the front. In the last part of Tamura's memoir, aptly titled "Writings of the Dead," Ōoka pulls out all the stops in an effort to imaginatively exorcise the images that persisted in haunting him. As with Tamura's experience by the river, the one he describes at the end of the novel is concentrated and composite. If the world Tamura described after leaving the officer's corpse can generally be characterized as one of light and life, the world he returns to after losing control of his narrative for the last time is one of darkness and death. Tamura begins with the psychological topography of the "land of the dead":

> It is naturally silent, like the quietude beneath the waters. The hills, trees, rocks, grass—everything seems to have passed down through this high space to settle here, on this natural bottom. God made these things high in the sky and then made them sink. He allowed them to pass through his enormous body and descend to this level.
>
> Having exhausted the time allotted for sinking, and being unable to move any further downward, everything was now immobile. (3:409)

This scene is characterized by stasis. In Tamura's inner world of symbolic death immersion there is initially no sound, no animation, no movement.

All is stock-still, as if frozen in space and time. Building on previous descriptions, Tamura portrays the land of the dead as if it were under water, an approach that augments the pervasive sense of heaviness, sluggishness, and unreality.

After portraying himself as an avenging angel going to chastise Filipinos/humans for disrespecting God and injuring His body, Tamura elaborates on the dark world of death he now not only dwells in, but acts in as well.[33] For the last time in the memoir, he reenters the surrealistic time and space of the *nobi.* This time, however, the images of the human figures theretofore absent finally become visible:

> The smoke from a single *nobi* was rising from the top of a hill. Swaying from side to side like seaweed, it stretched up higher and higher toward the fathomless sky.
>
> Where is the sun? Like God, it must be high in the sky, far above the waters filling the space in between.
>
> The grasses on top of the hill, pushed about as they were by the flowing waters, were swirling about. The flames, facing the low, dark forest surrounding the summit, fled off toward it as if being chased.
>
> There. A person. I shoot. I miss. He ran down the slope, and once out of range, confidently straightened up and briskly walked into the woods.
>
> There are more. Their upper torsos protruded above the swirling grasses. One, two, three.
>
> They approach me. As they alternately and mechanically expose and conceal themselves, the dark, featureless faces visible above the swirling grasses close in on me. I won't miss again.
>
> Where is the sun?
>
> A fire approaches. The sourceless fire closes in fast as it burns the surrounding grasses. It presses in, head raised, mouth open. The people on the far side of the smoke are smiling. (3:410)

Tamura's terminal death-in-life experience and profound conceptual and perceptual confusion are palpable in this description combining imagined images of God, *nobi,* and indistinct, shadowy figures. The abrupt, frequent alterations between past and present tense are clear indications of his struggle to regain control of his narrative.

In this climactic scene, Ōoka seeks to bring closure to an important part of his unresolved battlefield trauma by creatively inserting the people he never actually saw himself as he retreated through the mountains. The forward movements of the dark, featureless figures and fires, moreover, are strongly reminiscent of those of the young American soldier. Following the last sentence of the passage quoted above, Ōoka includes a detailed description of Tamura's hands holding onto his gun—the crucial image missing from his own memory of the encounter. And just before the point of no return—at the point of kill or be killed—"chance" intervenes to bring Tamura's traumatic experience to a wholly unanticipated end. In the passage that follows, Ōoka is not only able to give literal form to the psychological effect of chance, but also most directly express his experience of deadness:

> At that moment, I felt a blow to the back of my head. The sensation of paralysis spreads through my body. Yes, of course. I had forgotten. I was supposed to be struck on the back of the head by them. That's it! From the day I entered this mental hospital, I had been hoping for death. Now it has finally come.
>
> Why, then, am I still here? I cannot see anyone, but I can hear murmuring voices. The people are not visible, but they can see me and treat me any way they please. They can do anything they like: they can even lay me on an operating table and reset my [fractured] skull.
>
> I always thought that consciousness ended upon death. I was wrong. Even after death, all is not oblivion. I must tell this to them. I shout, "I'm alive!"
>
> But my voice doesn't even reach my own ears. Although they lack voices, the dead yet live. There is no such thing as individual death. Death is a universal event. Even after death we must be eternally awake. Day after day, we must make decisions. I must tell this to all humankind. But it's too late. (3:411)

The most salient aspects of this description of deadness are continued consciousness and radical alienation from both his body and the external world. Like Ōoka during his peak experience of walking down the high mountain ridge after leaving the plain's fires behind, all that reaches Tamura's ears are muted, unintelligible voices. Tamura, in other words, portrays himself stuck in a nightmarish inner world of death and meaninglessness, cut off almost completely from his fellow man. He will remain in this psychic prison of deadness, desymbolization, and alienation until he can bring himself to squarely face and work through deep-seated feelings of death guilt, self-recrimination, and loss.

The profound implications of the message Tamura struggles in vain to communicate to humanity will be turned to at the end of this chapter. Suffice it to say here that in order to effectively convey his insight regarding the lives of the dead, he must ultimately labor to repair the human bonds that were so traumatically severed during his protracted death-immersion experience. As I will show in the next two sections, such reconnection entailed struggles with the battlefield conduct of his comrades and, perhaps more important, with working out his relationship as a survivor to the war dead.

Cannibalism as an Extreme Form of Survival Egoism

As I noted in chapter 1, Ōoka bore ample witness to the frontline attitude and conduct of fellow soldiers in his memoirs. While he included positive assessments of a few exemplary young men, his primary focus was providing testimony on the egoism exhibited by the majority. Ōoka was deeply wounded by his older comrades' self-serving behavior. And he was appalled by eyewitness accounts of Sergeant Kurokawa's advocacy of hunting, killing, and eating a Filipino. It was, moreover, rumored that starving Imperial soldiers at Guadalcanal, New Guinea, Leyte, and Luzon had engaged in cannibalism.[34] Just as he struggled to make sense of his extraordinary experience of deadness and desymbolization, he struggled to come to terms with his comrades'—and by extension his own—survival egoism in fiction.

As Ōoka was writing *Fires on the Plain,* his concern with survival egoism was so all consuming that he excluded the few good men he could not bring himself to ignore completely in his autobiographical writings. As Ivan Morris has noted, there is no mention in the work of patriotism, esprit de corps, fighting spirit, courage, self-sacrifice, and the like.[35] The battlefield world Ōoka re-created was one of crushing defeat, deprivation, despair, illness, death, and ruthless, fraternal competition for survival. In fact, as the Imperial Army went down to defeat, the most immediate enemies were often not Americans or local guerrillas, but one's own brothers-in-arms.

Tamura broaches the subject of egoism early in his memoir. After being brutally ostracized from his company because of his tuberculosis, he passes a group of men digging trenches with sticks and broken pots as he is en route to the field hospital. While fully aware of what has just happened to him, they avert their eyes and return to their labors. Tamura summarizes his relationship with them as follows:

> Most were enlisted men I had been with since departing Japan for the front. While our shared sense of enslavement temporarily brought us together during the tedious days on the transport ship, the necessities of our day-to-day lives spent with seasoned veterans during the three months we spent in Manila turned us back into the egoists we had been in society. After we landed on Leyte, this egoism became all the more pronounced as circumstances worsened.
>
> Once I fell sick and it became clear that I had become a burden who could contribute nothing to the group, a distinct coldness came between us. When danger is not yet present, and one only has a premonition of its impending arrival, the instinct for self-preservation takes over and makes men more egoistical than necessary. (3:233–234)

In this passage, Tamura highlights the fragility of human relationships in extremity. Given the deep-rooted egocentrism of his comrades, their bonds are bound to be conditional, circumstantial, and highly unstable. All that still holds these desperate men together is mutual self-interest; as soon as Tamura can no longer contribute, he is abandoned by outfit and comrade alike.

Circumstances at the field hospital are even worse; medics compete for survival with their own patients, whom they must rely on for food. Only sick or wounded soldiers with provisions are admitted and nominally cared for; and those still able to walk are discharged once the supplies they brought with them run low. At the first sign of diarrhea, patients are denied food altogether. Rejected by his company and this medical facility, Tamura has little choice but to join fellow squatters who linger nearby. Without the margin to give or receive anything from one another, these radically marginalized men form relationships founded primarily on the tacit agreement not to steal food from one another. Tamura is approached by another soldier shortly after rejoining the group:

> "Hey, how much food you got?"
>
> He was horribly emaciated, probably one of the patients discharged after developing diarrhea. He was so weak that his entire body shook from the strain of standing long enough to hear my reply. When I told him I had

> six yams, he nodded with satisfaction and lurched back to his place. For some unknown reason, it seemed that it was necessary for the members of this group to know exactly how much food the others had.
>
> "Ha, ha. If you've got six, you're well off. Your company's generous. Mine gave me only two. And this is the last one I got left."
>
> As the soldier next to me said this, he took a yam out of his pocket and held it up to the group. He was a younger man who had arrived during my absence. Maggots writhed about in the bullet wound on his ankle.
>
> Stressing the paucity of one's resources under such circumstances clearly presented a delicate problem. Everyone fell silent. The one-potato man seemed to understood why.
>
> After saying, "Puh! Don't go worrying yourselves. I ain't askin' nobody for no food. I'm gonna pinch me some from over there tonight," he stared off toward the field hospital huts. (3:252–253)

In a subsequent exchange between Yasuda—an experienced, middle-aged veteran modeled on Butaichō—and Nagamatsu, the brutal reality of their situation is described and the topic of cannibalism broached:

> "Hey, listen, when things get like this, you can't afford to give a damn about anyone else; it's every man for himself. People can get by for a month or two on roots. And at some point . . ."
>
> "At some point, what?"
>
> "It just works out somehow, you idiot! What the hell good is it to think so far ahead now?" (3:261)

As Yasuda implies, "at some point" the struggle for survival can devolve into man eating man. Acts of survival egoism—be they harmless or radical—undermine the foundations of social living. To the extent that survivors engage in them, moreover, they contribute to social breakdown and destruction. As a burdened survivor, Ōoka's task was how to come to grips with and repair the damage brought about by such instinctual actions and in so doing recover trust and belief in his fellow man. As with his experience of deadness and desymbolization, formulation necessitated confronting and working through harsh frontline realities—in this case, the lengths he and some of his comrades were willing to go to in the interest of self-perpetuation.

Tamura displays his own survival egoism soon after rejoining the group of rejects. In a scene that closely parallels Ōoka's own experience,

Tamura walks off by himself when their position comes under bombardment. Although Ōoka didn't treat his conduct in such terms in his memoirs, in *Fires on the Plain* he was able to openly describe his alter ego's behavior as a self-serving act of abandonment:

> It was clear to me that the most heroic course was to return to the valley and help the wounded soldiers collapsed in the field. The urge I felt at that moment came as a complete surprise.
>
> I couldn't help but laugh out loud.
>
> Nothing could have been more absurd than the spectacle of my comrades, sacrifices to inane military strategy, running about like panicking insects before overwhelming, one-sided American firepower. To the very instant of their deaths, they hadn't the slightest idea who was killing them.
>
> What relation were they to me?
>
> Laughing more vigorously, I turned my back on the wounded, dying men below and continued up the trail. My stride would probably have been more dignified if I hadn't simply been acting on the spur of the moment to save my own hide. (3:270)

"What relation were they to me?" With these words, Tamura psychologically severs his bonds with his comrades in the interest of personal survival. After wandering alone through the tropical wilderness for ten days and killing the Filipina, however, he cries with joy upon being reunited with three compatriots from a different unit at the deserted hilltop farm. As with the rejects, delicate negotiations are required for acceptance into this group. Tamura has valuable social currency thanks to his salt. When he asks to join them, the senior officer informs him that they survived New Guinea by cannibalizing, and they won't hesitate to eat him if he slows them down too much. Their attitude changes completely, however, upon learning that he has salt. Tamura gains admittance by ritually dividing it among its members. These hastily formed bonds, however, dissolve along with the last grains of salt.

Tamura becomes increasingly unwelcome as his supply of salt runs low on the ensuing death march toward Palompon. His last few pinches, however, earn him some disturbing testimony from the bottom-ranking member of the group:

> "You've been hangin' around and talkin' respectfully to my squad leader, but you'd be better off on your own. I've been with him since New Guinea, and

> all he does is work us like farm animals. I don't recall him doing a single thing for us. He was nice to us back in barracks, but since he thinks he knows war, he's been cold as stone at the front. Keep hangin' around, and he'll take away all your salt. After that . . . well, in the end, you'll be driven off."
>
> "Is it really true that you ate human flesh on New Guinea?"
>
> After saying "Human?" he gazed up dreamily at the sky and fell silent for a time. "You'd better take it as a wild story . . . hey, I'll tell you an even more interesting one. It happened during withdrawal from Buna—a march far worse than this one. As I was walkin' along, I see this young soldier who had been shot in the chest and had crawled to the edge of the trail. He was more dead than alive. The young soldier said, "Kill that guy. He's a traitor." The guy he was talkin' about was the squad leader he'd been with. It turns out his squad leader had asked him to surrender together. When the young soldier refused, the guy just shot him and left him for dead. It's horrible. The squad leader didn't have to go and kill him." (3:339–340)

Tamura subsequently admits that he was capable of a similar act. After failing to cross the Ormoc Highway, the survivors scatter into the surrounding hills. Tamura decides to attempt surrender after watching a wounded comrade get cared for by Red Cross workers. His greatest fear was meeting a fellow soldier as he searched for an appropriate place to raise his white flag: "Had I seen one, I wouldn't have been able to embark on my sole path to survival. At that time, I probably would have killed the first comrade I came upon" (3:351).

While Tamura readily acknowledges his potential for killing a comrade to facilitate surrender, he adamantly refuses to consider the possibility that he might do so to avoid starvation. After witnessing a comrade with raised hands get gunned down mercilessly by a Filipina guerrilla and recalling the innocent woman he killed, he abandons all thoughts of surrender and returns to the deep mountains. Before long, he begins to starve. As he wanders about, he is never far from the stench of death, and he repeatedly comes across the corpses of his fallen countrymen, some, like those he saw in the coastal village, missing flesh from the buttocks. He realizes what has become of it one day when he sees a relatively fresh corpse and feels like eating it. After noting well-known cases of cannibalism such as the Medusa Raft Incident and rumors about New Guinea and Guadalcanal and expressing how difficult it is for him to imagine modern men eating one another or engaging in incest, he writes: "I felt I could ignore this social prejudice at that moment because I knew of extreme exceptions to it. Since I have lost memories from that time, however, I am unable to say whether my desire was *natural* or not. My memory loss was similar to that which occurs during the climactic moment of sexual intercourse" (3:358). Memory loss under such circumstances, whether the result of willful forgetting, repression, or biology, is a clear indicator of overwhelming, unbearable experience. In fact, memory loss itself can be understood as an extreme form of survival egoism. While Ōoka seems to have been reluctant to acknowledge this in "Before Capture," doing so in "Diary of a Madman" was one of his stated intentions.

Ōoka portrays the most extreme and devastating enactment of survival egoism when Tamura rejoins his comrades for the last time. As with the three soldiers he met upon returning to the hilltop farm, formal initiation into this cannibalistic group is carried out through ritual exchange. Instead of Tamura's making a salt offering, however, he is given—and eats—a piece of dried "monkey meat." When Tamura joins them, their food reserves are nearly exhausted. After Tamura "inadvertently" hands Yasuda his grenade, the competition for survival pits members of this marginal group one against the other.

In the climactic scene of fratricide and cannibalism, Ōoka is able to give full expression to his thoughts and feelings regarding the frontline survival egoism that so appalled and wounded him:

> I was enraged. If it was natural and inevitable for human beings to eat one another during extremes of starvation, then this world was no more than a remnant of God's wrath.
>
> If I could vomit and feel rage at that moment, then I was no longer human. I was an instrument of God, and it was now up to me to manifest His wrath. (3:395–396)

Ōoka accomplishes two important tasks in his unrestrained condemnation of this extreme form of survival egoism. At the same time that he gives full vent to his rage, indignation, and revulsion over the unacceptable reality of battlefield fratricide and fraternal cannibalism, he also expresses criticism and disgust concerning Tamura's survivor *egotism.* If cannibalism can be viewed as the height of survival egoism, then asserting that one survived because he was God's Chosen One is the pinnacle of survivor hubris, a point underscored in the final lines of the novel.

Creating an alter ego and exposing the dissembling, self-deception, and conceit contained in his memoir helped Ōoka to indirectly face and work through some of the survival issues he shied away from in his own autobiographical writings. Fully acknowledging and confronting radical acts of survival egoism, however, were but two important steps in the direction of fruitful formulation. Once the destruction of human bonds has been fully acknowledged, expressed, and condemned, the daunting task of repair yet remains. Tamura's postwar condition as presented in the second part of his memoir is a vivid testament to the alienation and meaninglessness that followed in the wake of his traumatic battlefield experience.

Although Tamura managed to remain in normal society for the first five years after repatriation, he was unable to reestablish meaningful relationships. This is conspicuous in his comments concerning his wife:

> Naturally, [she] welcomed me with open arms. When I saw her overjoyed expression, I too had a feeling akin to happiness. Something, however, seemed to keep us apart. It is perhaps best described as [the same as] the odd experience I underwent in the mountains of the Philippines. While this experience should have been insignificant because I only killed, but didn't eat, people, my one-sided memories nonetheless "came between" us. This is a lame metaphor, but it's the only way I can put it. (3:399)

While Tamura was able to get by for a time in peacetime society, rumors of the buildup of tensions on the Korean Peninsula symbolically reactivate repressed war memories. As previously shown, the return of the repressed is first manifest in the reemergence of his compulsive habit of bowing to his food. As his "one-sided memories" progressively reoccupy his mind and body, Tamura becomes ever more cynical about the possibility of meaningful human connection:

> When I looked into my wife's tear-filled eyes as I stood on the inside and she on the outside of those heavy [mental hospital] doors, I felt the full weight of what I had destroyed within her. What's so terrible, however, about destroying a heart? I'm a man who has killed bodies as well.
>
> I know, moreover, that my wife's heart is not the entirety of her being.

> As a madman, I know firsthand that every human exists in a condition of disintegration. Is love—be it between husband and wife or parent and child—not an impossibility for such internally divided individuals? (3:400)

As Tamura's repressed memories come back to haunt him—and return him psychologically to the battlefield past—the psychic numbing and intrapsychic dissociation familiar to him from the front are symbolically reactivated. Mistakenly assuming that his own disintegrated psychological condition is universal, he concludes that there can be no authentic, enduring human bonds.

Tamura's extreme postwar distrust, cynicism, and alienation are also manifest in his thoughts regarding his wife and doctor. After registering surprise over her willingness to agree to a divorce shortly after he enters the mental hospital, he claims that she continues to visit for the sole purpose of sexual liaison with him. This "fact" brings him to make the following radical declaration: "What the hell does it matter? Just as *all* men are cannibals, *all* women are whores. Let each do as they must" (3:403; emphasis added). The wellspring of Tamura's extreme cynicism is explicitly identified in an exchange with his doctor. Lamentably, Ivan Morris also chose to remove this passage from his English translation of the novel:

> "I'm probably not even [mentally] ill."
>
> "Ha, ha. That's what all patients say. It is also common for them to harbor ill-will toward their doctors. How about you?"
>
> ". . ."
>
> "Well, I'm sorry to have to say this, but you probably are ill. Your condition is called alienation. One of the secondary characteristics is distrust of others. In short, you distrust others because you can't trust yourself." (3:405)

Before Tamura can begin to repair the damage done to the social fabric by war-induced trauma and survival egoism, he must first recover belief in himself. Since he is so reluctant to face and work through his profound self-doubts concerning the full extent of his involvement in cannibalism as he arrogantly struggles to assert his integrity, his formulative efforts are substantially impeded. It is only at the end of his memoir that Tamura is able to make the confession—that he was hunting Filipinos to kill and eat—that could serve as a more viable basis for recovery and renewal.

In the end, Tamura was unable to satisfactorily explain his battlefield survival or find any meaning in it. While he struggles throughout his memoir to account for survival in terms of fate, chance, and God, he is clearly uncomfortable with all of these notions. Tamura steadfastly refuses until the end of his account to seriously consider the critical role that egoism played in his own survival. While he struggles in the first and last part of his account to justify survival in terms of divine intervention, in the second he is preoccupied with chance:

> Since my unwilling return to society, my entire life has become arbitrary. Before going to war, my life, based as it was on individual necessity, had at least as far as I was concerned a certain coherence and inevitability. After being subjected to arbitrary military authority on the battlefield, however, everything became a matter of chance. Survival, my present life—everything depends on chance. Without it, I probably wouldn't be able to see the wooden chair now before me.
>
> People, however, apparently can't accept chance. Our spirits are not strong enough to indefinitely bear the thought of life's being an unending succession of random occurrences. During our lifetimes, which are delineated by random birth and random death, we console ourselves by tallying up the limited number of things we bring about by our so-called free will and calling the coherent entity thus constructed our "life" or "character." There is simply no other way to think about it.
>
> This, too, is probably just nonsense. In actuality, I am doing nothing in this mental hospital at present but watching the movements of the heavenly bodies and leading a life disrupted night after night by sleep. In the sense that while I am engaged in them, I am able to forget about chance, the daily cleaning chores my doctor assigns me are not bad.
>
> . . .
>
> If there is a means of converting the chance that now dominates my life back into necessity, it will be by connecting my present existence with the life of chance forced on me by the military authorities. It is to this end that I am writing this memoir. (3:401–402)

Tamura's postwar condition as characterized in this extended passage is best appreciated in terms of impaired formulation. Struggle though he might to connect his "present life with the life of chance forced on [him] by the military authorities," his efforts are frustrated by his inability to resolve deep-seated feelings of guilt, self-recrimination, and loss or to find any meaning in survival. Consequently, he remains in a psychic condition characterized by separation, disintegration, and deadness.

Tamura initially searches for the meaning of survival in the wrong places. As I have shown in connection with Ōoka's battlefield experience, survival is meaningless to the extent that it depends on chance. For a modern man incapable of unshakable belief in the existence and control of a benevolent, transcendental being, meaning is virtually inseparable from social connectedness. As Tamura himself observes, the chain of events that resulted in alienation and nihilism was set in motion by the military authorities who forced him onto the battlefield against his will. Formulative recovery and renewal require examination and repair of traumatically severed human bonds. While painful, openly admitting the extent to which his own survival hinged on egoism could actually serve to reconnect him to rather than estrange him from his comrades. Survival egoism, after all, is something they had in common. At some point, recovery will also necessarily entail appropriate blaming and the conversion of static to animating forms of guilt. And essential to the overall project is acknowledgment and acceptance of the fact that human relations necessarily involve not only the living, but the dead as well. For Tamura to integrate his past and present selves and reconnect in meaningful ways with others, he must at some point attend to the spirits of the dead. At the end of his memoir, he takes an important step in this direction.

The All-But-Forgotten War Dead

During the chaos of battle and defeat and the protracted struggle for survival, it is impossible to adequately fulfill one's obligations to the dead or to mourn for them. Deprived of funeral rites and proper disposition of their mortal remains, the spirits of the dead are "homeless," "condemned to a miserable transitional existence in which they are capable neither of rejoining the living nor of settling comfortably among the other dead."[36] Even under normal circumstances, relationships between the living and the dead are an extremely complicated, delicate matter:

> Survivors' psychological needs include *both* connection and separation. . . . [There is] a tension between the need to remain close to the dead person and to stay in contact with evidences of him; the equal need to be rid of his body and of these same evidences; and in the process to absorb the fact of personal separation, the fact of death and image of loss. This is the survivor's "work of

> mourning," his struggle to reconstitute his psychic life in a way that can enable him to separate from the dead person while retaining a sense of connection with him, free himself from the deadness of that person and reestablish within himself, sometimes in altered form, whatever modes of immortality have been threatened by the death.[37]

In *Death in Life,* Lifton elaborates on this basic survivor conflict in relation to the dead: "The survivor is, from the beginning, torn by a fundamental ambivalence; he embraces the dead, pays homage to them, and joins in various rituals to perpetuate his relationship to them; but he also pushes them away, considers them tainted and unclean, dangerous and threatening."[38] In the extraordinary, death-saturated context of war and defeat and after seemingly pointless survival, the relationship between the survivor and the dead is especially problematic.

Ongoing psychic numbing, unresolved feelings of death guilt and self-recrimination, and impaired mourning, initially kept Ōoka from embracing, paying homage to, or joining in rituals to reestablish his broken connection with his fallen comrades. Instead, he maneuvered—both consciously and unconsciously—to reject the dead and suppress or repress memories of and feelings for them. Consequently, he was initially incapable of engaging productively in the guilt-centered struggles surrounding fidelity to the dead that could further formulative breakthrough.[39]

Tamura was psychologically and emotionally detached from his comrades at the front. When he was in isolation, his thoughts and feelings for his comrades were transferred to nature. Tamura consistently perceives and portrays elements of the natural environment in human—primarily feminine—terms. The ridgeline of some hills he sees are reflected to him as the curved back of a recumbent woman (3:237); another hill is described as looking like a person crouching down facing away from him (3:246); a lone dwarf tree resembles a standing man (3:241); palm trees abruptly transform into past lovers (3:275); reeds cluster together like a group of people (3:277); other reeds blanketing an isolated hill at the confluence of two rivers appear to him as pubic hair on a woman's genitals.[40]

Tamura not only perceives, envisions, and describes natural objects in human terms, but also responds to them as such. He clearly identified more closely with natural objects than with other people. The experience he describes having by the river is a good case in point. Tamura imagines death—and immortality—primarily in terms of the cessation of consciousness and of physical union with water. He seems to be wholly unconcerned with the spiritual dimension of human existence. The Japanese term for spirit or soul, *tamashii* or *reikon,* rarely appears in Tamura's memoir, and when it does it is used almost exclusively in relation to himself and the life essence of living human beings.

Given the hopeless circumstances, envisioning physical union with nature can be understood as a psychological maneuver to avoid unbearable thoughts of dying alone in a foreign land without proper funeral, burial, or memorialization. Tamura's way of thinking is consoling because it both provides for the natural disposition of his body and addresses his need for some form of symbolic immortality. Tamura, however, imagines merging with and living on in nature even before he is confronted with the abandoned, grotesque, dismembered, and animal-eaten corpses that are subsequently rarely out of sight, smell, or mind for long. One part of his animistic vision is especially revealing in this regard:

> One day, a deafening roar reverberated through the sky. A formation of large bombers was just passing over the narrow strip of sky immediately above me. They passed overhead rapidly, yet languidly. Wings outstretched like great phoenixes, they pierced the blue sky as they passed in and out of the clouds. The roar filled the sky, shook the ground, and rang deep within my ears.
>
> They injured "God's" body as they passed through the sky. . . .
>
> . . .
>
> Flies poured down. Filling the sky like so many flowers and buzzing loudly, they dove straight down toward my face. They were the blood of God. (3:369–370)

By this point, thoughts and feelings about God/Nature have completely replaced those for his comrades. Instead of concerning himself with the damaged, pierced, and mutilated bodies of his fallen countrymen, he transfers their physical wounding and hurt to the distant skies. Awareness of this defensive maneuver aids understanding of his subsequent depiction of himself as an avenging angel: instead of acting on behalf of his slaughtered and abandoned comrades, he psychologically sides with God/Nature and imagines himself venting his/her wrath on the arrogant men who would do him/her harm.

In the places where Tamura does write directly about his comrades, he does so in consistently negative terms. His memoir opens with his brutal rejection by his squad leader, comrades, and medics. This sets the psychological stage for his conspicuous lack of concern for others. Additionally, all the comrades he writes about are treated in terms of survival egoism. Their extreme self-interest and ruthless competitions for survival are used to justify his disregard for them. Moreover, his conviction that his death "in the corner of some unknown tropical field" is inevitable provides him with his universal excuse for not responding to or doing more for his comrades in need.

Tamura's thoughts and feelings for his fallen comrades were deeply but not completely repressed. They slip through in a number of places in his account before surfacing more fully in "Writings of the Dead." Several days after stumbling upon the hilltop farm, for instance, the following thoughts pass through his mind: "The gun and mortar fire gradually died down in the area surrounding the farm. It ceased completely to the south. I imagined the Japanese Army in that direction being completely wiped out, and corpses scattered throughout the forests and fields of that vast area. It was quite odd to picture the annihilation of my comrades as I lived on in my private paradise. Was I in fact hoping for their deaths? If so, I anticipated my own demise following my present satiation" (3:281). Once the immediate threat of death recedes, Tamura has the psychological margin to imagine his comrades going down to defeat on battlefields throughout Leyte Island. These thoughts clearly involve guilt over enjoying such comfortable circumstances while they continue to fight and die. As long as he hears the sounds of battle, he cannot completely forget that some of his comrades persist in resisting the enemy as he fights solely for self-perpetuation.

Tamura's fatal encounter with the Filipina can profitably be understood as a spontaneous expression of deep-seated feelings related to his fallen countrymen. Although he struggles to explain away the woman's death in terms of chance and accident, the significance of the immediate context for the killing must not be overlooked. After detailing the horrid condition of the corpses he sees in front of the church, Tamura speculates on how they died. Based on the evidence at hand, he concludes that they must have been attacked by locals while plundering the village. The Filipina was a member of the group that slaughtered his comrades and left their bodies to be eaten by animals. It will be recalled that Tamura reacted with rage when the woman continued to scream after he abruptly appeared before her. While he never considers his conduct in relation to his dead countrymen, the immediate context of the fatal encounter and his sudden outpouring of animosity strongly suggest that his conduct was a manifestation of his powerful subconscious desire to avenge their deaths.

A more subtle manifestation of Tamura's repressed thoughts and feelings for his dead comrades occurs in a similar, corpse-strewn setting and is also associated with the woman he killed. After watching a Filipina guerrilla gun down a comrade as he attempts to surrender, Tamura abandons thoughts of raising the white flag he had made (his loincloth tied to a stick). Upon mentally associating this guerrilla with the woman he killed, he sentences himself to die alone in the wilderness: "Once it became clear to me that however good my luck, I was proscribed from returning to the human world by the ghost (*bōrei*) of the woman I killed, I only continued living because I wasn't dead. I wasn't anxious. And I didn't hate the dead woman" (3:354–355). This passage, one of the few in the memoir including an explicit reference to the spirits of the dead, is clearly inseparable from profound feelings of guilt and self-recrimination.

After detailing the condition of the corpses he subsequently comes upon and describing a tense encounter with a routed, starving soldier like himself, he relates another telling experience:

> As the rain continued to fall in the evening, I lay down under the shelter of some thick foliage. In the distant fields long since devoid of fireflies, I could see a red flame. Just what kind of light could it be? It flickered more dimly and brightly as heavier and lighter rains passed by. Sometimes it looked like a vaguely defined circle of light submerged under deep waters.
>
> Because I, too, had a flame burning in my breast, I feared it.
>
> One evening, it began to move over the fields. Traveling at the height of a hand-held lantern, it waveringly approached over an impassible marshy area choked with reeds and water plants.
>
> I felt it was coming toward and would continue to press in on me. I steeled myself. The flame, however, suddenly veered off to one side, followed the dark outline of the ridge, rose slightly, and then disappeared from view.
>
> I was at a loss. I felt only dread, and then anger. (3:356–357)

The description of this red flame (*akai hi*), its movements, and his reaction to it strongly suggest its intimate linkage in Tamura's mind with the restless spirits of the "homeless" dead. Japanese folk beliefs regarding the flamelike lights (*tama-shi*) said to emerge from human bodies upon death support this interpretation.[41] Tamura's reactions to this enigmatic flame are expressions of his repressed, ambivalent feelings toward the war dead. At first, he is afraid of the flame, explaining that he too has one within himself. Whereas Tamura's flame represents the life principle of the living,[42] however, the flame that approaches him across the fields clearly represents the spirits of the dead. The anger Tamura subsequently experiences is similar to that felt toward the Filipina: it is generated from identification with the dead, from rage over the violence and pointlessness of their deaths and the way their bodies have been left to sun, wind, rain, and wild animals. It is, in short, the first intimation of the anxiety of responsibility that finally surfaces and is given direct expression in the final passages of the memoir.

Tamura's repressed feelings of guilt, responsibility, and rage thus find expression in ways both subtle and more obvious. In this connection, the points made in the first part of this section must not be forgotten: in numerous places in his memoir, Tamura describes himself experiencing profound sadness not in the distant past, but in the narrative present. Given the multivalence of the Japanese adjective "*kanashii,*" this feeling is clearly associated with grief and mourning. It is very telling that the only funeral service mentioned in the memoir takes place in a dream involving Tamura mourning his own death.

One of the important things Tamura fails to consider when thinking about cannibalism is the serious implications of this act to the dead. One of the earliest distinguishing features of early humans was the practice of burial and death-related rituals. Such death rites predate the relatively recent taboos of cannibalism and incest. Thus, the act Tamura contemplates—and engages in—in extremity involves not only transgressing the taboo against eating human flesh, but also neglecting the more fundamental obligation of the living to properly attend to and respect the dead. Even if circumstances made this impossible at the time, he surely would have felt profound guilt and self-condemnation after survival for ignoring this most basic social obligation.

It is thus significant that the only ritual Tamura engages in after survival is related not to his dead comrades, but to the plants and animals he feels deeply indebted to. This focus on the nonhuman, too, is best understood in terms of transference. Tamura was deeply indebted to the men who died in his place, but he was reluctant to acknowledge the extent to which he owed his life to them and loath to acknowledge or attend to their spirits.

At the end of the memoir, the feelings of guilt, sadness, responsibility, and indebtedness toward the dead that were repressed or transferred to nature finally find more direct and significant expression. In his spiritual vision, Tamura communed with nature in an animistic world of light and life. In "Writings of the Dead," he describes himself in the dark, largely static land of the dead. This marks a significant turning point in Tamura's attitude toward and relationship with his fallen comrades. He writes as follows after describing shadowy figures and *nobi* that press in on him and gazing down at the hands that grasp his rifle:

> I always thought that consciousness ended upon death. I was wrong. Even after death, all is not oblivion. I must tell this to them. I shout, "I'm alive!"
>
> But my voice doesn't even reach my own ears. Although they lack voices, the dead yet live. There is no such thing as individual death. Death is a universal event. Even after death we must be eternally awake. Day after day, we must make decisions. I must tell this to all humankind. But it's too late. (3:411)

In this passage, Tamura not only acknowledges, but also struggles to speak on behalf of the dead. Indeed, one detects here the first significant expression of the anxiety of responsibility Tamura felt as a burdened survivor. The implication of the message Tamura struggles in vain to convey to others is of great importance: death is never an isolated, discrete event; it inevitably has profound bearing on and implications for both immediate and ultimate human relationships. And if this is true of a solitary death, how much more so for the unnatural, premature, grotesque, and seemingly pointless deaths of tens or hundreds of thousands in a lost war.

In the final pages of his memoir, Tamura is also able to acknowledge and confront the spirits of those he has killed—Nagamatsu, Yasuda, and the Filipina. That he faces both his Japanese comrades and a Filipino is significant. The presence of the ghost of the young woman is both an indication of his deep sense of guilt over bringing her life to a violent, premature end and of inclusiveness in his thinking about the war dead.

While he is specifically joined in the realm of the dead by those he killed himself, their different nationalities, sexes, and ages enable them to serve as representatives of all those who died during the Battle of Leyte Island. The implications of this are profound: attending to the war dead cannot be restricted to one's own losses; at some point, it must come to include others whose lives were lost or shattered by the indiscriminate destruction and brutality of modern war.

By the time he finished writing *Fires on the Plain,* Ōoka seemed to have realized that his subsequent literary efforts to formulate his traumatic battlefield experience would have to take up where Tamura's leaves off—with the "homeless," all-but-forgotten war dead. Working through his relationship as a survivor to the war dead, however, required him to belatedly acknowledge, identity, and empathize with them. Tracing his movement from numbed, anxious rejection of the dead to his embrace of, mourning for, and remembrance of them is the task of the chapter that follows.

CHAPTER THREE

Lady Musashino and *In the Shadow of Cherry Blossoms*

PSYCHIC NUMBING AND DEEP-SEATED, unresolved feelings of death guilt and self-recrimination impaired Ōoka's ability to mourn for his dead comrades during the war and for many years after. He not only avoided funeral and memorial services at the time, but also maneuvered in his memoirs to reject the men of Nishiya Company as unworthy of further concern, sympathy, or grieving. After thirteen years of sustained literary struggle with the burdens of survival, however, he reached a crucial emotional turning point. The aim of this chapter is to trace Ōoka's difficult movement from anxious rejection of the war dead to his close identification with them and his empathy and unimpaired mourning for them by comparing and contrasting *Lady Musashino* (1950) and *In the Shadow of Cherry Blossoms* (1959).[1]

Ōoka conceived of *Lady Musashino* late in 1947, and it was serialized in *Gunzō* between January and September 1950. He began work on this romance (*ren'ai shōsetsu*) when serial publication of *Fires on the Plain* was interupted in 1949. *Lady Musashino* treats the complicated, adulterous relationships between two married couples—Michiko and Akiyama and Tomiko and Ono—and Tsutomu, a deeply troubled young veteran just returned from Burma.[2] In contrast to Ōoka's battlefield memoirs and *Fires on the Plain*, which are first-person narratives, Michiko and Tsutomu's tragic story is related by an aloof, omniscient narrator who comments ironically on the foibles and blind spots of each character while progressively exposing the sociohistorical, economic, psychological, and interpersonal factors that eventually result in Michiko's breakdown and suicide.

In this work, Ōoka was clearly concerned with the structure and dynamics of modern tragedy, and the unfolding of the carefully ordered plot gives the impression of characters being moved about like pieces on a chess board. In this immediate postwar game, however, it is the queen who is checkmated. The detached, ironic narrative perspective so conspicuous in the work is an accurate reflection of Ōoka's emotional distancing. This is particularly noticeable in his attitude toward and treatment of Michiko's suicide preparations and agonizing death, which for the most part are regarded through the eyes and consciousness of characters virtually incapable of sympathy, empathy, or mourning and from a safe, philosophical point of view.

While the narrative focus in the first half of the novel is primarily on Tsutomu and his struggle to adjust to life in postwar Japanese society, that in the second is on Michiko and the circumstances that give rise to her fatal breakdown. There are intimate thematic interconnections between Tsutomu and his female cousin, and this important point is highlighted in the following passage: "Both [Tsutomu and Michiko] inherited their facial features from the paternal side of the family; they resembled each other so closely that they easily could have passed for brother and sister. As they faced each other . . . hey both felt that they were seeing themselves transformed into the opposite sex" (3:55).

Lady Musashino revolves around Tsutomu and Michiko's troubled relationship. The narrative begins with Tsutomu's struggle to recover by renewing his relationship with the person he was most intimate with before going to war; it shifts midway to the profound effects this relationship has on her. The psychological dynamic is thus one of contagion: through contact with Tsutomu, Michiko's psychic condition increasingly comes to resemble his own. And while Ōoka clearly identifies and sympathizes with this young war veteran, he is ultimately unable to sympathize with Michiko. Since mourning becomes possible only when "one individual is capable of empathy with another,"[3] *dōjō*, or the lack thereof, is a highly significant aspect of the work.

Tsutomu's Postwar Condition

Tsutomu is haunted by his battlefield experience and periodically suffers symbolic reactivation of his past trauma:

> Occasionally, as Tsutomu stared down at the ground while walking along absorbed with some serious thought or another, he would abruptly have the feeling that the green fields of Burma were spreading out before him, and he would hear the booming of mortar fire and cries of pain and suffering. He couldn't raise his eyes for fear of seeing his vision become reality. When he would eventually come to his senses, he would realize that he was still in a corner of the outlying capital district. This realization, however, would have no effect whatsoever on the total disruption of thought this kind of experience brought on. (3:27)

Such descriptions vividly show how traumatic memory can precipitate breakdown and desymbolization almost instantly. Indeed, the narrator introduces the passage quoted above by observing that Tamura was "simply incapable of thinking things completely through" (3:27).

During one of the many solitary walks he takes through the Musashino countryside, Tsutomu has a related experience of spatial and temporal confusion:

> A small area of mixed-growth forest remained to the south of the open plain, and huge oaks towered over the expanse of light green grass. Tsutomu made his way toward them over the trailless fields. . . . Memories of being in the mountains of Burma revived in him. The trees in the tropical forests continually shed leaves regardless of season, and the footpaths that passed through them were narrow. While in Burma, Tsutomu recalled Musashino forests; now on the Musashino Plain, he thought of the Burmese woods. (3:51)

Psychologically speaking, Tsutomu has lost his grounding. His preoccupation throughout the novel with the geological history and formation of the Musashino Plain is intimately related to his efforts to resituate himself in the postwar world physically as well as psychologically.

Tsutomu's susceptibility to symbolic reactivation of his battlefield experience is but one of the legacies of his frontline trauma; psychic numbing was another. Emotional detachment is readily apparent in his reactions to news of his father's death. Tsutomu's father, a staff officer who rose to the rank of lieutenant colonel, killed himself with a pistol the day following Emperor Hirohito's announcement of Japan's unconditional surrender:

> When I write that Tsutomu's initial response to learning of his father's death was a feeling of liberation, the reader will probably think him a brute. This, however, was the case. After watching so many people die at the front, he knew how much trouble death spared one of. While he loved his father, he didn't have any particular feelings about his death. The dead passed and were gone. That was all there was to it. The same thing had nearly happened to Tsutomu himself. (3:26)

In his psychically numbed state, Tsutomu views death primarily as something that simplifies human relationships by liberating survivors of further concern and involvement. This formulation not only denies the reality of death and the solemn obligations of survivors to the deceased, but also serves to make mourning seem unnecessary.

Tsutomu's relationships with the living parallel his broken connections with the dead. He was just eighteen when he was conscripted out of university and sent to the front, and he lost his innocence there. When his unit retreated into the mountains, the volunteer nurses accompanying them were forced to exchange sex for food. Tsutomu's traumatic experience of defeat and his witnessing of extreme acts of survival egoism culminating in cannibalism strengthened the inner conviction he developed as an unwelcome stepchild that he could rely only on himself.[4] His traumatic frontline experience and exposure to unbridled decadence (*daraku*) in both the POW camp and postwar Japanese society robbed him of his trust and faith in humanity (3:25–26).

Tsutomu himself initially seeks to escape into depravity. After formally severing relations with his stepmother by giving her a part of his inheritance, he reenters the university and does little but drink and engage in casual sex. Significantly, Tsutomu's decadent postwar behavior involves reenactment of battlefield experience: "His curiosity and the cravings of his young body won out [over his scruples]. The memory of the smell of the hair of the [nurses] who abandoned their sense of shame for food lived on in him. After returning to Japan, he lost himself in carnal relations with loose coeds, finding pleasure in recalling the strange feelings he experienced in huts in the Burmese mountains when he smelled the fragrance of their sweat-soaked hair" (3:27).

Tsutomu's alienation, isolation, and inner deadness are palpable during a solitary walk he takes through the war-ravaged countryside. After passing the burned-out ruins of a hastily constructed airfield and following the Nogawa River for a time, he eventually reaches an enormous concrete airplane factory with all the windows broken:

> The factory grounds extended to an outlying building resembling a storehouse. The entire area was deserted. A piece of tin roofing that had come loose and hung down from the eaves vibrated audibly in the evening breeze.
>
> The slope falling away before him was covered with oaks. A natural trail followed the upper edge of the forest. Tsutomu [followed it for a time and] crouched down in the woods.
>
> All he could hear was the ominous sound of the tin sheeting being moved about in the wind. With the onset of dusk, the part of the sky visible beyond the forest that was punctuated here and there with the soft green of saplings progressively dimmed. Tsutomu was wounded in both heart and soul. (3:53–54)

Tsutomu attempts to heal himself through interactions with the natural environment and his renewed relationship with Michiko. These, in fact, are virtually inseparable in his mind. At the front, Tsutomu's thoughts and feelings for other people were transferred to nature. After the war, nature was the only thing Tsutomu was still capable of responding to. The narrator makes this clear from the outset: "Tsutomu had lost faith in people, but he still loved nature" (3:28). Tsutomu initially sees Michiko as an extension of the natural world. Through his increasing contact with her, he eventually succeeds in shifting the locus of concern from nature back to his fellow beings.

Tsutomu's Hope

The first thing Tsutomu does after repatriation is visit Michiko. One day in February as she sits outside on the verandah, Tsutomu abruptly appears from the back garden. After this initial reunion, however, Tsutomu avoids the Hake house and for a time gives himself up to liquor and women. The narrator suggests that his subsequent return to the Hake house in June probably represented his first positive step in the direction of recovery: "If he had stayed away from the Hake house partially out of respect for Michiko, and had felt like visiting after a long hiatus because he had grown tired of his life, there was hope for him yet" (3:27).

When Tsutomu acts on impulse to break his uncle's long-standing prohibition against entering the grounds from the back gate, the action is presented from Tsutomu's perspective. His conduct, of course, is symbolic: throughout his relationship with Michiko he wavers between his urge to flaunt social conventions and act on his feelings for her and his need to abide by them to avoid contributing to the destruction of the social web as he did on the battlefield. As he makes his way down toward the house, he notices a hollow in the ground he and Michiko often used while playing hide-and-seek, and "the feeling of complicity, the warmth of Michiko's body, and the fragrance of her youthful hair came back to him" (3:29). The tension between Tsutomu's psychological need for a vitalizing symbolic connection and his instinctual desire for physical relations is highlighted in the following passage. In the first two paragraphs, the reader is given direct access to his thoughts as he secretly observes Michiko and Tomiko talking on the verandah; in the third, the narrator comments ironically on the danger inherent in his ambivalent emotions:

> "From behind, she doesn't appear to have changed a bit since she married. What a strange face she pulled when I first came back! But she was happy right afterward. She's the only one who was truly glad to see me. Come to think of it, she was the only one who cried for me when I shipped off for the front. I've been a fool to stay away for so long. It must have been lonely since uncle died. She's all alone just like me.
>
> "Wait a minute. There is Akiyama. What a creep. There couldn't be any stranger bedfellows than that guy and Stendhal. Not being a reader myself I don't know well, but according to my buddy who knows French literature, all he does in his lectures is pull Stendhal down to his own level."
>
> It was fortunate for Akiyama that Tsutomu hadn't read the incestuous *Charterhouse of Parma.* If he had, he immediately would have felt like labeling the feelings he had for his cousin by a different name. (3:30)

Tsutomu is moved by sympathy and empathy for his cousin. Just as Michiko had genuine concern and feelings for him when he left for and returned from the front, he sincerely feels for her when he thinks of her loneliness after losing her father. His thoughts and feelings about Akiyama, however, reveal his profound ambivalence.

As Tsutomu clandestinely observes Michiko and Tomiko from the back garden, the two women are just discussing his degenerate behavior. Tsutomu emerges to join them on the verandah just after they agree that it would be best if he moved into the Hake house. Akiyama reluctantly agrees when Michiko suggests that a scandal might develop if he moved in with Tomiko.[5] After Tsutomu joins them, it becomes increasingly clear that his deep interest in the topography of the Musashino region is closely linked to his feelings for his unhappily married cousin:

> Tsutomu admired Michiko. When he gazed at her through the eyes of a young man who had moved beyond the habitual indifference that had developed out of the intimacy of their early years together, he was in awe of her simple beauty, which was untouched by the passage of time. What particularly attracted him were her precise, efficient movements. She was absolutely still when she had nothing to do. She never engaged in idle talk.
>
> Tsutomu's sensitivity to her economic, precise movements was probably something he picked up on the battlefield, a place of nothing but necessity and prohibition.
>
> Tsutomu had picked up the habit of scrutinizing the movements of things in general. For instance, he studied the workings of the spring in the garden. The clear, flowing water that bubbled forth moved pebbles along the streambed little by little. He crouched down on the bank of the flowing waters and gazed tirelessly at the movements of a single pebble as it gradually worked its way downstream—the way it rolled over two or three times, quivered in place for a moment, and then leaped four or five inches all at once. (3:49)

Tamura's preoccupation with the spring in the Hake garden and locating the headwaters of the Nogawa River that flowed through the valley below the house is part of his struggle to reconnect both literally and figuratively with a source of vitality. During walks he takes with Michiko through the Musashino countryside, while searching for the origins of the Nogawa and in the course of their later explorations of the Murayama Reservoir area, Tsutomu increasingly comes to see his cousin as his wellspring of recovery and renewal. Tragically and ironically, his chosen path to healing pushes Michiko toward the very condition he seeks to overcome.

As tensions mount between Akiyama and Michiko and Akiyama and Tsutomu, Tsutomu's sympathy for his unhappily married cousin deepens. Wanting to share his love of nature, he frequently invites her out on strolls through the countryside. One day, he asks her to join him on his quest for the source of the Nogawa River. When they come to a spring behind a Shinto shrine, Michiko feels a sudden impulse to embrace him as she watches him gaze with contentment at the water pouring forth from the base of a cliff. After further searching, they locate the river's true point of origination. When Tsutomu asks a man working in a nearby field what the place is called and he replies "Love Hollow" (Koi ga Kubo), Michiko goes weak in the knees. Tsutomu, however, is oblivious; at this point, he still looks upon the natural site before him, rather than the woman at his side as a life source.

As Tsutomu and Michiko grow more intimate, Akiyama's jealously and Michiko's suffering increase. Conscious that he is the root cause of their current marital difficulties, Tsutomu suggests to Michiko that the time has come for him to move out. When she melts into tears, he takes this as an expression of her deep love and concern for him. Tsutomu, however, resists thinking of her in passionate terms: "Once again, his respect for her won out. He felt it was blasphemous to imagine in Michiko the same thing he had discerned in the loose coeds he had known" (3:69).

The tragic course their relationship subsequently takes is largely conditioned by Tsutomu's traumatic battlefield experience. The following thoughts come to mind after he becomes conscious of their mutual love:

> As the unhappy child of a mother who abandoned her family, Tsutomu had been as far as one could be from the sentiments expressed by his privileged counterparts in the line "Family, I abhor you." At the very least, family to him had substance as the crystallization of his childhood longing.
>
> Now that he found himself in the position of family destroyer because of his love for his married cousin, however, he was shocked that he had come to think of the family as singularly fragile, as something that could be shattered with a single touch. At the front, he had watched many husbands die as they agonized about and grieved over the wives and children they were leaving behind. On the verge of death, one told him, "Even if you happen to make it back alive, don't tell my wife that I died like this." Politics, which makes no one happy, destroyed families in this way. Why couldn't he allow passion, which at least made him happy, to do the same? (3:80–81)

In this passage, one senses the surfacing of the anxiety of responsibility. And this anxiety cuts to the very heart of the matter—what his comrades ultimately fought and sacrificed themselves for and the solemn obligation of survivors to carry on their dying will. The comrade Tsutomu recalls died with concern for the protection of his family foremost in mind.[6] His last request was to spare his wife the pain of knowing the horrid circumstances in which he died. If Tsutomu were to act on his base impulses, he would not only be contributing toward the downfall of a family, but also betraying the dying will of his fallen comrades. In time, Tamura concludes that he must sacrifice his passion and act to repair the damaged social fabric on behalf of the war dead. This is precisely what he does when a violent storm forces him to spend the night with Michiko in a remote hotel.

In one of the many ironic parallels that comprise the structural dynamic of much of the novel, both Akiyama and Tomiko and Tsutomu and Michiko are off on separate trips when the storm hits. Whereas adultery is the explicit aim of the former couple, the latter leave home with the simple intention of spending a day exploring a point of geological interest. Given Tsutomu's rising anxiety about his responsibility, it is significant that the typhoon originates from Iwo Jima, site of some of the fiercest and most resolute fighting of the Pacific War.[7] Symbolically, this storm represents the angry spirits of the war dead. The fact that the time is the end of August—the month of surrender and Obon (Festival of the Dead)—serves to underscore this important connection.

In a scene explicitly linked to their experience on the way to and at Love Hollow, Tsutomu and Michiko walk together along a path above the Murayama Reservoir. The closer they drift toward acting on their feelings for one another, the worse the storm becomes. In the following passage, the narrator reveals the core of their troubles:

> Michiko recalled the time at Love Hollow when she first called her feelings for Tsutomu romantic love. She had changed this much in the less than two months that had passed since then. Was her life at that time false, and her life at present true? Or was her present suffering false, and her condition in the past true?
>
> As Michiko searched her soul in this way, Tsutomu was simply drunk with happiness. As they walked along together, he felt the unrestrained inti-

> macy they shared in the past returning. Why did they have to label their feelings romantic love and act upon them? (3:112–113)

Their fundamental mistake is to conflate genuine caring and concern for one another with passion. The brewing storm symbolizes the potential danger of physically consummating their relationship. After a reservoir official walks by and glares at them with obvious disapproval, Tsutomu ignores the No Trespassing (*tachiiri kinshi*) sign and leads an apprehensive Michiko into the forbidden zone.

The downward path they take through the forest, however, brings them not to the water's edge, but to a narrow promontory bordered by cliffs. Tsutomu puts his arms around her and their lips come together "naturally," as if "everything had been prearranged." Their respective reactions to their first kiss are very telling: "Tsutomu tasted something in Michiko's mouth that he was very familiar with. It had the flavor of an experience he had known sometime in the distant past. It was like the fragrance he smelled at his young mother's breast as a child. Michiko smelled Tsutomu and detected the scent of the dark thing she had sensed in him ever since his return from the front. Frightened, she opened her eyes and pulled away" (3:114–115). Tsutomu is attracted to Michiko as a source of the pure maternal affection he was denied in his youth. In contrast, Michiko senses the taint of death in him and instinctively fears contagion.

Their second, more extended kiss quickly becomes a trial for her. Since Tsutomu doesn't seem to demand anything further, however, Michiko is able to calm herself. She accepts their kissing as a natural expression of their childhood intimacy. But she realizes that this must be the only time. As if to punctuate her thoughts, the storm abruptly intensifies, and the buffeting winds and first drops of rain begin to reach them. After fleeing to a teahouse, they hear reports that the typhoon is approaching and the trains have stopped running.

In time, they find themselves face to face again, this time in a cheap room lit only by the flickering light of an oil lamp. When Tsutomu is "unable to restrain himself from certain behavior" (3:119), their kiss threatens to lead beyond the bounds of innocence. Michiko initially resists him and tells him stop, but her willpower weakens, and even though she continues to murmur "no," "her body open[s] before the force he brought to bear" (3:119). At the point of no return, however, Tsutomu is able to act on his rising feeling of responsibility and take an important step toward recovery and renewal:

> This was probably what Tsutomu had been waiting for. At that moment, however, he heard something outside.
>
> A thin, piercing sound arose in the wake of a crashing noise that sounded like the destruction of the facade of a building. The sound, which resembled the wail of a human voice, passed through the cacophony of the storm raging outside, entered into, and pervaded their room.
>
> Tsutomu looked around.
>
> Now he felt that the wailing sound was coming from Michiko's spirit as she crumbled before him.
>
> Her spirit seemed to be saying, "You must not do this. This alone you must do without."
>
> His own inner voice responded in kind, "This alone must not be done." If in her heart of hearts Michiko did not want this, then he must not do it. (3:119)

The first sounds to reach Tsutomu's ears clearly represent the collapse and destruction of the family.[8] These images of damage to the fundamental social unit are forewarnings of the serious consequences of adultery and incest. And at the crucial moment, the wail of Michiko's living spirit (*tamashii*) combines with the souls of the war dead to convey a common message: Do not succumb to the immoral demands of the flesh and exacerbate social breakdown; take the higher, spiritual path and contribute toward symbolic healing and recovery.

When Tsutomu relents, Michiko is overjoyed. While the immediate result of this fateful weekend is that Tsutomu has to move out of Hake house, in the long run his experience with Michiko enables formulative breakthrough. He subsequently loses interest in drinking and casual sex and begins to do some serious reading for the first time. His most important insights—which have direct bearing on his relationship with Michiko—emerge from his study of existentialism. After drawing on his frontline experience to critique the superficial understanding of those attracted to this philosophy in the wake of the war, Tsutomu hits upon the idea that forms the basis of his turning point experience:

> To Tsutomu, the existential philosophy en vogue seemed like a joke. While its advocates appeared to take irrationality and lowliness as human prerogatives, Tsutomu, who had grown sick and tired of baseness on the battlefield, had no desire to take pride in them. If there were such existentialists among the ants, they would no doubt say that their kind of existence was apheliotropic. This, however, would not be to their honor, nor would it have anything to do with what makes them work so diligently. Tsutomu felt that all animals, including humans, lived not by existence itself, but by the ideals their biological needs forced them to embrace. (3:130–131)

It is significant that Ōoka, who admitted in his battlefield memoirs to having no ideals himself, would have Tsutomu make this last assertion. The crucial issue here, of course, is the precise nature of these vital images. Tsutomu's newly discovered psychic lifeline comes to be intimately connected with the making and honoring of spiritual vows.

As will be detailed in the next section, things go from bad to worse for Michiko after Tsutomu moves out. By the time he visits her after another long hiatus, her suffering is readily visible in her face, which has become so gaunt that her eyes look unnaturally large. Tsutomu repeatedly tries to take her in his arms, but she will not allow it. After discussing the loss of part of her inheritance, the heightened cruelty this elicits from Akiyama, and Akiyama's affair with Tomiko, Tsutomu suggests that they could probably find happiness by forgetting society and doing as they pleased. Michiko, however, responds that, "Morality is our only strength" (3:154). After more pained discussion, she states that vows (*chikai*) are more sacred than morality, and then elaborates: "If we truly love each other and vow not to change, and we can honor our vows indefinitely, I think a time will come when the rules of society change and we will be able to be together in clear conscience" (3:155).

After a formal exchange of vows,[9] Michiko allows Tsutomu to take her in his arms and kiss her. Thus do Michiko and Tsutomu enact a rite of spiritual union. Despite her husband's infidelity and her ambivalent feelings for her cousin, Michiko will not allow herself to do anything that would compromise her moral obligations as wife and sole heir to the family legacy. Maintaining integrity in this way eventually brings her to sacrifice herself for the common good. The epigraph Ōoka chose for the novel—"Were the movements of Countess Dorgel's heart those of a bygone day?"

(Radiquet)—becomes significant here. The movements of Michiko's heart are clearly those of a woman who adheres to traditional morality rather than abandoning herself to postwar decadence and egoism. Far from being an anachronism, she deserves to be viewed as a paragon of virtue. The example she sets and the ideal she helps Tsutomu embrace prepare the way for his formulative breakthrough.

After exchanging vows, Michiko instructs Tsutomu not to visit until circumstances are such that they can be open and aboveboard with their relationship. She asks him to stay away from the Hake house until she writes that it's all right to visit. Within an hour of leaving, however, Tsutomu has already broken the spirit of their vows. Driven to desperation by pent-up sexual frustration, he impulsively makes an advance on Tomiko. As soon as she refuses him, he comes to his senses and feels a "biting sadness [pass] through his heart" (3:163). As with the *kanashimi* that repeatedly assailed Tamura as he composed his memoir, the sadness Tsutomu experiences is both an indication of his awareness of again having "injured the order of being"[10] and an indication of guilt and loss.

Tsutomu reaches his turning point in his struggle to repair his gravely frayed psychic lifeline by establishing a new basis from which to reformulate his relationship with society. His formulative breakthrough begins on top of a hill above the Murayama Reservoir, continues as he descends to the dam, and culminates as he approaches the Hake house. While telling himself that he revisits the area to gain an unimpeded view of the Musashino Plain, he is equally drawn back by nostalgia. Tsutomu's thoughts begin and end with Michiko and the vow they exchanged. By the time he has worked out the basis for his new connection with nature and society and worked through deep-seated feelings of death guilt, self-recrimination, and loss, his thinking undergoes a 180-degree change.

The physical context of Tsutomu's turning-point experience is significant. The overlook where his fruitful formulative process begins is an old Kamakura period (1185–1333) battlefield known as Shogun Hill (Shōgunzuka). American war planes engage in maneuvers in the skies above him. With an old battleground underfoot and modern warplanes overhead, Tsutomu engages in a serious, sustained effort to come to terms with his burdened past. As he works through each step of his anguished process of formulation, he physically moves from isolation in the mountains toward meaningful connection with people in the plains below.

After Tsutomu breaks the spirit of his vow at Tomiko's house, Akiyama shows up and takes a picture of them with Tsutomu's arm around Tomiko's shoulder. Akiyama subsequently shows the incriminating photo to Michiko. Before leaving for the Murayama Reservoir, Tsutomu receives an envelope from Michiko containing two pictures: the one he and Michiko took after making their vow and the one of him with his arm wrapped around Tomiko. While he sees only his own baseness in the latter, he senses sadness in the former:

> "This person has taken on a burden too heavy for her to bear. What's wrong with my wanting to take her away from that Hake house that is so unworthy of her? . . . But there was no way I could do it in a way she could accept. 'Vows'? Was it really so bad of me to feel like breaking something so insubstantial? If that's the way I actually felt, there's nothing I can do about it. If reality is right, then 'vows' are mistaken. If it hadn't come from her lips, I probably never would have believed in such a thing. 'Vows' and the like are the sour grapes of the weak. Akiyama's the detestable one. He's the one who put such ideas into her head. That guy is a perfect representative of all there is to being a husband. He is an embodiment of society itself." (3:195–196)

Tsutomu begins by sympathizing with and expressing concern for Michiko, whose "heavy burden" is to abide by social strictures despite the decadence and depravity of those around her. Immediately afterward, however, he defensively maneuvers to absolve himself of responsibility for betraying her trust by shifting blame first to Akiyama and then to society as a whole. Reluctant to accept personal accountability, he moves to blame and censure society for frustrating his relationship with Michiko. By the time he descends from Shogun Hill to the Murayama Reservoir, "Tsutomu was no longer thinking of Michiko. He was thinking of society. He was, however, thinking of it only as something that obstructed his love for her" (3:197).

While Tsutomu thinks nothing of breaking society's rules, he cannot bring himself to make Michiko do the same. This line of reasoning eventually leads him toward apocalyptic imagination. So thoroughly has he projected the blame for all his suffering and frustration onto society that as he gazes at a water tower, the idea of poisoning the reservoir and killing everyone in the greater Tokyo metropolitan area comes to mind. This is clearly an expression of his retaliatory desire to make the world suffer literally what he experienced symbolically at the front.[11]

Tamura is deeply shaken by these thoughts. This destructive imagery, however, helps facilitate confrontation with deep-seated feelings of death guilt and self-condemnation:

> The thought that came to him by the water tower lingered in Tsutomu's mind. "Well then, is that how wicked I am? If this is the conclusion I drew from my experience of defeat in Burma, then I am already probably one who can no longer associate with others. It was the height of reasonableness for Michiko to have refused to associate with me. The face in that photo she sent me is inhuman. And it's not just the face; the heart, too, is not that of a human being."
>
> Tsutomu felt like a convict who had had the word "veteran" branded on his forehead.
>
> "I had thought myself fortunate to have returned home after narrowly escaping death, but it probably would have been better to have died at the front. If I had, I would have been spared this self-reproach.
>
> "It would have been easy to die amidst the chaos of the jungle. If I think that I died then, what regrets could I possibly have about dying now?
>
> "What about dying together with Michiko? Ah, here's another of your wicked thoughts. What possible reason could she have to die? Do you want to go as far as murder?" (3:199–200)

Tsutomu moves here from projecting blame and evil out onto society to acknowledging its existence within himself. This is an important step toward taking personal responsibility. In the revelation that follows, moreover—that it would have been better if he had died at the front—one hears Ōoka's voice as well. Tsutomu's self-reproach is inseparable from the anxiety of responsibility. He feels terribly guilty over and is heavily burdened by survival. In contrast to Michiko, who has committed herself to putting the rules of society before her personal desires, Tsutomu struggles with the heavy burden of traumatic memory of and unfulfilled obligations to his fallen comrades. Desperate to escape from mounting feelings of guilt and self-recrimination, and his responsibilities to the war dead, he seriously considers suicide. Thus does Tsutomu begin with thoughts of killing others and end with thoughts of taking his own life. Subsequent thoughts of double suicide, however, bring on further waves of self-reproach.

Tsutomu reaches his turning point upon transferring thoughts and feelings back to the human world. After asking himself if he would even go so far as to murder to avoid the burdens he is so loath to shoulder, he looks off into the distance and sees Mt. Fuji illuminated by alpine glow. After realizing that this dormant volcano, which once stood for his enduring love for Michiko, is now associated in his mind with death, he is finally able to dispel his defensive, nature-centered illusions. He begins this process by observing that Mt. Fuji is so perfectly shaped and beautiful because it is a relatively young mountain. He goes on to imagine its being eroded and flattened out over the passage of geological time until it is reduced to the ugly form of a squat crab. This image ushers him toward formulative breakthrough:

> "Hell, am I thinking I'll be around to see Fuji reduced to the shape of a crab?! Of what use is that vision to me?" For the first time, Tsutomu began to wonder whether the geological interest that had possessed him since he returned from the front had been a kind of emotional fallacy.
>
> "Was [my interest in] the broad Musashino plateau I tried to assay by repeatedly climbing up to Sayama not just an illusion? What relation to me was the old Tamagawa delta that was formed innumerable years before my birth? And the Musashino woods people make so much of—were those trees not planted as windbreaks by generation after generation of farmers? Today's Musashino is factories, schools, airports, and the spacious houses of Tokyo citizens."
>
> As Tsutomu dispelled his geographical delusions, he also moved away from his vision of death. "If even a person like me wants to go on living at all costs, then I must make a fresh start with this as my foundation." (3:200–201)

Tsutomu's turning point hinges on the abandonment of his romanticized vision of nature and a symbolic return to the realities of contemporary human life. The basis for his newfound "psychic lifeline" is open acknowledgment and acceptance of the social nature of his physical environment, an insight that enables him to alter his psychological orientation from death and the nonhuman past toward life and a future of renewed social engagement.

As Tsutomu approaches the Hake house toward the end of his condensed formulative journey, his thoughts come full circle. Now, instead of simply trusting in their vow because it had come from Michiko's lips, he has come to the point where he can embrace it as his own existential ideal: "There probably is meaning in that silly vow. Given that society cannot be changed, the path toward life probably begins by setting one's own heart firmly in such a way. And if that's the only path there is, then it can't be helped, can it? I've been forsaken by her because of that stupid mistake I made, but it's not too late for reform. I'll show her I can honor my vow" (3:201).

As will be shown in the next section, even as Tsutomu negotiates a path toward recovery and renewal, Michiko suffers a traumatic desymbolization experience that culminates in suicide. Indeed, the climactic scene of the novel takes place immediately after Tsutomu reaches the Hake house. And, as indicated earlier, the domestic stage has been set for tragedy. Tsutomu's thoughts about and reactions to what he witnesses upon slipping through the back gate make it painfully clear that a crucial dimension of his traumatic war experience has been neglected.

Michiko's Sacrifice

Michiko is portrayed as a sheltered, "old world" woman committed to maintaining integrity by adhering to social expectation. Even though society's rules are restrictive, and biased against women, she nonetheless accepts them as the ground of her being. She steadfastly resists succumbing to the immoral postwar behavior that Akiyama, Ono, Tomiko, and Tsutomu engage in. Indeed, she is spiritually and emotionally wounded by their wanton conduct. What also distinguishes her from them is her capacity to have genuine concern for others and take personal responsibility for the deteriorated state of human relations among members of the extended Hake family.

Michiko is introduced as an unfortunate survivor. When the main action of the novel begins, she is sole heir to the family legacy: her two older brothers died after dissipating themselves in their youth, her mother was killed in an Allied air raid, and her father died of a heart attack the year after surrender. Michiko's response to her father's death provides a sharp contrast to Tsutomu's reaction to the loss of his father:

> Michiko cried and cried. She realized anew just how much her life had depended on her father. At the same time, she was probably aware of how little she had relied on Akiyama. Of all her scattered relatives, there wasn't a single person she could count on. Ono had his hands full with his business and wife. The only surviving family members of her military uncle who killed himself were his lowborn second wife and young child. Even before his death they had had little to do with one another. Only the son he had with his first wife had continued to come to the Hake house through the years. But there had been no word from him since he had been drafted out of university in 1943 and sent to the Burma front.
>
> Michiko felt completely alone. She wasn't sure if she'd be able to bear her isolation and go on living. Death exaggerates one's thinking, but the fact remained that the entirety of her life up to that point had been spent in her father's [protective] shadow. (3:17–18)

A fundamental aspect of Michiko's character is revealed in her relationship with and reaction to her brothers' deaths. Even after coming of age, she ignored the interest shown by her school peers and devoted herself wholly to her siblings. She naturally doted on Akiyama after marrying him when she was eighteen. Her feelings for her brothers, Akiyama, and Tsutomu were similar. Michiko needed an object for her love, but the love she felt and expressed was for the most part unrelated to passion. She reacted as follows to the loss of her brothers some three years after her marriage: "Somehow she felt that all the people she devoted herself to died. The thought suddenly occurred to her that perhaps it wasn't wise to love her husband too much" (3:8).

It was clearly in Michiko's nature to feel personally responsible for others. This disposition, in fact, is an essential part of her ethical sensibility. Unlike her counterparts, who by and large thought and acted solely in their own interests, Michiko was always painfully aware of the social ramifications of her behavior. Her difference from her younger cousin in this respect is highlighted in the following exchange:

> "Life is hard. As one who went to war, you should know that."
>
> "War is easy. All you have to do is preserve your own life. If things don't go well, you just die and that's the end of it."
>
> "In that case, life in everyday society is more difficult than life in war." (3:125)

The difficulty Michiko refers to stems from her awareness and acceptance of social interdependence. Unlike the battlefield, where survival egoism can and often does reign supreme, in peacetime society one is obligated to think of others as well as oneself and to make compromises in relationships.

Michiko's brothers die before they marry, and Michiko has had no children of her own. The Hake house is consequently left without a male heir. Upon the deaths of her parents, she becomes the sole inheritor of the family legacy. Her mother's thoughts on the cause of the family's misfortunes warrant special attention. While preparing the ground to build the Hake house, workmen excavating the hillside found old tombs. Taking this as an inauspicious sign, her mother insisted that construction be halted and they build elsewhere. Old Miyaji, however, would have none of it, and simply viewed the ancient gravesites as proof that the place had always been a suitable place to live. Michiko's mother interprets the hardships and losses they subsequently suffered as the curse of the grave (*haka no tatari*). Thus, the possibility is presented at the outset of the novel that the fall of the Hake house may in large part have stemmed from disrespectful behavior toward the dead. That Michiko's father was an atheist who refused to maintain a Buddhist memorial altar at home underscores this important point (3:187).

By the time of Miyaji's death, Akiyama has already grown tired of Michiko's body and begun to consider having an affair with Tomiko. It is not long before he moves from thought to action. As a traditional Japanese wife, Michiko can live with his adultery even though she doesn't like it. The precipitating factor of her psychological breakdown is her renewed relationship with Tsutomu. Trapped in a loveless marriage with a pompous university professor hell-bent on imitating the immoral conduct of Stendhal's fictional characters, she is initially prone to seeing her genuine feelings and concern for her troubled cousin in a romantic light.

As previously noted, Michiko's affections threaten to move in a dangerous direction during their search for the headwaters of the Nogawa River. After experiencing a sudden desire to embrace him near the shrine and then hearing the name Love Hollow, she begins to think of her feelings for Tsutomu in terms of *koi* (romantic love):

> Once Michiko became aware of her love, her first impulse was to suppress it. She no longer loved her husband. Be that as it may, however, she thought

> that as a wife it should have been impossible for her to harbor such feelings for another man. All the more so given that the man in question was her cousin Tsutomu. In light of her history of treating him affectionately as she would a younger sibling, at this point she felt it was the height of unseemliness to view him as an object of feelings that could be characterized as romantic love. (3:65)

Michiko's thinking of her affection for Tsutomu as romantic love has a traumatic effect on her. Ultimately, it is not her husband's coldness, cruelty, and infidelity that initiates psychological breakdown, but her socially unacceptable relationship with her cousin:

> Ever since infancy she had lived in her father's [protective] shadow. The peaceful, proper atmosphere that Old Miyaji created as a successful man from a respectable samurai family was everything to her. She had peace of mind to the extent that everything—her marriage, her love for Tsutomu—remained within this atmosphere. This held true even after her father's death.
>
> Now, however, her awareness of the "improper love" she felt for Tsutomu abruptly threw her into turmoil. (3:66)

Although Michiko's evolving relationship with Tsutomu robs her of composure and contributes substantially toward her psychological destabilization, she is eventually able to separate her sisterly feelings from passion. Her difference in this regard is at the root of much of the suffering and failed human relationships depicted in the novel: "It is interesting that while Michiko felt the mutual affection they shared as cousins to be a barrier to romantic love, Tsutomu saw it as its very foundation. Here, readers will probably be able to see the difference in the reactions of men and women concerning the heart of one in love. While women intuitively know how to distinguish *koi* from other emotions, men are apt to indiscriminately color every emotion they feel with romantic love" (3:71–72). Although Michiko nearly succumbs to Tsutomu's physical advances at the Murayama Reservoir, she is overjoyed when he relents. The vows they later exchange simultaneously involve symbolic affirmation of their spiritual union and a rejection of physical intimacy. Just as Michiko is instinctually able to distinguish romantic love from other feelings, she also knows that having an affair would only provide fleeting carnal pleasure at the expense of everything she holds dear.

While the ground for Michiko's tragic breakdown is prepared by her ambivalent feelings for Tsutomu, the seeds of final destruction are sown by Akiyama. While Michiko and Tsutomu are able to avoid crossing the line of propriety, they are engulfed and crushed by the conduct of those who cannot. The description of the immediate economic circumstances that set Michiko's trauma into motion is introduced self-consciously by the narrator: "Have I deceived the reader by not mentioning the matter of property until developments forced me to?" (3:137). After posing this jarring rhetorical question, the narrator articulates the external conditions that precipitate Michiko's breakdown.

Upon her father's death, Michiko became sole beneficiary of the family estate. The inheritance tax on the estate, which consisted primarily of the house and property, amounted to almost half its value. After tense and strained negotiations with Akiyama and Ono, Michiko agreed to give Akiyama power of attorney in exchange for his paying this tax. When Ono's business goes bad, however, he implores her to borrow money for him against her property. Soon after learning that Ono has lost the money Michiko lent him, Akiyama leaves her for Tomiko.

After Ono loses the money, Michiko is forced to endure Akiyama's abuse daily. Before long, he tells her that since they obviously no longer love one another, she loves Tsutomu, and Tomiko intends to leave Ono, they should be "logical" and formally separate. He gives her three days to make up her mind, and just before retiring to his study, he shows her the incriminating photos of Tsutomu and Tomiko (and himself and Tomiko). True to character, Michiko feels personally responsible for both Tsutomu's and Akiyama's immoral conduct. The following thoughts pass through her mind as she gazes at the photograph of her young cousin and Tomiko: "What worried her was the criminal look in Tsutomu's eyes. Her self-restraint certainly hadn't just been for her own peace of mind; she firmly believed that it had been for the good of the entire Hake family. It was painful, however, that as a result Tsutomu had been barred from the house and driven into this precarious position" (3:175). When she considers her husband's affair with Tomiko, which threatens to destroy their family, she concludes that "it was due to her own deficiencies that her husband's feelings had strayed so far afield" (3:184).

Michiko's turning point comes on an evening in November. Her breakdown is set into motion irrevocably when she realizes that her husband has not only left her, but absconded with the deed to the property as well: "It had been her disposition since marrying to shield her husband from the superior samurai airs put on by her father and brothers. After they died, the queen-bee instincts of a daughter who was sole heir to the family legacy led her to overlook her husband's adultery. Now that she had lost her property, she was deprived of the very meaning of her existence" (3:186–187). Thus, at the same time that Tsutomu is reestablishing his psychic lifeline on a new basis, Michiko is losing the foundations of her own. And, while Tsutomu finds a means of bringing symbolic meaning back into his life, Michiko discovers a way to make her unnatural death meaningful.

The narrator identifies closely with Michiko as she enters a condition of desymbolization and deadness:

> To Michiko, everything had now come to an end.
>
> The November rains fell through the night. The droplets hitting the old eaves leaked though the broken gutters and made for a strange concert that closed the old Hake house off from the world.
>
> Michiko walked alone from room to room. The familiar walls, the ceiling, the furniture so closely associated in her mind with her dead father—all were damp and dreary, and struck her as repugnant. She felt she had known this feeling from long before. Indeed, she realized that this had been the constant undercurrent of her life at the Hake house, which from childhood had seemed so happy and complete on the surface. Old Miyaji's logical life plan, too, had stagnated and fallen into decay over the years.
>
> Since he was an atheist, he didn't maintain a Buddhist altar in the house. So when she missed him, she would sit at the rosewood desk he always used before he died. Akiyama had used this same desk to write letters and the like, and now that he was gone she thought of him, too, as she sat before it. She had stopped loving him long before, but she had continued to protect him as part of the Hake household. His being a scholar was good social currency, and at her age it provided her with the most appropriate qualifications to be a "wife." Now that her husband was gone, she realized how comfortable she had been with this role. (3:187–188)

Michiko's thoughts increasingly drift toward suicide. When she recalls that Akiyama had asked their lawyer whether his power of attorney would continue to be in effect in the event of her death, she looks up the relevant clause in the new civil code and discovers that if she makes a will before dying she can leave two-thirds of her inheritance to whomever she chooses. After passing the rainy night contemplating death, she composes her last will and testament at dawn, then walks to Ono's house and entrusts it to him.

As Michiko makes her way toward the cemetery to pay a last visit to the family plots, the narrative perspective noticeably begins to withdraw from her like a movie camera pulling back from a close-up to a wide-angle view. This significant change in perspective is first apparent in the following passage:

> As she left Ono's house, crossed the Nogawa River, and hurried toward the Tama Cemetery where the spirits of her parents and siblings rested, it was unclear whether Michiko had firmly decided to kill herself or not. People can't definitively resolve to take such actions ahead of time. Many have reasons for killing themselves, and they frequently resolve to end their lives. Whether they actually carry their decision through or not, however, usually depends on contingencies of the moment. (3:192)

At this critical juncture, Ōoka introduces insights from his own battlefield experience. His main point here is that chance is the determinate factor in suicide. As the next section will show, to the extent that Ōoka shifts the focus of attention to what might be called the existential structure of suicide, he distances himself from identification and empathy with his female protagonist.

The description of Michiko's visit to the Tama Cemetery is the last to be presented from her point of view in any sustained manner. Upon reaching the family gravestones, she crouches, lifts a cover, gazes into the hollow containing the funerary urns, and thinks how much better it will be to join them than to continue enduring her present anguish. She thereupon implores her father's spirit for guidance. And, although the grave remains silent, she recalls the words he once spoke to her: "When I was a child, Japanese still killed themselves by cutting open their abdomens. Christianity proscribed suicide because masters would have suffered great losses if their slaves were allowed to kill themselves. Confucianism contains no such nonsense. Killing oneself when one's death has value and meaning—this is the great deed of a man of virtue. The traditional suicide performed in our country was the natural outgrowth of Confucianism" (3:194). Her father's thoughts on meaningful self-sacrifice have profound implications not only to Michiko's subsequent conduct, but also to that of those who died in and survived the Pacific War. The crux of the matter is *meaning*—the meaning of death or survival in the context of defeat.

As with Tsutomu's determination to never again be party to the destruction of the social web and his thoughts on his dying comrade's final request, one senses great anxiety in Ōoka's treatment of Michiko's suicide. If those killed in the war died for hearth and home, then it can be said that in sacrificing herself for the good of the extended Hake family, Michiko is carrying on their dying spirit. Michiko decides to kill herself after recalling her father's creed. Her subsequent act, however, is not only one of sustaining personal integrity: it is undertaken with the intention of counteracting evil (Akiyama's scheme to sell the house and use the money to start a new life with Tomiko), repairing the damaged social fabric (without the money, Akiyama's plans will be frustrated, and Tomiko will return to Ono), and supporting her poverty-stricken cousins (upon her death Tsutomu and Ono will each receive a one-third share of the estate). Michiko's suicide is thus a symbolic act of self-sacrifice in the interest of rectifying on the microcosmic level the decadence and depravity widespread in postwar society. As such, it warrants serious consideration as a noble act:

> At the very end, the vision of living happily with Tsutomu came to mind, but Michiko dismissed it. "That would be tantamount to following the same bestial path as Akiyama and Tomiko. Be that as it may, he was a boy prone to do things with Tomiko like wrapping his arm around her shoulder. That's it. If I leave my estate to him, even he will probably come to his senses." Concluding that she had to kill herself, Michiko left her father's grave.
>
> The autumn foliage surrounding the cemetery began to transform. She felt that everything was burning bright red and pressing in on her, and she could barely make out the path before her. (3:194–195)

Impaired Mourning

Tsutomu's turn toward life and Michiko's turn toward death occur contemporaneously. The divergent directions of these opposing psychological movements prepare the way for the tragedy that brings the novel to a close. While Ōoka seems to make good formulative progress in the early part of *Lady Musashino,* his preoccupation with chance, the impersonal dynamics of modern tragedy, and unresolved issues surrounding his relationship as a survivor to the dead and dying limited the extent to which he could identify with, empathize with, and mourn for Michiko as she took anguished leave of this life. His treatment of the climactic scenes that unfold on the domestic stage behind the Hake house and in an interior bedroom indicate that the specter of impending death symbolically reactivates the traumatic past, brings on psychic numbing, and seriously threatens all that had previously been gained. The novel ends literally for Michiko where it began symbolically for Tsutomu—with separation, disintegration, and death.[12]

The dramatic scene of Michiko's suicide preparations opens with a reenactment of Tsutomu's initial postwar approach to the Hake house. With a single minor exception, her actions on the verandah are related from Tsutomu's remote point of view. Significantly, as he stealthily makes his way toward the verandah, he is thinking and acting as if he were back on the battlefield:

> Tsutomu intended to climb over the hedge if the back gate was locked, but it opened unexpectedly as soon as he pushed it. "Now, that's odd—it was locked last time. Why would it be unlatched now? I'll have to ponder that one later."
>
> Once again, he went to the same cluster of Japanese rosebushes above the Hake spring he had crouched behind that afternoon in June. Since the leaves had fallen and the bushes were little but naked branches, he had to adopt the low-profile posture of a soldier to conceal himself. (3:201–202)

From his secret hiding place, Tsutomu sees Michiko on the verandah in her finest kimono and abstractly wonders if she's about to go out. He momentarily considers emerging before her but restrains himself upon recalling their vows, which by now have become his "one and only reason for living" (3:202).

Tsutomu cannot internalize or comprehend the scene unfolding before him. Like a psychically numbed soldier detachedly watching a comrade die, he regards Michiko's actions from a safe physical and emotional distance through uncomprehending eyes: "What's that white powder she's putting into the cup? There's quite a bit of it. Now, she's pouring cider in and it's foaming up. It appears to be some kind of medicine. But why on earth would she be thinking of drinking such a thing?" (3:202). Michiko stands and looks up toward the back gate just before drinking the deadly mixture. The following is the last important passage to be presented from her perspective: "Thinking 'this is the end,' Michiko gazed out toward the place Tsutomu had once appeared above the spring. After deciding to kill herself and leave her inheritance to him, she had intentionally unlocked the back gate" (3:203).

This scene effectively marks Michiko's abandonment. The Hake stage has been set for tragedy, and Tsutomu, the sole character marginally capable of empathy and compassion, departs without witnessing the final act:

> If he had only had the good fortune of guessing the nature of the substance she was dissolving in the cider, he surely would have run down to her immediately despite his vow not to come until called. If so, they might have had an opportunity to savor, if for [only] a moment, a happiness neither had dreamed of.
>
> Or perhaps they would have been able to do what had once crossed his mind, and die together.
>
> Tsutomu, however, departed in haste to avoid being defeated by the look in her eyes. Thus does fate ceaselessly weave the drama of human life, each in accordance with a person's own personal necessity. (3:203)

As he composed *Lady Musashino,* Ōoka was clearly better able to orchestrate tragedy than he was to merge psychologically and empathize with the woman inextricably caught up in it. Michiko's lonely preparations for death are initially regarded from Tsutomu's distanced, self-absorbed, and uncomprehending point of view. After his premature departure, the locus of narrative concern abruptly shifts to the metaphysical workings of fate. This shift can be understood as a form of defensive rationalization. Reluctant to relate to Michiko on a more personal, emotionally engaged level, Ōoka occupies himself with the impersonal circumstances that inexorably force Michiko and Tsutomu toward their respective tragedies. And since it is, strictly speaking, Ōoka himself weaving the drama of their lives, his narrative commentary on these matters is highly ironic.

Five years after undergoing his own battlefield trauma, Ōoka was apparently still loath to identify too closely with those fated to die painful, untimely deaths. Like his narrator and central male protagonists, Ōoka gingerly approaches Michiko's death and dying from without rather than from within. And while this affords him temporary protection from deep-seated feelings of death guilt and self-recrimination, siding with Tsutomu and discoursing on the impersonal workings of fate ultimately preclude the emotional opening up and empathy prerequisite to productively working through such traumatic loss.

Ōoka's treatment of the final interior scene is clearly marked by impaired mourning. For analytic purposes, it can be divided into three interrelated parts. Each in a sense involves a crucial aspect of Ōoka's ongoing struggle to come to terms with his traumatic battlefield experience—the anxiety of responsibility, the anxious denial of responsibility, and the inability to mourn. The first part is performed unconsciously by Michiko. From the time she begins to speak out deliriously until the moment of her death, she is psychically disintegrated and on the brink of insanity. As with her suicide preparations, her final moments are not treated from her perspective, but via the consciousness of another (Akiyama). Through an imaginary dialogue she has with Tsutomu, however, she is able to give uninhibited expression to the terribly conflicted but symbolically significant "movements of her heart." Akiyama plays the second important role in this climactic scene. Significantly, the narrative focus is not so much on Michiko as it is on her despicable, self-absorbed husband. Akiyama's reactions to and thoughts about his dying wife are those of an arrogant survivor anxiously maneuvering to ward off rising feelings of guilt and self-reproach. And the final integral part is taken by the narrator himself, who assays Michiko's death from a conspicuously aloof, philosophical position.

After failing both to sell the Hake house and to make a go of his relationship with Tomiko, Akiyama returns home to find Michiko asleep on the bed wearing her finest kimono. Her face, which is lightly powdered, shows traces of tears extending from the corners of her eyes down to her earlobes. When Akiyama realizes she has taken an overdose, he hurries to Ono's house and has him call a doctor. After examining her, the physician confidently declares that she will survive, and that the first sign of recovery will be delirious speech. Several hours after everyone else has departed, Akiyama hears deep sounds rising up from her throat. He thinks they sound like the "voice of her heart" and the "wail of a ghost" (3:222). The significance of this cannot be overemphasized. As in the first scene of sacrifice, in the hotel near the Murayama Reservoir, the reference to the wail of ghosts serves to link Michiko with the war dead.

Toward dawn, Michiko begins to call out tearfully for Tsutomu. Ōoka describes her psychic condition during the final moments of her life as follows: "Tears poured forth ceaselessly from her unseeing eyes and dampened her hair. Bereft of will and reason, only her heart still lived within her. Her heart was filled with love and jealousy, and it was being torn apart by despair" (3:224). Michiko is psychically disintegrated and near madness as she converses with an imaginary Tsutomu. The movements of her heart and soul that are reflected in her speech, however, reveal a woman whose thoughts and feelings are wholly directed toward another's well-being.

The first intelligible word Michiko utters is "Tomuchan," Tsutomu's childhood nickname. After telling him that she has left everything to him, she demands that he put an end to his immoral behavior. She then alternately scolds and forgives him in an affectionate, motherly fashion:

> "Tomuchan, you're a fool. The way you wear your army surplus clothes and act so important and boastful. It's foolish. What's so great about having gone to war? . . . You act so important. It's okay, though, those clothes."
>
> Michiko smiled happily for a time before again melting into tears.
>
> "It's hopeless for me. I must die. If I don't I won't be able to make you happy. What? What's that you say? You said let's go together. Fool. I know where I'm bound. The medicine's so bitter. Even mixing it with cider doesn't help. It's settled to the bottom of the cup. I have to drink this bitter, bitter mixture. Do you understand?" (3:223)

Toward the end of this feverish flow of emotion, Michiko demands that Tsutomu go on living and expresses her willingness to sacrifice herself to prevent him from having an affair with Tomiko: "No, you mustn't. Not you. You must live. Life is important. But no, you can't do that with Tomiko. It's simply not okay to do that with another man's wife. If you must—then do it to me. It's all over for me, so it doesn't matter what happens to my body. No, not like that. More gently. No, not that . . . oh, what does it matter. It no longer matters what becomes of this body of mine. I'll be dying anyway. No, not with Tomiko" (3:224). It is important to note here that Michiko's utterances do not contain the faintest hint of lust or sexual desire. Like her decision to end her life, offering up her body to Tsutomu is an expression of her determination to sacrifice herself in an effort to contain the senseless passions that threaten to destroy the extended Hake family.

When Michiko realizes that she is still alive, she implores Tsutomu to bring her more sleeping medicine. Her next-to-last words are direct expressions of unadulterated suffering and despair: "It hurts. It hurts so bad. Ah, I can't bear it, I can't stand this any longer. I don't want to, I've had all I can take" (3:226). The last thing to pass her lips is a cry for help. As with many soldiers at the front, however, Michiko's fate in *Lady Musashino* is to have her desperate pleas go unanswered.

Like Tamura at the end of *Fires on the Plain,* Michiko is as psychologically cut off from those around her as she is consumed by the anxiety of responsibility and the struggles to deliver her own message from the realm of the dead. In contrast to Tamura, who is unable to directly vocalize his message of fundamental human interconnectedness, Michiko is able to give full voice to her deep and abiding love and concern for Tsutomu. While her sacrifice may not in the long run bring about the renewal of human relations she hopes for, it nonetheless has great symbolic import. Like the sacrifices made by innumerable soldiers on battlefields throughout China, Southeast Asia, and the Pacific, Michiko's act is selfless and altruistic. In this sense, she acts in the same spirit as her military counterparts who laid down their lives as much in defense of hearth and home as for abstract concepts such as the godlike emperor, Imperial Japan, or the Greater East Asia Co-prosperity Sphere.

Tragically, as Michiko agonizes to deliver her message of interpersonal responsibility and revitalizing self-sacrifice, the only person in attendance is constitutionally incapable of listening sympathetically or accepting what she has to say. Michiko's final scene of death and dying is narrated almost exclusively from Akiyama's jaundiced perspective. The narrator describes his initial reaction to the realization that his wife has taken an overdose of sleeping medicine as follows: "As Akiyama stood in the middle of the room looking down at Michiko's sleeping face, he was taken by despair when he thought, 'It's always been like this, she's always been a woman who lived in her best clothes'" (3:220). An accurate reflection of her inner purity, decency, and integrity, Michiko's external appearance serves to bring out Akiyama's inner degeneracy.

The sharp contrast between husband and wife is further emphasized as Michiko exposes her true inner self. While his estranged wife is absorbed with painful thoughts of the well-being of another, Akiyama is consumed with thoughts solely of himself. After hearing her tell Tsutomu that she has left everything to him, Akiyama remembers the deed he had taken and returns it to its proper place. While the movements of her throat as she reenacts drinking the bitter mixture elicit a kind of biological sympathy and momentarily make him feel as if he were suffocating, he immediately maneuvers to deny personal responsibility and shift blame onto Tsutomu: "This has nothing to do with me. It's all because of him" (3:223).

Michiko subsequently calls out Tsutomu's name loudly over and over and, although Akiyama takes her in his arms and tells her he is the one she wants, he only does so to calm her down so the neighbors won't overhear her. As she continues to call out Tsutomu's name, Akiyama grinds his teeth, roughly shoves her away, and puts a pillow into her frantically searching arms. And when it finally becomes clear that she will not recover, he moves to push all blame away from himself: "When Akiyama realized that in the eyes of society he would be branded a man who drove his wife to suicide by pursuing his own pleasures, he hated her. 'Whatever people might say, she died because of *him.* I never dreamed that picture would have had such a profound effect on her. That was wrong. Be that as it may, it's not because of me that she's dying'" (3:225–226). Instead of guilt, self-reproach, sympathy, empathy, or sadness, Akiyama is consumed with hatred as his wife dies in agony before his eyes. The narrator subsequently condemns him for his lack of humanity:

> The last thing to pass through Michiko's lips was "Help me!" Akiyama shuddered when he heard the natural tone with which she made this utterance.
>
> Even then he was convinced that she died because of Tsutomu. He didn't realize that she killed herself because he abandoned her. This professor, so taken up with his literary lecture topics, was beyond the pale of humanity. (3:226)

The consistent focus on and portrayal of Akiyama during Michiko's death scene make it clear that at this stage in his formulative journey, Ōoka was still more deeply concerned with the inhumanity of men such as Akiyama than with Michiko's humanity. Akiyama is portrayed as an incarnation of arrogant, irresponsible, and destructive egoism. Like Tamura, he refuses to acknowledge the extent to which his own conduct contributed to the breakdown of human relations and death. In this sense, Akiyama is the antithesis of Michiko, a man doomed, perhaps, to remain outside or at best on the margins of civilized society.

The narrator takes the last important role in this dramatic scene of death and dying. As with her suicide preparations, Michiko's death is regarded with striking detachment:

> Ono and [his daughter] Yukiko finally arrived. Michiko continued to call out Tsutomu's name with everything she had. Her voice gradually weakened. Then she began to grope about near her chest as if to straighten her collar.
>
> "It hurts, it hurts so bad. Ah, I can't bear it. I can't stand this any longer. I don't want to, I've had all I can take."
>
> It was pure accident that Michiko's suicide attempt resulted in death. In the twentieth century, tragedy depends on accident.
>
> Ono was crying. He faced Michiko, whose breathing gradually slowed, and shouted, "You're terrible! How could you end your life so selfishly? Didn't you ever stop to think that by killing yourself, you'd also be killing those who love you?" (3:226)

Michiko's literary fate in *Lady Musashino* is to suffer and die in psychological isolation without receiving compassion, empathy, or understanding from those closest to her. As she is dying, her husband is despising her and her older cousin is taxing her for being selfish.

On the threshold of death, moreover, she seems to be abandoned by narrator and author as well. The jarring shift from her direct expressions of anguish to the nonhuman dynamics of modern tragedy can be seen as a defensive rationalization aimed at evading the complex emotions elicited by death and dying. As he wrote *Lady Musashino,* Ōoka was clearly still obsessed with chance, the factor he took to be the crux of both his traumatic encounter with the enemy and his failed suicide. In the novel, accident—synonymous in Ōoka's lexicon with chance—is proffered as the cause of Michiko's tragedy. In fact, Ōoka structured the work so that the determinant factor of her death was not overdose, but a congenital heart weakness. Michiko would have survived if not for this weakness. Therefore, Ōoka asserts through his narrator, her death was an accident, her tragedy a direct consequence of a random physical defect. Like his defensive rationalizations concerning the deaths of his comrades, this formulation fails to take full stock of the interpersonal, societal forces that contributed substantially to her breakdown, despair, and suicide.

Ōoka's preoccupation with the impersonal structure of modern tragedy leaves little room for the emotional responses its occurrence normally elicits.[13] While he could openly condemn Akiyama for his egoism, irresponsibility, and inhumanity, he didn't yet have access to the psychic resources he needed to openly identify and empathize with Michiko, to mourn or memorialize her loss. Ōoka returned from the Philippines with a poignant sense of the tragic, but eight years would elapse after writing *Lady Musashino* before his heart could go out to the individuals whose unnatural, premature deaths were brought about by forces largely beyond their control.

Emotional Turning Point

Ōoka reached a crucial watershed in his literary journey of survivor formulation in 1958. At the heart of this pivotal change was the newfound capacity to acknowledge, open himself up emotionally to, and empathize with his fallen comrades. Ōoka's emotional receptivity toward those he had theretofore anxiously maneuvered to push away ultimately enabled him to take up a survivor mission some eight years later.

Ōoka describes the emotional turning-point experience he had between January 13 and 20 in his "Writer's Diary."[14] It was surely no coincidence that this happened about the time of the anniversary of the virtual annihilation of Nishiya Company. His breakthrough process had two stages, both triggered by news of the *Gingamaru,* a training vessel to be dispatched to the Philippines to collect the remains of the war dead. In his diary entry for January 13, Ōoka writes that he was shocked (*shokku*) upon reading in the evening paper that the ship was scheduled to drop anchor near San Jose. This wholly unanticipated reminder of his dead comrades threw Ōoka into a state of turmoil that found expression in his behavior and the feverish thoughts coursing through his mind.

Ōoka drank heavily that night, and at one point was surprised to hear himself suddenly declare, "Father's going to the Philippines, too!" (15:119). Realizing that it would be impossible to make all the necessary arrangements to join the mission in a week's time, he considered flying to Manila and chartering a plane to take him on to Mindoro. In the following passage, he records the flood of thoughts and emotions unleashed by news of the *Gingamaru:*

> I'll have to get the address of the headquarters of the organization in charge of collecting the remains of the war dead from a newspaper somewhere. And I'll go to the Ministry of Foreign Affairs and see if they'll issue me a passport. I don't know if this will work out or not, but I must give it a try.
>
> Why didn't they invite me? I know where the men who died in San Jose are buried. I never imagined the *Gingamaru* would visit such an insignificant battlefield.
>
> I want to fall to the ground in San Jose and see if I can sob with abandon. If there are any people left who know how stoically we endured our time there, I'll meet with them. That is something I'm simply unable to convey to others. Come to think of it, I've probably forgotten myself. The only way to remember is to go back again. (15:120)

Ōoka specifies three main reasons for wanting to return to Mindoro. The first is that he knew where the remains of his comrades could be found. While he explicitly refers only to those buried in San Jose, he also knew where most of his comrades perished in the Rutay Highlands. His second motivation is the "fervent desire" to take part in the memorial service (*ireisai*) scheduled for February 28. Finally, he wants to see whether he is capable of uninhibited grieving. Ōoka seems to have been worried that he may already have put off mourning for too long. The lines immediately following the passage introduced above, however, make it clear that this was not the case: "The drunker I got, the more agitated my thoughts became. In time, the fatigue of my day of golf caught up with me, and I retired for the evening. I lay down and fell asleep wiping my tears with the edge of my bedsheets" (15:120). In his diary entry for the next day, Ōoka describes awaking with a hangover. Upon thinking more calmly and rationally he realizes that it will be impossible for him to join the mission.

The second stage of Ōoka's emotional turning-point experience, too, is provoked by news of the *Gingamaru.* He is stunned anew upon seeing footage on the evening news broadcast showing bereaved family members openly lamenting on the pier as the *Gingamaru* sets sail for the South Seas. When the broadcast ends, he retires to his study and composes a long requiem (*chinkonka*) addressed directly to the spirits of his fallen comrades. It opens as follows:

> *Listen up everybody!*
> *Itō, Shindō, Arai, Kuriyakawa, Ichiki, Hirayama, the other Itō;*

All you others whose names I've forgotten, all you friends
who died in San Jose—
Commander Nishiya, Platoon Leader Inoue,
Sergeant Ogasawara, Sergeant Nobe.
I report that the training vessel Gingamaru *left Tokyo today*
to collect your remains.
I report that today, after thirteen years, there are still
women crying for you on the pier.
There are people who still remember you,
you who were reduced to bones so long ago.
Even though they will not be able to reach your remains
in the mountains, bushes, or below ground,
A service will be held in San Jose.
Monks will recite sutras, pick up stones in San Jose,
bring them back,
And give them to your mothers and fathers, your brothers,
sisters, and children.
I pray for the monks to recite long sutras;
I pray for them to take only the exact number of stones.
(15:123–124)

After reporting on the *Gingamaru*'s departure and objectives, Ōoka turns to his own desire to take part in the mission and apologizes for being unable to do so. In explaining why he can't, he expresses the shame he feels as a burdened survivor. He begins by saying that while his return from the front was but "halfhearted," he nonetheless now has work that requires him to remain in country. He goes on to say, "It is shameful for me to be writing in such a way to dispel my gloom. This, however, is far from the only thing I am ashamed of" (15:124). Although Ōoka refrains from elaborating on the source of his shame, it is probably safe to assume that it had to do with what he did and failed to do at the front in the interest of personal survival (fight and die for his country) and his postwar behavior (rejecting, scapegoating, and forgetting his comrades).

As when he went to bed after his initial shock a week before, Ōoka was grieving as he composed his requiem. This is clear from the beginning and end of the poem. The twenty-eighth and twenty-ninth lines read as follows:

"Anyway, as I sit [writing] here at my desk tonight / Large teardrops fall one after another" (15:124–125). And his requiem closes shortly after these heartfelt lines:

> *When it was announced that the* Gingamaru *would depart,*
> *All your loved ones rushed to the pier,*
> *And cried there until the ship faded from view.*
> *While I restrain my desire to sob with abandon,*
> *I, too, have been softly weeping as I composed these verses.* (15:132)

Ōoka not only gives open expression to his grief in this elegiac poem, but also starts to identify with his fallen comrades to an unprecedented degree. He begins this, his first extended postwar effort to merge psychologically and emotionally with the war dead, by voicing the following realization:

> *No one [else] can understand how I feel.*
> *After all, I go on living in shame.*
> *I finally realized today, this very moment,*
> *that only you can understand.*
> *You, however, are but bones,*
> *Scattered over the ground, in the bushes.*
> *Bones have no ears,*
> *So they cannot hear; and even if they could,*
> *They have no mouths,*
> *No way to say "We know."* (15:124)

With these lines, Ōoka conveys his desire to commune directly with the spirits of his dead comrades. After accepting that it will be impossible to resolve his predicament by receiving a special message of understanding and forgiveness from them, he seems to realize that he must reach out to them himself. He initially does so by recalling their occupation of San Jose in a more honest, understanding, and sympathetic way:

> *Listen to me everyone.*
> *That indeed was an experience we and only we can understand.*

We were all weak soldiers, and the tides of war
had turned against us.
Upon reaching this place so far from home,
We were, in our heart of hearts, scared to death.
But we resigned ourselves to the situation.
We humbly intended to go down fighting, giving our all
Like true soldiers.
This in mind, we lost ourselves in fatigue duty;
Carrying baskets, leading water buffalo,
Under the scorching Philippine sun.
We never mentioned it,
but we were all thinking the same thing. (15:125)

Rather than dwelling on their incorrigible middle-class and survival egoism, Ōoka now asserts that even though the resolve went unspoken, they all harbored the same noble intention of sacrificing themselves. Thirteen years after the war, he reached the point where he could fondly recall the men in Nishiya Company as true brothers-in-arms.

After reassessing his comrades' intentions in this way, Ōoka recollects the battlefield reality that posed the most serious challenge to formulation—their premature, seemingly pointless deaths. In the following verses, he imagines how they prepared for the end, what they looked like at the moment of their deaths, and what became of their mortal remains afterward:

As feared, we were unable to resist the Americans when they
landed,
And we were scattered into the hills.
None among us had the good fortune of marrying the chief's
daughter.
We were shot to death and beaten to death;
We fell victim to malaria, we starved to death.
Kuriyakawa probably died with lips twisted, as was his way.
Shindō probably died with his glasses perched as usual on his
aquiline nose.
If Itō's large eyes were closed when he died,

He wouldn't have looked like himself.
Death itself, however, comes in an instant.
Did Shindō remove his shoes before dying?
Did he remove his gaiters as I did?
Legs splayed out heavily before him,
Bare feet in the grass;
Did the discoloration begin from the ankles?
Flesh consumed by maggots, bones exposed.
Did they drift away with the flowing waters? (15:125–126)

While identifying intimately with his comrades in this way, Ōoka is still reluctant to imagine what they might have been thinking and feeling as they approached and met their tragic ends. He surely knew that many of his comrades probably died in psychological torment and physical agony. In fact, their deaths occurred under the precise conditions believed to produce homeless spirits and angry ghosts (*onryō*). An important part of the weighty burdens Ōoka bore as a survivor concerned his budding awareness of the need to do something to put their troubled spirits to rest. The first practical steps in this process involve collecting their remains, giving them a proper memorial service, symbolically returning their spirits home, and honoring them. These, in fact, were the expressed aims of the *Gingamaru:*

The Gingamaru *has been sent to collect your bones.*
Try though they might, however, they'll be unable
to reach the remains in the mountains,
And will return with stones gathered only in San Jose.
But you will be able to return home, if only in form.
It's better to return than not to.
So thinking, your survivors made their impassioned petitions,
And cried for you on the pier.
Think of this, and be happy.
Return home and sit with pride at the Buddhist altar.
(15:126–127)

Recalling his fallen comrades with understanding and compassion, identifying with them, and beginning the work of mourning subsequently enabled Ōoka to act on his anxiety of responsibility in such a way as to convert static to animating forms of guilt. And, as previously mentioned, appropriate blaming was integral to this vitalizing process. Toward the end of his requiem, Ōoka takes an important step in this direction by enlisting the support of the spirits of the war dead to join him on a newly conceived crusade:

I have a request to make.
Transform into ghosts,
And appear before those
who once again seek to profit
from the despicable work of soldiers,
Even now, thirteen years after we were subjected to such bitter experiences.
I must ask this of you:
Because I live but halfheartedly,
And have no supernatural powers of my own. (15:127)

The full extent of the anxiety of responsibility Ōoka felt as he composed this impassioned requiem is palpable in the final lines concerning his plea for spiritual assistance:

I am doing all I can,
But regrettably, I am powerless.
Powerless, just as we were then,
When we carried those baskets,
Thirteen years ago in San Jose.
Even as ghosts, you may have no influence.
Nevertheless, we must try anything and everything.
Shouldn't we work together tirelessly?
We don't want our children and grandchildren
To suffer as we did, do we?!
Hear me, all of you! (15:130)

Thus does Ōoka come full circle in his relationship with his fallen comrades—from anxious rejection and condemnation to spiritually joining forces with them to oppose the greater forces responsible for war (and defeat). And, in so doing, he succeeds in moving from static to animating forms of guilt, from passivity toward survivor mission.

Ōoka closes his requiem with a moving description of a burial. That he could openly face and describe this excruciating frontline experience, one conspicuously absent from previous writings about the war, is a good indication of the substantial progress he made toward reconciling his relationship as a survivor with the war dead:

> *Hey, little Arai.*
> *You died before the Americans arrived.*
> *Didn't we dig your grave?*
> *Didn't we put a precious cigarette*
> *Between the fingers of the pale hands folded over your chest,*
> *And lower your body into the pit*
> *we dug for you with our own hands?*
> *Face Forward! Present Arms! Apply Soil!*
> *When the dirt cascaded over your face,*
> *You seemed to blink.*
> *Only your nose was barely visible.*
> *Commander Nishiya gave the order to cease and desist,*
> *Climbed down into the pit himself,*
> *And covered your face with a handkerchief.*
> *Then once again: Apply Soil!*
> *The pit was gradually filled in.*
> *We packed it down to prevent the natives from digging it up—*
> *We dared not raise a grave marker.*
> *This was twenty-five miles from San Jose.*
> Gingamaru *or not,*
> *Your remains are now in inaccessible mountains,*
> *Your bones will never be reached.* (15:131–132)

Lady Musashino and *In the Shadow of Cherry Blossoms*

In the March 8, 1958, entry of "Writer's Diary," Ōoka notes that he has just written the opening scene of a new novel called *Wind Gap* (*Fukoku*).

At the beginning of the entries for the fourteenth and sixteenth of the same month, however, he laments his inability to make any headway on the new project. This writer's block persisted for more than a month, breakthrough coming on April 16: "Informed of the suicide of my old friend, Sakamoto Mutsuko. She took an overdose sometime on the fourteenth, and arranged things so that she wouldn't be found for a full day afterward. By the time she was, it was already too late" (15:163). News of Mutsuko's suicide had a profound influence on his current literary project. As he noted two days later, "I probably can't make any progress on *Wind Gap* since there are no human beings yet. What if I imagine people walking in the gap, and add the person radical to the Chinese character for valley? Then the title would be *Fūzoku,* or *Manners.* I made up my mind. I didn't like the other title from the start. When a title changes, the story does, too. I asked *Chūō kōron* for another month's extension" (15:164). Thoughts of Sakamoto Mutsuko's life and death provided Ōoka with the impetus he needed to embark on the next important leg of his formulative journey. Significantly, the entry immediately following his decision to rename and reorient the novel briefly notes his attendance at her memorial service. Subsequently renamed and published serially between August 1958 and August 1959, *In the Shadow of Cherry Blossoms* (*Kaei*) is a moving prose requiem to his recently deceased friend.[15]

There are a number of significant parallels between Michiko and Mutsuko (Yōko in the novel). Both, in their own ways, were women who were more products of the prewar and wartime past than the contemporary postwar present. In "Writer's Diary," Ōoka recalls Mutsuko and another friend who took seriously ill about the time of her suicide: "A close friend of the deceased, Ishida Aiko, has been hospitalized after suffering a stroke, and there is little hope of recovery. It was another time when these two sat as young women at the counter of the [German] beer hall with patriotic marching songs in the air. The Ginza changed; they grew older" (15:163–164). Reflecting on Mutsuko's death, one writer suggested that Michiko in *Lady Musashino* bore a strong resemblance (*omokage*) to Mutsuko (15:163). And both ended their own lives by overdose.

The relationship of *Fires on the Plain* to "Before Capture" is essentially the same as that of *In the Shadow of Cherry Blossoms* to *Lady Musashino*—the latter of each pair of works supplemented (*ho'i*) the former. In *In the*

Shadow of Cherry Blossoms, Ōoka was able to confront and work through survivor issues that went unresolved in *Lady Musashino.* Thus, while both works center on female protagonists who suffer breakdowns ending in suicide, Ōoka's attitude toward and handling of Michiko's and Yōko's stories differ markedly.

Like the requiem Ōoka composed for his fallen comrades, *In the Shadow of Cherry Blossoms* is an elegy. The narrator consistently treats Yōko with sensitivity, understanding, empathy, and compassion. From the first line to the last line of the novella, Yōko's unfolding experience is primarily presented from *her* point of view. And even when the perspective does occasionally shift to other characters, they are the men who care for her most. Although the two most important people in her life—Matsuzaki and Takashima—are self-absorbed, irresponsible egoists, Ōoka endows them with a measure of understanding and sympathy that greatly exceeds that of their counterparts in *Lady Musashino.* Rather than dwelling on their destructive egoism and lack of humanity, Ōoka wholeheartedly devotes himself to bringing out Yōko's humanity. And rather than concerning himself with the impersonal structure and dynamics of modern tragedy, Ōoka focuses on the societal forces that combine to produce her tragic life as a marginalized, unloved, and unappreciated prostitute and mistress.

After reaching his emotional turning point with regard to his dead comrades, Ōoka was able to do for Yōko what he couldn't do for Michiko some eight years earlier—merge with her psychologically and emotionally from beginning to end and mourn and memorialize her loss. He surely had Sakamoto Mutsuko and his fallen comrades in heart and mind as he composed *In the Shadow of Cherry Blossoms.*

An Unbearably Burdened Past

Yōko was a heavily burdened survivor. She suffered repeated abandonment and betrayal in her youth, despaired and attempted suicide during the war, and survived the waves of devastating incendiary air raids that took the life of her "grandmother" and tens of thousands of other Tokyo civilians.[16] Yōko was not only severely traumatized by such experience, but also forced by circumstances to endure nearly two decades of postwar life as a bar hostess–prostitute and kept woman in the Ginza entertainment district. Like

Michiko, however, Yōko devotes herself to and sacrifices herself for those around her. She continues to endure her shameful, empty life in order to care for and support Matsuzaki and Takashima. It is only after being abandoned by the former at the outset of the novella and betrayed by the latter at the end that she brings her life of thirty-eight years to a premature end.

Yōko was born into a family of strife. She was just a year old when she was abandoned by her mother, who could no longer stand living with her abusive, alcoholic husband. Her father remarried, but her stepmother, Tetsu, could put up with him for only two years. When she left him, she took three-year-old Yōko with her. Tetsu subsequently led Yōko to believe that she was her real mother. As Tetsu struggled to start a Chinese restaurant in Tokyo, Yōko lived with her grandmother in Mishima, where she was frequently teased by neighborhood children, who called her *shirokko*. Not knowing that this was local slang for "foundling" (*hirokko*), she believed Tetsu's explanation that it meant "albino," that the children called her this because of her extraordinarily fair skin. At fourteen, Yōko learned the truth about her parentage during an argument with her stepbrother. Tetsu's betrayal added significantly to Yōko's growing sense of alienation from and distrust of people.

After a number of years in Mishima, Yōko and her grandmother joined Tetsu in Meguro. When the Chinese restaurant failed, Yōko had to quit school and go to work. She initially worked in a department-store cafeteria, but soon "graduated" to a German beer hall. And it wasn't long after that that she became a Ginza bar hostess. In time, the middle-aged president of a steel company took an interest in her and set her and Tetsu up in their own establishment. This all prepared the ground for her next major betrayal. Despite the man's repeated promises to be faithful, Yōko learns that he has not only fallen for another hostess, but also set her up with a bar as well. This development drives her to attempt suicide: "Yōko had dreamed of death since she was a young girl, but when her life became rife with trouble, she truly felt like ending it" (5:8). She subsequently takes an overdose, but is discovered in time to be saved. She is nursed back to health by a novelist she met about the time of her patron's infidelity, and moves into an Ōimachi apartment as his mistress after her grandmother is killed during the Allied air raid that destroyed the family home in Meguro as well.

Toward the end of her tragic, lonely, and shame-filled life alternating between being a bar hostess and kept woman, Yōko meets Matsuzaki, a married professor of Western art who, after nursing her back to health after she collapses with pneumonia, sets her up in an Akasaka apartment. Except for fleeting moments in her youth when she lived with her grandmother, the three years she spends with him are the best of her short life. While unbearably lonely during the interminable hours of his absence, Yōko is for a time able to avoid the degradation of the backstreet Ginza bar scene. It is thus telling that the novella opens at the point where Matsuzaki is leaving her. As when Akiyama left Michiko, abandonment—a psychological equivalent of death—is the precipitating factor of Yōko's breakdown.

While far from perfect, Matsuzaki and Takashima are endowed with the capacity to understand and to a certain extent sympathize with Yōko. The foundation of their insight into her character is their appreciation of the "dark shadows" of her unbearably burdened past:

> Matsuzaki's interpretation went as follows: When Yōko learned at age fourteen that she was not tied by blood to Tetsu, she became a child who never spoke except with her grandmother. And the painful awareness of being an outsider wasn't just something that made her withdraw into herself; she also believed that it was the main reason all the love she had directed toward Tetsu had been betrayed, and came to hate her.
>
> Matsuzaki also thought that the pleasure she had come to find in tormenting and debasing herself had its origins in this animosity. Before that bitter experience, there had been no distinction in her mind between Tetsu and her real mother. The habit she developed about that time of looking back on her past and ruminating on her unhappiness continued to the present day. (5:14–15)

Matsuzaki knows that the betrayal Yōko suffered early in life substantially shaped who she was. It was fitting that she would blame Tetsu; but since their sudden estrangement stemmed from her own altered awareness of their relationship, she couldn't help but condemn and despise herself at the same time. Yōko, like Michiko, tends to take personal responsibility for the tragedies that befall her and others.

Further access to Matsuzaki's thinking about Yōko's character and the way it was shaped by her troubled past is provided in a later passage:

> From the start, however, Matsuzaki was attracted by Yōko's innocence and her unrestrained, blowsy emotions. It was as if Yōko's kindheartedness had

been crystallized in childhood. Perhaps it came from being raised by her grandmother. To the present day, it continued to lend a young girl's artlessness to her facial expressions and behavior.

Even at thirty, Yōko hadn't had the slightest idea how to open a postal bank account. He himself had put a passbook in her hands for the first time. She had had no time to grow up. She had gone directly from the hands of her grandmother to the center of the Ginza, there to be covered by one man after another. Matsuzaki thought men constantly appeared at her door because they realized that when they were with her they could come into contact with this kindness. And Yōko was constitutionally incapable of turning anyone away. (5:18)

Matsuzaki's deep understanding of Yōko is palpable here. Despite a life of betrayal, abandonment, and shame, she has a far greater measure of humanity and goodness than those she interacts with. Like Michiko, she is a spiritually pure woman who genuinely cares about, is concerned with the well-being of, and feels for other people. Tragically, she lives in a heartless postwar social context in which the love she directs toward others is unrequited.

Takashima, too, regards Yōko with sensitivity and understanding. Like Matsuzaki, he is aware that the "dark shadows of her birth and upbringing" are inescapable (5:28). He is especially perceptive about the underlying psychology of her relationships with men:

In Takashima's mind, Yōko was made such that she couldn't bear the long hours a mistress had to pass in solitude. It was the same regardless of the man. She would sit alone in her room and come to feel that she was facing off with the whole of society. She simply didn't know how to dispel the thoughts that came to her at such times. While they were related to the heavy responsibilities everyone was burdened with from birth, he thought that her circumstances caused her to be assailed by them in a particularly direct and raw manner. It was thus fitting that she had become a bar hostess since she could at least forget these burdens as she shuffled from man to man.

Had she not had the habit of immediately becoming deeply involved with the men she was with, she could easily have led the life of the average Ginza woman. It was her nature, however, to experience waves of anxiety as she floated about in the twilight world of money, liquor, and passion. And when she did, she would flee back to the cloistered life of the mistress. Her relationship with Matsuzaki had been one swing of this pendular motion. He had a wife and child, but since he was not wealthy, it had been enough that their relationship had lasted for three years. Yōko now had to stand on her

> own once more. Nothing could be better than if she could bloom once again. This would probably be her last chance. (5:29)

Takashima understands the difficulty Yōko has with isolation and her sensitivity and vulnerability to societal expectation, obligation, and censure. Despite being forced by circumstance into her degrading line of work, she is burdened with a conscience that allows her no lasting peace of mind. She cannot help but become intimately involved with and feel personal responsibility for the men who come to her primarily for sex.

The narrator, too, stresses how burdened Yōko is by the past. And he makes it clear that this burden is lost on those who use her to dispel their own gloom: "The men in her life had no knowledge of her past. It didn't matter to them at all. Since all they wanted was for her to respond to their desire upon demand, their lust mounted when they saw that they could easily have their way with her" (5:60). With the possible exception of those with Matsuzaki and Takashima, Yōko's relationships with men take place solely on the debased physical level. Consequently, she is as spiritually alienated when with them as she is physically isolated when alone in her cramped Akasaka apartment.

While Yōko opens herself up to men both figuratively and literally, she receives little but money in return. To pursue Takashima's analogy, if her relationships are viewed in terms of emotional economics, there has never been a balance of accounts (5:86): Yōko always gives far more than she receives. As the narrator explains with succinctness and understanding, "Striving to satisfy everyone else, Yōko lost herself" (5:129). Since her body was the singular object of the men in her life, they were as blind to the emptiness in her heart as they were ignorant of her traumatic past. In the end, the dark shadows of her past and the degenerate postwar human relations based solely on physical interaction and material exchange force Yōko into a life of shame and suicide, which will be discussed in the next section.[17] Before we go on to that subject, however, it will be useful to examine the war-related aspects of Yōko's unbearable past.

Yōko survives through suppression and repression of traumatic memory. These fundamental psychic defenses are discernable in the following passage describing a rare return visit to Mishima: "The sun was high and there were no shadows in the square in front of Mishima Station. Although a friend whose desk used to be next to hers in grammar school had married into a family that ran a souvenir shop just two doors away, Yōko lived by suppressing such sentimentality. She went directly from the station to the taxi" (5:73). There are no visible shadows of the past in this scene of homecoming. Like the thoughts and emotions related to her childhood friend, they have been banished from consciousness. Yōko manages to keep the past at bay during the day she spends in Mishima, but it returns irrepressibly as she heads back to Tokyo that evening.

During her visit, Yōko goes with Tetsu to her grandmother's grave to pay her respects. On the train back to Tokyo, thoughts of her beloved grandmother, her estrangement from her stepmother, and the stasis of her own life symbolically reactivate deep-seated traumatic memory. The narrator prepares for this important scene as follows: "The sun began to set at Manazuru, and it was dark by Odawara. Yōko apparently fell asleep (*nettarashii*)" (5:78). It is significant that she only "apparently" dozed off. This vague description allows the four interrelated visions she has on the moving train to be taken as dreams, the return of the repressed, or a combination thereof.

In the first, she is back in wartime Tokyo walking through a scene of death and destruction following an Allied air raid. The streets are dark since there is a blackout in effect. Suddenly, she notices emaciated figures writhing about in what appears to be a school yard. As she passes by, they struggle futilely to get up off the ground. Yōko feels that they want to tell her something. When she looks at them more closely, she notices that the flesh of their arms and legs is not only hanging in tatters, but also continually raining down from their bodies. The more they struggle to rise, the more flesh they lose. She comes to with a start just as she is about to call out to them. While she knows that this dream is based on an experience she had during the war, she can't quite place it. This is not surprising, since memory of such traumatic experience can be deeply repressed. Since school yards were commonly used as relief centers, chances are Yōko had gone there in search of a missing relative. This conjecture is supported by the fact that immediately upon waking she wonders if her grandmother had been among the writhing victims.

In the next dream, Yōko returns to her Akasaka apartment to find it burned to the ground. She sees Matsuzaki stacking roof tiles as he straddles the wall adjoining the elementary school next door. When she tries to ask him why he is doing such a thing, she finds she cannot speak. Next, she sees him sitting on the bare foundation of the apartment and trying to put his seal on what appears to be a marriage certificate. No matter how hard or how many times he presses the seal, the proper mark is not made. When Yōko puts her hand on his shoulder to get a better look, she is shocked to see that his neck looks like that of a terminally ill man.

In the third dream, the past again intrudes into the present. Yōko is back at the Meguro house sitting across the table from her first patron. As he repeatedly brings his chopsticks to his mouth, rice tumbles out to the side, falling down onto and accumulating on his shoulder, and she thinks, "Oh, I hate it, I can't stand this" (5:80).

In the last dream, she looks out the train window and sees a billboard advertisement for *Snow White* on top of a movie theater. Yōko thinks that since she is playing the leading role, she must go see it. The train, however, will not stop for her. Gradually, she seems to realize that she is dreaming; she's never risen high enough in life to become a movie star. She tells herself over and over that she must wake up because it's unladylike to sleep on the train. The *Snow White* billboard, however, seems to be indelibly imprinted on the inside of her eyelids. Once again, she thinks, "Oh, I hate it, I can't stand this" (5:80).

These four dreams follow a past-present, past-present temporal pattern. This dynamic suggests that the unresolved, trauma-induced shadows of Yōko's wartime past ever threaten to intrude into, overlay, and darken her present and, by extension, her future life. Each of these dreams involves the inability to communicate or act, images of physical decay, and death and dying. Yōko's last dream is particularly prophetic. Like Snow White, Yōko has a fair complexion and is kindhearted and spiritually pure. Both, moreover, take poison. Yōko's world, however, clearly lacks a Prince Charming.

Toward the end of the novella, Yōko is assailed by similar images as she dozes in her Akasaka apartment. And this surfacing of repressed, war-related memory is again triggered by thoughts of death and dying—in this case, her decision to kill herself and the elaborate preparations she has made to that end. Yōko has two interrelated dreams at this time. While the first is firmly grounded in the past, the second—to be treated separately in a different context—has significant bearing on and implications for the present and future. The former involves one of Yōko's traumatic wartime experiences predating those that intruded into her dreams on the train: "Yōko dreamed incessantly in the cramped room of her apartment. Once again, it was during the war. She was walking by herself along a wide, dusty road wearing women's work pants (*monpe*). She was fleeing, but she didn't know where she was supposed to go. She only knew she had to meet someone and get something from him. There were innumerable people in front and behind her all moving in the same direction. They were probably trying to escape Tokyo after an air raid" (5:155).

Yōko eventually comes to a train and boards along with the others. It is packed with men who stare at her derriere, the outlines of which are conspicuous through the thin material of her *monpe* because she isn't wearing any underwear. After reaching a station where everyone scrambles to change to a train running on different tracks, someone takes Yōko by the hand. She turns to see a short, bald man grinning from ear to ear and holding out a thousand-yen bill. She takes the money, somehow knowing that if she goes with him she can reach her destination. When she looks at the reverse side of the bill, however, she is shocked to find a pornographic picture attached to it.

Upon awaking, Yōko realizes that this dream was based on a girlhood experience of being sent by her stepmother to meet a customer who said he would settle his account at the restaurant if Yōko came to his house to collect it. The man was her first patron—the owner of the steel factory—and the graphic sexual imagery she saw on the back of the bill was linked to the pictures he had shown her in his parlor. The outlines of this traumatic experience thus become clear. In the wake of a devastating air raid, Tetsu intentionally sold her innocent, unsuspecting stepdaughter to a dirty old man in the name of survival. The series of images that come to Yōko's mind are strongly associated with war, death, betrayal, survival egoism, loss of innocence, shame, and humiliation. Yōko's inability to come to terms with her unbearably burdened prewar and wartime past and the interminably empty life she leads in the present combine to produce her life of shame and suicide.

A Life of Shame and Suicide

In terms of his literary journey of survivor formulation, the crucial breakthrough Ōoka achieved in *In the Shadow of Cherry Blossoms* was to intimately identify and empathize with Yōko/Sakamoto Mutsuko as she departed this world in physical and spiritual anguish. With the exception of the actual moment of physical death, Ōoka's experience during and after the war was similar in essential ways to Yōko's. He, too, not only experienced prolonged psychic immersion in death, existential isolation, symbolic breakdown, despair, and failed suicide, but also endured a life of shame because of survival and capture. The commonality in their respective traumatic experiences coupled with Ōoka's newfound capacity to open himself up emotionally to the dead and dying enabled him to merge psychologically with Yōko and relate her tragic story from *her* perspective with unparalleled insight and sensitivity.

When Yōko is introduced at the beginning of the novella, she is already in a condition of psychic and emotional deadness. And the intimate identification of narrator and protagonist is palpable from the outset. With Matsuzaki's pretext for leaving her and background on their relationship removed, the work opens as follows:

> From the start, Yōko wasn't listening to what he was saying. . . .
>
> She was aware of his unwavering gaze on her hands as she continued to knit in silence, and she knew he was waiting for her to say something. Kindhearted though she was, she wasn't about give an opening to a man hesitating to broach the subject of breaking up. . . .
>
> Yōko raised her knitting to eye level. The green and brown plaid lap blanket she held in her hands was to have been for Matsuzaki's use when he prepared lectures in her apartment.
>
> Yōko, however, was not looking at the knitting that trailed down a foot or so below her outstretched arms. Instead, she was absorbing the details of the scene framed in the window beyond—the immobile, transparent autumn sky, the fading afternoon light on the roofs and walls of the buildings covering the slope from Reinanzaka to Mikawadai. (5:2–3)

So advanced is her psychic numbing that she does not react at all to being abandoned. As she gazes listlessly at the distant scene, her internal world is readily projected into and perceived in the surrounding environment.

Each component of the scene—the vacant, frozen sky of autumn, the last rays of light on the house-covered hill—is a reflection of her own stasis and deadness.

While the narrator unflinchingly portrays Yōko's psychic condition in this way, he does not do so impersonally or with emotional detachment. Indeed, he identifies and empathizes with her intimately throughout. This is readily apparent in the famous scene in which Yōko makes her lonely preparations to return to the Ginza after being abandoned by Matsuzaki. Following are excerpts from this extraordinary passage so reminiscent of Michiko's experience in the Hake house after Akiyama left her:

> Yōko gazed into the eyes that stared back at her from the depths of the cold mirror. The heavy air of that November evening, so still and thick that it would have reverberated if struck, closed her tiny room off from the world. The children playing in the neighboring school yard had apparently gone home; the ebb and flow of their voices had at some point receded into the distance. It was during these moments of quietude between the time the sounds of the day had died and those of the night had yet to be born that Yōko put on her face.
>
> The countenance reflected in the mirror had long since lost its resemblance to the Yōko of old. . . . She was determined, however, to put that face before her customers once more.
>
> The face in the mirror told her how wearisome it was to again be preparing herself to sell her charms. The cheeks that in the past had needed but a dusting of powder now had to be liberally covered with cream for the powder to take hold at all. The lips that had glowed like luscious fruit with a quick flicker of the tongue were now drawn and thin. They would have been shapeless without a good amount of bright lipstick.
>
> Yōko avoided as much as possible looking directly at the dark circles that had formed below her eyes or the crow's-feet that radiated outward from them. She used eye shadow to hide the lines of her eyebrows, which at some point had extended to droop down at their far ends. All she could do with the furrows that creased her brow was fill them in with powder. Since her face turned into a sea of wrinkles if she laughed with abandon, she had become a woman who could only smile gently. (5:44–46)

As with the opening passage of the work, this finely wrought description is replete with images of stasis and death. When Yōko gazes into the mirror, she comes face to face with Death itself. The conspicuous lassitude, or *monoui,* that assails her at such times is that of a woman long since grown tired of living. In this sensitive, restrained, and lyrical treatment of her experience, one senses deep understanding, compassion, empathy, and pathos.

Yōko has been exhausted by the empty, stereotypical pattern her life has followed for nearly two decades after the war. The narrator movingly conveys her world and weariness of life through an intimate description of her reactions to Shimizu's hackneyed proposal to set her up with her own business:

> She had the feeling that while she couldn't clearly remember when or with whom, she had experienced a similar scene time and again in the past. There was no shortage of men like Shimizu. After innumerable drunken one-night stands, however, they left no distinct impression.
>
> Ever since she had been a young woman, man after man had asked her to change bars after becoming intimate with her. Other men had been hurt as a result. Since they invariably behaved the same way themselves, they became indistinguishable, and simply receded into the obscurity of the past.
>
> Yōko was not particularly upset to be sitting next to this same kind of man making the same kind of proposal. It was all just wearisome. (5:95)

By this point in her life, Yōko is unable to feel much of anything at all. She neither experiences nor expresses frustration, anger, or sadness; all that remains is a pervasive, persistent sense of exhaustion and listlessness.

One of the two definitive images of Yōko's life is presented through a vision that comes to her shortly after visiting her grandmother's grave in Mishima:

> After passing through some dense woods, Yōko came to a pond filled with groundwater said to originate from the snowmelt of Mt. Fuji. The water gushed out noisily from the lower part of the dam, passed over some low-lying water plants, and splashed away vigorously. Even after being used by innumerable factories as it coursed through Mishima, it still flowed amply enough to merge with the Karino River and reach the sea.
>
> As Yōko crossed over the bridge with Tetsu, she gazed into the painfully clear, flowing waters. As she did, she reflected that while her life definitely began in Mishima, it stagnated in swamps and ditches before ever reaching the sea. She felt this would probably be the last time she saw Mishima. (5:78)

Although starting off as a pure, lively child, Yōko was mercilessly drained spiritually and sullied physically by factory hands as she struggled in vain to follow her own course. By the time she had passed only partway through the city, there was nothing left of her.

Yōko's means of enduring the exhaustion, emptiness, and stasis of her life were psychic numbing, alcohol, deathlike sleep, and the knowledge that at least Takashima needed her. Her primary line of defense was to feel nothing. Even when, upon occasion, emotion did begin to well up within her, she immediately took steps to kill it: "At the first hint of deep emotion, Yōko habitually suppressed it and called herself a fool" (5:90). Yōko knew only too well that numbness was necessary to her existence. During an exchange with Matsuzaki after he reenters her life toward the end of the novella, she states plainly that if she wasn't emotionally dead, she'd never have been able to continue working at the bar (5:144). The narrator provides the definitive statement in this regard:

> Yōko's mind was as devoid of memories of the previous night's liquor and sex as it was of hope for making a new start in Yugawara. The emptiness in her heart was the end product of twenty years spent adrift on the waves of Tokyo's consumer culture changing men as she would clothes. If it was questionable whether she had been alive before this time, then it was equally doubtful whether she was now.
>
> Qualitatively speaking, her life spent between liquor and men was one of death. Yōko, in effect, was already dead. (5:123)

Yōko takes some comfort in the knowledge that her psychological state is shared by others. The reader is given access to her thoughts upon returning to her apartment after yet another night of heavy drinking and physical servitude: "Returning home like this in broad daylight, Yōko was occasionally assailed by an awareness of the emptiness of her life. She had come to realize, however, that every one of the men and women around her had a hollowness of their own. The thought that they, too, lived as if they were dead was the mainstay of her existence" (5:123).

Heavy drinking is Yōko's second line of defense against the dark shadow of her past and the unbearable reality of her present life. She begins early in the evening before her customers arrive. Alcohol not only gives her temporary relief from mounting physical pain, but also enables her to get through night after night of her degrading profession. By drinking, she can forget herself for a time. Like her relationships with men, Yōko's life in the bar follows a fixed, unvarying pattern:

> Yōko would again be made aware of her advanced years when the younger girls got drunk and started to laugh in ways that were incomprehensible to her. By then, her legs would barely be able to support her [at the counter]. She would begin to worry about her makeup and spend long periods before the mirror in the washroom. Try though she might, she could not fix her face. Eventually, her legs would grow heavy and her knees would begin to buckle. If her old customers didn't show up to buy her highballs, her subsequent experience would be indescribably trying. If she could get drunk, she could talk more volubly and her legs would carry her more effortlessly. (5:49)

Although periodically tormented by traumatizing dreams, sleep was Yōko's last line of defense. One of her greatest pleasures was to close the blinds, stretch out on her simple bed on the floor, and fall asleep to the sound of children's voices. Sleep was as close as she could come to oblivion without actually dying. In the narrator's words, "She slept with the intention of disappearing from the world" (5:124).

Yōko was only able to endure the humiliation, emptiness, and deadness of her existence before and after her relationship with Matsuzaki because of her conviction that Takashima loved and needed her. He was the only man in her life who ever treated her like an ordinary woman. Once Takashima, too, finally betrays her by cheating her wealthy patron Nokata out of ten thousand yen, and it becomes clear that Nokata intends to use the incident as a pretext for leaving her, she is as thoroughly robbed of the foundations of her existence as Michiko was upon being abandoned by Akiyama. Yōko's net of postwar human relationships was too frayed and threadbare to support her weight when she needed it most. During the final week of her short life, no one saw fit to look in on her either at work or at her apartment. Yōko could not endure this last experience of abandonment and betrayal nor the seven days of near-total isolation that followed in its wake. Thus it was that she finally resolved to put an end to her empty life of unremitting suffering, shame, and loneliness.

Identification, Empathy, and Mourning

Ōoka was able to relate Yōko's tragic story with a measure of understanding, sensitivity, and compassion conspicuously absent in *Lady Musashino.* His treatment of her elaborate preparations for death make this clear. Yōko's final days at home are consistently presented from her perspective, from within rather than without. Her dying moments, moreover, are attended solely by a survivor-narrator not only capable of fully understanding her suicide, but of empathizing with her and mourning her loss as well.

Chapter 18 opens with the following lines: "Yōko's preparations had been complete for some time now. Having failed in her youth, she now knew exactly how much sleeping medicine she needed. She had been buying it little by little since Matsuzaki left her. At her age, she could never have returned to the Ginza without knowing that she could bring an end to her life any time she pleased" (5:148). It took Yōko more than three days to finish her elaborate preparations. During this time, she writes last testaments (*isho*) to Takashima and Tetsu, thoroughly cleans and tidies her apartment, pays a last visit to her old Meguro neighborhood, and goes to the public bath.

Yōko writes in her letter to Takashima that she doesn't blame him for the stunt (*itazura*) he pulled with Nokata—receiving ten thousand yen from him to buy a porcelain sake cup, selling it for twice the price to an antique dealer, and keeping all the money himself. True to character, she moves to take personal responsibility by telling herself that her powers of attraction were insufficient to keep Nokata's interest: if he had really cared for her, he never would have made an issue of such an insignificant sum of money. Thus, while Takashima's unethical conduct brings on her final crisis, she cares for him too deeply to hold him accountable: "It was a pleasure for Yōko to be able to write just before dying that she bore him no grudge" (5:150).

The narrator identifies closely with Yōko as she writes the testament she mails along with the key to her apartment to Tetsu: "As Yōko composed her letter, she had the feeling that someone else was writing it. When she read back through it, she felt that her true sentiments had gone unexpressed. In the end, however, she told herself that this was simply the way it was with farewell notes, and that it was fine if they just serve their practical purpose" (5:152). The narrator also conveys the altered state of consciousness she entered about this time: "As she wrote, she heard a sound on the tin roof above the kitchen. She heard light footsteps immediately afterward and realized it was a cat, but when she first heard the sound, she was so startled that she almost flew into the air. It was a day when the high-pitched voices of the children in the school yard next door sounded unusually loud. Yōko thought that these familiar voices struck her ears so forcefully because of her state of nervous exhaustion" (5:152).

Yōko begins her letter to Tetsu by expressing thanks for raising her from infancy despite the fact that she was not related by blood. After requesting that she take care of things after her death, she gives the following specific instructions: "Since I was a kind of foundling, I'll be to content if I am treated as one who died without any living relatives to tend her grave (*muenbutsu*). Please don't bury me in the family plot. I'd prefer to have my remains entrusted to some temple in Tokyo. Since I'll be dying in a good frame of mind, there is no need to cry for me. Please don't tell anyone about my death. The key money on the apartment should cover expenses" (5:151). To the end, Yōko is painfully aware of her position as a stigmatized, marginalized outsider. This holds true with regard to both her family and society. In the letter to her stepmother, Yōko faces, and accepts, the terrible reality of being forgotten, of being as isolated, marginalized, and unappreciated in death as she was in life.

After finishing her letters, Yōko takes three full days to clean and order her apartment. The narrator merges with her anew as she labors to remove from her physical surroundings the filth she knows cannot be purged from herself: "She intended to put everything in its proper place in short order. In actuality, however, she probably moved in slow motion. Occasionally, she felt as if her body were rising up and floating through the clouds. At other times, she became irritated and dashed from one end of the tiny two-room apartment to the other" (5:154). After thorough cleaning, her room begins to feel unbearably cramped and suffocating. As Takashima observed, when alone in her apartment like this she felt as if she were facing off with all of society. And this society had pressed in on her so mercilessly that it has ultimately deprived her of both movement and oxygen: "She thought she had done well to live in this apartment for three years. She felt as if she had lived interminably in this tiny room, which seemed to be crushed by the full weight of society" (5:154).

Just before the end, Yōko pays a visit to her old Meguro neighborhood. Their house had been destroyed during the war, and postwar renovation projects had erased virtually every vestige of her old haunts. The local Shinto shrine is the only remaining physical link to her past life there. Even memories of this sacred place serve as painful reminders of her identity as an outsider. It was on the grounds of this shrine that her mother had shown her a true albino. At the time, she had felt sorry for the boy because she already knew firsthand how sad and lonely it was to be different. The narrator's intimate identification with and empathy for Yōko are manifest in the following brief comment: "Yōko thought that she actually had been a *shirokko.* She had been so beautiful as a child that passersby would turn around to look at her. Now, this attractive *shirokko* was about to die" (5:155).

Yōko returns to her Akasaka apartment to complete her few remaining preparations. After being assailed by the haunting, war-related memory-dream that will be examined in the final section of this chapter, she awakes and goes to the public bath. Before returning, she puts on a new robe and leaves her old one neatly folded on the shelf. Back in her room, she spends a long time drying and braiding her hair. She goes through all this trouble so that there will be nothing to be ashamed of when she is discovered after death. Yōko has planned meticulously to ensure that her suicide will succeed: "She would do it Sunday night. She'd tell them when she left work on Saturday that she'd be going to Mishima to spend the night with Tetsu. If she mailed the key along with the letter on Sunday morning, it would surely arrive by Monday morning. Tetsu was senile, so even when informed of this urgent matter, she probably wouldn't reach Tokyo until Monday night or Tuesday morning. By then, there'd surely be nothing anyone could do" (5:152–153).

Yōko has a telling experience as she dries and braids her hair after laying out her deathbed: "She felt something rising up from the base of her chest and thought to herself, 'Am I finally going to cry?' In the end, however, only a low noise escaped before the feeling passed" (5:157). At this point, Yōko's psychic numbing is so chronic and advanced that she is incapable of emotional response. Now, just hours before her own death, she is unable even to grieve for herself.

The narrator psychologically and emotionally joins Yōko, empathizing with her most intimately between the time she takes her overdose and the moment of her death. Because she cannot bear the thought of dying in the dark, she puts off taking the sleeping medicine until Monday morning. Yōko, however, is not alone; the narrator is with her, and he stays by her side to the end:

> Yōko awoke to the sound of children's voices. The window gradually brightened. She had dreamed, but she made no effort to recall the dreams.
>
> Yōko went to the mirror, adjusted her makeup one last time, and then went straight to bed. She used belts to bind her legs together at the thighs and ankles, lay down on her back, and reached for the medicine beside her pillow.
>
> She felt a wave of anxiety over the possibility of having made a mistake that might result in survival. The same fear had arisen at precisely the same point when she had taken her overdose twenty years ago in the Meguro house. Yōko thought her fears contained the hope of failing and being saved. It was maddening. Even though she was sure she'd harbor no such hope this time around, misgivings had arisen after all. After she became agitated, there was no end to it. She was angry at everyone and everything—at Takashima, Matsuzaki, Junko, Iyako. She was galled it had taken so long to finish all her preparations. In quick, small gulps, she drank down the medicine.
>
> The dizziness and spinning of the room that followed immediately in its wake were the same as before. She thought, "What a filthy room." The voices of the children playing outside grew louder. As her mind and body progressively numbed and lost sensation, only the sound of their echoing voices still reached her. Children were peeking in on her through the window. They were mocking her, calling out *"shirokko, shirokko."* After that, all was darkness. (5:158)

While there admittedly is restraint in this treatment, the sensitive reader will sense that as when he composed his requiem to his dead comrades, Ōoka was quietly grieving as he re-created Yōko/Mutsuko's tragic life and death experience. As Tachihara Masa'aki has observed, this moving novella is "a pure, unparalleled requiem. While not readily apparent on the surface level of expression, [Ōoka] was surely weeping like a child behind the scenes."[18]

Indeed, abstract discourse on fate, chance, accident, and the like is conspicuously absent in *In the Shadow of Cherry Blossoms.* There is, in fact, but one remotely relevant comment mentioned in passing toward the close of the work: "Yōko postponed taking the overdose until dawn of the next day. If Tetsu would have seized the opportunity to call Takashima immediately upon receiving the letter Monday morning, Yōko's suicide attempt would have failed" (5:153). By this point in his formulative journey, the impersonal, metaphysical structures and dynamics of modern tragedy have clearly ceased to be of primary concern. In his battlefield memoirs and *Lady Musashino,* Ōoka defensively maneuvered to avoid deep-seated feelings of death guilt, self-recrimination, and loss by blaming the victim and attributing death to bad luck. As first seen in the requiem written for his fallen comrades, however, after successively facing and working through theretofore unresolved survivor issues, he eventually reached the point where he could open himself up emotionally to and identify and empathize with the powerless individuals whose lives were tragically destroyed by the macrocosmic and microcosmic workings of society. As will be detailed below, this opening up in turn enabled him to engage in more appropriate blaming, convert static to animating forms of guilt, and wholeheartedly devote himself to clearly identifying and rectifying fundamental social evils.

Memorialization, Social Injustice, and Survivor Mission

Ōoka memorializes Yōko/Mutsuko in two basic ways: by fully exposing her humanity and the truth of her tragic life of shame and suicide and by indelibly linking her to potent images of extraordinary beauty and profound significance. Indeed, despite Yōko's despairing thoughts of going unremembered and unmourned after death, Ōoka succeeds in immortalizing her in literature by relating her tragic story with unparalleled sensitivity, understanding, empathy, and compassion. In a sense, he belatedly gives her precisely what was so grievously lacking in her lonely, empty life as a mistress and Ginza bar hostess.

As indicated in this chapter, Yōko is remembered as a gentle, sensitive, kindhearted, spiritually immaculate, selfless woman who was not only prevented by circumstances largely beyond her control from following her natural course of maturity and development, but also forced to endure a lifetime of repeated abandonment, cruel rejection, and betrayal and of unremitting sexual servitude, unrequited love, shame, and humiliation. Through his loving treatment, Ōoka enables the reader to realize that in spite of sordid circumstance, Yōko had a measure of decency, integrity, and humanity wholly lacking in those around her. By intimately identifying and empathizing with her throughout her traumatic experience and telling the tragic story of her life with such care and understanding, Ōoka made it impossible for Yōko to be dismissed as a cheap Ginza whore. Rather, he shows how a fundamentally good and essentially helpless human being was exploited, progressively defiled, devitalized, and in the end mercilessly crushed by heartless, egoistical people and an indifferent postwar society.

And, as will be shown below, Ōoka also memorializes Yōko by indelibly associating her with a complex series of images of arresting beauty and enduring significance. He does this in three interrelated passages in the novella, the first toward the beginning and second and third toward the end. The first set of images is presented from Matsuzaki's perspective. As he walks away from Yōko's Akasaka apartment after breaking off relations with her, he thinks to himself that this will be the last time he visits the area and begins to recall how Yōko would come out to meet and send him off in fine weather. As he recollects the past in this way, the image of cherry trees (*sakura*) unexpectedly comes to mind, and he remembers the spring three years before when she joined him in Nara and they traveled to Yoshino:

> That had been the only trip worthy of the name they had taken together. The cherry trees of Naka-no-senbon were in full bloom. They were so beautiful that it was easy to ignore the drunken revelers under them. They climbed up as far as Saigyō's hut, and by the time they descended, the wind had died down and dusk had fallen. The fragrance of cherry blossoms that pervaded the air as they walked back down the quiet, now deserted mountain path was nearly suffocating.
>
> At one point, Yōko had said, "It was better to visit Yoshino than not to." Even if she forgot him, she would probably remember Yoshino.
>
> The two of them couldn't stay on in Yoshino, nor could they savor the elegance of dying together under the blossoms. When they looked up from beneath the trees, they saw petals so thin and fragile that the blue sky seemed visible right through them.
>
> The sun was high, the breeze warm, and the layered shadows of cherry blossoms trembled on the ground under the trees.
>
> As Matsuzaki gazed at the empty road before him, he thought, "If Yōko is a barren flower that will not itself bear fruit, she should be content to walk in the shadow of cherry blossoms." (5:20)

This experience was surely among the happiest of Yōko's life. Through a masterful use of poetic language and imagery, Ōoka succeeds in enshrining their fleeting and beautiful moment together that spring under the famous cherry trees of Yoshino.

At the end of this finely crafted, lyrical passage, Ōoka introduces the second defining image of Yōko and her life: she is a barren flower (*ada-*

bana), one that will never come to fruition, but only bloom briefly and beautifully before being scattered without leaving a trace. This image parallels that of Yōko being like a pure, flowing stream that stagnated in swamps and ditches before reaching the sea. Both suggest a life blocked from following its natural course. Yōko, however, is ultimately associated more closely with the shadow cast by the cherry blossoms than with the blossoms themselves. This is made clear by the work's title. It is as if Yōko were all too quickly deprived while still on the bough of the vitalizing light she desperately needed and too quickly came to be engulfed in the darkness below.

This downward movement is conspicuous in the second set of poetic images used to symbolize and memorialize her tragic life. Moved primarily by lust and the desire to dispel in small measure the increasing gloom, deadness, and emptiness of his own life, Matsuzaki seeks Yōko out again toward the very end of the novella. After tracking her down at a bar, he spirits her away with the promise of nighttime flower viewing. The two of them then take a driving tour through Tokyo, gazing at the blooming cherries by night. Yōko, who had been drinking heavily, eagerly looks out the windows on either side of the taxi and repeatedly exclaims, "How beautiful!" When they reach the row of cherry trees bordering the Aoyama Cemetery, they stop the car, and she runs out to get a closer look:

> With lips parted and head thrown back, Yōko stumbled from trunk to trunk as she receded into the distance.
>
> She said, "They're so beautiful, so beautiful!" over and over again.
>
> She also said, "I could eat them!" When told about the poet's vision of bodies being buried under the cherry trees, she murmured, "Exquisite!" (5:146)

In this passage, Yōko is presented in a state of near ecstasy. Here again, the cherry trees in full bloom are associated with beauty and fleeting but intense pleasure and joy. If the first set of images can be seen as the beginning, this surely heralds the end.

The final imagery indelibly associated with Yōko is introduced in a dream she has just before she kills herself. This follows immediately in the wake of her traumatic memory-dream of fleeing Tokyo during the Allied air raid: "The sun was high, and the shadows cast by the cherry blossoms were layered on the ground directly below them. It was Yōko who was buried at their roots. The shadows fell on her as well. The dark, heavy light passed through her to be absorbed into the earth. Beneath her, she saw it converging on a naked figure" (5:156–157). The last dream Yōko has before darkness finally descends upon her forever combines elements from the two other *sakura*-related passages. This time, however, she is not only alone, but transformed into an *adabana* petal scattered down into and now buried under the layered shadows cast by the sunlit canopy of flowers above. The sky-blue light visible through the thin, delicate petals in the first scene has darkened and now passes through Yōko herself as she lies below in the darkness. The image of *adabana* and the naked figure at the deepest reaches of the scene are strongly suggestive not only of her own life and death, but also that of others like her. Immediately below the surface beauty of postwar Japanese society are innumerable sacrifices, those consigned to live buried in the shadows; and further below them are the naked dead, the powerless, defenseless, and voiceless from whom society has extracted every drop of lifeblood and subjected to its fatal evils.

In linking Yōko with the *sakura*—the ultimate Japanese symbol of aestheticism, purity, spirit, and culture—Ōoka does much more than just beautify and memorialize her life and death. The images and their rich associations indicate his growing concern with exposing and actively opposing the evils present in prewar, wartime, and postwar Japanese society. This becomes increasingly clear upon consideration of the epigraph he selected, the treatment of Yōko's experience just before death, and the *omokage* (literally, "face shadow") dynamic at work throughout the novella.

The decisive shift in Ōoka's concern from the micro- to macrocosmic societal structures and forces that combine to shatter and destroy the lives of the powerless is implicit in the epigraph from Dante's *Divine Comedy:* "Please remember me. My name is Pia / I was born in Sienna, I died in Marena."[19] Pia, like Yōko, was treated mercilessly. Born to a family of means, she was married to an influential politician who locked her away and left her to die in isolation after falling for a beautiful, wealthy widow. Because Pia died unnaturally and prematurely, her soul could not migrate to Heaven. As Dante passed through purgatory, she called to him and uttered the lines quoted above. She also told him in simple terms that her husband knew the circumstances of her death.

Yōko was born in Mishima; she died in Tokyo. Her death, too, was the result of betrayal, marginalization, neglect, and abandonment. While immediate responsibility can be laid at the feet of her father, Tetsu, and the succession of men who deceived, used, and cast her aside, the fact that such heartless treatment was acceptable to society cannot be overemphasized. Yōko is therefore best viewed as a defenseless woman who was sacrificed at the altar of postwar society. Significantly, Ōoka, like Dante, positioned himself as a mediator between the living and the dead. Speaking on behalf of the deceased, he labors to expose the truth of her tragic life and death not only as a means of pacifying her restless spirit by ensuring that she will not go unmourned or unremembered, but also by calling on people to change society so that others need not suffer and be pointlessly sacrificed as she was.

Ōoka's shift in orientation toward engaging in appropriate blaming and attacking social evils can be seen most clearly toward the close of the work. The final passage, introduced in an earlier context, begins and ends with references to children. In the first instance, Yōko hears the happy, spirited voices of youths playing in the school playground next to her Akasaka apartment. Among other things, these voices serve to remind the reader that children are the future of any society. The second reference vividly demonstrates how deeply and permanently children can be scarred by rejection, cruelty, and lack of understanding, empathy, and compassion. Even in her last moments, Yōko cannot escape thoughts of being ostracized and mercilessly ridiculed for being different from her peers.

The mounting anger Yōko feels just before taking her overdose is also significant in this regard. This is the most intense emotion she is described as having during the final years of her life. She is initially enraged over having to suffer while on her deathbed her traumatic memory-dream of being "sold" to her first patron amid the attack on Tokyo. She is further agitated by the anxiety she experiences over possibly having made a misstep that might once again result in failed suicide and by the unwelcome realization that she still harbored hopes of survival. The embittered emotions that surface at the end of her life, however, are indicative of more appropriate blaming. After taking most of the responsibility for her life of shame and suicide onto herself, she is able to extend the concentric rings of accountability outward to encompass those who have let her down so badly. In truth, Yōko didn't really want to die. As Hiraoka Tokuyoshi writes of Michiko, Yōko, and one of the desperate soldiers described in *Fires on the Plain* who lingered on by the field hospital:

> None of them want to die, but they discern that they cannot escape death because of some great, invisible, heartless mechanisms [operating on them]. Even as they struggle to go on living, they become aware of the futility of their efforts. When their energy is exhausted and they decide to submit to their fate, they utter "I hate it, I can't stand it," and "Ahh." Consequently, their utterances do not mean "I hate to die." They are, rather, expressions of humans who, while still having infinite attachment to life, have no choice but to acknowledge that "[They] can't bear to go on living."[20]

It must be borne in mind, moreover, that individuals such as these die in great psychological and emotional turmoil—the very circumstances believed to produce homeless spirits and angry ghosts. For this reason, the mission to expose and address the social evils that bring about their untimely deaths is inseparable from pacification and memorialization. In the end, these too must be counted among the varied burdens of survival.

As Hiraoka's commentary implies, the deaths of these two women and of Imperial soldiers are of the same order. Ōoka subtly brings this important point home through a complex set of associations and resemblances. Like the thin, fragile cherry petals and layered shadows so intimately linked with Yōko, the *omokage* of other powerless figures doomed to meet premature, unnatural ends are visible in and through her. As far as *Lady Musashino,* the requiem to fallen comrades of Nishiya Company, and *In the Shadow of Cherry Blossoms* are concerned, these resemblances and associations can be schematized as follows: Tsutomu–the war dead; Tsutomu–Michiko; Michiko–the war dead; dead Nishiya Company soldiers–Mutsuko; Mutsuko–Michiko; Mutsuko–Yōko; Yōko–all those, including the war dead, whose lives were or are being destroyed and who were or are being sacrificed by society. Looking at these linkages and their important implications enables articulation of how Ōoka prepared the way for the last leg of his arduous formulative journey.

Like Ōoka's company commander, Tsutomu is indelibly marked by the deaths of his comrades. What's more, Tsutomu and Michiko are said to be mirror images of one another. Both, in a sense, are *omokage* of Tsutomu's father, an army officer who killed himself the day after surrender. And Michiko herself is intimately connected with the war dead.

The Nishiya Company dead were closely linked in Ōoka's heart and mind with Sakamoto Mutsuko, the *omokage* of Michiko. Yōko, in turn, was modeled on Mutsuko. While well-intentioned, both Yōko/Mutsuko and Ōoka's fallen comrades were ultimately powerless before the oppressive, destructive forces of their misdirected society. In contrast to Michiko, Yōko's entire life was one of self-sacrifice. But as with the men defending Mindoro, her death was a different matter: All of them in the end seemed to have been fated to die pointlessly without proper remembrance. Finally, Yōko is associated through *sakura* imagery with Special Attack Forces such as kamikaze.

Significantly, the first kamikaze forces were organized and deployed in the Philippines in October 1944. In *War Without Mercy,* John Dower draws attention to a 1942 Japanese article enumerating the symbolic linkage of *sakura* and kamikaze:

> The conception of purity associated with Shinto has been thought of hitherto as something pure white, as if it were something that had been thoroughly washed clean, like the white robes of a Shinto priest. The experience of the day the war broke out, however, has shown the error of such thinking; and this error is indeed apparent to those who have actually engaged in the rite of purification (*misogi*). The color of purification is faint red, tinged with the pinkness of blood; it is the color of life itself. It is this very warmth of life which has made the cherry blossom the symbol of the Yamato spirit.[21]

In a subsequent passage, Dower elaborates on these important associations as follows: "Virtually every act in which they engaged in one way or another connoted purity. The falling cherry blossom became the best known symbol of the young flyers, appearing in their poems, their songs, their farewell letters, and in the hands of the virgin schoolgirls who assembled to see them off on their final missions in the spring of 1945."[22] The intimate linkage between kamikaze and scattering cherry blossom is perhaps conveyed best in the poem Vice Admiral Ōnishi Takajirō dedicated to the first Special Attack Forces squadron:

> *Blossoming now,*
> *Tomorrow scattered on the winds,*

Such is the flower of life.
So delicate a perfume
Cannot last for long.[23]

The imagistic linking of Yōko and the *tokkōtai* has profound implications. Like young, idealistic kamikaze pilots, Yōko was sacrificed pointlessly. By this point in his formulative journey, it seems to have dawned on Ōoka that war was but one extreme way the powerless were crushed by greater social forces. Coming to full terms with personal issues surrounding death guilt and self-recrimination and opening himself up emotionally to and identifying and empathizing with his defenseless comrades not only enabled him to more inclusively embrace the myriad people sacrificed by society in times of war and peace, but also engage in more appropriate, purposeful blaming.

At this important juncture, it is important to note that Ōoka does not write about his compatriots in terms of victimization. Instead, he writes about survivors and sacrifices. The term "sacrifice" leaves room for a measure of personal accountability necessary for politically responsible activism. In addition, it can be employed to describe both passive and active manifestations—those who are sacrificed and those who willingly accept the obligations placed on them by society and knowingly sacrifice themselves. In other words, where there are Yōkos, there are also Michikos. As Ōoka notes in passing in his battlefield memoirs and subsequently makes clear in *The Battle for Leyte Island,* the Japanese military was not composed only of passive, poorly trained, and ineffective soldiers; it also had an ample number of committed, courageous men who fought with everything they had. In the end, the crucial challenge for burdened survivors such as Ōoka is to find value and significance in seemingly pointless sacrifice and survival. These are the roots of the anxiety of responsibility that was soon to become the driving force of his survivor mission. By the time Ōoka began serializing *The Battle for Leyte Island* some eight years after finishing *In the Shadow of Cherry Blossoms,* he had discovered in himself the capacity to do for more than ninety thousand what he was first able to do for his fallen comrades and Mutsuko/Yōko some thirteen years after his own naked survival.

CHAPTER FOUR

The Battle for Leyte Island

THE ANXIETY OF RESPONSIBILITY was the seed that took root and grew to full maturity during the two decades following survival. By 1966, it had blossomed into full-fledged survivor mission. For many years after returning from the front, Ōoka was much more concerned with his prisoner of war than his battlefield experience. This orientation is set forth explicitly in "Brothers-in-arms": "While there wasn't anything particularly novel to us about the battlefield, there certainly was in the POW camp. We were surrounded by a fence, and there was a PX. Nothing remained from the battlefield, but something surely did from our lives as prisoners of war" (1:233). "Homecoming," however, reveals the beginnings of a significant change in attitude. Ōoka writes as follows after describing how his recently disarmed and demobilized compatriots settle in for the long ocean voyage home:

> Most of the prisoners of war talked among themselves and recounted anew their personal experiences of defeat. In the POW camp, I wasn't inclined to take much interest in these stories; by and large, they concerned the overwhelming superiority of American weaponry and manpower, the inadequacy of rations supplied by the Japanese army, and the deliciousness of the first cigarettes and chocolate they received after capture. There was little variation one from the other.
>
> Now that I was about to part company with these men, however, I

> began to hold their stories dear. I walked from bunk to bunk listening to the defeat stories told by the soldiers of each division. (1:471)

Ōoka also makes a significant parenthetical comment in this regard in "Living POWs" (Ikiteiru furyo, 1949) while introducing the Japanese staff of the Leyte POW hospital:

> (Numerous different reinforcements were sent to Leyte, but I have no desire to go to the trouble of distinguishing one from another. I have made it a rule in my memoirs not to detail the battlefield experience of the prisoners of war I write about. To do so, I would have to write a general account of the Battle for Leyte Island. It would be pointless to patch together individual testimonies before the official battle history has been released. Since my intention from the outset has been to describe prisoners of war and not soldiers, how they fought before capture is unimportant.) (1:172)

This aside not only signals Ōoka's intention to eventually write an account of the Battle for Leyte Island, but also reveals his self-awareness of an important matter he had theretofore failed to take up in his war memoirs. In 1953, Ōoka reached the point where he could state his intentions directly. When asked by another prominent war writer, Noma Hiroshi, about his next literary project, he responded, "Well, if military men (*gunjin*) keep churning out their irresponsible stories, I think I'll just write my own account of the Battle for Leyte Island."[1]

Anxiety of Responsibility and Survivor Mission

The Korean War, the formulative breakthroughs he achieved in *Lady Musashino* and *Fires on the Plain,* the major emotional turning point he reached in 1958 and gave expression to in *In the Shadow of Cherry Blossoms* the following year, Japan's high rate of economic growth and accompanying slide toward neonationalism and remilitarization, and the Vietnam War not only combined to intensify Ōoka's anxiety of responsibility, but also enabled him to come to see the full significance and relevance of his traumatic battlefield experience. Indeed, by the time he returned to Mindoro Island in 1967, he had advanced to the point where he could directly address the spirits of his fallen comrades as follows:

> Twenty-five years after the war, my prisoner-of-war experience has virtually died, but the battlefield experience I shared with you has come back to life. That is what brought me back here. I had thought that no one would ever again want to go to war, that we would never repeat what we did in the past. This, however, was wishful thinking. After twenty-five years, a small group of scoundrels like those who drove us to war is still in power. Using lies and deception they now seek to force the same experience we went through onto our children. (2:570–571)

One of the main reasons it took Ōoka so long to begin work on his account of the Battle for Leyte Island was that he was waiting for the release of the official battle history.[2] Because the Battle for Leyte Island had ended in defeat and humiliation, military authorities were reluctant to make the details public. When the official history finally came out in 1970—the year after Ōoka finished serializing *The Battle for Leyte Island*—much had been altered, distorted, omitted, and concealed. With the Vietnam War raging on interminably and the United States continuing to use Japan as its major staging area for armed conflict (as it had during the Korean War), Ōoka finally concluded that he could afford to wait no longer.

The immediate impetus he needed to decisively embark on his survivor mission came in May 1966, when he attended a meeting of the Leyte Brotherhood. Toward the end of the meeting, Ōoka was asked to write the battle account of the Sixteenth Infantry Division, the corps that met the American invasion force on the east coast of Leyte Island on October 20, 1944.[3] While accounts of the First and Twenty-sixth Divisions had already been written, the experience of the Sixteenth had yet to be recorded because no officers had survived.[4] Ōoka readily agreed. And in the end, he didn't stop with the Sixteenth Division, but expanded the project to include the battlefield experience of all the soldiers who fought and died in the land, sea, and air engagements that effectively sealed Japan's fate in the Pacific War.

Through friends in the Leyte Brotherhood, Ōoka learned that contrary to his own experience, all the testimony he had heard, and everything he had read about the Battle for Leyte Island, Japanese soldiers actually fought well. After Ōoka agreed to write about the Sixteenth Division, brotherhood members showed him the battle account of the Twenty-sixth

Division and two American records—the official account of the Twenty-first Regiment (Twenty-fourth Division), which fought against First Division soldiers at Limon Pass (Breakneck Ridge), and a book of reportage about the Twenty-fourth Division's combat experience on Leyte Island.[5] The information contained in these accounts opened Ōoka's eyes to the fact that Japanese soldiers put up substantial resistance against their numerically and technologically superior enemies. This discovery didn't just add significantly to his anxiety of responsibility; it was also decisive in animating deep-seated death guilt.

Ōoka was also shocked to learn about this time that bereaved family members were reading *Fires on the Plain* as a *factual record* of the combat experience of Twenty-sixth and Sixteenth Division soldiers.[6] Having written for years about inferior Japanese soldiers who struggled egoistically to survive under abominable frontline conditions in the Philippines, he now felt strongly that it was his solemn moral obligation to correct the record by exposing the whole truth of Japanese battlefield experience in the Philippines.[7]

Awareness that Japanese soldiers fought well had significant ramifications. Now more than ever, Ōoka was convinced that the soldiers themselves were not primarily to blame for defeat. In *My Literary Life,* he describes the effect this knowledge had on his literary project:

> [My plans] were the same in that I intended to and actually did write a documentary account of how such a large number of men had to die pointlessly because they lacked supplies. Around 1953, all the [Japanese] materials I read were colored with an awareness of defeat. All that was said about the Twenty-sixth Division, for example, was as I described it in *Fires on the Plain:* the men were driven back before they were able to cross the mountains and attack Burauen [airfield]. While it was clear that some soldiers from the Sixteenth Division did join in the attack, survivors reported that upon landing, paratroopers immediately fled to their encampment and retreated with them without engaging the enemy. This simply was not the case. Because they gave up the attack midway themselves, survivors didn't really know what happened. These, however, were the only stories available at the time. I was shocked to read the American battle records and discover that the paratroopers actually did take part in the attack. From that time, my account began to take the form of describing how the campaign was lost even though there were many soldiers who fought effectively.[8]

The discovery that his countrymen performed remarkably well on Leyte Island provided Ōoka with the last element he needed to take up his mission of survivor illumination.[9] Armed with indisputable evidence that responsibility for defeat could not in all fairness be laid at the feet of the rank and file, he was now able to side with them as he unflaggingly endeavored to determine where it did lie. The following passage from *My Literary Life* is particularly instructive in this regard:

> It goes without saying that those who have never experienced war do not understand it clearly. The same can be said, however, for those who have had battlefield experience. Apparently, there were quite a few [professional] military men who read my account and had insights into their own experience. I myself did not understand [war] until I wrote [*The Battle for Leyte Island*]. Kanno [Akimasa] kindly brought to my attention the fact that the keynote in *A Prisoner of War's Account* was to sever all sympathy for the dead, and that, in reaction, or rather by a process of reversal, I came to feel like communing with them. It certainly is true that my insistence on "having no sympathy for those who died from the same cause that nearly ended my own life" reflected a kind of twisted psychology. Even though I actually did feel that way in the Philippines, I think I continued to insist on it afterward to compensate for the guilt (*yamashisa*) I felt over survival. When I learned how well many soldiers fought, my attitude changed completely.[10]

Robert Lifton observes that survivors such as Ōoka are burdened with an overwhelming "debt to the dead." Both death guilt and the anxiety of responsibility are related to a deep-rooted awareness of unfulfilled obligations. Survivors continue to be assailed by conscience in such a way until they can find a way of "repaying" those who died in their place.[11] Exhaustively researching and writing *The Battle for Leyte Island* was Ōoka's means of accomplishing this crucial task. Lifton identifies two predominant modes of survivor formulation: psychological nonresistance and survivor mission.[12] The latter, of course, is the most pertinent to appreciating how Ōoka managed to bring his journey of survivor formulation to a positive, enlightening conclusion. Significantly, the path Ōoka blazed in the direction of recovery and renewal during the two and a half decades after survival is strikingly similar in its general outlines to that traversed so painfully by other heavily burdened survivors:

We have seen that the dropping of the atomic bomb in Hiroshima annihilated a general sense of life's coherence as much as it did human bodies. We have also seen that mastery of the experience depended upon re-establishing form within which not only the death immersion but the survivor's altered identity could be grasped and rendered significant. This quest for formulation turns both *hibakusha* and concentration camp survivors into what has been called "collectors of justice." Beyond medical and economic benefits as such, they seek a sense of world-order in which their suffering has been recognized, in which reparative actions by those responsible for it can be identified.[13]

The Battle for Leyte Island

The Battle for Leyte Island is Ōoka's comprehensive narrative account of the land, air, and sea battles fought between Japanese, American, and Filipino soldiers that effectively signaled Japan's defeat in the Pacific War.[14] Ōoka began serializing this monumental 1,242-page work in *Chūō kōron* in January 1967, and the last installment appeared in July 1969.[15] To prepare to write this seminal work, he read all the available Japanese and English-language literature on the campaign (official battle histories, scholarly works, memoirs) and interviewed more than a hundred Japanese survivors.[16] Indeed, his commitment to examining every primary and secondary source related to the conflict earned him the nickname *shirabe oni* (research demon). Ōoka began to do his research in earnest in 1966, and he serialized *The Battle for Leyte Island* over an unbroken two-and-a-half-year period. The commitment, unwavering sense of purpose, and incredible stamina he brought to bear on this monumental project can leave no doubt that he was on a serious moral and ethical mission.

In "The Philippines and I" (Fuiripin to watashi, 1971), Ōoka looks back on his war-related writings and makes the following penetrating observations about their interrelationship:

> I became a novelist by writing "Before Capture," an account of my experience on Mindoro Island. My treatment of it, however, which was overly rational and aimed at personal understanding, was far from complete. By fictionalizing the experience of a routed soldier on Leyte Island, I sought to get at some of the things I didn't write about in "Before Capture." *Fires on the Plain* was a novelistic expansion of the verbatim notes I took on the story a Sixteenth Division soldier told me in the Leyte prisoner-of-war camp. In this

> way, my mind worked to supplement earlier works. As a former soldier, however, I regretted the lack of objective records related to the Battle for Leyte Island.
>
> Thus, my next project was to try to write a bird's-eye account of the campaign. (16:169–170)

The fundamental dynamic Ōoka draws attention to here—progressively supplementing earlier works by introducing and working through inadequately articulated or missing elements—holds true for his entire body of writings on the Pacific War. This passage also exposes a parallel and equally important progression; as he wrote about the war, the locus of concern progressively shifted from personal experience on Mindoro to the battlefield experience of individual soldiers on Leyte Island to attaining overall perspective and comprehension of the Battle for Leyte Island. This movement from microcosmic to macrocosmic perspective contributed greatly to Ōoka's formulative journey by enabling him to put his own and his comrades' battlefield experience in context.

While noticeable in his early war-related writings, Ōoka's interest in the overarching social structures and dynamics that condition individual experience is most conspicuous in *In the Shadow of Cherry Blossoms.* It is also integral to the series of historical pieces he wrote on the experience of men whose lives were lost or shattered about the time of the Meiji Restoration (1868). In the following passage from "Why I Wrote *The League of Heavenly Punishment*" (Naze *Tenchūgumi* o kaku ka, 1964), Ōoka describes how he came to realize the significance of politics to personal experience:

> My initial interest in the League of Heavenly Punishment was completely emotional. In 1941, Kikuchi Kan published *The League of Heavenly Punishment Presses On* in the *Mainichi Newspaper.* Today, I think that it is one of his weakest works, but at the time I was deeply moved by the fate of the *rōnin* [masterless samurai] who fled into the Totsukawa Mountains in Yamato after being routed.
>
> At that time, elder statesmen of the Restoration and the League of Heavenly Punishment were being lionized. While I came as a result to despise Meiji Restoration histories, I was nonetheless drawn to the league itself. I felt warmly disposed toward them because their belief in honoring the emperor, expelling the barbarians (*sonnō-jōi*) gained them nothing.
>
> When I myself subsequently experienced being part of a routed army in

> the Philippines, my sympathy for these men deepened. I decided that if I ever wrote a historical novel, it would be about the League of Heavenly Punishment. From 1948, I began to gather historical materials. My lack of study during the war came back to haunt me, however, and I had an extremely difficult time comprehending restoration histories.
>
> Since I had originally become interested in the league because of the poetry I sensed in their fleeing after defeat through the autumn foliage of the Totsukawa Mountains, it was hard for me to concern myself with the complicated dynamics of the restoration as a whole. As an amateur, I was unable to determine whether it was an absolutist or bourgeois revolution, and I had no interest whatsoever in the schemes and machinations of cunning leaders and strategists. I felt, however, that in order to convey the beauty of the League of Heavenly Punishment, I had to write about the August 18 political change in Kyoto that was the root cause of their failure. (14:134–135)

While the focus of Ōoka's concern remained firmly on the League of Heavenly Punishment, he came to see that in order to treat their experience fully he would have to deal with the macrocosmic political forces that conditioned their tragic experience. In the end, Ōoka left *The Gang of Heavenly Punishment* unfinished. After writing in detail about the political shift that sealed their fate, he abandoned the project at the very point where they had been defeated and were about to flee into the mountains.

Ōoka incorporated his insights into the importance of overarching political structures and dynamics to individual experience in his account of the failed Japanese campaign for the Philippines. He writes explicitly about this in "My Intentions in *The Battle for Leyte Island*" (*Reite senki* no ito, 1970):

> My war experience was that of one who entered the conflict as a conscript in 1944. I was a real greenhorn who had barely been taught how to hold a rifle. Consequently, I was an extremely ineffective soldier. At the time, the tides of war had turned against Japan, and things were going poorly everywhere in the Pacific. While I was such a weak soldier that I ended up being captured, I nonetheless wrote about my experience. The central theme of my [early] war literature involved consideration, based on my own battlefield experience, of how humans survive amidst the wretched conditions of war and how I myself did so. War, however, is a large-scale undertaking. Since war involves one country fighting against another, it is carried out on a level transcending individual interests. I was sent to Mindoro Island . . . and there were specific plans concerning troop positioning, how much ammunition was needed, and

> how the enemy would be counterattacked upon landing. These matters were decided by staff officers in Manila. More broadly, matters having to do with the entire Pacific region were determined by Imperial Headquarters. My personal experience was a product of these decisions. (15:481–482)

Masuda Kazutoshi has observed that by viewing the Battle for Leyte Island from a macrocosmic perspective, Ōoka was finally able to accomplish the task Tamura was unable to see through to completion in *Fires on the Plain*—"converting the chance that now dominate[d his] life back into necessity" by "connecting [his] present existence with the life of chance forced on [him] by the military authorities" (3:402).[17] Retrospectively viewing his traumatic war experience and survival as the natural outcome of macrocosmic factors unknowable at the time ultimately enabled Ōoka to restore integration and coherence to his life. Indeed, through researching and writing *The Battle for Leyte Island,* Ōoka was able to move from ignorance to understanding. In a telling anecdote related in "My Intentions in *The Battle for Leyte Island,*" he contrasts his severely limited grasp of the situation at the time with the full knowledge subsequently afforded by hindsight:

> Special Attack Forces first emerged during the Battle for Leyte Island. They even appeared over Mindoro. We saw them after withdrawing from the coast into the mountains. As we lay about absentmindedly toward dusk, we would hear the strained rattling sound our planes made as they passed overhead. The noise was so dismal that we thought, "We won't be able to win this war no matter how many of those they send." Because they only appeared at dusk, we called them "bat attacks." . . . There were only about five hundred soldiers like me on Mindoro. It was easiest for me to think that I was taken prisoner because the war was a totally lost cause with no redeeming value whatsoever. Through my research, however, I learned that the newly formed Special Attack Forces actually achieved outstanding results in the early battles using [modified] Zero fighters. . . . I realized for the first time that the terrible rattling sound I heard back then as the planes passed overhead was caused by the heavy bombs they carried, and my experience from twenty-five years ago was revived in me. (15:498–499)[18]

It is impossible for any individual soldier on the battlefield to gain an overall perspective on his unfolding experience at the time. In fact, a contemporaneous comprehension of the big picture is beyond the grasp even of the highest-level commander and strategist. Macrocosmic perspective on a massive, complex, and multidimensional land, sea, and air campaign lasting several months is attainable only after the fact, when the relevant records have been collected from individuals on all sides of the conflict and at every level of involvement. Even then, the historical record itself is often incomplete and problematic. This was particularly true of Japanese accounts of the disastrous Battle for Leyte Island. As Ōoka notes in his afterward to the work, "As is well known, Japan suffered some of its greatest losses during the Pacific War at Leyte Island. Because of the number and severity of strategic errors, it was the most humiliating battleground for former army and navy men. While the naval battle had been written about casually in terms of gamesmanship, there were virtually no comprehensive accounts of the land battles. The few that had appeared were little more than embellished tales" (10:608). Ōoka chose to call his book a battle account (*senki*) rather than a battle history (*senshi*) because of the incomplete, problematic nature of the documentary literature available at the time. In the postscript, he elaborates on this important matter:

> There are naturally limits on the amount of information an individual can gather about this kind of large-scale event. Since I am not a specialist in history or military matters, there may well be problems with my readings of and judgments on the documentary literature. It was not my intention, however, to write a battle history. [Instead] I describe a drama that was acted out on the circumscribed stage of Leyte Island. Since the Japanese and the Americans chose Leyte as the site of their decisive battle, its tropical spaces became the locations for a variety of unavoidable Japanese, American, and Filipino actions. Ultimately, I'd like to describe the work as a great collection of dreams that I as a novelist saw. There are many fundamental documents that still have not been made public. Strictly speaking, there is too little [historical] evidence to warrant calling my work a history. (10:609–610)

There were several other reasons why Ōoka avoided associating his work with battle histories. He knew that official battle histories were produced by professional military men and that they tended to concern themselves with key players, strategy, tactics, logistics, supplies, communications, and other technical matters related to modern warfare while giving little attention to the realities of soldiers' frontline experience. In addition, from reading through the memoirs of commanders and high-ranking staff officers,

Ōoka was certain that when the official battle history of the Battle for Leyte Island was finally released, it would be rife with distortions, embellishments, omissions, and cover-ups. Since Ōoka's survivor mission entailed exposing the whole truth and reality of Leyte battlefield experience in the name of all the soldiers who fought, suffered, and died there, he wanted to clearly distinguish his work from such conventional military accounts.

Speaking of his work as a great collection of dreams (*ōkina yume no shūyaku*) enabled him to convey that the bird's-eye perspective he was able to gain with the benefit of hindsight was not part of the experience at the time, but the subsequent product of exhaustive research and imagination. Ōoka's dream metaphor, moreover, is highly ironic. As will be detailed in the section on responsibility for defeat, Ōoka repeatedly describes the irrational, irresponsible, and inept strategies adopted by Japan's military leaders as pipe dreams; and those backward, unrealistic, and irresponsible plans produced the collective nightmare suffered by tens of thousands of frontline soldiers in the Philippines toward the end of the Pacific War.

By characterizing *The Battle for Leyte Island* as a drama (*geki*), Ōoka draws attention to the fact that the work focuses on human beings. Although he examines strategy and tactics thoroughly, he does so in large part because they had direct bearing on the battlefield experience of the men burdened with enacting the role of soldier on the "circumscribed stage of Leyte Island." In "My Intentions in *The Battle for Leyte Island*," Ōoka explains how the advent of conscription led to the birth of modern war literature. Once wars came to be fought by nonprofessionals, profound tensions inevitably arose between the demands of patriotic duty and the dictates of conscience, and survivors wrote about their experience with a new focus on the (im)morality of modern warfare (15:489–490). He goes on to praise the authors of *War and Peace, All Quiet on the Western Front,* and *The Naked and the Dead* for keeping their sights set firmly on the human dimensions of armed conflict. Toward the end of the piece, he humbly writes that the value of his own work will be found here as well:

> As I wrote *The Battle for Leyte Island,* I realized that war is not a simple matter of victory and defeat. The same basic principles at work in everyday society are also at work in war. The intentions, desires, weaknesses, and emotions of the various people who make up the military are as important in war as they are in peace. There is still no official Japanese battle history of the

> campaign for Leyte Island. Even when one finally appears, it will be little more than a military record. Because novelists take the standpoint of keeping humans in sight throughout the course of war, they can explore issues never touched on in official accounts. The birth of the genre of war literature in contemporary times can be traced to writers who paid particularly close attention to the human dimensions of war. If my work has any significance, it will be precisely in this regard. (15:502)

Realities of Leyte Battlefields

Ōoka dedicated *The Battle for Leyte Island* to dead soldiers (*shinda heitaitachi*). With this dedication, he announces from the outset that his foremost concern in the work is the soldiers whose lives were sacrificed during this fateful campaign. And while he devotes the most space and attention to the battlefield experience of his own countrymen, he also writes with understanding and sympathy about American soldiers,[19] and in the epilogue gives serious consideration to the profound effect the conflict had on the Filipino people.

Consoling and Honoring the War Dead

Clearly, one of Ōoka's central aims in *The Battle for Leyte Island* was consoling (*chinkon*), honestly remembering, honoring, and memorializing the war dead.[20] As previously mentioned, proper separation from and sustained meaningful connection to the dead is difficult under normal circumstances. In the following passage, Robert Lifton comments on survivors' usual means of dealing with their ambivalent feelings toward the dead: "A universal solution to the dilemma is the survivor's participation in *rites de passage*—funeral ceremonies—which speed the dead on their 'journey' to another plane of existence, and 'incorporate the deceased into the world of the dead.'" The fundamental dilemma Ōoka faced with regard to the war dead—both his own Nishiya Company comrades and those who died fighting in the Battle for Leyte Island—was that no such rites de passage had been adequately conducted. It wasn't just that his comrades had died under extraordinarily violent circumstances on foreign soil, but that many of their bodies had been abandoned on the battlefield as well. Ōoka clearly felt they were homeless spirits who had been denied proper separation from, and continuity with their survivors. And, as Lifton stresses, "The survivor must reject the dead (especially the newly dead) until he can place them safely within a mode of immortality."[21]

Ōoka makes the following declaration near the beginning of the work: "War requiems and the tears of bereaved family members are probably not sufficient to console the spirits of dead soldiers" (9:59). Such being the case, what can be done to put their troubled souls to rest? As if in response to this implicit query, Ōoka introduces the opening stanza from Wilfred Owen's poem "Anthem for Doomed Youth" and comments explicitly on how he incorporated Owen's insights into his own mission as a collector of justice:

> *What passing-bells for these who die as cattle?*
> *—Only the monstrous anger of the guns.*
> *Only the stuttering rifles' rapid rattle*
> *Can patter out their hasty orisons.*[22]

> From here on, I intend to describe in as minute detail as possible the things I have judged to be realities of the battles fought on Leyte Island. I will re-create the roar of 75-mm mortars and the reports of Model 38 rifles. This, I believe, is the only means of consoling the spirits of those who died in combat. And this is all I can do. (9:59)

Ōoka was committed to telling the whole truth of the Battle for Leyte Island. As previously mentioned, before he began this mission of survivor illumination, people generally assumed, as had Ōoka himself, that the campaign ended in such decisive, humiliating defeat because of soldiers' lack of fighting spirit and poor battlefield performance. This mistaken view had its origins in and was perpetuated by the defensive stories told by survivors, the self-justifying memoirs of high-ranking military men, the miserable scenes witnessed and recorded by war correspondents who visited the island toward the end of the campaign, and the negative depictions in works such as *Fires on the Plain.*[23] After years of struggling to formulate his own traumatic battlefield experience, Ōoka knew that self-justification, scapegoating, and ignorance were at the root of these uniformly negative representations of his comrades' battlefield performance. While he doesn't deny the existence of cowardly, ineffective, and egoistical soldiers, his primary focus in *The Battle for Leyte Island* was to correct the record by establishing how bravely, resolutely, and effectively many of his compatriots fought. And this untold story of the disastrous campaign for the Philippines had profound relevance to remembrance of the war dead. As Ōoka writes about the Sixteenth Infantry Division:

> The American records I have drawn upon up to this point enable recognition of the fact that the division probably resisted to the full extent of the manpower they actually had at their disposal. While American records, too, contain exaggerations and can't be taken completely at face value, it can be said that for a corps that was [initially] routed at the shoreline, they gave a hundred and ten percent in the battles at Buri Airfield, Tabontabon, Kiling, and Dagami.
>
> I have closely followed the American records . . . in order to redeem some of their honor and calm the spirits of the men who died fighting in hopeless battles. (9:306)

Ōoka carried out his survivor mission of exposing and recreating the realities of Leyte battlefields with bereaved family members in mind. Official wartime notifications contained but five brief lines related to the approximate time and location of death. The bereaved naturally hungered to learn more about the specific circumstances under which their loved ones perished. Ōoka touches on this important dimension of his work in the afterword: "The greater the [battlefield] losses, the greater the number of bereaved family members who want to know how and in what kind of places their fathers, elder brothers, and sons fought and died" (10: 609). In "The Philippines and I," he describes how this matter progressively came to the fore as he wrote the work: "My initial intention was to grasp the totality of the Battle for Leyte Island. As I wrote, however, it increasingly became a matter of enumerating where and how each and every soldier died" (16:170).

Keeping his sights firmly set on reproducing the battlefield experience of the individuals who fought and died in the Battle for Leyte Island enabled Ōoka to accomplish more than keeping a face on war, consoling the troubled spirits of the dead, and comforting their bereaved families; it also facilitated the work of mourning. As when he composed his lyrical requiem for his fallen comrades from Nishiya Company in 1958 and his prose elegy for Mutsuko/Yōko the following year, there can be little doubt that Ōoka was quietly grieving throughout the time he researched and wrote *The Battle for Leyte Island.* Indeed, the work in a sense can be understood as a great, sustained memorial for all the soldiers who died in the Philippines. He highlights this dimension of his work in the concluding passage of the postscript:

> Mr. Mamiya [Haruo's] older brother, Masaoto was an adjunct in the First Division's Fifty-seventh Regiment; Suzuki [Takao's] brother Tsukida Teruhiko served as headquarters sergeant in the Forty-ninth Regiment of the same division. I can easily imagine that they edited and produced the maps for this book with such commitment and devotion because they saw their work as a kind of mass for the repose of the spirits of their deceased brothers and the other war dead. Similarly, I, too, wrote this book while thinking of my comrades from Nishiya Company who died on Mindoro Island and the eighty thousand compatriots who died on Leyte Island. I feel that it has been through their protection and guidance that I have lived to see this book through to fruition. (10: 610–611)

In *The Battle for Leyte Island,* Ōoka reproduces soldiers' battlefield experience with extraordinary realism and immediacy. Before we examine representative passages, it is useful to comment on the dynamic that helps make this possible. To this end, it is worth recalling that Ōoka compared the relationship between himself and Mutsuko/Yōko to that of Dante and Pia in *The Divine Comedy.* Like Dante, Ōoka saw his role as writer in *In The Shadow of Cherry Blossoms* as that of medium between the living and the troubled spirits of the dead. And just as the famous Italian poet heard Pia call out to him as he passed through purgatory, Ōoka heard Yōko's soul implore him to convey the full truth of her tragic life and death to the people of this world. Ōoka takes this same role in *The Battle for Leyte Island;* this time, however, he heard not one, but thousands of souls cry out to him.[24] In *The Collective Self,* Kamei Hideo observes that Ōoka describes soldiers' battlefield experience on Leyte Island as if "possessed" (*tsuita*).[25] This is a fitting way to view the role he serves in conveying the realities of Leyte battlefields: he acts as a medium through which the testimonies of the war dead are channeled to the realm of the living. Ōoka closes his magnum opus with the following powerful statement: "The testimony of the dead is multifaceted, and their voices are audible to those who would listen. The soil of Leyte Island continues to tell their tale" (10:547).

The Opening Battle

At the outset of his battle account, Ōoka focuses on reproducing the experience of the men of the Sixteenth Division charged with meeting the massive American amphibious force that reached Leyte Island in October 1944. He begins with the intensive naval bombardment that initiated the fierce, bloody battles that were to rage on for almost two months:

> The weather was clear on October 20. The offing became increasingly visible with the arrival of dawn, and as the sun began to rise, lookouts saw an unbroken line of black along the horizon. It was formed by ships. At 0600 hours the six battleships in Leyte Bay opened fire. After two hours, cruisers and destroyers entered deeply into the bay and commenced their bombardment. They had no specific target. The entire thirty-kilometer coastline between San Jose and Dulag was covered with shells from the waterline to two kilometers inland.
>
> Kincaid's Seventh Fleet carried every type of shell except armor piercing. Large shells for destroying fortified mortar emplacements and pillboxes, shells designed to kill and maim personnel, and incendiary phosphorous shells were fired haphazardly. One explosion followed so closely after the next that there was no pause in the thunderous sounds. According to one survivor, it was like the constant howl of a typhoon. (9:63)

In this introductory passage, Ōoka supplements the experiences of eyewitnesses with detailed information concerning the weather, identity of the enemy forces, and type of projectiles used to soften up the shoreline. The reader first sees through the eyes of a sentry near the water's edge and then hears the deafening roar of high explosives echoing in a survivor's ears. By grounding his descriptions in the senses, Ōoka embodies the perspective and heightens the realism.

Ōoka next turns to the expectations of the soldiers dug in along the coast. While well aware of the enormous destructive power of the preparatory bombardment they would be subjected to, the soldiers had been persuaded by staff officers that they need not be overly concerned because no matter how many shells were fired, it was impossible to hit every position. Many did, in fact, survive the initial onslaught. As Ōoka is quick to add, however, "It was no easy matter . . . to withstand the deafening roar, which continued for four hours without interruption" (9:64).

Ōoka subsequently reproduces the experience of the bombardment itself and describes the first casualties:

> The men saw batteries fortified with palm trunks and mud get blown away with their foundations, and they watched palms trees burn from the ground up until the fronds at the top caught fire and sent flames up into the sky like roman candles. Comrades right next to them one second would suddenly disappear, and when they returned to their senses, they would realize that the flesh of their own thighs had been torn open. Some of the dead were lying on their sides with their hands clasped over their chests as if in sleep. There were other corpses in similar positions, but their cheeks had been shattered and their eyeballs had sprung from their sockets to dangle down toward their pillows of soil. There were headless bodies, bodies missing arms, missing legs, bodies with entrails spilling out from rent-open abdomens. All around them were human bodies broken apart and twisted in ways that defied imagination. (9:64)

This description condenses the visual imagery permanently imprinted in the eyes of the survivors. After witnessing the fiery destruction of their batteries and the surrounding trees, the gaze is fixed on the terrible effects of high explosives on fragile human bodies. In this way, Ōoka stresses that indiscriminate physical dismemberment and mutilation are incontrovertible battlefield realities. Ōoka refuses to allow the death and physical destruction of combat to be downplayed, sidestepped, beautified, or ignored. It cannot be overemphasized, moreover, that there was no way to properly attend to these shattered and fragmented bodies. Kamei has rightly observed that abandoned corpses are a leitmotif of *The Battle for Leyte Island.*[26] Through repeated, detailed description, they become in the minds of the reader, as they did in those of survivors, images indelibly associated with combat.

In the next section of his sustained, multifaceted treatment of the opening engagement, Ōoka directs attention to the varied reactions of officers and soldiers:

> The air was filled with the strangely pungent odor of gunpowder and freshly turned earth. There were big-talking noncoms who cowered with upturned eyes, and cadets who inexplicably emerged from their trenches and wandered about with their arms dangling limply at their sides. Some recruits buried their faces in the dirt and sobbed. Even veteran noncoms wondered if their bodies would miraculously fly up out of their trenches in a crouching position, be blown back through the trees, and then float back to earth.
>
> Among the noncoms, however, there were also men who were thinking, "Think I'll die before taking some American soldiers with me?! Ha!" There

> were also enlisted men who were themselves surprised by their ability to keep their eyes open, raise their heads above their trenches, and look out upon the sparkling ocean that spread out before them. These differences in response depended more on physical constitution than on spirit. Some soldiers had dull nerves and criminal tendencies. Others, who had nerves of steel and burned with the desire to destroy [the enemy], were able to keep their heads and continue to aim and fire their machine guns accurately throughout the bombardment. Honest and diligent men who refused to let themselves rest before fulfilling their assigned duties also fought with great determination. Even men previously assumed to be meek, men who had never before spoken with raised voices, suddenly began to bellow words of encouragement to their comrades. (9:64–65)

Ōoka frames this detailed depiction of frontline soldiers' conduct and performance with sensory descriptions—the smell of gunpowder and overturned soil and the booming shouts of men spurring their comrades to redouble their efforts. Conspicuous in this treatment is the unpredictability of human behavior in extremity. Some of those assumed to have nerves of steel quickly crumbled, while others expected to quake in their boots found the capacity to function effectively amid the death, destruction, and chaos. Ōoka's comment about the importance of physical constitution is telling. He resists approaching soldiers' combat performance in terms of "spirit." In so doing, he implicitly rejects the emphasis military leaders and ideologues placed on *yamatodamashii* (Japanese spirit). The focus on physical constitution, moreover, is consistent with his treatment of battlefield experience: it is the composition of the material body that primarily determines how a soldier performs under severe stress, and it is the corporeal self that is destroyed and dismembered when struck by flying bullets and metal fragments. Thus, Ōoka insists that battle be approached in concrete, as opposed to abstract, terms. Instead of spirit, he highlights the willpower, determination, and strong sense of obligation of the soldiers who fought well. It is also worth noting that he does not stand in judgment of those who were unable to function at this level; while honestly acknowledging their debilitation, he nonetheless describes their experience, too, with empathy and understanding.

In the final passage of his sustained reproduction of the opening engagement, Ōoka takes issue with conventional treatments of war and forcefully sets forth his own thoughts on the matter:

> From ages past, war tales have been written by people with dispositions diametrically opposite to the men just described. In such works the causes and outcomes of battle are pursued in storybook fashion by stressing strategy and tactics. This is because such war tales cannot be written without focusing on brilliant generals such as Shokatsu Ryō or Sanada Yukimura.[27] Actual battles, however, are carried out by men with dispositions wholly unconnected with strategy or ninja. These men, members of every military rank from private to general, often make battles take courses that have little to do with tactics or war tales.[28] Despite the fact that the Battle for Leyte Island was fought with a critical lack of supplies and according to makeshift strategies, it continued for two months because of the bravery and determination of men such as these. (9:65)

It was clearly Ōoka's intention to write a new kind of battle account centered on the soldiers and officers burdened with carrying out the ill-conceived orders of their distant superiors. This is not to say that he ignores the leaders and strategists in Imperial Headquarters and the Southern, Fourteenth Area, and Thirty-fifth Armies. What he does consistently do, however, is connect their decisions directly to the experience of the men in the field. And in the process, he demonstrates clearly that it was they themselves, and not the soldiers, who bore the primary responsibility for defeat.

Ōoka subsequently details how the men of the Sixteenth Division stoutly defended their positions until they were overwhelmed by their superior enemies. The Americans brought their organized resistance to an end by October 30, and the 3,000 survivors withdrew into the rugged coastal mountains. Although there were many wounded and they were desperately low on food and ammunition, the survivors of the opening battle nevertheless continued to engage the succession of patrols sent out against them. Indeed, in the end, at least 150 soldiers from the Sixteenth Division took part in the subsequent attack on Burauen and Buri airfields some two weeks later.[29] In the following passage, Ōoka praises these stalwart men in the highest terms:

> Even after losing more than 200 men when they were ambushed by the Americans as they sought to break through to the east, soldiers from the Sixteenth Division did not abandon the scheduled attack. It is unclear whether they crossed over the ridge and sought to break through from a different valley or avoided the valleys and followed the ridgeline until they could

descend to the plains. Be that as it may, it is to the honor of the division that 150 men joined in the attack on Buri Airfield on the morning of the Sixth.

It is unclear whether they attacked at dawn on the sixth rather than dusk on the fifth because they encountered an American patrol or hesitated when the paratroopers they were expecting failed to materialize. The attack force was apparently composed primarily of remnants from the Twentieth and Ninth Regiments. In light of the battles the division had to fight up to that point and the harsh conditions they endured [in the mountains], this was one of the bravest actions undertaken during the entire course of the Battle for Leyte Island. (10:97)

The Battle of Leyte Gulf

In addition to detailing the experience and lauding the performance of soldiers in the Sixteenth Division, Ōoka also devotes ample attention to conveying the gruesome realities of the sea battles that took place between October 24 and 26. In the following passage, he recalls the experience of sailors on the enormous battleship *Musashi* and then quotes at length from a survivor's spine-chilling, eyewitness account:

> The sinking of the *Musashi* was replete with misery. When this largest of battleships swung into action, wholly unforeseen situations arose. To defend against aerial attack, the main guns fired incendiary shells called *sanshikidan.* When the warning buzzer sounded, gunners manning the numerous antiaircraft machine guns on the deck had to seek cover immediately. During the heat of battle, however, buzzers either didn't go off or were inaudible, and many men were blown from the deck into the sea. After the big guns fired, smoke engulfed the ship, and the men were unable to see the enemy planes as they dove in for the attack.
>
> Sea battles produced scenes of misery not witnessed on land: appendages raining down from the sky, chunks of flesh plastered to walls, cascades of blood pouring down stairways, and death down in holds from which there was no escape. We mustn't forget that these sea battles were filled with harsh realities of a wholly different order from the things depicted in the memoirs of admirals and deck officers:
>
> "There was no one around me. I struggled to return to my position through the viscous, sticky blood on the deck as if moving in slow motion. The dense objects under my feet were scattered chunks of human flesh. And they weren't just on the deck; they were plastered like so many pieces of clay all over the surrounding metal structure, and crimson droplets fell from them one after another. Half a beet-red face was pressed up against one side of a torn-up piece of decking as if rubbing cheeks with it. There were two young

> soldiers collapsed nearby whose clothes had been stripped off. They had both apparently been thrown into that position by the gun blasts. Only a single foot protruded from one's pants leg. Their skin had taken the brunt of the blast. The outer fascia—which looked like that of a skinned frog—was peeled back and still oozing blood. Someone was writhing near the base of the machine-gun emplacement. He was spread flat out under a gun barrel that had been flipped upside down on top of him. His neck was twisted around and he was facing upward. The barrel pressing down heavily against the side of his neck sizzled as it seared further into his flesh. I proceeded forward and saw a young emergency worker with a child's face dragging something springy behind him as he squirmed over the deck. His jaw was clenched, and his face, which was already showing signs of death, was the color of earth. Upon closer inspection, I saw that he was dragging his entrails. They were light peach in color and looked strangely moist and shiny. With unsteady, quivering hands, the youth struggled with everything he had left to force his intestines back into his ripped-open belly. Suddenly a wheezing sound emerged from his throat, he pitched forward onto the tangled cords of his entrails, and then froze in that position. He continued to grope at his intestines with his scorched fingertips until he took his last breath. A convulsion ran through his body. I dashed away still watching him from the corner of my eye." (Watanabe Kiyoshi, *Umi yukaba muzuzuku shikabane*)
> (9:175–176)

Once again, Ōoka leads into a vivid account of combat experience with a sharp critique of conventional treatments of battle. As he writes in the second paragraph, "We mustn't forget that these sea battles were filled with cruel realities of a wholly different order from the things depicted in the memoirs of admirals and deck officers." As with those of their army counterparts, the written recollections of high-ranking naval leaders normally center on strategic decisions, tactics, and the general course of engagements. Conspicuously absent are the cruel realities that are experienced by the individuals who must take physical part in war. Ōoka insists that the human experience of armed conflict be unflinchingly detailed at the ground, or, in this case, deck, level rather than from the physically and psychologically removed level of the bridge. Since war is actually carried out by individuals, the only means of fully exposing its brutal realities is to approach it from the standpoint of those physically engaged in it. It should go without saying that if the basic truths of combat are forgotten or obscured by abstractions, it becomes all the more likely that naive, idealistic young men will once again be willingly led into war.

To make absolutely sure that the most definitive experiences of battle are remembered, Ōoka introduces a survivor's firsthand account of what transpired on the deck of the *Musashi* during the disastrous Battle of Leyte Gulf. As with his treatments of his own frontline experience, the power of the descriptive language comes from the indelible imagery of carnage imprinted in Watanabe's mind during his psychic and physical immersion in death. As with the portrayal of the soldiers of the Sixteenth Division during the bombardment that opened the Battle for Leyte Island, the unwavering focus in this profoundly disturbing passage is on human bodies literally vaporized and blown to pieces. In this description, however, there is an added element: among the many bodies that have been torn apart, shattered, and pulverized are those of extremely young men, of youths with the faces of children. Just as the vulnerability of the human body in war must not be forgotten, so people must realize that much of war is carried out by a nation's youth. And a further point also must be borne in mind: if the mortal remains of soldiers are scattered and vaporized in this way, around what can survivors such as Watanabe and bereaved family members organize their rites de passage? Indeed, all they have are the immediate, detailed accounts of the circumstances under which their comrades' and loved ones' lives came to a sudden, violent, premature, and grotesque end. In this sense, such faithful reproduction of battlefield reality is itself a kind of memorial.

The Special Attack Forces

In addition to re-creating the experience of the soldiers from the Sixteenth Division who opposed the American landing and that of sailors on the *Musashi* during the Battle of Leyte Gulf, Ōoka devotes considerable attention to the experience and performance of the Special Attack Forces that flew for the first time during the Battle for Leyte Island. In his treatment of these suicide attack units, Ōoka takes great pains to delineate between the tactic of crashing bomb-laden planes into enemy ships and the men upon whom it fell to do so.[30] He also clearly distinguishes the Special Attack Forces pilots who fought in the Philippines from those who flew months later in the Battle for Okinawa. Some of these relevant contextual matters will be touched upon before I turn to consider Ōoka's re-creation of their combat experience and assessment of their performance.[31]

As Ōoka wrote in the late 1960s about the Special Attack Forces engaged in one-way, self-destructive missions in the Philippines, he was well aware of the negative associations that had built up around them. In *War,* he observes that people generally associated kamikaze pilots with being unskillful and out of control (he cites the term "kamikaze taxi driver" as a case in point).[32] He points out, however, that such a pilot would never have come anywhere near his target. When the Special Attack Forces were first organized, participation was mostly voluntary, pilots were well trained and experienced, and planes were in good condition. This was not the case during the Battle for Okinawa. By the latter stage of the war, participation had increasingly become compulsory, many of the pilots were young and inexperienced, and they had to fly their missions in worn-out training planes. In the following passage, Ōoka distinguishes between the Special Attack Forces pilots who flew in the Philippines and their Okinawa counterparts, and between the suicidal tactic itself and the pilots who enacted it:

> By the time of the Battle for Okinawa, great numbers of young student reserves were sent out on suicide missions. These youths left heartrending testaments that can be seen in collections such as *Kike wadatsumi no koe* and *Aa dōki no sakura.* While participation was ostensibly voluntary, these Special Attack Forces pilots were actually coerced into flying missions in inferior, second-rate planes. Their tender hearts were deeply wounded by the contradiction between the lofty reputation of the Special Attack Forces and the meanness of base life, and the writings they left behind are some of the most devastating to emerge from the war.
>
> At the time of the Battle of Okinawa, it is said that before heading for their targets, some pilots made mock attacks on headquarters. There was also a great increase in the number of planes making emergency landing on small islands because of "mechanical failures." . . . Enemy soldiers record observing Special Attack Forces planes that, rather than attacking, drifted unsteadily down into the sea as if the pilots had lost consciousness.[33]
>
> The last leader of the Special Attack Forces, Rear Admiral Ugaki Matome, commander of the Fifth Air Fleet, records in his *Sensō roku* that by this stage half of the flights ended in "emergency landings." There were also technical officers who suggested abandoning the tactic after the hit rate dropped to 7 percent.
>
> The spiritual anguish imposed on pilots by this tactic defies imagination. It was better when they could still believe that they could save their homeland by offering up their lives. By Okinawa, however, special Attack Forces pilots knew this was no longer possible—and they were right.

> Although they persisted in mouthing statements about certain victory, there wasn't a single professional military man who still believed in the possibility of Japan's winning the war. They were solely motivated by thoughts of saving face. Their pronouncements were a cover for their plan to enter into peace negotiations after a battle victory. I think the most abominable aspect of the Special Attack Forces was forcing young men to die in vain in the name of a great, eternal cause.
>
> Regardless of these difficulties, we can't help but be proud of the fact that the four hundred planes sent out in the Philippines achieved almost as many direct hits (111 vs. 133) and the same number of near hits as the nineteen hundred planes dispatched during the Battle for Okinawa. (9:264–265)

In numerous places, Ōoka describes how skillfully and effectively army and navy Special Attack Forces pilots fought in the Philippines. After detailing their attacks and the severe damage they inflicted on American ships and personnel during the campaign for the Philippines, Ōoka asserts that Japanese can take pride (*hokori*) in their combat performance.

Vice Admiral Ōnishi Takajirō, commander of the First Air Fleet, was the senior officer in the Philippines given charge of organizing and leading the Special Attack Forces. Upon arrival in Manila on October 17, he was shocked to discover that there were only thirty planes at his disposal for the decisive battle scheduled to commence within the week. Since the Shō, or Victory Operation, assumed that Vice Admiral Kurita Takeo's main attack force would have substantial air support as it approached and entered Leyte Bay, Ōnishi concluded that his "only recourse was to attach 250-kilogram bombs to the Zeros he had at his disposal and have each one make deadly strikes directly into enemy ships" (9:262).

Lieutenant Seki Yukio was subsequently selected to lead the navy's Special Attack Forces. In the passage that follows, Commander Tamai describes Seki's reaction upon being asked to take charge of these new suicide units:

> "Captain Seki pressed his lips tightly together and remained silent. With elbows on the table and his head with its long, combed-back hair supported between his hands, he kept his face down and eyes closed as he sank deeply in thought. He remained absolutely still. One second became two, two became three, three became four, four became five . . .
>
> "Suddenly his hands began to move, and I thought he was about to run his fingers through his hair. Instead, he calmly lifted his head and said, *'By*

> *all means please let me do this.'* His tone of voice was clear and decisive; there wasn't the slightest hint of hesitation." (9:262–263)

Ōoka draws attention to the way in which Commander Tamai employs stereotypical military language to stress Captain Seki's composure and firm resolve in making up his mind. Rather than dwelling on Seki's decision, however, Ōoka imagines what must have crossed his mind during the period of silent contemplation immediately preceding it. As with Ōoka's treatment of the shoreline experience of the men of the Sixteenth Division and the sailors on the *Musashi,* he emphasizes excruciating aspects of Special Attack Forces pilots' experience rarely if ever mentioned in the memoirs of staff officers or official battle histories:

> Pilots, of course, had to be ready to die at any time. At this stage of the war, however, when American air power and antiaircraft defenses had been strengthened substantially, taking off on a mission had become tantamount to death. A pilot might make it back three times, but he was sure to be shot down the fourth. When forced to choose a course of action holding absolutely no chance of survival, however, humans cross into a qualitatively different world.
>
> During the heat of battle, people cross this line unexpectedly easily. For a wounded pilot, crashing into an enemy vessel is not only a means of making inevitable death honorable, but also of giving vent to his wrath. Some men reflexively act to sacrifice themselves and save their comrades by covering grenades that fall into their trenches with their own bodies. I feel, however, that between the time they decided in barracks to take part in a suicide mission and the time they set out several days later, and between the time they actually took off and the time they reached their objectives, *tokkōtai* pilots were forced to endure life at its cruelest. (9:263)

Ōoka identifies closely with Captain Seki—and by extension all Special Attack Forces pilots—and imagines the profoundly disturbing psychological and emotional effects of living with the knowledge of certain, violent death within a matter of days, hours, or minutes.

In chapter 10, "Shimpū" (Divine wind), and subsequent chapters, Ōoka draws liberally upon American battle records to produce minute descriptions of some of the most destructive suicide attacks. He begins by correcting the record: "The first fruits of Special Attack Forces attacks are normally attributed to Captain Seki for sinking the escort carrier *St. Lo* off

Samar Island during the height of the Battle of Leyte Gulf on October 25, 1944. However, if the value of the Special Attack Forces is seen not in the extent of damage, but in the self-sacrificing spirit of daring certain death to crash into enemy ships, then this honor must go to the pilot who hit the escort carrier *Santee* earlier that same morning" (9:257). Following are selections from his descriptions of two of the most destructive Special Attack Forces engagements. The first took place on the first day of the Battle of Leyte Gulf, the second as a massive American invasion fleet shaped a course for Mindoro Island (December 13):

> Protected by four Zero fighters, the five Special Attack Forces planes of Lieutenant Seki Yukio's Shikishima unit took off from Mabalacat Airfield at 0725 hours. Their targets were the four carriers and six destroyers ninety nautical miles to the east of Tacloban. This group of escort carriers under Rear Admiral Clifford Sprague had been pursued since morning by Vice Admiral Kurita's fleet.
>
> Kurita's ships had broken off the chase at 0910 hours, and the attack came just as the five escort carriers that had narrowly escaped destruction had turned into the wind to receive their returning planes.
>
> Since they came in just above the surface of the water, the Japanese planes were not picked up by radar. They suddenly climbed to five thousand feet and then dove down vertically. There was no time to launch a counterattack.
>
> After flying over the stern of the flagship, *Kitcan Bay,* one plane did an abrupt wingover. It missed the bridge, hit the starboard side, fell to the sea, and exploded, causing many casualties on deck.
>
> Two other planes headed for the *Fanshow Bay,* but luckily were shot down before they reached it. The two remaining planes making for the *White Plains* passed through the 40-mm antiaircraft fire, rose up 150 meters, and then dove down sharply. One, trailing smoke, turned to crash into the *St. Lo.*
>
> To give sailors worn out from four hours of combat time to rest and have coffee, the *St. Lo* had slowed down considerably. The Special Attack Forces plane exploded after it pierced through the flight deck. This explosion detonated the seven torpedoes and shells stored in the hold. The planes on deck were thrown hundreds of feet into the air, and fire spread back to the stern. The *St. Lo* sank at 1115 hours.
>
> Another plane, apparently choosing its target as it circled the group of warships, finally dove down on the *White Plains.* Sailors on board clearly saw tracer bullets hitting it, but the plane kept coming. Fifty-six hundred meters in front of the ship, it turned, swooped in just above the flight deck, and exploded before crashing into the sea. Human body parts and fragments

from the plane rained down on the deck, injuring eleven men. (9:259–260)

. . .

Special Attack Forces attacks on the convoy were apparently delayed because it was unclear what course it would take. According to [Samuel E.] Morison's *History of Naval Operations in WW II,* as the convoy swung around the southern tip of Negros Island and was about to enter the Sulu Sea just before 1500 hours, it came under attack by a single VAL (Type 99 carrier-based bomber). Because it abruptly emerged from behind the mountains, it wasn't picked up on radar. The two bombs it carried exploded simultaneously when it crashed into the *Nashville*'s bridge, obliterating command headquarters. A violent tremor passed through the entire ship. The explosion ignited the powder magazines of the 5-inch and 40-mm guns. A total of 133 officers and men were killed and 190 injured.

. . .

This was the most effective attack carried out by a Special Attack Forces pilot to date. Judging from the large number of casualties, his plane must have been carrying two 250-kilogram bombs. Only a skilled, experienced pilot could have maneuvered such an encumbered aircraft directly into a flagship. Japanese records make no mention of any naval units being sent out that day. While there is no precise information on the time or point of origin, army records show that six planes from the Hakkō, Kyokkō, Gokoku, and Yasukuni units were dispatched. Was one of these planes misidentified as a Type 99 bomber? Or did a naval Special Attack Forces pilot who had made an emergency landing on Negros attack on his own? (10:203–204)

Ōoka includes detailed descriptions of successful suicide attacks both to reproduce battle realities and to bring home to the reader how difficult it was to evade intercepting fighters and pilot such bomb-laden planes through curtains of antiaircraft fire to hit an enemy ship.[34] He also notes that at the time, American soldiers, too, felt that the Japanese Special Attack Forces were impressive. When asked if they would volunteer to fly on similar missions if they found themselves in the same situation, 70 percent of the American pilots reportedly answered in the affirmative (9:263). Ōoka reserves his highest praise for the small number of Special Attack Forces pilots who *accomplished* their missions. Toward the end of *The Battle for Leyte Island,* he lauds the battle performance of the fliers who brought their suicide missions to successful conclusions: "I cannot help but hold in reverence the Special Attack Forces pilots who first decided of themselves to resolve the issue of life and death on their own terms and were then able to maintain flawless control of their planes until the instant they fatally crashed into their targets. . . . The men who kept their objectives clearly in sight to the very end even after having been handed death sentences were great (*erai*)" (10:520).

Ōoka was so deeply impressed by the courage, willpower, consummate skill, and selflessness exhibited by successful Special Attack Forces pilots that he felt them worthy of inclusion in the modern mythology of the Japanese people.[35] Rather than dwelling on the egoism, baseness, and degeneracy of commanders, strategists, or common soldiers like himself, Ōoka labors to unearth and prominently display these shining examples of what his countrymen were capable of. And he was well aware of the important role they could play in inspiring later generations: "There were men among us who were able to overcome unimaginable spiritual anxiety and agitation to attain their goals. Their achievements are wholly unrelated to the stupidity and corruption of their leaders at the time. That there was room for such strong willpower—the likes of which has disappeared without a trace—to emerge from that desolation must be our hope for the future" (9:265). In this statement, one can again detect the anxiety of responsibility. Implicit is Ōoka's conviction that the Japanese as a people have an obligation to carry on the dying will of the men who sacrificed themselves in the Philippines and the belief that the willpower necessary for doing so could reemerge from the spiritual and moral corruption and degeneration of postwar Japan.

The Battle of Limon Pass

Some of the fiercest, most brutal, and ghastly fighting occurred in and around the rugged, labyrinthine topography in the vicinity of Limon Pass, and Ōoka's vivid, impassioned re-creations of the horrible experience of the soldiers who fought and died there are among the most powerful, unforgettable, and significant in *The Battle for Leyte Island.* These bloody battles, fought mainly between soldiers from the Fifty-seventh and Forty-ninth Regiments of Japan's First Division and the Twenty-first Regiment of the U.S. Twenty-fourth Division, took place over the ten-day period between November 4 and 15. The fighting on November 8, the day a powerful typhoon hit the island, was perhaps the worst. Ōoka exerts himself to reproduce the brutal realities of this most devastating and haunting of Leyte battlefields. He begins with the American perspective:

> The Americans attacked during the typhoon. According to Twenty-fourth Division battle records, the plan was to take advantage of the wind and rain to break through Japanese defenses. A flamethrower corps and some 42-mm chemical mortars arrived just before the attack. The mortars had been used to good effect during the attack on Hill 522 above Palo. They were filled with white phosphorous, and when detonated ten meters above ground by time-delayed fuse, they rained fire down upon men in the trenches below. . . .
>
> . . . The fighting on the eighth and ninth was the grimmest of the battles for control of Limon Pass. After four consecutive days of combat, the Americans' blood was up. They were hell-bent on reaching the main ridgeline that day. They were furious at the Japanese who forced them to engage in such a miserable battle.
>
> Their minds were consumed with thoughts like "Why the hell do we have to fight here? Did we come all these thousands of miles to the Philippines just so the rich back home could get richer and our wives could get laid by pompous assholes?" They became even more enraged when they thought that while they were laying their lives on the line and fighting in the rain, staff officers and war correspondents were back in Palo and Tacloban dancing with local girls. (9:398–399)

The typhoon that hit Leyte on the eighth provided a fitting metaphor for the fighting; from the outset, Ōoka portrays the battles that raged on and around Limon Pass that day as the violent expressions of intense, pent-up emotions. Drawing on American battle records, reportage, and memoirs, he paints a clear picture of the psychological state of the enemy: their "blood was up," they were "hell-bent" on reaching their objective that day, they were "furious" at the Japanese for putting up such resolute resistance, and they were "consumed" with anger and frustration over the difficult, odious, and deadly job they had to do while others took it easy. Ōoka then turns to what the Japanese soldiers were thinking and feeling on that fateful morning: "The Japanese soldiers, too, had worked themselves up into a fit of rage. They felt it was unfair that the Americans could rely on their material superiority, and they were consumed with anger over all the comrades who had been killed during the previous three days of fighting" (9:399). The implications of all this are clear; given no other outlet, all these pent-up emotions would be vented on one another in combat: "The result was hand-to-hand fighting in the rain pitting hatred and abhorrence against wrath and indignation" (9:399).[36]

After establishing the emotional tone of the battle in this way, Ōoka turns to the physical context of this gory battlefield drama:

> At 0700 hours the soldiers from F and L Companies poured out of their foxholes on the eastern slope of the north ridge and climbed upward through the rain. Because the rain was light, their flamethrowers were effective despite strong winds. The cogon grass ahead of them was dried and ignited almost instantaneously. Japanese soldiers emerging from their foxholes were burned to death. The entire north ridge was enveloped in smoke and flames, and a flock of birds that rose up in fright was swept away toward Carigara in the gale-force winds.
>
> According to American records, the Japanese, too, set the grass ablaze with gasoline. The fires constantly shifted directions depending on the wind, now moving toward the Japanese, now in the direction of the Americans. The flames moved insanely over the slopes. (9:399–400)

Having firmly set the physical stage and backdrop, Ōoka unfolds one of what Kamei Hideo has called his "hell screens."[37] But the "hell screen" Ōoka opens on the realities of the Battle for Limon Pass contains an added element: the haunting screams of men dying in unendurable agony:

> The wounded collapsed on the grass struggled in vain to escape the flames. The screams raised by Japanese and American soldiers being roasted alive and the cacophony of the entire ridge going up in flames were enough to drown out the stutter of machine-gun fire.
>
> Hearing the sounds of terribly labored breathing, Japanese soldiers waiting in their trenches for the fires to pass raised their heads to see where it was coming from. A scarlet-faced soldier was just crawling past. They called to him, but he didn't seem to hear them. Gasping horridly, he dragged himself along by clinging to the roots of singed cogon grass. He was bright red from the waist down; there were nothing but crimson stumps where his legs should have been.
>
> There was simply no escape. Young soldiers were assailed by the heart-withering thought that their lives, which should at least have lasted for seventy years, would end after just twenty-five. American soldiers came in the wake of the rain and flames. Even after they passed by, there was still nowhere to go, so the men stayed in their trenches and became snipers. In the end, they too were burned to death. (9:400)

In this unforgettable passage, Ōoka portrays the Battle of Limon Pass as a fiery hell on earth. Like the sailors trapped in the holds of the *Musashi,* the soldiers hunkering down in trenches could not escape. In the midst of this scene of unmitigated horror, blood-curdling screams, and searing death, the spotlight comes to rest on a lone, legless youth dragging himself over scorched earth. This man is blood brother to the young sailor who struggled in vain with his entrails. Shattered youth, shattered bodies; premature, absurd, grotesque, and excruciating death—these, Ōoka seems to insist, are the unchanging, undeniable, and ultimately wholly unacceptable realities of Leyte battlefields.

Ōoka's description of the battle that raged through the rain, wind, and flames is but one integral component of his treatment of the overall battlefield experience of First Division soldiers at Limon Pass. While the fighting was especially bad on November 8, Ōoka stresses how resolutely and effectively they fought before and after that time. In fact, these men continued to resist their numerically superior and better-equipped opponents until the official order to withdraw finally reached them toward the end of December.[38] In one brief sentence, Ōoka summarizes what they were up against: "In short, at Limon Pass Japanese soldiers of every rank were burdened with the task of fighting desperately to make the impossible possible" (9:437).

By drawing liberally on official American battle accounts, Ōoka firmly establishes how well soldiers of the First Division fought. In chapter 14, "The Regimental Flag," he quotes at length from the official field report made by Colonel William J. Verbeck, commander of the Twenty-first Regiment:

> The 21st Infantry was committed to action against strong hostile forces at PINAMOPOAN, LEYTE ISLAND, PHILIPPINE ISLANDS, on 5 November 1944. Elements in contact were 57th Infantry Regiment, 49th Infantry Regiment, and small units of the 1st Infantry Regiment all of the First Division, and a Battalion or more of the 1st Division Artillery including some 15 m guns. During the period 5 November to 16 November 1944 the Regiment was directed to "maintain the initiative at all costs." During the period the 21st Infantry suffered 630 battle casualties, and killed and counted 1,779 enemy. The twelve day period resulted in an advance of 2,000 yards of difficult terrain over a series of six ridges South of PINAMOPOAN, now called BREAKNECK RIDGE.
>
> All who contacted the enemy were impressed with his excellence in battle. Little was noted of reckless charges, needless sacrifices, or failure to

> observe known tactical principles. The most outstanding enemy characteristic was his excellence in fire discipline and control of all arms. Without exception enemy fire was withheld until the moment when its delivery in great volume would give greatest effect. (9:443–444)

Colonel Verbeck's field report clearly establishes that the men of the First Division consistently exhibited tightly organized, disciplined, and effective fighting. It goes on to describe how the Japanese concealed their fortifications ingeniously, avoided night attacks, tenaciously held their positions even when surrounded or outflanked, and used sniper and mortar fire to devastating effect. At the end of his report, Colonel Verbeck praises the sophisticated battle tactics employed by his Japanese opponents: "The enemy used reverse slope defense tactics effectively. Every reverse slope in the area was well defended. Every foot of the terrain attacked was utilized properly for defense. His utilization of the terrain for defense was exceptionally good."[39]

In this field report, which Ōoka quotes in its entirety, Colonel Verbeck consistently depicts Japanese fighting at Limon Pass as intelligent, resourceful, reasonable, tightly organized, coordinated, and effective. In the following passage, Ōoka comments on the report and explains why he incorporated it:

> Since this report was written for the purpose of battlefield instruction, it is probably somewhat exaggerated for cautionary purposes. Nonetheless, it is one of the most immediate descriptions of how our First Division soldiers fought. The respect and high esteem Colonel William Verbeck had for his opponents is self-evident. This report, one he wrote in the field on November 15 right after the battle, is ample proof of his sincerity in meeting in Tokyo after the war with Lieutenant General Kataoka, commander of the First Division, to commend the Fifty-seventh Regiment for putting up such a good fight. I think this field report is the best offering that can be made to the soldiers that died fighting so well at Limon Pass. (9:447)

The Experience of Defeat

While clearly far from the only frontline reality, at some point Japanese soldiers throughout Leyte Island experienced defeat. In *The Battle for Leyte Island,* Ōoka effectively reproduces this experience by treating it on three basic levels—general, specific, and individual. The dynamic of this approach can perhaps best be conveyed through cinematic analogy. Like a film director, Ōoka begins his visual sequences of each stage of defeat with a distant, wide-angle shot. After establishing the overall context, he closes in on a more detailed scene involving the collective experience of a group of men at a particular location and time. Finally, he grounds and personalizes the experience by lodging it in an individual. Indeed, on the third and most immediate level, the audience gazes at the unfolding hell screen of total defeat through the eyes of a survivor.

Approaching soldiers' experience of loss at the general, specific, and personal levels enables Ōoka to thoroughly re-create and expose the all-but-unimaginable battlefield actualities that defined the latter stages of the failed campaign. Through masterful literary representation of routed soldiers' experience, Ōoka develops six key motifs: privation, starvation, abandoned corpses, fraternal atrocity, surrender, and cannibalism. And in contrast to his memoirs and early fiction, he for the most part refrains from blaming, condemning, or rejecting the desperate men in the field who struggled against all odds (and each other) to preserve their lives. Ōoka describes their hellacious, inescapable experience of defeat with great sensitivity, understanding, empathy, and compassion. Indeed, as with his treatment of the other integral realities of Leyte battlefields, Ōoka's primary role is that of medium.

To personalize the experience of defeat, Ōoka draws most heavily and frequently on the testimony of Private Itō Waichi, the model for Private Tamura in *Fires on the Plain.*[40] There can be little doubt that Ōoka identified very closely with this man. Like Ōoka himself, he was effectively a noncombatant who wandered through harsh mountain terrain after being routed by a vastly superior enemy and was taken captive after witnessing the fruitless deaths of virtually every one of his comrades. In contrast to Ōoka, however, Private Itō seems to have been open and honest about his battlefield conduct from the beginning. Of all the Japanese soldiers in the main prisoner-of-war camp on Leyte Island, he alone readily admitted to surrender (10:444). Since Private Itō was an extraordinarily rare survivor capable of relating his battlefield trauma free of self-justification, embellishment, or concealment, Ōoka could be confident that his testimony was a good reflection of the truth of his own and, by extension, much of his comrades' harrowing frontline experience.

The Battle for Leyte Island has just begun at the point when Ōoka introduces Private Itō in chapter 17, "The Spinal Mountain Range": "Called up in 1941, Private Itō Waichi, a medic attached to the Sixteenth Division's Fourth Field Hospital, was the gentle son of a Nishijin, Kyoto, weaver. By nature, he did not like war. He had a hard time during the occupation of Luzon. He was subjected to malicious talk about intending to become a spy throughout the time he worked in hospitals in Naga and Legaspi because he befriended Filipinos to learn English and Tagalog. Consequently, he was still a private after three years of military service" (9:514). Since his early battlefield experience is relevant to his later conduct, it will be touched upon briefly before turning to his representative experience of defeat.

When the Americans reached Leyte Island, Private Itō was working in a sanatorium in the coastal town of Dulag. Because of the great influx of casualties following the opening American bombardment, he joined other medical personnel in transporting overflow patients to the Fourth Field Hospital in Tacloban. Upon arrival, however, the men were given a severe dressing-down for leaving their assigned positions during combat. They were ordered to return to Dulag immediately, this time on foot. Dawn was breaking about the time they reached Palo, and before long naval bombardment began anew. After digging in and waiting for the shelling to end, Private Itō and his group proceeded south along the coast while listening to the sounds of heavy fighting in the nearby foothills. Prevented by American tanks from continuing on toward Dulag, they changed direction and made for Sixteenth Division Headquarters in Dagami. Upon reporting at headquarters, they were again harshly reprimanded for being deserters.

Ordered to support a Ninth Regiment machine-gun company regrouping near Kiling, they set off again. Soon after departing, however, a heated firefight broke out ahead of them. At this point, the senior ranking medical officer, a first lieutenant surgeon, made a shocking proposal: "Look, there's no way we're gonna win this war. Our deaths will be worthless. If we hide out around here, the Americans'll come to us. Let's surrender together" (9:516). Ōoka comments on this proposition as follows:

> This should have been an unutterable proposal for an Imperial Army man expected to take "not suffering the shame of capture" as his guiding principle. Medicine, however, is a peaceful practice undertaken by intelligent men.

> While no one dared to say so openly, soldiers everywhere felt that the war was unwinnable. This relatively high-ranking enlisted surgeon was able to express what was secretly on everyone else's mind. There are numerous examples from other Philippine battlefields of army surgeons surrendering with their staff and patients. This, however, is the only case I know in which a medical man proposed to do so the day following an enemy landing.
>
> This same officer subsequently dropped out with another first lieutenant surgeon while crossing over the spinal mountain range. Private Itō and those with him at the time believed they did so in order to surrender. However, neither of these men survived. (9:516)

In commenting on this incident, Ōoka does not stand in judgment, but explains why enlisted medical officers entertained, expressed, and acted on thoughts of capitulating more readily than others. While he clearly felt that the second day of the battle was too early for this kind of proposal, he does not in any way imply that this man was a coward or egoist. Rather, he directs attention to the fact that this highly intelligent man had the nerve to air the thoughts and feelings shared by beleaguered Japanese soldiers on battlefields throughout the Pacific. In fact, acknowledging, accepting, and openly speaking the truth requires its own kind of courage. If there is criticism in this passage, it is not explicitly aimed at this surgeon, but implicitly directly at Japan's military leaders, who clearly lacked his essential type of courage and honesty.

Because this jarring proposal was made so soon after the battle began, Private Itō and his comrades rejected it. Ōoka observes, however, that this incident had a profound influence on Itō's subsequent behavior. The men eventually managed to join the combat unit in Kiling. After collecting the wounded, they searched in vain for the Fourth Field Hospital, which had been relocated to Dolores, a town on the western side of the central mountain range near Ormoc. They had no choice but to retrace their steps to Dagami. Before long the number of medical personnel converging on Dagami swelled to 150. Although a makeshift field hospital was set up around a cluster of huts to the west of the town, it was all but useless because it lacked basic medical supplies.

In chapter 21, "The Battle for Burauen," Ōoka provides a good summary of the conditions the men of the Sixteenth Division faced after being routed in the opening battles:

> The [Sixteenth] Division had already been in the mountains for a month. They had to supplement the meager provisions they still retained with the bananas, papayas, and potatoes they were able to gather themselves. By rationing and eating meager portions, they had made their provisions last. Many had died or been incapacitated by malaria, diarrhea, and malnutrition. By this point, the daily attrition rate was seventy-five men per day.
>
> After the American offensive of November 3, they lost half of their officers above the rank of company commander, and they were forced to abandon their fortified foothill positions in Dagami. Division Commander Makino led his remaining men to a cluster of native huts high on the slopes of Mt. Lobi, where they established a bivouac.
>
> From the end of October, the division had been sending the sick and wounded over the mountains to Ormoc. They also dispatched small groups of healthy soldiers to procure provisions. Since these men weren't given any food for the journey; they had to fend for themselves along the way. Many sick and wounded died or were killed by American patrols in the rain and fog of the spinal mountain range.
>
> Even if they managed to reach Ormoc, the army refused to give them any food because they looked so disreputable. Knowing that if they returned to Dagami without fulfilling their mission they would only be slapped in the face and harshly reprimanded, they opted for building makeshift shelters and living off the land in the foothills above and behind Ormoc. They chose locations as far as possible from the fighting. These men, in short, became so-called reserves (*yūhei*). (10:93–94)

Private Itō was among one of the groups of healthy soldiers and walking wounded that was sent over the central mountain range. He and a number of other medics were ordered to escort thirty patients to Ormoc, requisition provisions and medical supplies, and then return with them to division headquarters in Dagami. The group had to make their way through the mountains by chopping their way through cold, trailless rain forest. The terrain was so rugged and inhospitable that some days they advanced no more than a kilometer. The march was more than the sick and wounded could handle, and before long they began to collapse by the side of the path:

> For a time, medics were able to help their weakened patients hobble along by physically supporting them. As they continued their forced march without food or water, however, even the healthy began to reach the limits of their strength. Some of the wounded, saying they could go no further, pressed their hands together and begged to be allowed to die where they lay. Since

> none had the strength to carry them, they tried to scold them into getting back up on their feet. When this failed, all they could do was leave them a grenade and press on. (9:517)

Eventually, the men manage to cross the mountains, descend to Lake Danao, and reach Thirty-fifth Army Headquarters in Ormoc. Private Itō despairs after they report to a staff officer and he berates them as deserters and refuses to give them the food and medical supplies they request. Realizing that it would be useless to return to Dagami empty-handed, they decide to report to the Fourth Field Hospital, which had been combined with the Thirty-fifth Army Hospital and relocated to Valencia. The conditions confronting them there are appalling:

> The Valencia hospital consisted of little more than wounded laid out on bare floors. It was so severely understaffed and overburdened that soldiers were not tended to for five or six days at a time. Most, moreover, were so badly injured that they were beyond help. While those judged to be in need of operations were sent on to the supply hospital in Ipil, death frequently preceded diagnosis. Besides, only commissioned officers were sent to the rear. Noncoms and soldiers missing arms and legs just like their superiors were left on the floor with maggots infesting wounds still roughly wrapped in field dressings.
>
> "Medic, please remove the maggots. It hurts, it hurts terribly."
>
> Implored in this way, all the newly arrived medical men could do was extract the squirming larvae from between the gaps of their bandages. At the time, Private Itō honestly thought to himself, "How can we possibly win the war under such conditions?" (9:518)

It is significant that this combined medical facility was situated near Thirty-fifth Army Headquarters. Even near the central base of operations for the Battle for Leyte Island, the most basic equipment and supplies necessary for conducting and sustaining the war effort are conspicuously lacking. The unconscionable conditions Private Itō witnesses in this "hospital" make him begin to have serious doubts about Japan's prospects of winning the war. And here again, it is not cowardice, but battlefield reality that causes this fundamental question to form in his mind. Ōoka is quick to add, however, that this was just the beginning of his difficulties (9:518).

When Ōoka returns to Private Itō's trials and tribulations, the Battle for Leyte Island is on the verge of collapse. With the implementation of the

Wa Operation to retake airstrips near the east-coast town of Burauen, half of the Fourth Field Hospital staff is ordered to proceed to the area to provide medical support. Accompanied by a squad of soldiers, the thirty medics retrace their steps to Lake Danao and then begin the climb back up into the mountains. While Private Itō doesn't recall precisely when or where, he clearly remembers coming upon a valley containing more than two hundred Japanese corpses and the body of a black American. Within the context of Private Itō's personal experience, this is the first of a series of images related to the central motif of abandoned, unburied Japanese dead, which will be taken up separately.

The group presses on until they reach a road passing straight through a long, narrow valley. Since it looks like a likely place for ambush, the officer in charge of the escort squad orders the medics to wait while he takes his men forward. Before they pass halfway along the road, shots ring out from the top of the hill to their left, four to five men fall, and the remaining soldiers take cover and return fire. The officer eventually leads his men back, says they cannot make it through, and orders everyone to stay in place until further notice. Ōoka provides direct access to Itō's thoughts at this juncture: "Private Itō thought that the reason they continued to linger there idly until the Wa Operation was called off and they were ordered to withdraw to Ormoc was that deep in their hearts none of them wanted to go on to Burauen. Had the clearing before them been their only obstacle, they could easily have broken through by night" (10:96–97).

Ōoka is careful not to contribute to the mistaken impression that the conduct of groups such as this was somehow representative of that of the Japanese soldiers who fought in the Battle for Leyte Island. Immediately following Private Itō's thoughts on why his group abandoned the attack, Ōoka comments on who survived to testify about their battlefield experience and who did not. He does not judge the men who could not bring themselves to join in the last-ditch attack at Burauen, but he does openly praise the small number who did:

> Private Itō doesn't remember what day in December this took place. And it's not necessarily because these events transpired more than twenty years ago that his memory was dim. Soldiers forced to take part in an odious operation through the rains of the central mountain range lose their sense of space and time almost immediately. Ultimately, those in the Sixteenth Division who

> participated in and survived the Burauen Operation were men such as these who didn't take part in the attack because of accident or injury. Private Itō vaguely recalls thinking that the attack was scheduled for December 8, the day the Imperial Rescript [declaring war against the United States] was issued. Soldiers on Limon Pass and on battlefields throughout Leyte Island looked forward to this date, harboring hopes that something significant might occur.
>
> Even after losing more than 200 men when they were ambushed by the Americans as they sought to break through to the east, soldiers from the Sixteenth Division did not abandon the scheduled attack. It is unclear whether they crossed over the ridge and sought to break through from a different valley or avoided the valleys and followed the ridgeline until they could descend to the plains. Be that as it may, it is to the honor of the division that 150 men joined in the attack on Buri Airfield on the morning of the sixth. (10:97)

If there is any implicit criticism in this passage, it is clearly not directed toward the men of the Sixteenth Division. Ōoka understood and sympathized with the soldiers who decided to passively wait in a safe place for the battle, and, by extension, the war, to end. While he praises in the highest terms the men who joined in the attack after all they had been through, he does not do so at the expense of their comrades who did not. Instead, he subtly directs his criticism at those who initiated, conducted, and irresponsibly insisted that the battle be continued despite every sign of imminent failure. Just as Emperor Hirohito had the power and authority to declare war against the United States at the time of Pearl Harbor on December 8, 1941 (December 7 in Hawaii), so did he have the power and authority to bring it to an end exactly three years later when it became obvious to everyone in the field from bottom-ranking soldiers to Thirty-fifth Area Army commanders that the "decisive" Battle for Leyte Island, and thus the Pacific War itself, had become a lost cause. The failure of the Wa Operation and the American counterlanding at Ormoc the following day clearly signaled the turn toward total, irreversible defeat.

It is thus fitting that Ōoka returns to recreating Private Itō's experience in the chapter titled "Defeat." He contextualizes this survivor's personal experience of suffering and loss by making effective use of the cinematic technique mentioned at the beginning of this section. Ōoka opens with an overview of the condition of routed Japanese soldiers throughout the island, describes the general experience of the men withdrawing from the vicinity of Limon Pass toward Palompon, and then pans south to provide a general view of the situation of troops near Burauen:

> By this time, the soldiers remaining on the abandoned battlefields of Leyte Island had fallen into a chaotic state. Battle records suggest that the First and 102d Divisions withdrew with some semblance of order. Because they were advancing on the heels of the Americans who were driving westward, however, scattered skirmishes broke out everywhere. The time for being concerned about disorderly ranks or men dropping out one after another had long since passed.
>
> The Sixteenth and Twenty-sixth Division soldiers abandoned near Burauen and Albuera encountered even more miserable conditions. With the American army in control of the Ormoc Highway, they were unable to leave the rain and fog of the central mountains for the next two months. (10:311)

In this opening passage, Ōoka emphasizes that the remnants of the divisions to the south faced the most miserable (*hizan*) conditions. The men of the Sixteenth Division had not only met the overwhelming American invasion force at the opening of the Battle for Leyte Island, but also endured a full month of bivouacking and fighting enemy patrols in the mountains before taking part in the attack on Burauen. Unlike the men dug in at Limon Pass, moreover, they had not been resupplied. Thus, when the tides of war turned against them, they experienced defeat at its worst.

After setting the general stage in this way, Ōoka focuses in on the collective experience of Sixteenth Division soldiers once all hope of victory was gone:

> The scattered units apparently came together near Lake Danao. Toward the beginning of the battle, the Imabori Detachment (Twenty-sixth Division, Twelfth Regiment) passed by this volcanic lake twelve kilometers northeast of Ormoc as it marched along the mountain path leading from Dolores to Palo. Sixteenth Division soldiers, too, repeatedly walked by its shores as they moved back and forth between Ormoc and their positions over the mountains to the east. With the failure of the Wa Operation, the feet of Sixteenth Division officers and men naturally turned toward this familiar body of water.
>
> These men had taken part in the Burauen attack after sticking it out in the mountains without being resupplied for fifty days following the American landing. Virtually every staff officer and company commander had died in combat, and Division Commander Makino Shirō and the small number

> of men in his charge all suffered from malaria, tropical ulcers, diarrhea, and malnutrition. As previously noted, the official order to withdraw was never issued to the Sixteenth Division. Their circumstances were all the more miserable because units pulled back helter-skelter. Few soldiers had rifles. Harried by American patrols and Filipino guerrillas, they gradually worked their way northward through the trailless forests of the spinal mountain range in search of the water and fish of Lake Danao. (10:311–312)

Lake Danao acted as a great magnet for routed, sick, and wounded soldiers. Its attraction was not only its familiarity, but its potential as a desperately needed food source. To the men unable to break through American lines to reach Palompon, this lake stood as one of their final symbols of hope.

After providing this midrange view of the movements and conditions of the men converging on Lake Danao, Ōoka zooms in to expose an unforgettable scene of soldiers' collective experience of defeat:

> All that remains of the circumstances these defeated soldiers faced are the fragmented memories of the few who survived. The bleached bones of dead Japanese soldiers were scattered everywhere. Using them as trail markers, the routed followed them to the north. Most were barefoot because by now their boots and *jikatabi* had been torn to shreds. Those who still carried rifles abandoned them. All that remained on their equipment belts were their mess tins—their most essential tool for survival.
>
> Squatting along the sides of the path were sick, utterly exhausted men. Facing the passing soldiers, they silently held out their mess tins. Their gestures were those of beggars. The men who still had the strength to keep moving were starving and on their last legs. They had absolutely nothing to give. Knowing this, the beggars said nothing and simply stared at them with open, lifeless eyes. Wasted away as they were by starvation, their movements were mechanical and repetitive. They died one after another. (10:312)

Ōoka handles this tragic scene with sensitivity and compassion. He empathizes not only with the dying men being abandoned, but with those who were incapable of assisting or comforting them as well. This passage effectively exposes conditions of absolute privation. This, one of the definitive realities of the defeat experience, is crystallized in the haunting image of the beggar. Once proud soldiers of the Imperial Japanese Army, these men have been reduced by combat, injury, disease, and starvation to pathetic figures mechanically enacting hopeless gestures for help. Accompanying their awareness that they would receive nothing was the knowledge that it was only a matter of time before their own bleached bones would be added to those of their dead comrades. When Private Itō was confronted with the horrendous conditions of the combined medical facility in Valencia, he asked in all seriousness how Japan could possibly win the war under such conditions. The implicit question here is how the war could even be continued, or more specifically, how these men could be asked to fight on in such appalling circumstances.

Immediately after describing this indelible scene of hopelessness, privation, and demeaning death, Ōoka turns to Private Itō's personal experience. He, too, surely passed through this ghastly gauntlet of beggars and bleached bones. And at some point en route to Lake Danao, he encountered the terrible aftermath of fraternal atrocity. Clearly, where there were passive beggars, there were also men willing to do anything in the name of self-perpetuation:

> Private Itō Waichi of the Sixteenth Division's Fourth Field Hospital was withdrawing through the central mountains after guerrillas kept him from reaching Burauen. He was part of a twenty-man unit that still retained its military structure. They met a young transport soldier carrying a sack filled with rice. When informed that it was impossible to reach Burauen, the young man relinquished his load. He seemed to feel that he had fulfilled his duty by delivering the rice into the hands of a bona fide unit. When a noncom took out a piece of paper and wrote him a receipt, he looked relieved and turned back.
>
> Private Itō subsequently saw a similar transport soldier who had been stripped naked, tied to a tree with his leather belt, and strangled. Since guerrillas killed by cutting the throat from ear to ear with a machete, Itō was convinced that the young man had been murdered by his own comrades. (10:313)

By this stage, the battle had devolved from one against the American and Filipino enemy to one of comrade against comrade. It was survival of the fittest. Since transport soldiers were under strict orders to give their precious loads only to organized units, Private Itō believed that this young man was probably killed when "reserves" demanded his rice and he refused. They killed him to prevent exposure of their crime. In his comments on this brutal incident of fratricide, Ōoka expresses a measure of criticism conspicuously absent from his other treatments of soldiers' conduct in extremity. As is clear from the following passage, however, he criticizes them less for perpetrating the acts themselves than for refusing after the fact to admit that their conduct was wrong:

> Among these "reserves"-turned-robbers the gunners were said to be the worst offenders. Since their work involved transporting heavy artillery pieces and ammunition, they were stronger than the average foot solider. Once their artillery pieces were destroyed, they became "reserves" and used their superior physical strength to prey upon others. They justified themselves by claiming that after their field pieces became useless there was nothing for them to do, that they were not duty-bound to fight on with rifles, and they didn't know how to use them anyway.
>
> A survivor who had been a gunner in the Sixteenth Division's Twenty-second Artillery Regiment said, "We had no choice in the matter. That was our only means of survival." To the present day, he never even imagined that what he had done had been wrong. (10:313–314)

After detailing and commenting on this fraternal atrocity, Ōoka quickly returns to the central motif of privation. He describes how the remnants of the Sixteenth and Twenty-sixth Divisions ate anything they could find—snakes, lizards, frogs, tadpoles, worms. Mostly they ate wild grasses. Since few had matches, these things had to be consumed raw. After weeks of ingesting such marginal food, all the men suffered from diarrhea. The trail was thus marked not only by the bleached bones of their dead comrades, but by loose feces as well. Given the importance in Japanese culture of purity and proper handling of and respect for the dead, it is difficult to imagine a more unacceptable and appalling situation.

Ōoka builds on his treatment of the defeat experience of the remnants of the Sixteenth and Twenty-sixth Divisions in chapter 29, "Mt. Canguipot." Again employing the technique of moving from generalized to personalized experience, he recreates the increasingly brutal realities of Leyte battlefields:

> The defeated soldiers moved from the east side of the spinal mountain range toward Lake Danao. The rains fell steadily in the central mountains even when Mt. Canguipot was clear. Since patrols from the Ninety-sixth Division had penetrated deeply into the foothills, the men had to move through the dense forests five hundred meters above sea level. Units of the Sixteenth Division had passed back and forth through these thickly wooded areas so

> many times that distinct trails had formed. They were marked by the bleached bones of the dead.
>
> Their provisions were completely exhausted. Those who still carried rifles discarded them along with their ammunition belts and bayonets. They looked like specters as they moved in groups of threes and fives with like-minded comrades carrying nothing but the mess tins used to boil wild grasses swinging at their sides.
>
> By the end of January, the main force of the Twenty-sixth Division had abandoned their positions at the headwaters of the Talisayan River and were traversing along the western side of the spinal mountain range. To avoid the American patrols based in Ormoc, they followed the paths threading through the high mountains, and some eventually joined the men from the Sixteenth [Division] at Lake Danao. But since it was a volcanic lake, there were no fish to be had. Before long they came under attack by the guerrillas, who knew they were gathering there.
>
> It is thought that by the middle of February, most of the soldiers of the Sixteenth and Twenty-sixth Divisions had crossed the mountain path connecting Lake Danao and Dolores. North of this path were the highest mountains of northern Leyte. Because the dense tropical forests that covered their slopes were always enveloped in thick clouds, water droplets were continually falling from the high canopy of branches above. Decomposing leaves covered the ground so thickly that as the men walked through they sank down to their shins.
>
> Leeches came down with the rain. They attached inside ears, on eyelids, anywhere they could take hold, and gorged themselves on the soldiers' thin blood. Upon awaking in the morning, men found them hanging in front of their eyes like rope curtains. (10:437–439)

In this depiction of the movements of and circumstances faced by men of the Sixteenth and Twenty-sixth Divisions, Ōoka adds several new images that vividly capture essential aspects of the experience of defeat. Now the starving, beleaguered men who staggered along trails lined with their comrades' scattered bones have themselves come to resemble a progression of ghosts. Rather than eating the small animals they chance upon, their own lifeblood is being drained by such creatures. And the final, haunting image of starving, desperate men with battened leeches dangling down in front of their eyes is strongly suggestive of imminent, grotesque, and degrading death.

After describing how these "specters" subsequently come to a remote corpse-strewn battlefield, Ōoka makes a significant comment related to the central motif of the abandoned dead: "They came upon what appeared to be the site of recent battle, and there were Japanese corpses and the body of a black soldier on the ground. Because the Americans collected all their dead, few Japanese soldiers ever saw enemy remains. This writer knows of just three exceptions: the body of the black man seen in the vicinity of Burauen, the soldier from the Eleventh Airborne Division found near Mt. Lobi, and the black soldier described here" (10:439). It is worth pausing at this juncture to consider how and to what ends Ōoka employs so many graphic descriptions of abandoned, unburied bodies in *The Battle for Leyte Island.*

Ōoka's presentation of images related to the dead can, for the purpose of analysis, be treated by geographical area: the initial battlefields on the east coast, Limon Pass, and the mountainous corridor between Burauen and Dolores. As previously shown, the first vivid description of the dead appeared in the context of the opening battle. The main focus there was on bodies broken, shattered, and scattered. Given the intensity of the American bombardment and the invasion that followed in its wake, it was impossible to properly attend to these first casualties.

Drawing on American battle records, Ōoka provides the following description of what the men from a tank company witnessed as they made their way toward Jaro on November 28:

> When the tank force entered Alangalang at 0900 hours, the town was completely silent. The local inhabitants had fled the area. All they heard from time to time was the sound of dogs barking down side streets. Corpses of Japanese soldiers could be seen here and there on the road. They must have been hit by artillery, since they were all missing arms and legs. The corpses were still fresh, because the Americans had shelled the town the previous day. Exposed as they were to the tropical sun, however, they had already begun to swell. They had, moreover, apparently been eaten by dogs—the bones near the buttocks of some of the bodies were clearly visible. (9:310–311)

Now the bodies that were initially described as being blown apart are swelling in the sun and being consumed by animals.

The next important series of corpse-related imagery comes from Limon Pass. By this point, intensive battles have raged on for many days, and both sides have suffered heavy losses. In the aptly named "Death Valley" chapter, Ōoka details the aftermath of heated fighting near the Limon River:

> For the next forty-eight hours the riverbed of the Limon River was pounded unremittingly with artillery shells. The three-hour bombardment directed at the tree-covered slopes between the northern extremity of the heights above the highway and the northern bank of the river from 1500 hours to nightfall stripped the whole area of foliage down to the bare earth. The rear guard of the First Infantry Division suffered mounting casualties as they struggled to break through to the riverbed to join the frontline fighting. Neither the Japanese nor the Americans had the margin to collect their dead, and corpses missing arms and legs swelled in the sun or were swept downstream by the rising waters of the Limon River until being deposited on the rocky strands below. The battle ended in Japanese victory, but the First Division paid dearly. It is thought that they probably lost as much as a third of their total fighting strength. (9:548)

While Ōoka notes here that during the heat of the battle neither side was able to gather in its dead, it is safe to assume that when the Americans eventually forced the Japanese back and took control of the area, they recovered as many of the bodies of their fallen comrades as was humanly possible. Given the subsequent course of the battle and the progressive slide toward complete defeat, the Japanese were unable to do the same for their own dead.

Ōoka makes this point explicitly in a subsequent passage describing a narrow ravine on the southern side of the Limon River that provided the primary access to the valley floor once the Americans gained control of the northern heights: "The American gunners set their sights on this steep-sided corridor. Since there was neither time nor place to attend to the many soldiers killed by the incessant shelling rained down by the men of Sprague's platoon, the bodies progressively swelled up, putrefied, and turned to bleached bones in the narrow defile. These images of death had a profound effect on the morale of First Division soldiers. The men referred to this two-hundred-meter-long gorge as 'Death Valley'" (9:560–561).

Private Itō's experience essentially paralleled that of the Sixteenth and Twenty-sixth Division men who after defeat struggled through rugged mountains to reach Lake Danao and later sought to break through to the north. As has been shown, his own and his comrades' experience of defeat is repeatedly punctuated with death imagery. Ōoka, moreover, makes repeated references to the bleached bones that lined the mountain path leading to Lake Danao. Indeed, as the men of the First Division had their "Death Valley," the men of the Sixteenth and Twenty-sixth had their "White Bone Highway" (10:233).

Reviewing the series of images Ōoka builds up around the abandoned, unburied war dead, one sees bodies blown apart by naval bombardment; relatively fresh dog-eaten corpses; dismembered, putrefying bodies swelling in the sun; bodies progressively skeletonized; and finally, bodies reduced to scattered, bleached bones. What is the significance of such imagery? Why was Ōoka at such pains to implant these images in the reader's mind? Kamei Hideo addresses these important questions as follows:

> In light of the structure of the work, these corpses are mute, direct, material witnesses to the tremendous pressure brought to bear on individual soldiers. It is very symbolic that descriptions of bleached bones begin to appear just at the point when the Imperial Army's fighting strength had reached its limit and soldiers were being ordered to attack on all fronts. These bones were harbingers of the decisive turning point in the battle. Ōoka probably took advantage of every opportunity he could find to incorporate references to descriptions of bodies he came upon while reading through battle accounts and testimonies. Officers and strategists not only had far better chances of battlefield survival, they also had greater opportunity afterward to write accounts to justify themselves and their conduct (unmasking them is another central aim of *The Battle for Leyte Island*). For those permanently deprived of the ability to speak or write, leaving images of themselves in the eyes of their surviving comrades was the sole remaining means of conveying the truth of war.[41]

Kamei stresses that through repeated reference to abandoned corpses, Ōoka enables the war dead to symbolically testify about their experience of war and defeat. He also makes the important observation that the skeletal remains not only foretell, but in substantial ways symbolize, defeat. While it is important to emphasize the dead themselves, one must not neglect to consider the survivors in whose eyes these images were indelibly imprinted. In fact, such consideration facilitates appreciation of the anxiety of responsibility and the obligations of survivors to the dead. Writing *The Battle of Leyte Island* was Ōoka's literary means of consoling the restless spirits of the war dead by reproducing the full reality of their battlefield experience and absolving them of blame for defeat. What, however, could be done about the physical remains scattered throughout the battlefields and mountains of Leyte Island? In the end, properly attending to their mortal remains was a solemn obligation that would have to go unfulfilled.

There can be little doubt that through repeated, graphic descriptions of the bodies of the abandoned, unburied war dead Ōoka sought to transfer to the reader images indelibly left in the minds and hearts of battlefield survivors. The repeated description of these images, moreover, raises the fundamental question of who and what was responsible for such unacceptable battlefield realities. Ōoka in no way criticizes soldiers in the field for failing to attend to the dead. From his own experience on Mindoro he knew that this was impossibile. It thus behooves us at this point to reconsider the statement introduced previously: "Because the Americans collected all of their dead, few Japanese soldiers ever saw enemy corpses." The profound implications of this line should now be clear: the Japanese military didn't fail to adequately care for just their healthy, sick, and wounded soldiers, but their dead as well. Indeed, what Ōoka progressively brings to light in *The Battle for Leyte Island* is the Japanese leadership's utter disregard for life and human rights. Woefully lacking in the basic materials they needed to conduct modern war, the leadership increasingly came to see the soldiers themselves as expendable materiel.

After recalling how the routed soldiers of the Sixteenth and Twenty-sixth Divisions came upon hundreds of relatively fresh corpses, Ōoka turns to one of the most appalling realities of Leyte battlefields. When hope for survival at Lake Danao was shattered by lack of food and repeated guerrilla attack, the men had little choice but to return to the mountains. It was rumored that Thirty-fifth Army Command Headquarters had been relocated to Palompon. The soldiers' last hope for survival was to make it to this town on the west coast in time for evacuation to Cebu. To reach Palompon, however, routed soldiers from southern battlefields had to cross the east-west-running Ormoc Highway, which at this point was firmly in American hands. Try as they might, they were only rarely able to break through. Some men gave up, returned to the central mountains, made primitive shelters, and tried to survive as best they could. In the following passage, Ōoka broaches and then elaborates on the delicate matter of fratricide and cannibalism:

> Rumors of cannibalism occurring during the latter stages of the Battle for Leyte Island emerged from this area. Since these men virtually never came across guerrillas or American soldiers, all they could do was eat each other. During the Burauen Operation, men banded together to rob transport soldiers of their loads, but after the attack was called off, such prey was no longer available. It is believed that at this point solitary soldiers themselves were killed and eaten.
>
> There are no witnesses to cannibalism, and no perpetrators have come forward. Soldiers, moreover, have always enjoyed talking about this gruesome subject. Rumors of isolated companies caught in the snows of northern Manchuria or Mongolia or routed soldiers in the jungles of New Guinea and Guadalcanal eating one another spread throughout the Pacific. And Leyte Island had all the necessary conditions to give rise to such rumors.
>
> Many recall seeing bands of dangerous, evil-looking soldiers, and men invariably traveled in groups of twos and threes. When they encountered another group, they would indicate that they still had strength to resist by saying "Hey," and then moving on. Walking alone at night was strictly forbidden. Similar stories are also told about Luzon and Mindanao.
>
> A certain soldier from the Sixteenth Division met another man who had enlisted in the same year as himself. He was with a noncom from a different company. The man offered him some dried "monkey meat," but he sensed something was wrong and declined. That night, the man divulged his secret and asked the soldier to help kill the noncom, prepare his body for consumption, and then search out an American encampment where they could surrender together. The man fled the scene in revulsion.
>
> I incorporated this anecdote in *Fires on the Plain.* The soldier from the Sixteenth Division is still alive. In his case, however, the act was never consummated. There is nothing but hearsay concerning men actually committing the deed itself.
>
> It is said, however, that in the northern mountains of Luzon individuals from different squads within the same company ate each other out of vengeance. There is also testimony of a soldier who witnessed a sick comrade gnawing on a human arm "with fingers attached." Others came upon the butchered body of a Filipina. (10:439–440)

Ōoka treats the issue of fraternal cannibalism with a conspicuously calm and measured hand. Indeed, he initially seems to take great pains to leave the possibility open that defeated Japanese soldiers may not actually have engaged in fraternal killing and cannibalism. In the absence of eyewitnesses or direct confessions, everything hinges on rumor and hearsay.[42] At the same time, however, Ōoka also presents evidence suggesting that some of his countrymen may well have killed and eaten each other in the northern mountains of Leyte Island. Importantly, he notes that the area "had all the necessary conditions to give rise to such rumors." In fact, Ōoka firmly established these conditions himself via descriptions of the privation that went hand in hand with defeat. There is, moreover, the Sixteenth Division soldier's—Private Itō's—firsthand account of being offered a highly suspect piece of dried meat. And at the end of the passage, Ōoka introduces more concrete evidence related to possible cannibalism on Luzon.

It is significant that Ōoka makes direct reference to *Fires on the Plain.* The implications of the differing ways he approaches the issue of fraternal cannibalism in his early and later work will be pursued at the end of this section. Suffice it to say here that whereas in the novel he leaves no room for doubt regarding whether men were killing and eating one another on the battlefield, and to a great extent presents their conduct as representative, in *The Battle for Leyte Island* he highlights the fact that Private Itō, the real-life source for the story, neither engaged in nor witnessed such behavior himself.

The last time Private Itō figures prominently in Ōoka's treatment of the experience of defeat is when he surrenders. Given the problematic nature of this act, Ōoka refrains, as he did in his discussion of cannibalism, from identifying him by name. Here, he writes about the experience of a Sixteenth Division medical private. After narrating how Private Itō abandoned his weapon in full view of the other members of his group as they struggled northward through the mountains after leaving Lake Danao, Ōoka describes how he finally reached the point of despair: "It had been more than two weeks since he had had anything to eat. As he walked along, his awareness suddenly became attenuated. Apparently, he also became hard of hearing. There was a constant ringing in his ears, and he could barely make out what his friends were saying. While absentmindedly picking at his ear, he dug out a mass of earwax as big as the insides of a snail. Feeling utterly miserable, he broke down in tears" (10: 442).

It was about this time that Private Itō began to seriously consider surrender. The idea was first planted in his head by the first lieutenant surgeon on the day after the Americans began bombardment of the eastern coast of Leyte. He was convinced that this senior surgeon later dropped out en route to Burauen with the intention of raising his hands. Ōoka describes

Private Itō's psychology at the end of his ordeal with great sensitivity and understanding:

> He was an active-duty soldier who had been part of the occupying force on Luzon for three years after taking part in the battles on the Bataan Peninsula. During that time, he had grown thoroughly sick and tired of his occupation life of arbitrary punishment, obscene talk, and "gifts" appropriated from the local inhabitants.
>
> He was the eldest son of a Nishijin, Kyoto, weaver who had lost his father as a child and been raised by his mother and two older sisters. With the escalation of the war, the shop received fewer and fewer orders, and their lives became increasingly difficult. He despised the military men who had such an adverse effect on the world. In the end, he was sent to what seemed to be the ends of the earth and forced to put his life on the line in a hopeless battle. It was all so inane. By now he had had more than enough. He still valued his life.
>
> He resented having been born in a country with an emperor on high that demanded him to sacrifice himself pointlessly. In his heart of hearts he agreed with the surgeon who had suggested allowing themselves to be captured after the Americans landed. At the time, however, he had lacked the courage to act. He was afraid of what might have happened had he raised his hands—he could have been tortured or killed.
>
> Toward the middle of February, he and his group came to a wide road where some jeeps were passing back and forth. When he saw a Filipino walking leisurely along the road wearing a straw hat, he longed for civilian life. (10:442–443)

Ōoka's sympathies clearly lie with this gentle medical man who had endured so much hardship at the front; there isn't the slightest hint of criticism in this extended passage. By presenting Itō's sincere thoughts and feelings with such empathy and understanding, Ōoka again implicitly directs criticism toward Japan's leadership. Through Private Itō, he stresses the undeniable reality of the situation: the decisive Battle for Leyte Island and thus the Pacific War itself was already a lost cause. This being the case, it was not only idiotic, but also unconscionable to force the desperate, routed, and starving men in the field to fight on to the death. Ōoka, moreover, doesn't approach Itō's surrender in terms of cowardice or survival egoism, but in terms of courage. After suffering through years of hateful, abusive, and rapacious military life; helplessly watching as his comrades died of wounds, sickness, and starvation; witnessing the horrible aftermath of fraternal atrocities and the innumerable dismembered, abandoned, and unburied bodies of his compatriots, Private Itō finally resolved to take matters into his own hands. Even if his emperor and country refused to place any value on his existence, he still did.

While Itō found the courage within himself to honestly face, acknowledge, accept, and act in accordance with the incontrovertible realities of defeat, Japan's leadership clearly did not. In fact, when the Decisive Battle for Leyte Island (Reite kessen) was officially abandoned, Imperial Headquarters not only ordered the desperate men on Leyte to fight on to the death while living off the land, but also went on to commit the entire country and people to Hondo kessen, the Decisive Battle for the Homeland.

While Private Itō could easily have crossed the road with his companions that night, he stayed behind and concealed himself. He passed the night in prayer. By this time, he had lost all faith in gods and Buddhas, and the only thing he could still believe in was his mother's love. Visualizing his mother in his heart, he prayed for safe surrender. When vehicles began moving back and forth on the road the next morning, he emerged in front of a jeep with hands held above his head. The American soldier who happened to be driving by casually pulled over, said "Okay, come on," helped him in, gave him a cigarette, and then drove off.

The final scene of the protracted tragedy of Japanese defeat at Leyte Island was enacted near Mt. Canguipot, a 395-meter-high peak a few kilometers inland from the northwest coastal town of Villaba.[43] For routed soldiers throughout the island, this rocky peak represented their last hope of survival. Troops from northern battlefields such as Limon Pass began withdrawing toward the western coast late in December, and by New Year's Day, Thirty-fifth Army Headquarters had been reestablished near Palompon. In the end, about fifteen thousand routed soldiers from throughout the island managed to reach the vicinity of Mt. Canguipot. In time, they faced the same desperate circumstances as their comrades who sought to survive high in the central mountains.

Over several days in the middle of January, about eight hundred First Division soldiers were evacuated by boat to Cebu Island. These were the last to escape the island in any significant numbers. When American cleanup operations in the area intensified toward the end of the month,

Thirty-fifth Army Headquarters was relocated to some caves beneath the rocky cliffs of Mt. Canguipot. The Americans initiated a second offensive toward the end of February, and the beleaguered Japanese suffered many casualties. Army headquarters was relocated to Cebu at the end of March. About ten thousand Japanese soldiers—many of them sick and wounded—were for all intents and purposes abandoned after the Battle for Leyte Island was officially called off.

As with his other treatments of the experience of defeat, Ōoka handles the final tragic drama enacted near Mt. Canguipot with remarkable sensitivity and understanding. This can be seen in his description of how the peak was reflected in the eyes of the desperate men who struggled to reach it: "The mountain itself had an appearance befitting the name Kankipō, or Jubilation Peak.[44] There was a sheer, seventy-meter cliff on the eastern side of the summit, and its purplish-blue rock face was dyed red at sunrise and sunset. Since it towered above the surrounding hills, it was clearly visible from a great distance. Routed soldiers seeking to reunite with their units took heart when they thought that their comrades would be there, and they marched on with their eyes glued to its lofty, rock summit" (10:430).

In the following passage, Ōoka conveys what soldiers were thinking and feeling as they saw in the New Year:

> Leyte Island was quiet on January 1. On this day, the ten thousand men . . . who gathered on the west coast near Mt. Canguipot cooked rice and celebrated the New Year. Some, facing in the direction of the Imperial Palace, paid their respects, prayed for Imperial Japan's eternal good fortunes in war, and renewed their resolve to be become pillars of the nation on that solitary island in the South Seas. Others, thinking that there was no way in hell that they could accept being saddled with the preposterous duty of making a last stand in such a remote place, resolved to find a way of escaping from the island. (10:376)

Ōoka is careful to acknowledge the New Year's resolutions both of men of unshakable conviction and of those who, like Private Itō, had reached the point of resolving to act on their own behalf. While he clearly holds the men committed to sacrificing themselves for their country in high esteem, he does not do so at the expense of those who can no longer bring themselves to do so. Whether facing with reverence or turning their backs in disgust, the conduct of both groups is centered on the Imperial Palace. Here again, the locus of concern is more with the unreasonable and unrealistic orders emanating from Tokyo than with the varied responses they elicited in desperate men in the field.

The remnants of the Imperial Japanese Army that converged on Mt. Canguipot were initially fortunate in that they arrived during the harvest. As a result, they for a short time had food to eat. Like a swarm of locusts descending on a cultivated field, however, the ravenous Japanese soldiers quickly consumed everything in sight. By the beginning of March, there was nothing left in the area to sustain them. While they planted crops themselves, none lived long enough to see them come to fruition.

Like that of the men who struggled to survive on the cold, wet slopes of the central mountain range, little is known about the fate of the ten thousand men abandoned on the western coast of Leyte; once again, all that remains are the fragmentary memories of a few survivors. In the epilogue to *The Battle for Leyte Island,* Ōoka carefully re-creates the final acts of the closing drama of battlefield defeat on Leyte Island:

> It can be assumed that by this time, formal military organization had already broken down. When foraging for food, small groups worked out better. According to Private Horigome, since these groups operated independently, they repeatedly separated from and ran into each other. Each member of a group went out in search of food on his own. [Survival] etiquette dictated that even if a member of the group happened to find something to eat, he would neither share it nor be asked to. Personal possessions, too, were neither lent nor borrowed. Unmitigated egoism became the foundation of this most marginal and fragile social order.
>
> Once human relationships had broken down this far, it was reportedly easy for the men to end their lives. Sick soldiers killed themselves for simple reasons: because of wounds to their invaluable legs, because they had no prospect of acquiring any more food, because of chronic diarrhea. They would abruptly drop out of the group, hug their grenades (if they still had them), and pull the pins. Or they would attach their belts to tree branches and hang themselves. A good number who lacked the strength or spirit to end their lives by their own hand were captured as they lay prostrate in the woods more dead than alive. (10:510–511)

Ōoka treats the last moments of his Leyte comrades respectfully and nonjudgmentally. While he identifies survival egoism as the foundation of their marginal social order, he has come to understand it as the natural, inevitable consequence of defeat, privation, and official prohibition of surrender. In stark contrast to his treatment in his battlefield memoirs and *Fires of the Plain,* Ōoka neither stresses nor lingers over the things people did in the name of self-perpetuation. By this point, he has come to see that given their extremity, they had no other choice. Rather than highlighting and commenting at length on extreme acts of survival egoism, Ōoka directs attention to the psychological and emotional effect of the radical atomization of human relations. As the body needs food, so does the spirit require meaningful human connection. The men who took their own lives in the forests on the slopes of Mt. Canguipot did so under conditions of existential isolation: psychically separated from their brothers-in-arms, forsaken by their country, and stranded in a remote area of an isolated foreign island thousands of miles from home, they found death preferable to a life of continued spiritual and physical anguish and degradation.

As foretold by Private Itō's experience on the way back from Burauen, however, where there are men who will quietly die begging or by their own hand, there are also those who will prey on the vulnerable and defenseless. At the end of his in-depth treatment of the experience of defeat, Ōoka returns to the issue of fraternal cannibalism. As in his prior treatment, he begins by stressing that desperate soldiers were only *rumored* to have killed and eaten one another in the foothills surrounding Mt. Canguipot. Instead of presenting more concrete, detailed evidence at the end of his discussion, however, this time he provides it right up front:

> Filipinos from the town of Villaba recall seeing the corpse of a young Japanese soldier with all the flesh removed from the buttocks and thighs in a valley to the north of Mt. Canguipot. It was rumored in the Palo prisoner-of-war camp, moreover, that a soldier captured in the same area about this time was carrying a charred human arm.
>
> This was hearsay, but a survivor from the Twenty-third Division actually saw with his own eyes the dismembered corpse of a Filipina on Luzon Island. In addition, the corpse of an officer lacking buttocks flesh was seen on Mindanao and believed to have been eaten out of vengeance. The reality of the existence of these mutilated corpses cannot be denied. (10:511)

Ōoka clearly had little doubt that a number of Japanese soldiers engaged in cannibalism during the final stages of the failed campaign for Leyte Island. In fact, he subsequently states that cannibalism was surely one of the reasons so few survivors emerged from the Mt. Canguipot area. Ōoka, however, makes an important observation immediately after counting cannibalism as an undeniable reality of Leyte battlefields: "This is not, of course, to say that all starving soldiers resorted to this kind of behavior. When it comes to overcoming moral restraints, there are always individual differences; in the exact same circumstances, some will cannibalize and others will not" (10:511). While Ōoka takes care to delineate between those who did and did not cannibalize, he does not go on to condemn the one or praise the other. Instead, he places primary emphasis on the circumstances that can bring forth such atrocious behavior. He makes this significant point most forcefully toward the end of his discussion:

> The isolated islands of the Philippines were like damaged ships floating on the ocean. As during a time of famine, moreover, there was no food to be had in an entire area. The animalistic dimension of the human being is large indeed. While peacetime society is founded on the restraint of the animal within, in war the beast is not only freed but prodded to take action. While this is necessary to make men into good fighters, other animal instincts are released at the same time. This is why war is inevitably accompanied by rape and torture. Thus, when confronted by absolute famine conditions, it is only natural that men would revert to their primitive past of consuming one another. (10:513)

In the end, Ōoka concludes that cannibalism was the natural outcome of the extraordinary circumstances of war, defeat, abandonment, and privation. While Tamura reached an ostensibly similar conclusion toward the end of the first part of his memoir, the respective manner of presentation and implications are strikingly different. Articulation of these differences goes far toward showing how far Ōoka had progressed on his formulative journey.

In the climactic scene of cannibalism in *Fires on the Plain,* Ōoka has Tamura make the following declaration: "I was enraged. If it was natural and inevitable for human beings to eat one another during extremes of starvation, then this world was no more than a remnant of God's wrath. If I could vomit and feel rage at that moment, then I was no longer human. I was an instrument of God, and it was now up to me to manifest His wrath" (3:395–396). When Ōoka had Tamura proclaim these impassioned words of condemnation, he himself was still clinging to a scapegoating formulation in which he sought to transfer his own deep-seated feelings of survivor guilt and self-recrimination onto others. Conspicuous in Tamura's declaration is extreme animus, anxious rationalization aimed at denying his own potential for engaging in such an act and the burning desire to punish *others* for *their* evil.

In *The Battle for Leyte Island,* Ōoka handles the issue of fraternal cannibalism with remarkable composure and sensitivity. Completely absent is any trace of rage, blame, or condemnation of the individuals who resorted to killing and eating one another in a last-ditch effort to survive. By the time Ōoka was completing his survivor mission, he had reached the point where he could understand and sympathize even with his comrades who killed and ate their brothers-in-arms. As will be detailed in the following chapter on responsibility for defeat, Ōoka ultimately held the military leaders in Imperial Headquarters morally accountable for creating the circumstances that led to these most appalling manifestations of unbridled human nature.

Ōoka, however, does not allow disturbing images of defeat—piteous beggars; abandoned, unburied bodies; trails lined with bleached bones and feces; strung-up and strangled young transport soldiers; cannibal-mutilated corpses—to stand for the entirety of Japanese battlefield experience during the Battle for Leyte Island. While fully acknowledging the realities of defeat, he nonetheless directs attention toward the many men who fought bravely, resolutely, and effectively against an overwhelmingly superior, vastly more modernized opponent. The images of the First Division men battling on Limon Pass, the Sixteenth Division soldiers who rallied to attack at Burauen after months of hardship, and the skill and exemplary self-sacrifice of Special Attack Forces pilots who crashed their bomb-laden planes into their targets must not be forgotten. In the epilogue, Ōoka makes a direct statement concerning whom he holds in the highest esteem: "We must not forget that the battles in the Philippines were fought in a context of face slapping and brutal arbitrary military punishment, and according to a strategy of attrition. It was only natural that there would be many deserters and suicides. I, however, respect those soldiers who despite these conditions of slavery found reasons to fight unrelated to the allegiance demanded of them by the army, and did so well" (10:515). In praising these men, Ōoka again takes care to divorce their courageous conduct from indoctrinated allegiance or patriotism. He holds in highest regard those individuals who found personal reasons to fight. And Ōoka will not allow these paragons to be co-opted by the very forces that not only abused them and failed to take care of them, but also forced them to pointlessly sacrifice their precious lives in the name of an utterly hopeless, long-lost cause.

In *The Battle for Leyte Island,* Ōoka conducts a solemn rite of passage for the spirits of his fallen comrades by thoroughly and unflinchingly recreating their battlefield experience, absolving them of responsibility for defeat, and belatedly conferring upon them the quality of glory, honor, respect, and immortality they deserved. He clearly felt that the troubled souls of the war dead could be consoled only by honest and accurate memory and proper memorialization. He also seemed to have realized that the work of mourning had to be carried out fully before the living could begin to reassert the continuity of life and move with confidence and vitality into the future. Before the path toward recovery and renewal could be envisioned and blazed, however, another crucial matter had to be attended to—finding meaning in the seemingly meaningless deaths of nearly ninety thousand of his countrymen. In the end, Ōoka sought to make their deaths meaningful by painstakingly learning and passing on the vital lessons of defeat in the Battle for Leyte Island and the Pacific War. The fruits that developed from this aspect of his survivor mission were simultaneously gifts to posterity and offerings to the spirits of the war dead.

Responsibility for Defeat

In *Embracing Defeat: Japan in the Wake of World War II,* John Dower writes with great understanding and insight about the experience of defeat and the weighty burdens of survival:

> What do you tell the dead when you lose? It was this question, rather than the moral or legal perspectives of the victor, that preoccupied most Japanese as they tried to absorb the issues of war responsibility, guilt, repentance, and atonement. This was only natural—not because of cultural differences, but because the world is different when you lose. Where the victors asked who was responsible for Japanese aggression and the atrocities committed by the imperial forces, the more pressing question on the Japanese side was: who was responsible *for defeat?* And where the victors focused on Japan's guilt vis-à-vis other countries and peoples, the Japanese were overwhelmed by grief

> and guilt toward their own dead countrymen. The victors could comfort the souls of the dead, and console themselves, by reporting that the outcome of the war had been great and good. Just as every fighting man on the winning side became a hero, so no supreme sacrifice in the victorious struggle had been in vain. Triumph gave a measure of closure to grief. Defeat left the meaning of these war deaths—of kin, acquaintances, one's compatriots in general—raw and open.[45]

Dower's two main points here—that the Japanese were most concerned after the war with responsibility for defeat and the meaning of their soldiers' deaths—are highly relevant to Ōoka's survivor mission. With regard to *The Battle for Leyte Island,* however, Dower's first question must be expanded to encompass who *and what* were responsible for such terrible loss. While Ōoka gives serious consideration to moral accountability, he also approaches Japanese defeat in the Battle for Leyte Island and the Pacific War in terms of systemic failure and backwardness. And for Ōoka as well, finding significance in his comrades' deaths was a pressing matter. As has been shown, his Herculean efforts to thoroughly formulate responsibility for defeat were inseparable from this moral project.[46] In the end, Ōoka gave meaning to the sacrifices of his comrades by drawing out the vitalizing lessons of their miserable experience of war and defeat. Learning and passing on these costly lessons was also his primary means of making his own survival meaningful.

In *The Battle for Leyte Island* Ōoka fulfills the two solemn obligations taken on by survivors in the Leyte Brotherhood—not allowing their horrible experience of battle and defeat to be forgotten, and doing everything in their power to ensure that Japan would never again be involved in such a war.[47] Ōoka formulates the responsibility for defeat by examining the Battle for Leyte Island in terms of systemic failure; strategic, tactical, and technological retardation; moral responsibility; and conspiracies of silence.

Systemic Failure

Although the imminence and inevitability of defeat was clear to an unbiased eye as early as the summer of 1944, top leaders in Imperial Headquarters had become blind to reality. Rather than acting decisively to bring the war to an end after the Combined Fleet was crippled in the Battle of the Philippine Sea and Saipan was lost, staff officers dreamed up radical new battle plans. The code name for the operation, announced on July 24, was Shō, or Victory.[48] The Shō Operation called for an all-out, concerted surprise attack on the American amphibious fleets at the perimeter of a reconfigured Absolute National Defense Sphere. It was premised on winner-take-all air, sea, and land battles waged at one of four anticipated locations: the Philippines, Taiwan/Ryukyu Islands, homeland, or Kuriles. Although the Combined Fleet lost irreplaceable aircraft carriers and hundreds of planes in the Battle of the Philippine Sea, it was thought that if all available land-based air forces were deployed in support, the great battleships *Yamato* and *Musashi* could be used to deal a devastating blow to the enemy invasion force.

The sustained air battles fought off Taiwan a week before the American landing at Leyte effectively doomed the Shō Operation before it could even be implemented. Because of the grossly exaggerated damage reports made by inexperienced pilots, the navy thought that it had scored a major victory against Admiral Halsey's fast carrier fleet.[49] Ōoka describes the reaction in Tokyo to these erroneous reports as follows: "The announcement made by Imperial Headquarters drove the people, who had begun to harbor serious misgivings since the fall of Saipan, into fits of ecstasy. The emperor issued a rescript commending the Combined Fleet, great celebrations were held in Tokyo and Osaka, and Prime Minister Koiso proclaimed that 'victory is now upon us!'" (9:44).

Damage reports on enemy ships were grossly exaggerated, but assessments of their own losses were surprisingly honest and accurate: Imperial Headquarters acknowledged the destruction of 312 planes. This loss of desperately needed land-based and surface-based air power just days before the decisive battle undermined a crucial component of the Shō Operation. What ultimately proved to be fatal, however, was the navy's failure to disclose to its army counterparts that they had learned soon after the air engagements ended that Admiral Halsey's fast carrier fleet was not only unscathed, but also shaping a course for the Philippines.

The navy's silence on the actual outcome of the Taiwan air battles contributed substantially to failure. Once it became clear that the Americans were converging on Leyte, Imperial Headquarters ordered implementation of the Shō Operation effective midnight, October 19. The plans for the Philippines had all been premised on the decisive battle being fought at

Luzon. Upon being informed that Admiral Halsey's fleet had been destroyed, however, army strategists in Imperial Headquarters abruptly changed the site to Leyte Island. And the costs of this last-minute shift were unimaginably high: "Thus did the Japanese army commit the fundamental error of ineffectively sending incremental reinforcements to a decisive battleground that required superior troop strength from the outset. By their own hand, they became mired in a war of attrition" (9:57).

Ōoka underscores the fact that the root cause of the army's strategic mistakes was the navy's reluctance to divulge the truth about the actual outcome of the Taiwan air battles. Had the navy been more forthcoming from the outset, the Shō Operation might not have ended in such utter failure:

> The navy section of Imperial Headquarters did not report to the army section that no damage had been done to the enemy's mobile fleet. While this is unbelievable when viewed from the present, the navy was probably thinking of the face they would lose if they admitted that they had gained nothing after being honored by the emperor and raising the people's hopes. No matter how difficult to admit, however, this fact should have been revealed.
>
> With the decisive battle just days away, the American mobile fleet was still intact. This meant that airfields and shipping throughout the Philippines were in imminent danger of coming under attack by more than a thousand planes.
>
> If the army section had known this, the decisive battle probably wouldn't have been suddenly shifted to Leyte, Prime Minister Koiso would not have exclaimed that "Leyte is Tennōzan," the three divisions comprising the decisive attack force would not have been transported to the island through hazardous waters, and only the Sixteenth Division and the reinforcements sent from the Visayans and Mindanao would have been sacrificed.[50] Moreover, the circumstances that led to the abandonment and starvation of ten thousand troops might also have been avoided. (9:45–46)

Ōoka formulates responsibility for the debacle primarily in terms of systemic failure and group responsibility:

> French historian Marc Bloch is of the opinion that these kinds of errors in leadership cannot be reduced to personal responsibility, but originate from the organizations in which individuals operate. . . .
>
> The old Japanese military has been described (by Maruyama Masao) as a "system of irresponsibility" based on the nominal high command of the emperor, but apparently this isn't just the special characteristic of monarchies.[51]

> Bureaucratic command structures inevitably emerge even in the military organizations in democratic countries. The result is a labyrinth of innumerable written orders, continually revised and rewritten strategic plans, and mountains of "secret" and "top secret" documents. Meddling by outsiders is neither allowed nor feasible. Even section functionaries on the inside cannot make sense of them. With sectionalism comes competition, which inevitably leads to jealousy and incessant quarreling. Such a system operates smoothly as long as it is fueled by victory. Once the slide toward defeat begins, however, the flaws all emerge at once.
>
> Why did the Imperial Navy that so scrupulously maintained radio silence before the attack on Pearl Harbor commit the blunder of exposing their fleet's movements to the Americans by thoughtlessly exchanging messages before Midway? Did Yamamoto Isoroku become an idiot in just six months? No, maintaining tight control over an entire military organization made arrogant by victory was beyond the ability of a single combined fleet commander.
>
> It can safely be said that the navy clearly foresaw that by 1944 the comparative naval strengths of America and Japan would be ten to one. Despite this knowledge, they could not say "no" to initiating the war. They couldn't stand before the emperor and people and admit the inadequacy of their military preparedness and armaments. This, however, was not simply a matter of the vanity and moral weakness of the military leadership. The navy on the whole had become so superannuated that it could no longer function in a rational manner. Behind the silence of the "silent navy," there was nothing at all. (9:46–47)

Given this perspective, the central question becomes how Japan's formerly successful military organizations became so degenerate and dysfunctional. Put differently, Ōoka faced the challenge of explaining why the Japanese lost nearly 90,000 men during the Battle for Leyte Island when the Americans lost only 3,405 (10:500). In the extended passage introduced above, Ōoka makes three important observations in this regard. Although he writes specifically about the Imperial Navy, his comments are equally applicable to the army. His first important point is that the navy had been "made arrogant by victory"; the second is that the slide toward defeat made inherent systemic flaws "all appear at once;" and the third is that the navy had become "so superannuated (*ryōkyūka*) that [it] was no longer able to function in a rational manner." As will be elaborated on below, these elements—hubris, crises-induced systemic breakdown and decrepitude—are integral to Ōoka's central thesis that stunted, uncoordinated modernization was the cause of Japanese failure in the Battle for Leyte Island and in the Pacific War. Martial successes—not only in the early stages of the Pacific War, but also in the Sino-Japanese and Russo-Japanese Wars—bred arrogance, overconfidence, and irrational contempt for the enemy. These fostered the chronic conservatism, complacency, and ossification that in turn gave rise to backward strategies, tactics, and technology and to counterproductive, draconian treatment of troops. The debilitating weaknesses of having made little or no progress in crucial areas of modern warfare became painfully apparent once Japan took on a highly adaptable, technologically advanced, fully modernized enemy.

Uncoordinated Modernization

Ōoka argues that in the Battle for Leyte Island and the Pacific War Japan ultimately fought against—and was defeated by—the character and particular circumstances of its modern history. He writes as follows, for instance, about the failed Battle of Leyte Gulf: "[The naval historian James A.] Field has written that rather than fighting the American fleet in the Battle of Leyte Gulf, the Combined Fleet was fighting its own history. . . . By history Field meant the great loss of planes and pilots Japan suffered during naval engagements in the Solomons and Marianas. Taken more broadly, however, it could be said that the Combined Fleet was fighting against the history of the Imperial Navy, or to go even further, Japan's entire modern history" (9:244).

Ōoka approaches the Battle of Limon Pass in similar terms:

> All these critiques [of the army's handling of the Battle of Limon Pass] were made with the benefit of hindsight. If we don't learn from history, however, we will be stuck forever at Limon Pass. These are not problems that can simply be traced to the nature of the old Japanese army; they were the products of the overall political and economic conditions Japan faced as it sought to join the modern scramble for colonies. On Limon Pass, as in the Battle of Leyte Gulf, the whole span of modern Japanese history was at work. Like the sailors of Vice Admiral Kurita's fleet, First Division soldiers at Limon Pass fought against Japanese history itself. (9:620–621)

Ōoka fleshes out his central thesis by scrutinizing the Shō Operation and the specific strategies, tactics, and technologies Japan employed during the main land and sea engagements of the Battle for Leyte Island. Examination of his treatment of why and how these efforts failed as they did facilitates appreciation of his contention that retarded, uncoordinated modernization was the tap root of disaster in the Philippines and the Pacific War as a whole.

Pipe Dreams

Ōoka consistently characterizes the overall Shō Operation, the specific strategies for individual land and sea engagements of the Battle for Leyte Island, and Imperial Headquarters' last-ditch plan to fight the Decisive Battle for the Homeland as "desktop" or "dream" plans. He writes about the Shō Operation as follows:

> When one compares American and Japanese strategies [for Leyte Island], one realizes the great extent to which each party saw through the other's intentions. The plans themselves were actually quite straightforward. Both sides settled on the location objectively appropriate to their respective battle strengths. The decisive factor, however, is whether a country has the fighting power and materiel it needs to actually carry out their plans. This is the essence of war. In the final analysis, the Japanese military lost because all they had were conceptual, desktop plans. (9:34–35)

By the middle of 1944, staff officers in Imperial Headquarters had clearly begun to lose touch with reality. This was readily reflected in unsound and unrealistic operational plans. Their fundamental weakness was impracticability:

> Field praises Japanese strategy [in the Shō Operation], but he also points out that the navy as a whole lacked the "high level of mediocrity" necessary for [successfully] conducting modern warfare. He observes that to actualize large-scale, coordinated battle operations, each individual must function in a sphere that is an extension of his everyday rational thinking and strive to keep mistakes to an absolute minimum. Since this was lacking in the Shō Operation, which involved decoys, wild frontal attacks, and other extraordinary measures, things did not go well. (9:245)

As will be subsequently shown, this holds true for the land battles as well.

Just before it became obvious that the Americans were converging on Leyte, the Combined Fleet's forces were spread out between Japan and the South Seas. The Second Fleet, centered on the battleship *Yamato,* was anchored at Lingga taking on fuel and supplies. The mobile fleet was in the Inland Sea training new pilots and receiving replacement aircraft. Unless the mobile fleet went to Lingga to refuel, there was a real danger of running out of fuel during the upcoming battle. While the fleet in the South Seas had plenty of heavy oil, it was low on ammunition. For logistical reasons such as these, the Combined Fleet's plans of staging a coordinated surprise attack as soon as the enemy began their invasion were frustrated from the start (9:161). In the end, the various fleets didn't converge on Leyte until five days after the American landing. In the "Naval Engagements" chapter Ōoka details and appraises the naval portion of the Shō Operation:

> If Leyte Island was allowed to slip into enemy hands, the Combined Fleet would lose its last opportunity to stage a coordinated attack. Although they were unprepared, the two fleets had no choice but to set sail from the north and south and attempt to crush the enemy's strategy of landing in force at Leyte.
>
> The strategy the Combined Fleet adopted to this end, a clever combination of decoy and frontal assault tactics, was a finely wrought Japanese masterpiece. The original plan was to bring Rear Admiral Shima Kiyohide's Fifth Fleet (two heavy cruisers, one light cruiser) down from Hokkaido, add two light aircraft carriers and two battle carriers (battleships with rear landing decks), and send it south as a decoy force. It would then lure the American mobile force to the east of Leyte Island northward to where Vice Admiral Ozawa Jizaburō's main mobile fleet of four aircraft carriers would strike. The surface force, which would in the meantime have forced its way through from the south, would then enter Leyte Gulf, destroy the transports, and foil the enemy's landing.
>
> This was the deformed strategy thought up at this critical turning point in the autumn when American occupation of Leyte Island threatened to cut off access to southern resources. Risking the loss of an entire fleet by using it as a decoy was beyond the pale of reasonable naval engagement. It also went against the global naval tradition that developed from the time Nelson advocated gaining control of the seas by destroying the main enemy fleet. It did accord, however, with the new naval strategy that had emerged since Guadalcanal of supported troop landings.
>
> The enemy's island-hopping strategy forced revision of the concept of "destroying the main naval force." Now the islands themselves were immediately made into air bases, and strategies as a whole began to center on air power. Occupation by ground troops was necessary to gain such air bases. For the navy, destroying landing forces came to be as important as destroying the enemy fleets themselves. (9:161–162)

As will be detailed below, because of Vice Admiral Kurita's and his staff's old-headedness, the Imperial Navy's strategy resulted in extinction rather than domination. While incorporating a number of innovative elements, the navy's plans were still premised on the sacrifice of a third of its fleet. As a result of the heavy losses of planes in the Battle of the Philippine Sea and the Taiwan air engagements, the decoy force used to lure Halsey's mobile force to the north would be defenseless. Ōoka is quick to remind the reader, moreover, that even if the navy's extraordinary plan had succeeded, the Japanese wouldn't have been able to make the island into an air base or hold it for very long because plane production was flagging. The only things localized success would have accomplished were slowing down the American advance and providing "boasting rights" for the navy, which could then have claimed that it fought well in its last engagement (9:162).

While Ōoka doesn't directly label it as such, the army's plan for the Sixteenth Division to single-handedly meet the enemy invasion surely qualifies as a purely conceptual, desktop plan. Because of the false reports concerning the outcome of the air battles off Taiwan, overconfidence, and serious underestimation of the size and strength of the enemy amphibious force, it was assumed that a single division would be sufficient to keep the Americans at bay until substantial reinforcements could be transported to the island. In reality, however, Sixteenth Division soldiers were outnumbered four to one, and their defenses collapsed within a matter of days. As strategists in Imperial Headquarters increasingly lost touch with contemporary battlefield reality, moreover, they were also deprived of their ability to consider how the enemy might react to their plans. Ōoka assesses the opening battle as follows:

> The strategic mistakes made at the outset of the Battle for Leyte Island stemmed from the army's making judgments based solely on its own convenience. Judging from prior American behavior and based on the hasty conclusion that the invasion force would consist of two divisions, it was assumed that the enemy would take their time in establishing their beachhead before pushing inland. They estimated that it would be at least a week before they pushed out into the Leyte plains. In short, they were incapable of imagining that if they shifted to a strategy of defense-in-depth, the enemy might move inland more rapidly.
>
> This wasn't just a weakness of the Thirty-fifth Army. The Japanese army on the whole [repeatedly] committed this kind of error. The strategic plans

> made by staff officers who had their heads filled with dream tales of Okehazama surprise attacks and Tannenberg routs were based on the assumption that their enemies would just sit on their hands while the officers concocted their brilliant Napoleonic surprise attacks. They were incapable of imagining what the enemy would do after they initiated a particular course of action. The plans [the Japanese officers] made for the Battle for Leyte Island repeatedly reveal one-sided thinking. (9:96)

Ōoka faults the Imperial Army for its lack of realistic, practical imagination on the one hand and its enduring anachronistic fantasies of come-from-behind victory on the other. As with their navy counterparts, army planners were living more in the idealized past than responding reasonably to the unsettling realities of the present. In short, the operational plans dreamed up in Imperial Headquarters toward the end of the Pacific War were debilitatingly old-headed and impractical. And what was true of Japanese operational plans for the overall Battle for Leyte Island was equally so of the tactics and technologies employed in individual land and sea engagements.

Operational plans for the Battle of Limon Pass, for instance, were at great variance with battleground actualities: "The frontage of Limon Pass was so narrow that the indiscriminate concentration of troop strength there only provided enemy gunners with easy targets. This desktop plan founded on the tactic of 'breaking through the bottleneck' (*airo aishutsu*) was made by men who were wholly ignorant of the topography of the central mountains" (9:369). Positioning troops according to inaccurate maps rather than confirmed topographical data not only set soldiers up for slaughter in the narrow confines of Limon Pass, but also resulted in entire regiments becoming hopelessly lost and effectively put out of commission.

While troop placement was bad, the army's repeated use of outmoded battle strategies proved to be even worse. In the following passage, Ōoka stresses how old-headedness and ossification contributed substantially to defeat in the Battle of Limon Pass:

> Of course, unlike European countries, Japan had no opponent nearby who could mobilize a million troops at a time for massive engagements. The Japanese were outnumbered even in the battles they fought at the end of the Siberian Railway during the Russo-Japanese War. Consequently, Japan immediately adopted the German strategy of outflanking with inferior troop

> strength (*ressei hōi*). (Germany, like Japan, was a young, rising nation. To prevail on both the French and Russian fronts, it had to adopt such overextension strategies.) Standard Japanese army practices such as perfunctory mobile operations and reliance on fighting spirit grew out of these skeletonized fin de siècle German stratagems.
>
> Although the evils of these practices had already become apparent during the Russo-Japanese War, victory made the army arrogant, and they didn't properly learn their lessons. During the thirty years before the outbreak of the Japan-China war, they made no headway at all.
>
> The old Japanese army was an organization with a unified command structure extending from the emperor generalissimo at the top all the way down to the foot soldier at the bottom, and each constitutive unit was susceptible to conservatism and formalization. While the half-baked strategy of *ressei hōi* was employed over and over against ill-equipped Chinese soldiers, the enemy managed to escape every time.
>
> The effort to outflank the British army, which by then could be resupplied by airdrop, ended in Japanese defeat (Burma front). Even when a wedge was thrown into opposing landing forces, it did not lead to decimation of the enemy (New Guinea). The Imperial Army employed the same strategies—and reaped the same poor results—time and time again.
>
> Immediately upon encountering the enemy, the vanguard of the First Division spread out to the right. This was little more than patterned behavior. Only a single perfunctory patrol was sent out on the left to Hill 218 (five kilometers to the northwest). Clifford was thus able to outflank them with ease.
>
> Against an enemy employing such sound strategies, the raids (*kirikomi*) conducted by the Forty-ninth Regiment at Capoocan and Culasian held little chance of success. Wild frontal assaults and *ressei hōi* were two of the Imperial Army's hackneyed strategies. (9:619–620)

In this extended passage, Ōoka exposes some of the causes of defeat in the land battles waged on Leyte Island. He initially draws attention to the fundamental unsoundness of Japanese aspirations of becoming a world military power. The incontrovertible realities of being an island nation with limited natural and human resources necessitated the adoption of risky compensatory stratagems that inevitably ended in untenable overextension. Like the Imperial Navy, moreover, the Imperial Army quickly became conservative, complacent, and ossified. This, as Ōoka suggests, can best be understood in terms of systemic failure; the chronic and debilitating tendency toward self-defeating conservatism was apparently latent in the very nature of Japan's military organism. Early martial successes exacerbated this predisposition. With victory came egotism and hubris, which had the deleterious effect of rendering military leadership all but incapable of learning anything from their own battlefield experience.

The Japanese army not only failed to modernize their military tactics, but underestimated and irrationally despised their opponents as well.[52] Toward the end of the first volume of *The Battle for Leyte Island,* Ōoka observes that long before the outbreak of the Pacific War, Japanese strategists had begun to hold their enemies in such contempt that they simply stopped bothering to study them. One of the main reasons the army sent only a perfunctory patrol out to Hill 218 was their presumption that the Americans would never attempt a bold outflanking maneuver. In the following passage, Ōoka traces the origins of this self-defeating tendency: "At the time of the Manchurian Incident and the Japan-China war, the Japanese military gathered more intelligence on the organization, equipment, and fighting strength of the enemy before engaging them in battle. Subsequently, however, they came to arbitrarily despise their opponents. South of Central China, they made no effort to learn about their enemies' troop movements. The pattern of blindly pushing forward only to be caught unawares was already more or less established by this time" (9:613).

The Ta Operation, Imperial Headquarters' makeshift plan to reinforce and resupply Leyte Island, was also unrealistic, impractical, and ineffective. The aim of this operation was to transport two and a half divisions and the necessary food and ordnance from Manila to Leyte. The first major problem was a severe shortage of transport ships. The second was that by the end of October the Japanese had lost control of both skies and sea. At the time this operation was being formulated, the actual results of the Taiwan air battles had become clear, and the crucial Battle of Leyte Gulf had already ended in stunning defeat. To make matters worse, Japan lost 439 planes and a number of warships during the November 5–6 aerial raids on Manila. Far from being a viable staging area for massive transport operations, the capital was coming under frequent attack, and Manila Bay was quickly turning into a ship's graveyard.

As will be treated in greater detail in the context of moral responsibility, at this critical juncture both the Fourteenth Area and Southern Armies requested that Reite kessen be called off and that the decisive battle be waged at Luzon as originally planned. On November 8, however, Imperial

Headquarters commanded that the Battle for Leyte Island be carried forward. In the end, nine transport convoys were organized and sent to Leyte Island. While the first two were relatively successful, subsequent efforts resulted in mounting loss of life, equipment, and supplies. Ōoka estimates that as many as ten thousand men died en route to Leyte (10:504).

The operational plans for taking back the airstrips near Burauen (Wa Operation) were no different. This extraordinary plan envisioned a coordinated surprise attack by paratroopers (Ten Operation), crash-landing soldiers (Gi Operation), the newly arrived Twenty-sixth Division, and remnants of the Sixteenth Division.[53] Ōoka describes the Wa Operation with biting irony: "The grand scope of the plan and the way it accorded so well with the Japanese penchant for surprise attacks made it a fitting crown for the whole Battle for Leyte Island" (9:496). Dreamed up by staff officers in the Southern Army, this operation was a response to intelligence reports that the American air forces on Leyte Island had just received two hundred new B-25s and P-38s.

While intelligence on the type and number of enemy planes was accurate, that concerning their whereabouts was not. By the time the attack began on November 5, the Americans had abandoned use of these airstrips. Like the overall Battle for Leyte Island itself, the army had neither the troops nor the supplies it needed to effectively carry out the Wa Operation. Because of the roughness of the terrain, the Twenty-sixth Division was unable to get their artillery pieces over the mountains from the west coast, most of the paratroopers were shot down or scattered upon landing, and the 150 or so remnants of the Sixteenth Division who managed to join in the attack did so a day behind schedule. Ōoka highlights the fundamental unreasonableness of the Wa Operation in the following terms:

> The Fourteenth Area Army never imagined it would be so difficult to get over the mountains. Since they had no aerial photographs of the western side of the central mountain range, their knowledge of the topography was vague at best. They proposed the Wa Operation assuming that it would be easy to improve the path enough to get artillery into position. In actuality, however, the path was so deteriorated it could barely be followed at all; it was a major undertaking simply to make it passable.
>
> . . . The Wa Operation thus became a raid sans artillery support.
>
> Lieutenant General Tominaga's Gi and Ten Operations, too, contained unrealistic elements. Making crash landings and dropping paratroopers onto

> airfields were acts of desperation. While sounding courageous, they went against fundamental martial practices. In the end, they amounted to little more than disturbance tactics; they were obviously inappropriate in light of the relative number, efficiency, and maneuverability opposing aircraft exhibited in the air battles that had been fought up to that point. These operations can be understood as variations on the Special Attack Forces; they were unreasonable plans made by men who were at their wit's end. Nothing whatsoever was gained by combining two unrealistic plans. (10:76)

While never put fully into practice, the final operational plan conjured up in Imperial Headquarters was no less conceptual and unrealistic than the others under discussion. This operation, code-named Ketsu, or Decisive, called for the coordination of a massive counterlanding at Carigara with a breakthrough by First Division troops at Limon Pass:

> The Thirty-fifth Army began to entertain thoughts of this strategy on October 28 when they were still ignorant of the actual situation [on the east coast]. It was similar to the Wa Operation in that it, too, was a purely conceptual plan. Since it was never actually carried out, it is not described in battle accounts. Its code name, however, sporadically appears in them. There are references to a "Ketsu Operation" on December 11, after the Wa Operation failed. On that day, the First Division prepared to light beacon fires atop Three Knob Hill. The Ketsu Operation was the general name for the plan Imperial Headquarters adopted in March 1945 to fight the Decisive Battle for the Homeland. The use of this code name in the field indicates great ardor. This operation, too, however, was ultimately abandoned because of the American move toward Mindoro Island on December 15. In *Leyte Battle History,* the following item appears for December 14: "Ketsu Operation cancelled." (9:596–597)

The outrageousness and impracticality of this last-ditch operation cannot be overemphasized. At this point, control over the skies and seas was firmly in American hands, the Ta and Wa Operations had ended in miserable failure, Manila was under frequent attack, First Division defense positions at Limon Pass were on the verge of collapse, and the December 7 American counterlanding at Ormoc had effectively put an end to any real hopes of a comeback. Thus, in the face of every sign of imminent defeat, Imperial Headquarters persisted in having pipe dreams of a come-from-behind victory. This time, fresh reinforcements were to be transported directly from Pusan and Taiwan to Leyte. The operation was subsequently called off, but not before these transports had been attacked by enemy submarines. In the end, virtually all supplies were lost en route; only one-half to one-third of the troops reached Manila alive (10:197).

Macrocosmically and microcosmically, each operation Imperial Headquarters came up with was more fantastic, impracticable, and irresponsible than the last. From the A-go Operation to Reite kessen, from Reite kessen to Hondo kessen; from Ta to Wa, from Wa to Ketsu—truly, as John Dower has observed, "Long after it had become obvious that Japan was doomed, its leaders all the way up to the emperor remained unable to contemplate surrender. They were psychologically blocked, capable only of stumbling forward."[54] As the specter of defeat loomed ever larger, staff officers in Imperial Headquarters conjured up even more outlandish and inhuman operations. The Ketsu Operation, taken up after belated acknowledgment of defeat in the Battle for Leyte Island, was symptomatic of both psychological and ethical bankruptcy. Now the "decisive battle" was to be fought in the home islands:

> Based on the "Outline of Imperial Army and Navy Strategy," the concept of fighting the Decisive Battle for the Homeland was agreed upon by Imperial Headquarters on January 20, 1945. The operation called for the mobilization of fifty new divisions between February and August. These divisions would be positioned along the entire length of the Pacific Coast. The defenders would have no rifles and grenades, but it was thought that if they could temporarily check the enemy advance with gasoline bombs, Special Attack Forces held in reserve could destroy the American warships. (10:434–435)

Ōoka consistently characterizes the Ketsu Operation as Imperial Headquarters' "dream" plan. Indeed, top strategists in Tokyo clung so insistently to their hopes in the kamikaze that they refused to relent even after atomic bombs had devastated Hiroshima and Nagasaki. The rich multivalence and irony of Ōoka characterizing *The Battle for Leyte Island* as a "great collection of dreams" should by now be clear.

Backward Tactics and Technology

The following discussion of Ōoka's treatment of the decisive role that antiquated tactics and technologies played in defeat will commence with the Battle of Leyte Gulf and then turn to representative land battles. In the extended passage that follows, Ōoka states his reasons for writing about this naval engagement,[55] outlines its main elements, and makes a significant comment on this crucial phase of the Shō Operation and the way it was enacted:

> The main subject of this account is the land battles fought on Leyte Island. Because the Battle of Leyte Gulf fought between October 24 and 26 had such a decisive impact on them, however, it cannot be passed over lightly.
>
> As is commonly known, this was the largest, most decisive battle fought between the Japanese and American navies. The Combined Fleet was defeated after investing 80 percent of its force. The Americans consequently gained control of the seas around Leyte, and the land battles lost their potential to be decisive. Imperial Headquarters, however, hung their hopes on the Special Attack Forces, which made their first appearance during this sea engagement. Until the end of the war, Imperial Headquarters continued to dream that the enemy might stop fighting if only their hand could be burned by our resistance.
>
> The naval engagements were carried out over a vast, four-hundred-nautical-mile area extending from the northeast of Luzon to the Sulu Sea, and from there to the southwest of Leyte. It was the biggest battle in world naval history. While the Japanese navy ultimately lost because it had insufficient air power, the plan the Combined Fleet came up with at the time—one of its most ingenious—created the possibility for localized battle success. In terms of both strategy and enactment, this battle can be seen as a classic example of our spirit. (9:160)

At the end of the passage, Ōoka states that the Battle of Leyte Gulf was symbolic of Japanese spirit (*seishin*). The Special Attack Forces that were first employed during the Shō Operation were the embodiments of strategists' dreams of achieving a single battle victory before moving toward negotiated peace. The plans for the naval operation were emblematic of Japanese potential for innovative thinking. Finally, the way the battle actually unfolded represented how conservatism and ossification resulted in crippling backwardness in military tactics and technology.

Throughout *The Battle for Leyte Island,* Ōoka notes that the Imperial Army and Navy were ultimately incapable of effectively conducting modern warfare. In the course of presenting his thesis that Japan was fighting against its own history in both the Philippines and the Pacific, he draws particular attention to the navy's anachronistic tactics and technologies:

> Leading up to the Battle of the Inland Sea,[56] Imperial Japan rose while strengthening its capital ships. While Japan succeeded in destroying the decrepit Chinese and Russian navies, the weakness of being a country without natural resources emerged once the country took on the United States and Britain. There is no reason to doubt the courage of our fallen army and navy men. The navy, however, found no margin to foster the practices—such as accurate damage reporting—necessary for modern naval warfare.
>
> There were clever strategists in the Combined Fleet. On the whole, the Shō Operation can be described as a combination of Japanese cunning and daring. It contained the unreasonableness, however, of envisioning in too fine detail the great naval engagements that would be fought over a six-hundred-nautical-mile area. Movement over such an extensive area cannot be coordinated without an efficient system of communications. Since Japanese communications were woefully inadequate, the fleets did not move according to plan. (9:244–245)

Ōoka makes three important points here. The first is that historically speaking the navy increased its power and influence by concentrating on the development of battleships. As will be shown below, however, the navy's dogged reliance on big battlewagons was one of the root causes of defeat in the Battle of Leyte Gulf. While such warships may have worked well against their turn-of-the-century foes, they were wholly ineffective against the aircraft carrier–based fleets of their more advanced opponents. The Imperial Navy, moreover, failed to adequately train their crews for contemporary combat. While Ōoka cites damage reporting as a primary example, he notes elsewhere that the abusive, draconian treatment of soldiers had a profoundly deleterious effect on both morale and combat performance. Ōoka's final point concerns technology. The Japanese military not only lacked the fighting strength and basic supplies it needed to successfully carry out the Decisive Battle for Leyte Island, but the technology and technical know-how as well.

While the Shō Operation failed primarily because of insufficient air power, Ōoka emphasizes the significant role played by the Imperial Navy's tactical backwardness. The most serious weakness was overreliance on enormous battlewagons: "Because the Imperial Navy didn't have enough escort ships . . . and didn't take proper precautions against submarine attack, three heavy cruisers were lost in the Palawan Strait. This resulted from the navy's preoccupation with deciding naval engagements with great battleships. The navy didn't begin to build [escort] destroyers in substantial numbers until 1943. By then, is was already too late. Here, too, 'history' was at work"[57] (9:244).

While an inadequate number of escort destroyers made Japan's great battleships vulnerable to submarine attack, insufficient air support made them easy prey for American carrier-based planes. Ōoka goes on to comment at length on the obsoleteness and ineffectiveness of such behemoths:

> The sinking of the *Musashi* in the Battle of the Sibuyan Sea was a highly symbolic event. As is well known, the *Musashi* was sister ship to the *Yamato.* Construction was begun in March 1938. Upon completion in August 1943, the *Musashi* was added to the Combined Fleet's forces. Since the navy was already plagued by lack of heavy oil, however, it was neither used in operations nor were its guns used for target practice. Its enormous hull merely rolled about at the Lingga naval base.
>
> Naval ships, too, express the spirit of a people. The *Yamato* and *Musashi* revealed our country's desire to catch up with and surpass the West. Displacing 72,000 tons and equipped with nine 46-centimeter guns, it was the most powerful battleship in the world. A shell fired at an angle of forty-five degrees rose twice as high as Mt. Fuji and sailed a distance of forty-one kilometers. . . . Built with the know-how of Japan's most preeminent shipbuilders, its capabilities were kept top secret, and it quickly became the object of legendary awe and faith. When confronted by surface-based planes that could attack within a range of two hundred nautical miles, however, it was sunk without a fight.
>
> About the time that construction began, concerns were being raised in navy inner circles by "carrier men" such as Yamamoto Isoroku and Ōnishi Takijirō. Since the Battle of the Inland Sea, however, it had been naval tradition to use battleships to determine sea engagements. Yamamoto and Ōnishi were powerless in the face of this bias. The Americans had organized their fleets around aircraft carriers; with the exception of the main batteries, all battleships had been refitted with antiaircraft guns to provide cover. The Imperial Navy was thus defeated by the U.S. navy's flexibility (*jūnansei*). (9:173–174)

Like the operational plans for the Battle for Leyte Island, Japan's huge capital ships were telling expressions of Japanese spirit. In his treatment of both the Shō Operation and the *Musashi,* Ōoka highlights the ironic contrast between the grandiosity of Japan's dreams and aspirations and the pathetic outcome of its efforts to realize them. In the case of the Battle of

Leyte Gulf, naval tradition itself was at the root of defeat. As will be shown below in the discussion of Kurita's failure to force entry into Leyte Gulf and of the Battle of Limon Pass, the chronic conservatism and rigidity of the Japanese army and navy proved to be fatal handicaps when fighting against their highly rational, flexible, fully modernized Western opponents.

Ōoka interprets Vice Admiral Kurita's refusal to carry out the prime directive of the Shō Operation as the tragic outcome of traditional naval battle practices. Like the old-headed thinking that led to the construction of enormous, ineffective capital ships, Kurita's conduct during the pivotal battle reflected his inability or unwillingness to adapt to rapidly changing times. One of the most innovative elements of the naval portion of the Shō Operation was using the enormous firepower of the Combined Fleet's great battleships to attack transports in Leyte Gulf and the American beachhead. After describing the circumstances that led to the American mistake of leaving the San Bernardino Strait unguarded, Ōoka explains why Kurita failed to take advantage of his opportunity to lead his attack fleet directly toward and into Leyte Gulf:

> There were also contradictions involving Kurita's fleet. We have already seen what transpired when Kurita encountered Sprague's escort carrier group after passing through the San Bernardino Strait. Had he been determined to remain faithful to the aim of the Shō Operation, he would have ordered a number of his ships to attack [the escort carrier group] and led his main force toward Leyte Gulf. Here, too, however, the bias of determining battles through naval engagement can be seen. As a result, time and ammunition were wasted chasing a defenseless group of escort carriers.
>
> Since it was unheard of for a mobile force to have only seven escort destroyers (even if they were mistaken for heavy cruisers, they were still far too few in number), it is conceivable that during the course of the battle they would have realized they were attacking converted escort carriers. Wishful thinking (*ganbō*) that they were engaging the American mobile force, however, operated to block sound rational judgment. (9:225–226)

In the end, Vice Admiral Kurita made six major course changes. Ōoka takes the turn he made away from Leyte Gulf and toward Sprague's group of escort carriers as a clear indication of his reluctance to act in accordance with the dictates of the Shō Operation. He stresses, moreover, that as with the navy's willingness to attack against all odds in the Philippines, its failure to inform its counterparts in the army about the actual outcome of the Taiwan air battles, and Imperial Headquarters' Ketsu Operation, emotion once again overshadowed rationality.

Ōoka underscores this important point by describing the role that fear played in the navy's actions. He begins by reiterating that the Shō Operation was premised on risking the annihilation of the entire fleet in order to force entry into Leyte Gulf. This meant certain death for the men in Kurita's attack force. Ōoka notes that they had had numerous brushes with death even before encountering Sprague's group of escort carriers: on the twenty-third they had watched helplessly as submarines sank three of their heavy cruisers. During the intensive air raids the following day, they witnessed the destruction of the *Musashi.* Because of their rising dread, driftwood and whitecaps were continually being mistaken for torpedoes and mines, and submarine alerts were repeatedly sounded and cancelled. In the end, Ōoka suggests that their wishful thinking concerning the identity of the enemy they encountered after emerging from the San Bernardino Strait was inseparable from the terror they felt over being burdened with carrying out a suicide mission: "The probability is high, however, that their fear was expressed both in the judgment the officers and men in Kurita's fleet made when they left Lingga that concentrating on transports in Leyte Gulf was an unworthy action and in their noble-sounding desire to fight a decisive battle with the enemy mobile fleet" (9:227). In the following passage, Ōoka laments Vice Admiral Kurita's failure to enter Leyte Gulf and concludes that he and his officers were simply too inflexible to accept or to act according to the new tactic:

> For the Japanese navy, however, the Shō Operation was do-or-die. To the men in the naval section of Imperial Headquarters at the time, and for Japanese today, Kurita's hesitation at the crucial moment was emotionally unacceptable. To enable him to reach his objective, Nishimura's fleet had been destroyed, and Ozawa had left the empty flight decks of the four carriers he used as decoys exposed to American fighter attack. This was all done so that Kurita's fleet could force its way into Leyte Gulf. Our hearts tells us that Kurita sowed the seeds for unending regret by turning away. But even if his fleet had succeeded in destroying the Leyte beachhead, they would have had virtually no chance of survival. Lieutenant Colonel Tanemura's *Imperial Headquarters' Secret Journal* reveals that the army section in Imperial Headquarters viewed this operation as "suicidal." From the standpoint of

> Japan's overall fighting power, the *Yamato* and the other big ships [in Kurita's fleet] that escaped were liabilities because they consumed an enormous amount of heavy oil even when at rest. The Shō Operation reflects the navy's apocalyptic thinking. Since this would be their last chance, they were willing to risk everything. If they happened to emerge victorious, it would be a godsend; and if they went down in defeat their role in the war would be finished.
>
> By strange coincidence, this plan was well adapted to countering the Americans' new amphibious attack strategy. At the crucial moment, however, the vanguard battle force disobeyed orders. The *Yamato* and ships under it in the main attack fleet refused self-destruction. In the thoughts that coursed through the minds of Kurita's staff officers at that time—if die we must, then let it be while engaging the enemy fleet, it can't be helped if all we have in range are empty ships, etc.—one can see systemic rejection of the new battle mode. (9:238–239)

Ōoka was clearly ambivalent about Vice Admiral Kurita's conduct. On one hand, he deeply regretted the decision to abandon the attack after such great sacrifices had been made to facilitate it, and saw it as yet another striking example of the psychological inflexibility and decrepitude that brought on overwhelming defeat in the Battle for Leyte Island. At the same time, however, he was able to understand and sympathize with Kurita and his men. While incorporating ingenious and innovative elements, the Shō Operation was desperate, reckless, and premised on suicidal attack. In this sense, the "new" naval tactic differed little from that of the Special Attack Forces. In short, it was not only unreasonable but also unconscionable to order the main battle force of the combined fleet to sacrifice itself in an all-out attack on Leyte Gulf. While Kurita and his staff's resistance to progressive modes of combat exposes one of the root causes of defeat, their refusal to destroy themselves is readily comprehensible in human terms. The heart of the problem would appear to lie in Imperial Headquarters, where psychically numbed strategists progressively came to see little difference between the use of the limited natural resources at their disposal and the human resources they sought to exploit in compensation.

In the end, Ōoka does not hold Vice Admiral Kurita personally responsible for not entering Leyte Gulf. True to his central thesis in *The Battle for Leyte Island,* he explains the failure of the crucial naval phase of the Shō Operation in historical rather than personal terms:

> The root cause of Commander Kurita's hesitation just when there was a possibility for the Shō Operation to achieve localized success need not be sought in his character or his lack of experience leading a large-scale naval operation. I think it should be viewed as the outcome of historical factors. A variety of circumstances led to low morale among the men of Kurita's fleet. This was reflected in the rash of false alarms and inaccurate firing. Accurate fire, which was at the heart of earlier Japanese victories in the Yellow Sea and Sea of Japan, was rarely seen in the naval engagements off Samar Island.
>
> Japan had to compensate for its lack of fighting strength with highly trained pilots and gunners. There were limits, however, to these human resources, and replacements came too late. The Japanese navy, too, which at the beginning of the war was manned by volunteer sailors and fishermen, was composed primarily of conscripts by the time the Shō Operation was put into effect. At this point, slave training and feudalistic ship life became serious handicaps. The replacements, who should have arrived at the battlefield in high spirits, were instead filled with hatred and resentment toward their superior officers and the military. The Shō Operation failed because of the accumulation of innumerable products of modern Japanese history such as these. (9:246–247)

According to Ōoka, in the Battle of Leyte Gulf the Combined Fleet fought against and was defeated by the character of its own modern history. Lack of adequate air power, overly complicated strategic plans, poor communications, backward tactics and technology, poor training and draconian treatment of soldiers, and old-headedness caused failure of the crucial naval phase of the Shō Operation and resulted in the fruitless deaths of tens of thousands of men in the field.

Ōoka treats the land engagements fought during the Battle for Leyte Island in similar terms. As with naval strategy, tactics, and technology, backwardness led to overwhelming defeat and pointless loss of life. One of the Imperial Army's most fundamental errors was expecting too much from a single-division force. This was an important origin of defeat in both the opening battle on the east coast and the pivotal Battle of Limon Pass:

> The wisest strategy for the First Division would probably have been to place the Forty-ninth Regiment on Three Knob Hill and keep the First Regiment in reserve to the south of Cabulan. Had they adopted this approach, however, they immediately would have been criticized for lack of fighting spirit. This is related to the Japanese army's anachronistic predisposition of

> thinking of a single division as a more powerful fighting force than it actually was. Ever since the Franco-Prussian War of 1870, Western armies had taken the corps (two divisions) as the basic tactical unit and substantially increased the number of heavy artillery pieces assigned to it. Japan's old-headed leadership, however, had the bad habit of viewing a single division with fewer than forty field pieces as a decisive fighting force. (9:618–619)

This is yet another clear example of stunted, uncoordinated modernization. While the West quickly learned the lessons of the Franco-Prussian War and modified their military organizations accordingly, the Imperial Army did not. Ōoka initially seeks to accounts for this failing in historical terms:

> Eighteen seventy was the third year of the Meiji period, the time when the Japanese army was first established. The Franco-Prussian War caused the military government to abandon its devotion to France and adopt the strategies of the German victors. Major Meckel, one of Moltke's disciples, was invited to Japan, and the framework for the Japanese army was put into place over a three-year period. Given the new government's [constrained] financial circumstances, however, it was all they could do to establish a single-division structure. They simply didn't have the wherewithal to organize their army on a corps basis. And this [antiquated] organizational structure went unchanged until Limon Pass. (9:619)

While fiscal limitations may have kept the fledgling Meiji government from establishing a new military organization along corps lines, there was little to prevent it from doing so at a later date. The fact that the army would doggedly stick with the same outdated organizational structure for seventy years after Western armies moved on demonstrates the self-destructive conservatism and rigidity that characterizes Japan's former military institutions.

Lack of heavy artillery also contributed substantially to defeat. After the Franco-Prussian War, Western armies not only converted to a corps-based organizational structure, but also significantly increased the number of field pieces assigned to each of these tactical units. In the Battle of Limon Pass, the Americans had 160 pieces of heavy artillery, the Japanese, 27. When test smoke was released to determine the extent of enemy counter-fire, more than a thousand rounds fell upon the site within fifteen minutes (9:437). To conceal the locations of their precious field pieces, the Japanese could fire only sporadically, and to be effective, they had to fire with pinpoint accuracy. In the following passage, Ōoka provides Commander

Kataoka's assessment of the state of the Battle of Limon Pass and then comments on how far behind the times the Japanese army was in terms of artillery:

> In his December 5 report to the [Thirty-fifth] Army . . . Division Commander Kataoka said that even though the First Division was positioned for a holding action, they were actually fighting showdown battles daily. It was infantry against artillery. It wasn't just that he was lacking the minimum number of field pieces needed for modern battle; he also had to rely on the system of telephone-based sightings that had become the standard since the Russo-Japanese War. Once American shells destroyed the power lines, the Japanese could no longer mask their inferior troop strength with accurate fire.
>
> Ever since Napoleon—or to take it back even further, ever since Charles the VIII's soldiers swept over Renaissance Italy in the fifteenth century—it had been common knowledge that artillery gunners decided victory or defeat in land battles. It is not an overstatement to say that the army leadership's neglect to overhaul their practices even after experiencing the full force of heavy artillery and tanks at Nomonhan determined defeat at Limon Pass. (9:616)

Ōoka makes it clear that it wasn't just the Imperial Army's failure to keep pace with military developments in the West that proved to be fatal in the Battle of Limon Pass; the army also neglected to properly learn the important lessons afforded by their own past experience. In short, turn-of-the-century victories over China and Russia made Japan's military leaders arrogant, complacent, and conservative, and this in turn stymied the modernization process.

Even when Japanese strategists did show signs of innovation and progressiveness, their men in the field were often incapable of acting in accord with the new plans. Vice Admiral Kurita's failure to enter Leyte Gulf is a good case in point. The new tactics developed by top-level staff officers for defense of the east coast of Leyte Island and the way they were modified by strategists in the field provide another good example of this fateful dynamic in the context of land battle. Like their comrades fighting at Limon Pass, the men of the Sixteenth Division, burdened with meeting the American landing force, were outnumbered four to one. But in the end, flawed defense tactics proved to be their undoing:

> It can be said, however, that what ultimately proved to be fatal to the Sixteenth Division men charged with defending Leyte Island was the Thirty-

> fifth Army's half-baked directive to fight the Americans at the shoreline. The [Fourteenth Area] Army accepted Imperial Headquarters' instructions to make defense-in-depth their basic tactic. Army staff headquarters sent these instructions complete with precise casualty figures on the [preinvasion] naval bombardment of Saipan. Strategists in the field, however, felt that they would lose face if they didn't find fault with these directives.
>
> Innumerable points were raised and debated at the joint meeting held in Manila. Some said that the casualty statistics were irrelevant because the fortifications on Saipan had been incomplete. Others observed that there were differences between defensive battles on small islands such as Saipan and large islands such as Leyte. Field commanders were of the opinion that if they abandoned the shoreline defensive installations they had just spent six months constructing, it would not only have a bad effect on morale, but also undermine all the training they had done up to that point.
>
> In the end, Lieutenant General Suzuki opted for a compromise plan. [Along with defense-in-depth] "strong, resolute resistance" would also be put up at the shoreline, and "part of the force would have to suffer rapid attrition to this end." This overly ambitious plan called for units surviving the naval bombardment to fight holding actions as long as possible before falling back to foothill positions. (9:96–97)

Despite receiving clear directives to adopt new defensive tactics developed from serious study of recent battle experience,[58] Suzuki, an experienced commander with a long, distinguished record of battlefield successes, half-heartedly reverted to an outmoded approach that had proved to be ineffective time and again. Here, too, face prevailed over reason. As with the other anachronistic strategies and tactics under consideration, the results of Suzuki's compromised defense tactics were catastrophic. While a number of shoreline positions survived the opening bombardment, the overwhelming invasion that followed in its wake quickly overran them. As could have been anticipated, moreover, the sudden failure of coastal defenses precipitated the collapse of defense-in-depth positions as well (9:97). In large part as a result of this flawed defense tactic, the Sixteenth Division suffered 50 percent casualties during the bombardment and was completely routed by the fourth day of battle.

In his formulation of responsibility for defeat, Ōoka also singles out the Imperial Army's penchant for defense-by-attack tactics as particularly unreasonable, ineffective, and devastating to men in the field. The use of this tactic was particularly crippling toward the latter stages of the Battle of

Limon Pass. By this time, the main focus of the land battles had shifted south to the airfields near Burauen, and the First Division was, in Commander Suzuki's words, "fighting showdown battles daily." At this critical juncture, the soldiers who were struggling just to hold their positions were given orders to attack on all fronts. The origins of this outrageous directive, too, lay in overestimation of the capabilities of a single-division force: "This was the [Fourteenth Area] Army's way of spurring the First Division, which had only been blocking the enemy's southward movement, and the Forty-ninth and First Regiments, which hadn't been able to break through to the Carigara Plains, into more decisive action. At the core of this thinking was the Japanese army's anachronistic notion that a single division was a powerful tactical unit that could and should have been able to decide such battles on its own" (9:544). Ōoka goes on to explain why the army made such unreasonable and irresponsible demands on the men at Limon Pass:

> There is an extremely practical way of interpreting this attack. In a nutshell, the army, aware of the decline in divisional fighting strength, judged that ordering an all-out assault would bring about just the defense they desired.
>
> This ploy—a standard means of defense with inferior troop strength—was frequently used at the China front. The concept—one formulated far behind lines—grew out of distrust in the fighting spirit of frontline soldiers. This tactic was only rarely employed when the Japanese army's battle strength was at its peak during the Russo-Japanese War, but as the conflict dragged interminably on in China, it at some point became standard practice. (9:546)

In the epilogue of *The Battle for Leyte Island,* Ōoka succinctly summarizes his main findings on why and how the Shō Operation ended in such resounding defeat:

> [Defeat in] the land, sea, and air battles for Leyte Island determined Japan's loss of the war. When Japan lost its aircraft carriers in the Battle of the Philippine Sea, the Combined Fleet was deprived of its ability to function as a naval force. It was believed, however, that by acting in concert with all the shore-based air forces in the Philippines, the navy could still vie with America's mobile attack force. Because of an unexpected decline in army, navy, and air force fighting strength, however, the final outcome was the destruction of the Combined Fleet and the attrition of shore-based air power.
>
> The army's land operations were premised on navy and air force victory.

Consequently, after control of the air and sea was lost, the army was unable to provide divisional reinforcements with food and ammunition, and defeat was the natural outcome. Japan, however, was at a critical crossroads. If Leyte was lost, it would be impossible to access the natural resources of the South Seas, and this in its turn would make it impossible to continue the war. Because Japan's existence depended on the outcome of the land battles, the Combined Fleet came up with the unprecedented tactic of using battleships as troop transports. The army, too, proclaimed that "Leyte is Tennōzan," persisted in haphazardly sending in supplies for the decisive battle, and in the process wasted both resources and human lives.

Because Leyte was the biggest Pacific island battles were fought on, the Americans and the Japanese made a number of mistakes. Because the decrepit Japanese army and navy didn't have either the fighting power or military know-how and technology to wage modern warfare, however, the errors made by the Americans did not have any serious consequences. From start to finish, the battles proceeded according to American initiative. The supplies the Japanese army transported to the decisive battleground merely fueled attrition, and the men were progressively driven toward total, naked defeat.

Many issues remain concerning the details of the strategies employed. Examples include the Sixteenth Division's half-baked shoreline defense, the First Division's confusion at the outset of the Limon Pass engagement, the hesitation of Kurita's fleet, and the unreasonableness of the strategies developed for the surprise attack at Burauen. These, however, were but ripples on the surface of the overall operation. Generally speaking, because of its defective communications, premodern firepower technology, and the army's premodern tactics of directing artillery fire by telephone-based sightings and deciding battles by means of wild, frontal attacks, Japan had no chance of winning. (10:518–519)

Moral Responsibility

An examination of Ōoka's formulation of responsibility for defeat would be incomplete without consideration of his treatment of the crucial matter of moral responsibility. While Ōoka realized that the Japanese military's "system of irresponsibility" precluded meaningful assignation of individual accountability, he clearly felt that it was incumbent on him to articulate collective responsibility. In short, even though Ōoka argues that fundamental historical factors—lack of natural resources; insufficient fighting strength; stunted, uncoordinated modernization; and the like—were the root causes of defeat in the Battle for Leyte Island in particular and the Pacific War in general, he nonetheless held top leadership groups in

Imperial Headquarters morally accountable for the wholly unjustified waste of human life.

Ōoka's treatment of Imperial Headquarters' moral responsibility revolves around five key points: the enduring pipe dream of entering into peace negotiations after achieving a local battle victory, stubborn refusal to listen to commanders in the field, the abandonment of ten thousand desperate soldiers after the Shō Operation was called off, willingness to sacrifice hundreds of thousands of Japanese lives in the Decisive Battle for the Homeland, and postwar cover-ups and conspiracies of silence.

The most appropriate time to have moved to bring the war to an end was after defeat in the Battle of the Philippine Sea and the loss of Saipan:

> With the failure of the plan to carry out a surprise attack at the perimeter of the Absolute National Defense Sphere (A-go Operation), the Imperial Navy was deprived of the fighting strength and strategy it needed to destroy the American mobile fleet. On July 18, 1944—the same day that Imperial Headquarters acknowledged the loss of Saipan—Tōjō [Hideki] dissolved his cabinet and stepped down as prime minister, and Army General Koiso Kuniaki replaced him to form a new one. With the resignation of the naval minister, General Yonai Mitsumasa, it was clear to anyone who could look objectively at the war situation that these changes signaled a turn toward bringing hostilities to an end. (9:26–27)

Rather than capitulating, however, strategists in Imperial Headquarters dreamed up the Shō Operation. This strategic plan was not meant to win the war. Upon arriving in Manila on October 30, Hattori Takushirō, chief of staff of the strategy section of Imperial Headquarters, confided as follows to Major Kobayashi Shūjirō, staff officer of the Fourteenth Area Army: "Actually, Imperial Headquarters intends to score a victory at Leyte and then sue for peace" (9:283).

Imperial Headquarters had another opportunity to reconsider their plans after the Shō Operation officially went into effect at midnight, October 19. General Yamashita Tomoyuki, commander of the Fourteenth Area Army, and his new chief of staff, Lieutenant General Mutō Akira, were strongly against the army's last-minute decision to change the site of the decisive battle from Luzon to Leyte Island. Ōoka highlights the rationality, prudence, and practicality of these two high-ranking officers. After researching the amphibious assault tactics used at New Guinea, Yamashita knew that when General MacArthur reached Leyte, he would have the requisite fighting strength, firepower, and supplies. Ōoka describes General Yamashita's position as follows:

> It was General Yamashita's realistic judgment that regardless of the outcome of the Taiwan air battles, based on the sound tactics the enemy had employed up to that point, there could be little doubt concerning their confidence or that they would be well prepared when they landed at Leyte Island. Their own troops on Leyte, however, were not positioned properly, defensive installations were incomplete, and there was no stockpile of supplies. Even if they belatedly reinforced the island, there was little prospect of a positive outcome. If they failed, they would be unable to wage the decisive battle at Luzon. The chances of success were slim at best, and if they didn't succeed, they ran the risk of losing the Philippines. There was no reason to depart from the original plan; in accordance with it, only holding actions should be undertaken at Leyte Island. (9:54)

Imperial Headquarters and the Southern Army, however, were dead set on fighting the decisive battle at Leyte: "Staff officers in the Southern Army heartily approved of Imperial Headquarters' plan to fight the decisive battle at Leyte. With both Imperial Headquarters and the Southern Army against him, Yamashita's opposition was futile. To have pushed any further would have risked insubordination" (9:55).

The next opportunity to reconsider Reite kessen arose after the Combined Fleet was soundly defeated in the Battle of Leyte Gulf. Although this clearly signaled failure of the Shō Operation, Imperial Headquarters again refused to accept reality. Obsessed with realizing their pipe dream of suing for peace after achieving a single battle victory, they hung all their hopes on the Special Attack Forces: "Until the very end of the war, they continued to dream that the enemy might stop fighting if only their hand could be burned by our resistance" (9:160).

Imperial Headquarters had another prime opportunity to call off the operation about two weeks after defeat in the Battle of Leyte Gulf. During a series of brief but intensive air raids by American surface-based fighters on November 5 and 6, Japan lost 439 new planes and a number of warships. This loss of irreplaceable air power and shipping made it all but impossible to continue the Ta Operation. The third and fourth convoys set to transport the Twenty-sixth Division, three First Division companies, and sixty-six hundred tons of supplies and equipment were about to depart for Leyte. As has been shown, at this crucial juncture, General Yamashita again sought to persuade the Southern Army to reconsider its position. On November 7, he sent Fourteenth Area Army Chief of Staff Mutō to Southern Army command headquarters to present their case to Staff Officer Itamura. When Itamura was incredulous and reiterated that Reite kessen was being conducted according to Imperial Headquarters' directive, Mutō became enraged and fired back: "Both Imperial Headquarters and the Southern Army are blind to the actual battle situation. Is it allowable to force so many officers and men to die in vain? The [Fourteenth] Area Army is no longer responsible for the defense of Luzon. Is this really what you want?" (9:471). Later, Ōoka paraphrases Mutō's bitter remarks as follows: "both Imperial Headquarters and the Southern Army had lost the flexibility of mind to acknowledge reality" (10:2).

Although Itamura refused to respond directly to Mutō's poignant questions, the Southern Army officially requested that Imperial Headquarters abandon the Ta Operation (and thus Reite kessen) five days after their meeting. Imperial Headquarters responded by dispatching Lieutenant General Wachi Takaji to Manila to take over as Thirty-fifth Army chief of staff. He came with orders not only to push the Decisive Battle for Leyte Island forward, but also to redouble reinforcement and resupply efforts. Ōoka is quick to remind the reader of the results of these irresponsible decisions:

> Anyway, this is how the last opportunity was lost to avoid bundling up the Twenty-sixth Division and sending them off to their deaths. It goes without saying that scraping the Ta Operation and keeping the Twenty-sixth Division on Luzon would have had no effect whatsoever on the overall state of the war. The two companies of the Eleventh Regiment remaining on Luzon also faced miserable starvation conditions after they fled into the mountains. The pitiful outcome of having only three hundred of the twelve thousand men from the Twenty-sixth Division . . . survive, however, probably could have been averted. So, at least, bereaved families would think. (9:472–473)

Imperial Headquarters subsequently had yet another chance to alleviate the suffering and limit the senseless loss of life on Leyte Island. After the collapse of the Wa Operation, the enemy counterlanding at Ormoc, the withdrawal of First Division troops from Limon Pass, and the American invasion of Mindoro Island, top military leaders in Tokyo finally realized that the Shō Operation had failed. Instead of accepting defeat and acting responsibly to spare their naked, starving soldiers additional suffering, however, Imperial Headquarters ordered them to fight on to the last man while living off the land.

In the epilogue, Ōoka provides detailed figures on the number of Japanese army, navy, and noncombatant deaths. He estimates that including the reinforcements who lost their lives en route to Leyte, a total of ninety thousand men perished in the Battle for Leyte Island. It must be remembered, moreover, that nearly a quarter of this number died of disease, starvation, and suicide *after* General MacArthur officially declared the battle over on Christmas Day 1944. Toward the end of *The Battle for Leyte Island,* Ōoka takes Imperial Headquarters' leadership to task:

> It is the responsibility of statesmen to ensure that these kinds of extreme conditions never arise in normal society. If citizens were ever faced with them, court judges would immediately order emergency evacuations. Needless to say, it was the military's responsibility to do the same for the soldiers under their command. By adopting the strategy of conducting holding actions throughout the Pacific, Imperial Headquarters shirked its fundamental responsibility to its men. . . .
>
> . . . It was a crime to sacrifice citizens for a fairy tale like Hondo kessen. It was scandalous to command people to lay down their lives while considering desperate, stopgap measures like suing for peace after achieving a localized battle victory. (10:514–516)

Conspiracies of Silence

When Ōoka took up his survivor mission in 1967, the official military history of the Battle for Leyte Island had still not been made public. And the situation hadn't changed when Ōoka's last installment appeared in *Chūō kōron* in July 1969. The official military history—*The Army Shō Operation, volume 1: The Decisive Battle for Leyte Island*—was finally released by the Self-Defense Forces' Office of War History at the end of 1970. In his 1971 postscript to *The Battle for Leyte Island,* Ōoka comments on the specific circumstances that moved him to want to produce his own account of the failed campaign:

> As is well known, Japan suffered some of its greatest losses during the Pacific War at Leyte Island. Because of the number and severity of strategic errors, it was the most humiliating battleground for former army and navy men. While the naval battle had been written about casually in terms of gamesmanship, there were virtually no comprehensive accounts of the land battles. The few that had appeared were little more than embellished tales.
>
> The greater the losses, however, the greater the number of bereaved family members who want to know how and in what kind of places their fathers, elder brothers, and sons fought and died. My 1953 resolve to write my own account was inseparable from my indignation over career military men's callousness and the embellished tales they were producing. (10:608–609)

These callous (*taida*) former commanders and staff officers and their embellished tales (*funshokusareta monogatari*) enraged Ōoka. Having spent eight years struggling with his own traumatic frontline experience in memoirs and fiction, he immediately sniffed out former Japanese leaders' self-justification, evasion of responsibility, and blame shifting.

Like Private Tamura and his battlefield memoir, Japan's military leaders could not wholly conceal and remake the past, and fatally incriminating truths managed to slip through their meticulously constructed defenses. Indeed, as in *Fires on the Plain,* one of Ōoka's central aims in *The Battle for Leyte Island* was to bring the issue of moral responsibility to the fore by fully revealing the hidden truths of the troubled past. He draws special attention to four significant conspiracies of silence: the origins of the Special Attack Forces, the specific circumstances surrounding Vice Admiral Kurita's failure to force entry into Leyte Gulf, the fateful all-out attack order issued to First Division soldiers at Limon Pass, and Imperial Headquarters' last-ditch plans for a counterlanding at Carigara. In the context of his treatment of the fourth—the Leyte Ketsu Operation—Ōoka delineates group responsibility for the continuance of the Battle for Leyte Island long after it had already been lost.

The deployment of the Special Attack Forces was inseparable from Imperial Headquarters' self-serving pipe dream of suing for peace after achieving a decisive battle victory. Military leaders in Tokyo imagined they could "burn the enemy's hand" sufficiently enough to make them want to bring an end to hostilities by having pilots crash bomb-laden planes into American warships. Cognizant after the war of how negatively this reflected on them, they made every effort to cover their tracks and make it appear as if this inhuman tactic was developed spontaneously in the field. As Ōoka indefatigably worked through mountains of battle records, memoirs, and scholarly studies, he came upon evidence that clearly indicated that the special attack Forces were actually the brainchild of Imperial Headquarters: "While surviving staff officers continue to claim that they were formed voluntarily by men in the field, the outlines of this tactic could be seen at Pearl Harbor, and serious research was begun after defeat at Guadalcanal. There is much evidence indicating that Imperial Headquarters resolved to make use of it at the same time they decided to go forward with the Shō Operation" (10:519–520).

Unsuccessful attempts were also made to conceal the details surrounding Vice Admiral Kurita's conduct during the Battle of Leyte Gulf. Since his behavior reflected so poorly on the Imperial Navy, former leaders were loath to have the truth be known. Here again, however, disturbing realities from the wartime past could not be hermetically sealed off from the present. In the "Naval Engagements" chapter, Ōoka writes as follows about the conclusions that could be drawn from the inconsistencies, omissions, and contradictions in the public record, and then comments explicitly on the conspiracy of silence they pointed to:

> The reality that emerges from the accumulation of suspicious evidence and the confused testimonies, justifications, and restatements of commanders and staff officers is that Kurita's fleet was not only deficient in fighting spirit, but also had had no intention of forcing their way into Leyte Gulf . . .
>
> . . . The aforementioned [incriminating] details do not appear in the *Records of Battle and Seaweed* (*Sensō roku*). This work, too, was published after the war. No one can see the [relevant battle] records. The records covering the period from January 1 to April 2, 1943—the period when the navy shifted to a defensive stance—are also missing. After the war, Rear Admiral Kuroshima, a former Combined Fleet staff officer, [purportedly] left them on a train.
>
> It must not be forgotten that all the battle histories and memoirs written by former military men about the Greater East Asia War contain deliberate fabrications. This history is being written with ample consideration given to concealing the shame of former military men and defending the pride of the individuals involved. (9:237)

The self-serving efforts of former military men to recover lost honor and self-esteem came at the expense of honest confrontation and working through of the past.

One of the most significant cover-ups Ōoka was able to uncover was the catastrophic all-out attack order issued at the end of November to the beleaguered men at Limon Pass. The results of this unrealistic, anachronistic, and irresponsible attack-as-defense directive were so disastrous that references to it were almost completely expunged from the public record. Ironically, one of the first clear references to the order's existence appeared in the official history of the battle released in 1970. As Ōoka clearly implies in the following passage, although the paper trail was obscure at best, there could be little doubt that the suicidal, all-out attacks that took place at Limon Pass on November 20 were initiated by Imperial Headquarters' directive. The army, however, attempted to keep their part in this fiasco out of public memory:

> The order to attack on all fronts on the twentieth is not mentioned in Major Tomochika's memoirs or the *Battle Record of the First Division.* There was no reference to it until the official battle history was released in 1970. In the postwar period when only the miseries of the Leyte battles were being talked about, the issuance of this order was naturally concealed out of consideration for bereaved family members. In actuality, however, it was precisely at this point in time that the greatest number of sacrifices were made. We must remember that the military is not only an organization that undertakes such heartless, stupid actions, but also one that covers them up afterward. (9:605)

While Ōoka grants a certain amount of legitimacy to considerations of the feelings of bereaved family members, he clearly felt that clarification of moral responsibility ultimately had to outweigh them. In fact, rather than sparing grieving families additional suffering, the primary objective of this conspiracy of silence was to shield former Imperial Headquarters staff officers from blame. Without honest confrontation with the realities of the past, the vital lessons of defeat, too, were in danger of being forgotten along with the guilt, humiliation, and shame of Japan's military leaders.

The last important cover-up Ōoka brings to light has to do with Imperial Headquarters' outrageous plan to land major reinforcements at

Carigara well after the Shō Operation had obviously failed. While references to the Leyte Ketsu Operation, too, were kept out of the public record almost completely, the code name itself appears in the field records kept by frontline units at Limon Pass. The decision to implement this dream plan was made on December 11, about a week after the Wa Operation collapsed and the Americans counterlanded at Ormoc. The aim of the plan was to break through the impasse at Limon Pass by coordinating the landing of the Tenth Division's Thirty-ninth Regiment with an all-out push forward by the First Division and Sixty-eighth Independent Brigade. As Ōoka bitingly observes, however, "Imperial Headquarters' illusions naturally came to be modified by necessities in the field" (10:197).

After establishing how unrealistic and irresponsible the Leyte Ketsu Operation was, Ōoka turns to the matter of cover-ups, blame shifting, and moral responsibility: "The details of this operation don't appear in *Imperial Headquarters' Secret Journal* or in Colonel Hattori's *Complete History of the Greater East Asia War.* While all the blame was shifted onto the Southern Army, the public record clearly indicates that responsibility for going forward with these purely conceptual, desktop plans that caused additional, pointless sacrifices actually lies with the Second Section of Imperial Headquarters" (10:196–197).

In Chapter 28, "The Chi Operation," Ōoka provides a telling example of Japan's definitive "system of irresponsibility."[59] In preparation, he describes how Prime Minister Koiso was deeply embarrassed during his December 30 audience with the emperor. When Hirohito told him that he had been informed that Reite kessen had been abandoned and pointedly asked Koiso how he intended to explain himself to the nation after proclaiming that "Leyte is Tennōzan," Koiso could only respond that this was the first he had heard of it and that he would decide how to handle the situation after thoroughly looking into the matter. As it turns out, Imperial Headquarters also neglected to tell the army minister about this major change in strategic orientation. Ōoka comments as follows on the breakdown of communication among these branches of the Japanese military:

> The secretism of the army and navy high command that led them not to inform Prime Minister Koiso or the army minister of this decision was a malignant cancer that emerged at the time of the Marco Polo Bridge Incident. As circumstances worsened, this disease brought about ever greater

> harm. The army and navy didn't communicate with one another either. Toward the beginning of this battle account I described how the army became hopelessly mired in the Battle for Leyte Island because the navy never saw fit to inform them that the results of the Taiwan air battles had been grossly exaggerated. (10:372)

During the Supreme War Direction Council meeting held on the afternoon of the thirtieth, Prime Minister Koiso complained to Army Chief of Staff Umezu that had he been told about the decision earlier, he wouldn't find himself in his present predicament. Several days after the location of the decisive battle was shifted to Luzon, the two men had the following exchange: "'The army doesn't appear to be engaging in a decisive battle at all. Shouldn't you be going at it a bit more vigorously?' To this, Umezu responded, 'I'm only the emperor's chief of staff. Since the battle is being conducted by commanders in the field, there's nothing I can do about it'" (10:372–373).

After detailing how the top military leadership both in Tokyo and in the field repeatedly engaged in cover-ups, conspiracies of silence, and blame shifting, Ōoka delineates the primary groups responsible for sustaining Reite kessen in the face of every sign of defeat:

> Determining whether the Battle for Leyte Island was continued at the insistence of Imperial Headquarters or the Southern Army is a delicate matter. In terms of the chain of command, the [Fourteenth] Area Army only had direct contact with the Southern Army, and in many written accounts—particularly in the memoirs partial to General Yamashita—the Southern Army is always given the villain's role.
>
> It is clear that three days before the American landing the Southern Army recommended to Imperial Headquarters that the decisive battle be fought at Leyte Island (Imperial Headquarters was already in agreement with the Southern Army on this matter), and that after witnessing the increase of enemy air power at Tacloban, they sent a telegraph on November 12 requesting Imperial Headquarters to call off the operation. This time it was Imperial Headquarters' turn to have its way. Disregarding the Southern Army's request, they assigned Lieutenant General Wachi as the new chief of staff for the Thirty-fifth Army and demanded the continuance of Reite kessen. Even after the Wa Operation failed, they ordered implementation of the Ketsu Operation at Carigara. The battle histories have very little to say, however, about this plan.
>
> Hattori Takushirō's *Complete History of the Greater East Asia War* can be

viewed as a rough draft of the official battle history. Colonel Hattori himself had been the section chief of staff at the time, and he concealed compromising material. This colonel had directed army operations from the outbreak of hostilities. Hattori was dismissed because of the policy changes made after Miyazaki took over as section chief and because of his arbitrary decision concerning his February 1945 plan to fortify Okinawa. Since Reite kessen can be considered as his personal failure, the strings of Imperial Headquarters' leadership were concealed in the *Complete History of the Greater East Asia War.*

Thus, the ungracious role fell to the Southern Army. It was not the case, however, that from November they were unwaveringly opposed to continuing Reite kessen. It was the Southern Army that persisted in clinging to the utterly unrealistic plan of destroying the enemy even after they landed at Mindoro on December 15.

Twelve hundred kilometers of the South China Sea lay between Mindoro Island and the place in Indochina where the Southern Army reestablished its headquarters. In addition to their apprehensions over the supply line to the home islands being cut, they surely feared that the American army might have had plans of [bypassing Mindoro and] proceeding directly to Saigon. Even their initial insistence that the decisive battle be fought at Leyte Island involved this kind of self-protective egoism.[60] (10:373–374)

Lessons and Legacies of Defeat

The profound anxiety of responsibility that energized Ōoka's survivor mission was closely related to one of the main burdens of survival: ensuring that his comrades in the Philippines and elsewhere hadn't suffered and died in vain. He sought to give meaning to their sacrifices by learning from their terrible war experience. Mastering the lessons of defeat and rectifying lingering social evils in light of them was a viable means of avoiding repetition of past mistakes, sparing posterity from the miserable experience of their forefathers, and calming the spirits of the war dead.

As Japan rebuilt its war-ravaged country and economy in the geopolitical context of the Cold War, collective memory of the horrors and deprivations of the Pacific War quickly faded. And the outbreak of the Korean War just five years after surrender made one thing painfully clear: the unequal postwar relationship between the victor and vanquished made ongoing complicity in armed hostilities unavoidable. Within a year of the signing of the San Francisco Peace Treaty and the nominal end to the

American Occupation of Japan, it was all too apparent that many of the costly lessons of defeat had gone unlearned.

Nineteen fifty-three was an important year in this regard. As Ienaga Saburō notes, during the Ikeda-Robertson conference, "the United States and Japan agreed to promote militarism among the Japanese people in a bid to increase public support for rearmament," and the "Ministry of Education did a volte face on the official interpretation of the war." After this, conservative Japanese politicians and former military leaders began to more openly look back on the Greater East Asia War with a dangerous, revanchistic eye. Minister of Education Okano Seigō, for instance, spoke as follows before the Diet: "I do not wish to pass judgment on the rightness or wrongness of the Greater East Asia War, but the fact that Japan took on so many opponents and fought them for four years . . . proves our superiority."[61] This year also saw the publication of former Colonel Hattori Takushirō's *Complete History of the Greater East Asia War.*

For Ōoka, the controversial ratification of the U.S.-Japan Security Treaty in 1960, the outbreak of the Vietnam War and Japan's support of it, the appearance of increasingly strident revisionist works such as Hayashi Fusao's *Affirmation of the Greater East Asia War* (1963), and ever-tightening Ministry of Education control of the contents of history textbooks were the last straws. By this time, it was obvious that Japan had not only failed to internalize the costly lessons of defeat, but was also in serious danger of sliding back toward the misguided militarism of the past. To Ōoka and many other distinguished artists and intellectuals, this was wholly unconscionable; it was, in fact, tantamount to gross disrespect for the war dead.[62]

Ōoka knew that the silence concerning the past had to be broken before the lessons of defeat could be grasped and acted on. At well over a thousand pages, *The Battle for Leyte Island* does this in a big way. To master the lessons of the past, the basic facts surrounding the Battle of Leyte Island, and by extension the Pacific War, had to be fully exposed, and responsibility for defeat clearly delineated.[63] In Ienaga Saburō's words: "A careful confirmation of the truth about the Pacific War and making these facts as widely known as possible are the only ways to avoid another tragedy. It is a solemn obligation incumbent on those who survived the conflict, a debt we owe to the millions who perished in the fires of war."[64]

Exposing the cover-ups, omissions, and conspiracies of silence in the writings of high-ranking military men and clearly establishing responsibility for defeat enabled Ōoka to get at some of the most instructive truths of the disastrous campaign for the Philippines. He refused to allow those responsible for making the decisions that led to such wanton, pointless destruction and loss of life to cover their tracks or shift blame onto others.

Ōoka makes his most insightful and powerful statement in this regard following his revelation of how Vice Admiral Kurita's dubious conduct during the Battle of Leyte Gulf was intentionally obscured in the official record:

> It must not be forgotten that all the battle histories and memoirs written about the Greater East Asia War by former military men contain deliberate fabrications. This history is being written with ample consideration given to concealing the shame of former military men and defending the pride of the individuals involved. And now, twenty-five years after the end of the war, the trend toward contemporary Japanese militarism has led to the further seasoning of such accounts. History is not simply a narrative of past events; it is always a reflection of the present. (9:237)

Ōoka was aware that the past was purposefully being distorted and made more palatable for public consumption to further neonationalist goals of remilitarizing and recovering lost face. Ironically, it was this kind of insidious manipulation of history that paved the way toward Japan's war of aggression in the first place. Ōoka resolutely set out to articulate the lessons of defeat in large part to counter the dangerous erosion of consciousness caused by historical revisionism and contemporary propaganda campaigns.[65]

Lessons

According to Ōoka, one of the most fundamental lessons of defeat has to do with Japan's physical and historical limitations. First and foremost, the Japanese government and people have to come to acknowledge, accept, and act in accordance with the reality of being a small island nation with finite human and natural resources:

> Because of the geographical conditions of the Western Pacific Ocean, Japan had no choice but to develop a defensive naval force. . . . Forced to fight a

> war with a two-year reserve of oil and no real prospect of victory, the navy could only adopt the risky strategy of attacking Pearl Harbor with a defensive force. Because of inadequate fighting strength, however, it could not take advantage of its initial successes and push the war through to a positive conclusion.
>
> The navy reluctantly became mired in a war of attrition, and when its fighting power hit bottom, risky plans to attack in the Marianas and at Leyte reemerged. And even if they had for a time prevailed in one of these battles, it could not have led to overall victory because they lacked the means to capitalize on success. All these attacks did was postpone [inevitable] defeat. In any event, by the end of 1944, the energy we needed to sustain the war was already exhausted. (9:246)

Ōoka addresses this matter most concisely in the context of his discussion on how the major battle came to be waged at Leyte: "The decisive factor . . . is whether a country has the fighting power and supplies it needs to back up their plans. This is the essence of war. In the final analysis, the Japanese military lost because all they had were conceptual, desktop plans." (9:34–35)

Viewed in light of the international political context of the mid- to late 1960s, Ōoka's assessment of the failure of the Battle of Limon Pass takes on special significance:

> All these critiques were made with the benefit of hindsight. If we don't learn from history, however, we will be stuck indefinitely at Limon Pass. These are not problems that can simply be traced to the nature of the old Japanese army; they were the products of Japan's overall political and economic conditions as she sought to join in on the modern scramble for colonies. At Limon Pass, as in the Battle of Leyte Gulf, the whole span of modern Japanese history was at work. (9:620–621)

To break through the impasse symbolized by Limon Pass, the Japanese must overcome their past.

Ōoka knew that at a time of rampant imperialism and colonialism, Japan had to modernize rapidly to maintain independence. Grave problems began to arise, however, when the interests of Japan's leaders moved beyond preserving sovereignty to competing with other developed nations in the modern scramble for colonies. In political terms, the crucial issue concerned the structural independence of supreme command. Unbridled by party politics or the will of the people, the militarists were able to have their way. As a result of reckless aggression in Korea, Manchuria, and Mongolia, Japan became hopelessly mired in a costly war of attrition first in China and then throughout the Pacific and Southeast Asia. Since the Japanese militarists lacked the natural resources and manpower they needed to effectively wage and sustain modern warfare, they increasingly sought to compensate with unsound tactics such as *ressei hōi* and *kirikomi.* In time, they found themselves hopelessly overextended.

Ōoka stresses that Japan's national aspirations had to be kept in line with the actualities of the country's limited material and human resources. More important, his government and people had to absorb two related lessons. First, "it is wholly unacceptable in the name of patriotism to venture forth into other countries to pillage and kill."[66] Second, one eventually reaps what is sown: "The history of the battles fought for Leyte Island teaches Japanese and Americans—peoples prone to amnesia—the terrible consequences of seeking to profit on another peoples' land. It also shows the damage done to that land itself. Finally, it demonstrates how the harm done to others eventually comes to be visited on oneself" (10:547).

A further lesson of defeat relates to the flawed character of Japan's military institutions. The course and final outcome of the Pacific War clearly indicate that the Japanese military was a system of irresponsibility susceptible to secrecy, sectionalism, and internal breakdown. Sectionalism was one of its most debilitating and self-destructive characteristics. Rather than operating in a collaborative, coordinated fashion to realize the common goal of victory, the Imperial Army and Navy were locked in constant rivalry. In time, this chronic divisiveness developed into a malignant, terminal cancer.

Hubris, conservatism, and ossification were equally debilitating systemic weaknesses of the former Japanese military organism. Overcoming these chronic maladies required radical treatment aimed at fostering and maintaining greater mental flexibility and a healthier respect for the enemy. With regard to the latter, Ōoka surely would have concurred with the following assessment:

> The hawks' first miscalculation was the inability to defeat China. Their second was in attacking the United States and England. A famous student of war, Mao Tse-tung, found wisdom in Sun-tzu's *Art of War:* "Know your

> enemy and know yourself, and you can fight a hundred battles without disaster." Mao wrote that war, the highest form of struggle, is the most difficult social phenomenon to understand correctly. Yet man inevitably goes to war and when he does, his mistakes arise from ignorance of the enemy and himself. Japan's defeat stemmed from just that "ignorance of them and us," what Ishiwara Kanji, Shigemitsu Mamoru, and other leaders later called the result of mistaken "comprehensive assessments" and "in-depth analyses."[67]

Hubris, conservatism, and ossification were at the heart of defeat. After making initial advances in strategy, tactics, and technology, the former Japanese military settled into fixed, patterned martial practices despite their ineffectiveness. The lack of ongoing adaptation and modification eventuated in crippling underdevelopment. As Ōoka concludes in relation to the Battle of Leyte Gulf: "The Imperial Navy was beaten by the U.S. Navy's flexibility" (9:174).

Two more lessons that had to be internalized concerned irrationality and preoccupation with face. In combination, these two psychological weaknesses contributed substantially not only to defeat, but to gratuitous destruction and loss of life as well. The former military's progressive loss of objectivity, prudence, and practicality stemmed from an overinflated sense of self and overconfidence engendered by Japan's successes in the early battles of the Pacific War. In his discussion of the navy's rash decision to continue the war even after defeat in the crucial Battle of the Philippine Sea, Ōoka makes the connection between systemic ossification and irrationality clear: "The Japanese navy on the whole had become so superannuated that it could no longer function in a rational manner. Behind the silence of the 'silent navy' there was nothing at all" (9:47). Arrogance, irrationality, and dreaming characterized each major turning point of the latter stages of the war.

Preoccupation with self-image also kept Japan's wartime leadership from accepting defeat. Like sectionalism, the excessive concern with face was a malignant cancer present from the outset of hostilities in the Pacific: "It can safely be said that the navy clearly foresaw that by 1944 the comparative naval strengths of America and Japan would be ten to one. Despite this knowledge, they could not say 'no' to initiating the war. They couldn't stand before the emperor and people and admit the inadequacy of their military preparedness and armaments" (9:46). The former Japanese military's inability to honestly acknowledge and deal with the reality of defeat in the "decisive" Battle of the Philippine Sea drove strategists to conjure up ever more radical and impracticable recuperative measures. Reite kessen and Hondo kessen were self-destructive face-saving maneuvers.

Excessive considerations of face were also at the root of the fatal, last-minute decision to change the site of the battle from Luzon to Leyte Island. Here again, the Imperial Navy was psychologically incapable of owning up to the truth: "The navy section of Imperial Headquarters did not report to the army section that no damage had been done to the enemy's mobile fleet. While this is unbelievable viewed from the present, the navy was probably thinking of the face they would lose if they admitted they had gained nothing after being honored by the emperor and raising the people's hopes. No matter how difficult to admit, however, this fact should have been revealed" (9:45–46).

Inability to register the reality of failure in the Battle for Leyte Island also played a significant role in the scandalous decision to go forward with the Ta Operation. In his prudent, realistic plea for the Southern Army to reconsider its position, General Yamashita explicitly mentions the matter of face: "At this critical juncture, they should forget about face, act decisively to end further reinforcement, direct soldiers on Leyte to conduct holding actions as originally planned, and concentrate on preparing to defend Luzon" (9:470).

Face saving was also at the root of the unconscionable Ketsu Operation. In a last-ditch attempt to evade personal humiliation, top leaders in the army section of Imperial Headquarters were willing to sacrifice hundreds of thousands of troops and noncombatants in the Philippines, Iwo Jima, Okinawa, and the homeland: "The men in Imperial Headquarters didn't want to lose face before the emperor and the nation and reacted aggressively when cornered" (10:515). In every instance, the outcome of these desperate, irresponsible face-saving maneuvers was pointless destruction and loss of life. The radically self-centered conduct of Japan's top military leaders is comparable to the most egregious and abominable acts of survival egoism perpetrated by routed frontline soldiers. The scale of the damage brought about by their immoral actions, however, places them in a class of their own.

Ōoka's examination of the Battle for Leyte Island and the Pacific War leaves no doubt that obsessive concern with face was the root cause of the mass death and destruction that attended the final stages of the conflict. And this fundamental psychological weakness continues to cause great harm. To the present day, excessive concern with maintaining positive self-image inhibits coming to terms with the burdened past, internalizing the vitalizing lessons of defeat, mourning, repentance and atonement, and reconciling with other countries.

Two additional lessons of defeat have to do with the former Japanese military's devaluation of life and disregard for human rights. Ōoka probably would have concurred with Ienaga Saburō's assertion that "an outlook that regarded life so cheaply and devised the Kamikaze attacks was at the root of all Japan's misadventures."[68] Utter disregard for human life and individual rights was conspicuous throughout the Pacific War. This held true not only for Japanese troops and civilians, but also for foreign soldiers and noncombatants. This tendency was given official expression in the rescript declaring the Greater East Asia War: "The entire nation with a united will shall mobilize its total strength so that nothing will miscarry in the attainment of our war aims." The crucial phrase calling for strict adherence with international agreements on the conduct of war and the humane treatment of prisoners—one included in declarations of hostilities at the outset of the Sino-Japanese and Russo-Japanese Wars—is conspicuous by its absence.[69] Japan's military leaders were clearly committed to using any and every means to gain victory.

The former Japanese military's devaluation of life and contempt for personal rights is also readily apparent in the mistreatment of soldiers. Since they could be called up for the cost of draft-notice postage, conscripts were routinely referred to as *issen gorin* (less than a penny). Soldiers and sailors were frequently slapped in the face and subjected to abusive corporal punishments such as being stripped, hung upside down, and beaten with hardwood sticks. The penalty for men who erred in the handling of horses was eating horse dung.[70] As with the desperate face-saving maneuvers discussed above, such brutal, degrading treatment was self-defeating. In his discussion of the Battle of Leyte Gulf, Ōoka comments directly on the detrimental effects of these cruel practices: "At this point, slave training and feudalistic ship life became serious handicaps. The replacements, who should have arrived at the battlefield in high spirits, were instead filled with hatred and resentment toward their superior officers and the military (9:247).

The abusive treatment Japanese soldiers were subjected to at the hands of their superiors not only resulted in poor battlefield performance, but also contributed significantly to the perpetration of atrocities. Ienaga comments as follows on what the renowned political scientist Maruyama Masao refers to as the "transfer of oppression": "The inevitable side effects of training to 'breed vicious fighters' was a penchant for brutality against enemy prisoners and civilian noncombatants. Men under constant pressure would explode in irrational, destructive behavior. Individuals whose own dignity and manhood had been so cruelly violated would hardly refrain from doing the same to defenseless persons under their control. After all, they were just applying what they had learned in basic training."[71]

The contempt with which Japanese military leaders regarded human life and individual rights can also be seen in the directive for the main force of the Combined Fleet to sacrifice themselves in the Battle of Leyte Gulf, the willingness to develop and deploy Special Attack Forces, the order for the fifteen thousand stranded troops on Leyte to fight to the last man while living off the land, and the mobilization of fifty new divisions to meet the American invasion of the homeland armed with little but bamboo spears and gasoline bombs. By drawing attention to such matters, Ōoka makes it clear that the former Japanese military was not only plagued by strategic, tactical, and technological backwardness, but was severely retarded morally and ethically as well:

> In the end, one reaches the common-sense conclusion that once the Battle for Leyte Island had failed, Imperial Headquarters should have given field commanders throughout the Philippines the freedom to surrender. If they had, the useless deaths of both Japanese and American soldiers on Luzon, Mindanao, and in the Visayan Islands and the miserable mass starvation and cannibalism that occurred in the mountains could have been averted.
>
> This conclusion, however, was reached with the benefit of hindsight. Given the country's limited land area and lack of natural resources, it has been historical necessity since the Meiji Restoration for Japan to sacrifice its people to enter the ranks of modern nations. (10:516)

Ōoka surely felt that the time had long since passed for Japanese leaders to end their long history of sacrificing the people in the interest of self-aggrandizement. In the epilogue of *The Battle for Leyte Island,* he sets forth his thoughts concerning the proper relationship between the government and people, and closes by castigating the old Japanese military for its moral bankruptcy:

> The foundation of military strength is the citizenry of Japan. Conscription is a necessary condition for the establishment of modern nations. When carried out by an authority of supreme command operating independently of politics, however, it is little more than slavery. The old Japanese military exploited their conscripts like farm animals. They reckoned that if they sacrificed twenty million people, America would propose bringing an end to the war.
>
> . . .
>
> Modern wars can't be carried out without professionally trained military forces. Foot soldiers must be conditioned to attack through hailstorms of bullets and defend their positions with their lives. . . . This kind of conduct depends on systematized education and the existence of professional military men who will sacrifice themselves for the nation. It is cruel and heartless, however, to impose these things on the populace as a whole. In addition to the interests of the nation, each citizen has the fundamental right to pursue his own domestic happiness. Accordingly, it is incumbent on the military to order surrender once they can no longer maintain the conditions necessary for conscripts to fight. This is the reason other countries provide prisoners of war with the same provisions as their own soldiers and make international agreements to settle accounts after war. The old Japanese army, however, did not inform the people of the existence of these international agreements, ordered them "not to suffer the shame of capture," and insisted on suicide before being taken prisoner. (10:515–516)

Our consideration of Ōoka's treatment of the lessons of defeat would be incomplete, moreover, if we didn't take account of the harsh realities of Leyte battlefields. In *The Battle for Leyte Island,* he forcefully brings home to his readership the fact that there was nothing holy, glorious, or "great" about the Greater East Asia War. For those physically engaged in combat in the Philippines and elsewhere, it was painful separation from family, hearth and home, brutal degradation, traumatic immersion in symbolic and physical death, killing, maiming, torture, rape, pillaging, wanton destruction and loss of life, sickness, deprivation, despair, and meaningless death. Indeed, there was nothing abstract about the experience at all; it was the flower of the nation's youth crushed in the mud hundreds and thousands of miles from home, young men with the faces of children hopelessly struggling to replace extruded intestines into rent bellies and dragging their legless torsos over scorched earth; inert faces with eyes sprung from the sockets, bodies lacking heads, arms, legs, or wholly vaporized; swollen, animal-eaten corpses left to sun, wind, and rain; once-proud men reduced to lifeless, starving beggars; desperate men embracing and detonating grenades or hanging themselves; former brothers-in-arms killing, butchering, and eating each other in the struggle for survival; remote mountain paths marked by the feces of the dying and the bleached bones of the abandoned dead.

Legacies

In *Embracing Defeat,* John Dower writes about the universal tendency to focus primary attention on one's own losses: "People in all cultures and times have mythologized their own war dead, while soon forgetting their victims—if, in fact, they ever even give much thought to them."[72] While this may very well be the case, the study of Ōoka's body of writings on the Pacific War suggests that it is possible for individuals—and by extension collectives—to extend concern to encompass extranational victims once they have squarely faced and worked through suppressed or repressed issues of guilt and responsibility and adequately mourned, honored, and memorialized their own dead. Indeed, it was only toward the conclusion of his long, torturous journey of survivor formulation that Ōoka was able to give serious consideration to the sufferings and losses of the Filipino people. And this was surely no afterthought; it was the ethical fruit of thorough survivor illumination.

In the epilogue to *The Battle for Leyte Island,* Ōoka writes about Filipino experience in relation to the Pacific War and postwar history. With regard to the former, he discusses the damage brought about by Japan's and America's fateful decision to wage their decisive battle on Filipino soil. In connection with the latter, he examines political developments in the Philippines after the war. Lastly, Ōoka takes up the profoundly disturbing parallels between the postwar dispositions of that country and his own.

In *Return to Mindoro Island,* Ōoka openly acknowledges the terrible harm caused by Japan in the Philippines: "Twenty-five years ago, we occupied this land and killed, raped, and pillaged in order to carry out a war upon which the fate of our nation was said to hang" (2:449–450). In *The Battle for Leyte Island,* he states unequivocally that local inhabitants suffered most from the conflict. While the initial effect of the Japanese occupation of Leyte was minimal—there were few troops, and the military allowed the existing government to continue administering civilian affairs—this relatively benign period came to an abrupt end when guerrillas became more active toward the end of 1943. To counter this rising threat, reinforcements from the Sixteenth Division were sent to the island. Following this second invasion, many civilians were wounded or killed when they were caught in the cross fire (10:521).

Before the beginning of the Battle for Leyte Island in October 1944, the most substantial and harmful effect on the Filipinos accompanied Japan's strategic shift to constructing airfields and fortifying coastal defenses. To these ends, local inhabitants (including women and children) were used as slave labor, their harvests were appropriated, and private homes and public facilities were dismantled for building material. With increasing frequency and viciousness, the self-proclaimed Japanese "liberators" arrested, tortured, and summarily executed those suspected of aiding and abetting guerrilla forces. Ōoka wryly observes that by this point, "there was no one who still believed in [the ideals of] the Greater East Asian Co-Prosperity Sphere" (9:25).

Japanese practices of taking harvests during occupation and appropriating food from civilians while engaged in military operations eventually destroyed the fragile agricultural economy. To convey a sense of the extent of Filipino losses, Ōoka provides a chart listing the total number of livestock (water buffalo, cows, horses, pigs, goats, sheep, chickens, ducks, turkeys) in 1939 and 1945. During this six-year period, the Filipinos lost one-half to two-thirds of the farm animals they depended on for their livelihood.

Ōoka is equally critical of the United States. The extensive damage brought about by the massive, indiscriminate army and naval bombardment of the cities, towns, and villages occupied by Japanese troops vastly exceeded that caused by the Japanese. Eighty percent of the country's public facilities and 60 percent of private property were destroyed in this way. As with the introduction of Japanese military script moreover, PX-based black markets contributed substantially to the further decline of the economy and public morality. By January 1945, there were nearly 260,000 American troops on Leyte Island, and incidents of rape and robbery were legion. And like their Japanese counterparts, the Americans set up numerous brothels staffed by local girls.

Turning to postwar developments, Ōoka begins by pointing out that during the fifty-year period between 1895 and 1945 the Filipinos suffered four masters: the Spanish until 1898, the prewar Americans until 1941, the Japanese until 1945, and the postwar Americans after that. He goes on to introduce a telling anecdote about the lesson a Filipino grandfather passed on to his grandson: "The Spanish were not good. The Americans were bad. The Japanese, even worse. The returning Americans, however, were the worst of all" (10:526). Ōoka devotes a substantial number of pages in his epilogue to establishing the fact that rather than liberating the Philippines, General MacArthur reoccupied the country in the interest of American Far East strategic policy and Filipino and American capital (10:500, 525). In support of the first claim, he describes how MacArthur mobilized four and a half divisions and sacrificed roughly the same number of American lives "liberating" Cebu, Negros, eastern Mindanao, Panay, and other Visayan islands as he did in gaining control of Leyte itself. These outlying islands were not only of negligible military value, but were also largely in guerrilla hands. MacArthur's relentless mopping-up operations significantly augmented the suffering and loss of the Filipino people:

> [General MacArthur] carried out the liberation of the Philippines to the fullest extent. As we have seen, he sent regular soldiers even to minor islands in the Visayas such as Bohol, where they slaughtered the small bands of Japanese troops they encountered. He never seemed to worry that as a result of this strategy, the calamities of war would be spread to every corner of the country. As a consequence of the battle mode of thoroughly bombarding enemy positions, Filipinos' houses were razed, and many noncombatants were killed and wounded. . . . It is highly dubious whether this was an appropriate strategy for liberating a friendly nation said to be the bastion of democracy in the Far East. (10:532–533)

While the Philippines achieved nominal national independence in 1946, Ōoka stresses that the country was effectively recolonized. Like the Japanese several years later, the Filipinos ended up with what John Dower has called "subordinate independence."[73] In March 1946 the United States

Congress passed the Philippine Rehabilitation Act, approving a $620 million loan for the new government. This, of course, came with strings attached. To obtain these funds, the fledgling administration had to accept a clause granting Americans the same rights to conduct business in the country as their own nationals. Meeting this provision necessitated constitutional amendment. When this was accomplished the following year, the Bell Trade Act went into effect. In its wake, the government signed a separate agreement on military bases that granted the United States ninety-nine-year leases at Subic Bay, Clark Air Base, and fourteen additional sites. In this way, "America put the Philippines under harsher colonial rule than before the war. What it all amounted to was making the country into its advanced military base in the Far East" (10:539).

There can be little doubt that Ōoka was aware of the disturbing parallels between the postwar dispensations of the Philippines and Japan. Toward the end of *The Battle for Leyte Island,* he notes that American leaders quickly realized that in light of its strategic position, highly developed infrastructure, high rate of literacy, and the peoples' tendency to "worship the powerful," Japan would make a better bastion of democracy than Taiwan or the Philippines (10:543).

As with the Philippines, the United States quickly moved to make Japan into an advanced (Cold War) military base. John Dower tallies up the cost of Japan's postwar "independence" as follows:

> Although in the end the peace treaty would involve scores of nations, the Americans controlled the peacemaking process; and the exact price Japan would be called upon to pay for incorporation into a Pax Americana became apparent only bit by bit. Rearmament under the American "nuclear umbrella" was but one part of that price. The continued maintenance of U.S. military bases and facilities throughout the country was another. Okinawa was excluded from the restoration of sovereignty (just as it had been excluded from the occupation reforms) and consigned as a major U.S. nuclear base to indefinite neocolonial control. . . .
>
> . . . It was only after embracing the separate peace and passing through the grand ceremony of a formal peace conference in San Francisco in September 1951, however, that the Yoshida government learned how high the costs of independence would actually be. As it turned out, the U.S. Senate refused to ratify the peace treaty unless Japan agreed to sign a parallel treaty with the Nationalist Chinese regime in Taiwan—and, beyond this, to adhere to the rigorous American policy of isolating and economically containing the

> People's Republic of China. . . . The U.S.-Japan security treaty and a related "administrative agreement" that accompanied it also turned out to be more inequitable than any other bilateral arrangement the United States entered into in the postwar period. The Americans retained exceptional extraterritorial rights, and the number of military installations they demanded was far in excess of what anyone had anticipated. . . .
>
> . . . To the conservatives, this was a high but unavoidable price to pay for independence and security in a dangerously riven world. To much of the populace, the difference between occupation and the limbo of "subordinate independence" was hardly discernible and certainly nothing to cheer about. Officially, sovereignty was restored at 10:30 P.M. on April 28, 1952. The streets, everyone reported, were strangely quiet.[74]

Ōoka ironically observes that the Filipinos and Japanese were the only Asian countries to think of American Occupation forces as a "liberation army (*kaihōgun*)" (10:544). And Dower notes that while Japan enjoyed a fleeting honeymoon in which the country was "locked in an almost sensual embrace" with its conquerors, it increasingly became clear that "the Americans could not or would not let go."[75] In the end, Ōoka concludes that Japan and the Philippines are two of the most unfortunate countries in Asia:

> Although the invaders were unaware [of their role as victimizers], the fact remained that the Filipino people on whose soil the battles were fought were their victims. Since the Philippines was chosen by the Japanese and Americans as the site of their decisive battle, the land was ravaged and a great number of civilians were killed. And this was not all; after the war their country was reoccupied by the Americans, and they were put under an even more oppressive yoke of [neo]colonial rule. Since big landowners and procurement capital were protected, the industrialization of this commonwealth nation that had once been the most democratic in the East lagged behind that of subordinate countries that emerged after the war such as Korea and Taiwan. Today the Philippines is the country in greatest danger of having a premodern uprising or revolution.
>
> Along with Japan, a country of high economic growth that due to export capital, the mobilization of economic animals, and the expansion of the Self-Defense Force is presently witnessing a revival of the old ideal of the Greater East Asian Co-Prosperity Sphere, the Philippines is fast becoming the most miserable nation in Asia (10:547).

To Ōoka as a battlefield survivor, Japan's postwar political circumstances were wholly unconscionable. In *Return to Mindoro Island,* he informs his countrymen that they have a solemn, outstanding debt to the war dead to overcome the humiliation of subordinate independence and reinstate full political and military autonomy. Ōoka knew, however, that the attainment of these national goals had to be preceded by a thorough purging of Japan's corrupt body politic. Without such reform, there was a real danger that the achievement of these aims might lead his nation back down the same disastrous path of fruitless war and self-destruction. These important matters will be turned to in the concluding section of this study.

Conclusion

Lingering Obligations

Robert Jay Lifton notes that while studying Hiroshima survivors' experience, he became "impressed by the relationship of death guilt to the process of identification—to the survivor's tendency to incorporate within himself an image of the dead, and then to think, feel, and act as he imagines they did or would." He goes on to write that "identification guilt can become thoroughly internalized and function as conscience." A similar dynamic is clearly at work in *Return to Mindoro Island.* As mentioned at the outset of this study, moreover, throughout the nearly two decades between the formal completion of his journey of survivor formulation and his death in 1988, Ōoka served as conscience for his nation by keeping memory of the Pacific War and the millions of war dead alive. Writing about the Nazi death camps, however, Terrence Des Pres cautions us that "conscience . . . is a social achievement. At least on its historical level, it is the collective effort to come to terms with evil, to distill a moral knowledge equal to the problems at hand. Only after the ethical content of an experience has been made available to all members of the community does conscience become the individual 'voice' we usually take it for."[1] This is the formidable challenge facing Japan today. The crux of the matter concerns the motivating force behind and the practical means of fostering such conscience.

Return to Mindoro Island is particularly illuminating here. Ōoka describes himself communing with the Japanese war dead on three separate occasions during his trip back to the Philippines in 1967: just before reaching Leyte Island by plane, at Limon Pass, and while overlooking the Rutay Highlands. Initially, following a general, third-person introduction, he identifies intimately with and addresses the spirits of fallen *tokkōtai* pilots:

> By the time you were aware of the dark spots approaching from the direction of the sun, it was too late. The American pilots were more cunning and skilled than you were, and they maneuvered unpredictably before your eyes. They approached with incredible speed and riddled your planes and bodies with bullets.
>
> They dropped down like bolts of lightning from the invisible heights above you to interrupt your course. They fired round after round and then slipped away through the airspace below. Or before you realized it, your body was pierced with bullets, and you sank into the darkness of death without ever knowing whether it was your plane or consciousness that was slipping away.
>
> If fortune smiled on you and you were able to proceed unimpeded by any harrying, encumbering enemy, you made for your target barely visible in the distance amid the shimmering waves and began to dive sharply. When long-range antiaircraft fire began to explode around you, you had to grasp the joystick firmly to stabilize your wildly pitching aircraft and stay your course.
>
> In order to crash your planes into the enemy ships, you had to hold on even when your wings sheared off and you were hit by bullets. These things occurred in a world known to you, and to you alone. (2:444)

While critical of the inhuman tactic itself, Ōoka was deeply impressed and inspired by the incredible willpower and unwavering commitment of the Special Attack Forces pilots who managed to overcome adversity, reach their targets, and carry out their missions. In fact, as has been shown, he felt that these exemplary men were not only worthy of incorporation in contemporary Japanese mythology, but also represented Japan's hope for the future.

The profound implications of Ōoka's position become increasingly clear upon consideration of his experience at Limon Pass:

> The sky is clear and there is a gentle breeze. All I see are the grass-covered ridges bathed in sunshine. It was the monsoon season when the men of the

First Division's Fifty-seventh Regiment fought here twenty-five years ago. On November 8, the fourth day of the battle, a typhoon swept over the island. In the midst of the wind and rain, the grass blazed as grimy soldiers on both sides engaged in what amounted to hand-to-hand combat.

Most of the men who died in battle are buried in this area near the highway. It is believed, however, that where the mountains are high and deep to the southeast, the bones of the dead still lie exposed to the elements.

Although the soldiers came to Leyte with faith in certain victory drummed into them, they simultaneously harbored the rational fear that they might be the next to die. Once they received their orders and were sent to the front, however, they had to overcome this fear. Some fought believing that by dying defending these small ridges they could save their homeland and families. They fought on literally intending to become guardian spirits of the nation, and they were progressively slaughtered by America's superior weaponry.

This battleground was wholly different from those on Mindoro Island. I felt a clutch at the heart. As we read sutras and wept, I had the illusion that the dead were rising up here and there from the grass-covered slopes.

What do their spirits demand? Life in the Japanese military was miserable, and some probably thought of death as liberation. Some, however, truly believed they were dying for the emperor. There were also those who hated the Americans for interfering with the resolution of the Japan-China war, and wanted to kill the enemy to the last man and eat his flesh. They felt that their deaths could prevent their wives from being raped and their children from being bludgeoned to death. . . . In this way, they sought to give meaning to their deaths.

At the instant of death they could have been thinking of nothing but slaughtering the American devils. They died consumed with animus, and their bones are now exposed to the elements on a foreign land thousands of miles from home.

Given this, what can we as survivors do? Carry on their will to kill the enemy to the last man. Unfortunately, there hasn't been another war with the United States, Japan is covered with American military bases, and the naval ports once used by the Combined Fleet are now frequented by America's nuclear aircraft carriers and submarines.

Bound to the land as they are, the spirits of the men who fought and died along the narrow frontages of Limon Pass surely cannot know of such things. Our mission as survivors must be to free our homeland from these conditions. (2:452–453)

The pressing anxiety of responsibility Ōoka experienced on Leyte Island is also palpable during his return trip to Mindoro. After hiring a local guide and traveling by jeep and foot as near as possible to the Rutay Highlands, Ōoka separates himself from his Japanese traveling companions, guide, and escort officer and walks up a grassy slope to a place affording an unimpeded view of their former mountain encampment. He then kneels down, bows his head, and recalls the horrible battlefield experience he endured with his brothers-in-arms. After recollecting how out of their own misery they had belittled the Special Attack Forces they saw flying overhead en route to attack the enemy at San Jose and how they had no way of knowing at the time that those airmen were inflicting heavy damage on the American beachhead and shipping, Ōoka states that as a survivor he was not only able to learn about what happened on Leyte and Mindoro, but also witness postwar developments in the Philippines and Japan. At this point, he again communes with the spirits of the dead:

> Twenty-five years after the war, my prisoner-of-war experience has virtually died, and the battlefield experience I shared with you has come back to life. That is what brought me back here. I had thought that no one would ever again want to go to war, that we would never repeat what we did in the past. This, however, was just wishful thinking. After twenty-five years, a small group of scoundrels like those who drove us to war is still in power. Through lies and deception they now seek to force the same experience we went through onto our children.
>
> You died, I survived. The way Nishiya Company conducted itself was stupid and poor. We were, for the most part, middle-aged men sunk deeply in thought in an effort to forget our misery. We failed to find a decisive reason to use the weapons forced into our hands. This was the consequence of our lacking high morals to live by.
>
> The *tokkōtai* pilots who attacked the San Jose beachhead and the men from Yamamoto Company who held out . . . for thirteen years [after the war] did. "We didn't!" I shouted.
>
> I will not say what I promised my comrades then and there. It is my practice not to speak before I act. After some twenty-five years, I finally resolved to accept the fate that had brought me this far. (2:570–571)

Ōoka never does elaborate on the promise he made to the spirits of his dead comrades. If he remained faithful to his policy of action before words, then he may never have fulfilled his silent vow. Several other possibilities, however, come to mind. Perhaps Ōoka silently promised to travel back to Mindoro again some day to collect their remains. In the end, however, declining health prevented him from doing so. Another possibility is that Ōoka promised to carry on their dying will by doing everything he could to defend his country, spare posterity of their ungodly experience of defeat, and shake off the humiliating shackles of subordinate independence. It is important to recall here that he revisited Mindoro just months after he began serializing *The Battle for Leyte Island.* His promise to the spirits of his fallen comrades thus preceded the full realization of his mission of survivor illumination. Evidence supporting this interpretation can be found in *War.* In this work, he divulges that as his nation began its fateful move toward full-scale hostilities he chose the lower, selfish path of domestic exile. Immediately following this painful admission, he asserts that he will never again acquiesce in such a way.[2] The implications of this should be clear: far better to put one's life on the line fighting domestic evil than to allow oneself to be forced into engaging in an unjust war abroad.

In "To Lake Danao" (Danaoko made, 1967), Ōoka describes how members of his Japanese tour group set up small Buddhist altars near major Leyte battlefields, make offerings of food, read sutras, play the national anthem and military songs, and use megaphones to shout messages to the spirits of the dead. Ōoka, however, has no desire to call out like this. "As a survivor and veteran," the sole message he wants to convey is "I will get the enemy for you" (2:608). Immediately following this declaration, however, he raises a crucial question: "Where, however, is the enemy?" By leaving this question unanswered, Ōoka sets an important challenge for his nation. Clearly, one of the primary tasks of the Japanese people must be to locate—and overcome—the enemy within.[3]

Ōoka ends his formal mission of survivor formulation by articulating how his countrymen can fulfill the outstanding debt they owe to the millions who perished in the flames of war. Through his own personal struggles, he learned that the only sure way to come to terms with the past was to squarely face the facts concerning the Pacific War and to work through deep-seated feelings of guilt, self-recrimination, and loss. And what holds true for the individual may very well hold true for the group as well. Ōoka's journey of survivor illumination offers an inspiring microcosmic example of a viable means of collectively mastering the burdened past.

Observations the Mitscherlichs make in *The Inability to Mourn,* their groundbreaking psychological study of German responses to the Second

World War, can help shed light on Japan's ongoing dilemma with regard to the Pacific War. They state unequivocally that "without a working-through of guilt, however belated, there [can] be no work of mourning." It thus follows that since there has yet to be a thorough, honest confrontation with and working-through of responsibility, the Japanese have been unable to mourn adequately even for their own fallen countrymen.[4] And this mourning, as has been suggested, appears to be prerequisite to properly attending to the dead of others.

A further observation the Mitscherlichs make is also highly apropos to the Japanese case. In the following passage, I replace the word "Germans" with "Japanese": "The primary 'intellectual task' of all thinking Japanese must be very cautiously to expose for what they are the self-deceptions that are substantially contributing to the creation of a new erroneous self-image. . . . What matters is how each individual and each group manages to become aware of its own specific self-deceptions and thereby learns to overcome them."[5]

Completion of his twenty-five-year-long literary journey of survivor formulation enabled Ōoka to unburden himself. And this was not all; through his body of writings on the Pacific War and subsequent endeavors to keep memory of the war alive and remind his countrymen of their solemn, moral obligations to the war dead, he symbolically bequeathed to his compatriots the moral compass he had found and employed to such good effect during his struggles with the many, varied, and overwhelming burdens of survival. Now it is up to present and future generations to take it up and use it to open up their own personal and collective paths toward reconciliation. To see this project through to completion, they will need courage and fortitude comparable to that of the best *tokkōtai* pilots. And the final outcome of this most patriotic of missions would not be death and (self-) destruction, but healing, recovery, and renewal. I close with hopes that Ōoka's comments in the *Yomiuri Newspaper* on the twenty-ninth anniversary of defeat can provide inspiration and direction for this long-overdue ethical quest for a better, brighter, more peaceful, vital, and responsible future: "It's unpardonable that we have yet to thoroughly work through the matter of war responsibility. But even now is not too late. How about this: Why don't we work to improve our nation and reform our corrupt politics with a democratic fervor equal to that of the American people?"[6]

Appendix: Selected Works by Ōoka Shōhei

Selections for this appendix were made according to the following criteria: (1) providing a fairly comprehensive enumeration of Pacific War–related works pertinent to the present study, and (2) providing representative examples of works in other areas and genres. Readers interested in more-detailed, exhaustive compilations should refer to the Japanese sources on which this appendix was based: Ikeda Jun'ichi's "Nenpu" (Personal chronological history) in volume 18 of Iwanami shoten's *Ōoka Shōhei shū* (Collected works of Ōoka Shōhei) and Ishida Hitoshi's "Nenpu" in Kadokawa shoten's *Kanshō Nihon gendai bungaku,* vol. 26: *Ōoka Shōhei/Takeda Taijun* (Appreciating modern Japanese literature, vol. 26: *Ōoka Shōhei/Takeda Taijun*), ed. Yoshida Hiroo et al.

1929.
Translation of Paul Claudel's *Rimbaud* in *Hakuchigun.*

1932.
October: "Yokomitsu Riichi shi no *Haha*" (Yokomitsu Riichi's *Mother*) in *Sakuhin.*
Translation of Andre Gide's "Stendhal: Preface to *Armence*" in *Shōsetsu.*

1933.
October: "Kawakami Tetsutarō no bunshō ni tsuite" (About Kawakami Tetsutarō's literary style) in *Bungei hyōron.*

1934.
May: Begins serialization of autobiographical novel, *Seishun* (Youth) in *Sakuhin* (suspended after three installments).
June: "Tampen shōsetsu ni tsuite" (Regarding short fiction) in *Bungei hyōron.*

1935.

May: "Jiido to Yokomitsu Riichi" (Gide and Yokomitsu Riichi) in *Bungei tsūshin.*

1936.

May: "Sutandaaru" (Stendhal) in *Bungakkai.* "Shōsetsu no omoshirosa ni tsuite" (The interest of fiction) in *Bungaku dokuhon.*

June: "*Aka to Kuro*: Sutandaaru shiron no ni" (*The Red and the Black:* A second essay on Stendhal) in *Bungakkai.*

1939.

April: Translation of Alain's *Stendhal* published by Sōgensha.

1941.

May: Translation of Stendhal's *Life of Haydn* published by Sōgensha.

1942.

November: Translation of Albert Thibaudet's *Stendhal* published by Aoki shoten.

1944.

May: Translation of Honoré de Balzac's *Stendhal* published by Shōgakukan.

1947.

August: Edits Sōgensha's *Nakahara Chūya shishū* (Collected poems of Nakahara Chūya).

1948.

February: "Chikamatsu Shūkō 'Kurokami'" (Chikamatsu Shūkō's "Black Hair") in *Hihyō.* "Furyoki" (Records of a POW) [subsequently renamed "Tsukamaru made" (Before capture)] in *Bungakkai.* Translations by Sakuko Matsui ("Prisoner of War: The Prelude to Capture"), 1967; and Wayne P. Lammers ("My Capture"), 1996.

April: "San Hose yasen byōin" (San Jose field hospital) in *Chūō kōron.* Translation by Lammers, 1996. Translation of Stendhal's *De l'amour* (first half), published by Sōgensha.

August: "Reite no ame" (The rains of Leyte) in *Sakuhin* [subsequently divided into two works and retitled "Takuroban no ame" (The rains of Tacloban) and "Paro no yō" (The sun of Palo)]. Translations by Lammers ("Rainy Tacloban," "Sunny Palo"), 1996.

November: Translation of Stendhal's *De l'amour* (second half).

December: "Nishiyatai shimatsuki" (Nishiya Company chronicle) in *Geijutsu.* Translation by Lammers, 1996. Translation of Stendhal's *Charterhouse of Parma* (first part) published by Shisakusha.

1949.

January–February: "Kutsu no hanashi" (Boot talk) in *Shōsetsukai.*

March: "Ikiteiru furyo" (Living as POWs) in *Sakuhin.* Translation by Lammers,

1996. "Sen'yū" (Brothers-in-arms) in *Bungakkai.* Translation by Lammers, 1996.

July: "Furyo tōbō" (Prisoner escape) in *Shūkan asahi.* "Furyo no kisetsu" (Seasons of a POW) in *Kaizō bungei* [subsequently renamed "Kisetsu" (Seasons)]. Translation by Lammers, 1996.

August: "Nishiyatai funsen" (Nishiya Company's hard fight) in *Bungakkai.*

October: "Hitō ni tsuita hojūhei" (The conscript who arrived in the Philippines) in *Sekai no ugoki.* "Mindorotō shi" (Record of Mindoro Island) in *Tōhoku bungaku.* "Kensetsu" (Construction) in *Bekkan bungei shunjū* [subsequently combined with "Gaigyō" (Field work) and renamed "Rōdō" (Labor)]. Translation by Lammers, 1996.

December: "Gaigyō" (Field work) in *Kaizō.* "Kaijō nite" (On the high seas) in *Bungei.* "San Hose no seibo" (The Virgin Mary of San Jose) in *Bungaku kaigi.*

1950.

January: "Shussei" (Bound for the front) in *Shinchō.*

January–September: *Musashino fujin* (Lady Musashino) in *Gunzō.*

February: "Angōshu" (Decoder) in *Fūsetsu.*

March: "Hachigatsu tōka" (August 10) in *Bungakkai.* Translation by Lammers, 1996.

May: "Shūgeki" (Attack) in *Shinshōsetsu.* "Konomiya shinjū" (Love suicides at Konomiya) in *Bungakkai.*

June: "Haisō kikō" (Journey of the routed) in *Kaizō bungei.*

August: "Waga fukuin" (My demobilization) in *Shōsetsu kōen.*

September: "Jochū no ko" (Maid's child) in *Bekkan shōsetsu shinchō.* "Atarashiki furyo to furuki furyo" (New prisoners and old) in *Bungei shunjū.* Translation by Lammers, 1996.

October: "Kikan" (Homecoming) in *Kaizō.* Translation (titled "Going Home") by Lammers, 1996. "Tsuma" (My wife) in *Bekkan bungei shunjū.*

November: "Sanchū roei" (Mountain bivouac) in *Bungakkai.* "Hoshō no me ni tsuite" (Concerning a sentry's eyes) in *Bungei.* "Ane" (Big sister) in *Shinchō.* "Watashi no shohōsen: *Musashino fujin* no ito ni tsuite" (Self-prescription: Concerning my intentions in Lady Musashino) in *Gunzō.*

1951.

January: "Furyo engei taikai" (The great POW variety show) in *Ningen* [subsequently renamed "Engei taikai" (Variety show)]. Translation by Lammers (Theatricals), 1996.

January–August: *Nobi* (Fires on the plain) in *Tembō.* Translation by Ivan Morris, 1957.

March: "Ie" (Family) in *Bungakkai.* Translation of Stendhal's *Charterhouse of*

Parma (second part) published by *Shinchō bunko*. "Yukai na renchū" (Pleasant company) in *Shōsetsu shinchō*.

April: "Bungakuteki seishun den" (Life of a literary youth) in *Gunzō*. Ōoka et al., eds., *Nakahara Chūya zenshū* (Complete works of Nakahara Chūya) published by Sōgensha.

June: "Haha" (Mother) in *Chūō kōron bungei tokushū*.

August: "Chichi" (Father) in *Bungei shunjū*.

September: "Kikyō" (Back home) in *Shōsetsu shinchō*.

October: "Shinkeisan" (Mr. Nerves) in *Gunzō*.

November: "Saikai" (Reunion) in *Shinchō*.

1952.

January–May 1953. *Sansō* (Oxygen) serialized in *Bungakkai* [incomplete].

July: *Shi to shōsetsu no aida* (Between verse and fiction) published by Sōgensha.

August: "Kindai Yooroppa bungaku to watashi" (Contemporary European literature and myself) in *Bungei*.

1953.

February: "Furiwakegami" (Parted hair) in *Ooru yomimono*.

February–August: *Keshō* (Makeup) in *Asahi shinbun*.

May: "Yuu aa hebui" (You are heavy) in *Gunzō*.

June: "Wasureenu hitobito" (Those I can't forget) in *Bekkan bungei shunjū*.

August–December: "Waga shi, waga tomo" (My mentor, my friend) [about Kobayashi Hideo] in *Shinchō*.

August: "Yasunari tōge" (Yasunari pass) in *Bungei shunjū*. "Sensō to bungaku" (War and literature), dialogue with Noma Hiroshi, in *Jinmin bungaku*.

September: "Watashi no bungaku techō" (My literary notebook) in *Gunzō* [subsequently renamed "Sokai nikki" (Evacuee's diary)].

October: "Sōsaku no himitsu: *Nobi* no ito" (Creative secrets: My intentions in *Fires on the Plain*) in *Bungakkai*.

1955.

May–October: *Hamuretto nikki* (Hamlet diary) serialized in *Shinchō*.

June: "Nanfutsu kikō" (Travels in the South of France) in *Bungakkai*.

July: "Numazu" (Numazu) in *Bungei shunjū*.

September: "Mahiru no hokōsha" (Pedestrian at high noon) in *Shōsetsu shinchō*.

December: "Girisha gensō" (Greek fantasies) in *Bungakkai*.

1956. January. "Hibara" (Hibara) in *Bungei shunjū*.

February: *Zarutsuburuku no koeda* (Sprays of Salzburg) [travel essays] published by Shinchōsha.

May: "Waga zangei" (My confessional) in *Bungei*.

September: "Hakuchigun" (Idiot's group) in *Bungakkai*.

1957.
January: "Mizu" (Water) in *Gunzō.*
January–March: "Chinkonka" (Requiem) serialized in *Bungei* [incomplete].
January–November: *Mebana* (Female flower) serialized in *Fujin kōron.*

1958.
January–June: "Sakka no nikki" (Writer's diary) in *Shinchō.*
January–December 1959: *Gendai shōsetsu sakuhō* (Writing modern fiction) in *Bungakkai.*
August–August 1959: *Kaei* (In the shadow of cherry blossoms) in *Chūō kōron.* Translation by Dennis Washburn (*The Shade of Blossoms*), 1998.
December: *Asa no uta* (Morning song) [about Nakahara Chūya] published by Kadokawa shoten.

1959.
July: "Boku wa naze bungaku seinen in natta ka" (Why I became a literary youth) in *Gunzō.*

1960.
January: "Sakasasugi" (Inverse cedar) in *Gunzō.*

1961.
January–December: *Jōshikiteki bungaku ron* (A commonsense view of literature) in *Gunzō.*
June–March 1962: *Wakakusa monogatari* (Tale of young grasses) in *Asahi shinbun* [subsequently renamed *Jiken* (The Incident)].
October: "Kurokami" (Black hair) in *Shōsetsu shinchō.*

1962.
July: "Kobayashi Hideo no sedai" (Kobayashi Hideo's generation) in *Shinchō.* *Bundan ronsōjutsu* (The art of literary debate) published by Sekkasha.

1963.
January: "Sensō bungaku wa fukkatsushita" (The revival of war literature) in *Gunzō.*
May: "Soren kikō" (Travels in the Soviet Union) in *Bungei.*
October: "Tenchū" (Heavenly punishment) in Shōsetsu shinchō. "Kyohei" (Call to arms) in *Bungei shunjū.*
November–September 1964: *Tenchūgumi* (Gang of heavenly punishment) serialized in *Sankei shinbun.*
December: "Yoshimura Toratarō" (Yoshimura Toratarō) in *Sekai.*

1964.
May–June: "Bungakuteki Chūgoku kikō" (Literary travels in China) in *Chūō kōron.*

1965.
January: "Anekōji ansatsu" (Assassination of Anekōji) in *Shōsetsu gendai.*

March: "Takasugi Kensaku" (Takasugi Kensaku) in *Bekkan bungei shunjū.*
May: "Waga biteki sennō" (My aesthetic brainwashing) in *Geijutsu shinchō.*
June: "Oba" (Aunt) in *Gunzō.*
August: "Watashi no sengo shi" (My postwar history) in *Bungei.*

1966.
February: "Ryōma koroshi" (Ryōma's murder) in *Shōsetsu gendai.*
March: "Haha rokuya" (Mother: Six nights) in *Gunzō.* Stage adaptation of Stendhal's *The Red and the Black.*
July: "Watanabe Kazan" (Watanabe Kazan) in *Shōsetsu shinchō.*
December: "Waga bungaku ni okeru ishiki to muishiki" (Conscious and subconscious in my literature) in *Warera no bungaku 4,* published by Kōdansha.

1967.
January–July 1969: *Reite senki* (The battle for Leyte Island) serialized in *Chūō kōron.*
April 13–15: "Fuiripin kikō" (Travels in the Philippines) in *Asahi shinbun.* April 27: "Mukashinagara no kusa no oka" (The grass hill unchanged from the past) in *Asahi shinbun.*
June: "Danaoko made" (To Lake Danao) in *Bekkan bungei shunjū.*
"*Nobi* no shima in tazunete" (Visiting the island of *Fires on the Plain*) in *Fujin kōron.*
September: *Arishihi no uta* (Poems of bygone days) [about Nakahara Chūya's poetry] published by Kadokawa shoten.
October: Ōoka et al., eds., *Nakahara Chūya zenshū* (Complete works of Nakahara Chūya) published by Kadokawa shoten.

1968.
September: "Heidomo ga yume no ato" (The remains of soldiers' dreams), dialogue with Agawa Hiroyuki, in *Fūkei.*

1969.
March: "Watashi no bungaku o kataru" (About my literature), interview with Akiyama Shun, in *Mita Bungaku.*
August: *Mindorotō futatabi* (Return to Mindoro Island) in *Umi.*
August 13: "Hachigatsu jūgonichi: ken'i e no fushin ga yomigaeru hi" (August fifteenth: The day my distrust of authority comes back) in *Kyoto shinbun.*
October 18: "*Reite senki* no ito" (My intentions in *The Battle for Leyte Island*), lecture at Yamanashi Eiwa Junior College.

1970.
January: "Chinkonka" (Requiem) in *Bungei* [completed].
May 16: "Senchū kara sengo e" (From war to postwar), lecture at Seijō University.
May 30: "Sensō to bungaku" (War and literature), lecture at Seijō Junior College.

October: "Sensō to bungaku" (War and literature), dialogue with Furuyama Komao, in *Kikan geijutsu.*

December: *Sensō* (War) published by Daikōsha.

1971.

January: "Takibi" (Bonfire) in *Shinchō.* Edits Chūō kōronsha's *Teihon Tominaga Tarō shishū* (Standard collection of Tominaga Tarō's poetry).

February: "Zakkan: Mishima Yukio no shi" (Mixed emotions: Mishima Yukio's death) in *Shinchō.* "Ikinokotta mono e no shōgen" (Testimony to survivors) in *Bungei shunjū.*

July: "Nikutai wa moroi" (Flesh is weak) in *Sankei shinbun.*

August 7–8: "Fuiripin to watashi" (The Philippines and myself) in *Yomiuri shinbun.*

September: "Sensō, bungaku, ningen" (War, literature, people), dialogue with Ōnishi Kyojin in *Gunzō.*

1972.

January: "Shirabe oni" (Research demon) in *Omoshiro hanbun.* "Sensō, bungaku, ningen" (War, literature, people), dialogue with Kaikō Takeshi in *Chūō kōron.*

April: "Heishi to kokka" (Soldier and nation), dialogue with Yūki Shōji in *Chūō kōron.* "Nihonjin no guntai to tennō" (The emperor and the Japanese army), dialogue with Shiba Ryōtarō in *Shiō.*

May 15–19: "Sakura to ichū" (Cherry and ginko) in *Asahi shinbun.*

August: "*Nobi* ni okeru Futsu bungaku no eikyō" (The influence of French literature in *Fires on the Plain*) in *Mita bungaku.*

November: *Sensō to bungaku* (War and literature) [collection of dialogues] published by Chūō kōronsha.

November 3: "Rubangutō no heitaitachi" (The soldiers on Lubang Island) in *Asahi jaanaru.*

1973.

January: "Watashi no naka no Nihonjin: Okada Tasuku" (The Japanese within me: Okada Tasuku) in *Nami.* "Sengo, Bukkyō, ai" (Postwar, Buddhism, love), dialogue with Takeda Taijun in *Bungei.*

January–February: "Natsume Sōseki to kokka ishiki" (Natsume Sōseki and national consciousness) in *Sekai.*

March: "Kokka, Nampō, sensō" (Nation, South Seas, war), dialogue with Oda Minoru in *Gunzō.*

May: *Yōnen* (Childhood) [autobiography] published by Shiō shuppansha.

June: *Moya* (Sprouting fields) [collections of pieces related to travels in America] published by Kōdansha.

July: *Sutandaaru ronshū* (Collected essays on Stendhal) published by Tachikaze shobō.

October–August 1975: *Ōoka Shōhei zenshū* (Complete works of Ōoka Shōhei)[15 vols.] published by Chūō kōronsha.

November: "Jinnikugui ni tsuite" (On cannibalism) in *Shinchō*. "Sensō no naka no ningen" (Man in war), dialogue with Yoshida Mitsuru in *Bungei shunjū: me de miru Taiheiyō Sensō shi*.

1974.

January: *Nakahara Chūya: yurikago* (Nakahara Chūya: Cradle) published by Kadokawa shoten.

May: "Rubangutō no higeki" (The tragedy on Lubang Island) in *Chūō kōron*.

June: "Rekishi shōsetsu no mondai" (The problem with historical fiction) in *Bungakkai*. "Kyokugen no shi to nichijō no shi" (Death in extremity and death in everyday life), dialogue with Ishihara Yoshirō in *Shūmatsu kara*.

July: "Rekishi to rekishi shōsetsu" (History and historical fiction), dialogue with Honda Shūgo in *Gunzō*.

September: "Rubangutō senki" (Battle record of Lubang Island) in *Rekishi to jinbutsu*. *Tominaga Tarō: shokan o tōshite mita shōgai to sakuhin* (Tominaga Tarō: Life and works as seen through his correspondences).

November: "Waga bungaku seikatsu" (My literary life), interview for special edition on modern writers with Akiyama Shun, Nakano Kōji, and Kanno Akimasa in *Umi*.

1975.

June: "Sensō to bungaku" (War and literature), dialogue with Noma Hiroshi in *Daisan bunmei*.

June–July: "Mori Ōgai ni okeru kirimori to netsuzō: *Sakai jiken* o megutte" (Contrivance and fabrication in Mori Ōgai's *Incident at Sakai*) in *Sekai*.

July: "Watashi to sensō" (War and myself) in *Shūkan Yomiuri*.

November: *Seinen: aru jiden no kokoromi* (Youth: An attempt at autobiography) published by *Chikuma shobō*.

1976.

June: *Bungaku ni okeru kyo to jitsu* (Truth and fiction in literature) published by Kōdansha.

November: "*Reite senki, Furyoki, Nobi*" (The Battle for Leyte Island, Records of a POW, Fires on the Plain), interview in *Heiwa kyōiku*.

1977.

March: "Seiji to muku" (Innocence and politics), dialogue with Yoshida Hiroo in *Kokubungaku*.

August: "*Mindorotō futatabi:* sono ato" (After *Return to Mindoro Island*) in *Umi*.

August 13: "Sanjūsannenme no natsu" (The thirty-third summer) in *Yomiuri shinbun*.

September: "Heitaiari no senjō futatabi" (Back to the battlefield of the army ants), dialogue with Furuyama Komao in *Bungei shunjū.*
December: *Aru hojūhei no tatakai* (A certain conscript's war) [collection of short works] published by Tokuma shoten.

1978.
April: *Waga fukuin, waga sengo* (My demobilization, my postwar) published by Tokuma shoten. *Muzai* (Not guilty) [collection of court trial stories] published by Shinchōsha.

1979.
May: "Ippeisotsu no shiten kara" (From the perspective of the common soldier), dialogue with Oda Minoru in *Shisha.*
June: *Saisho no mokugekisha* (The first witness) [collection of detective stories] published by Shūeisha.

1981.
March: *Seijō dayori* (Tidings from Seijō) published by Bungei shunjū.
August 8: "Hachijūichinen: kaku no kiki" (Nuclear crisis, 1981), interview in *Shinano shinbun.*
August 15: "Shishatachi no koe o kike" (Heed the voices of the dead), interview simultaneously in *Tokyo shinbun* and *Nichū shinbun.*
September–December: *Nagai tabi* (The long journey) [about convicted and executed Class B "war criminal" Okada Tasuku] serialized simultaneously in *Tokyo shinbun* and *Nichū shinbun.*

1982.
January: "Aru B kyū senhan" (A Class B war crime) in *Hō to Seisaku.*
May 21: "Kaku sensō no kikensei haramu" (The escalating threat of nuclear war) in *Asahi jaanaru.*
June–March 1984: *Ōoka Shōhei shū* (Collected works of Ōoka Shōhei) [18 vols.] published by Iwanami shoten.
August: "Ippeisotsu toshite: watashi no sensōron" (As a common soldier: My thoughts on war) in *Asahi shinbun.*
September: "Sensō bungaku ni okeru shinjitsu no omomi" (The importance of truth in war literature), dialogue with Iio Kenji in *Seishun to dokusho.*

1983.
January: "*Nagai tabi*: sono ato" (After *The Long Journey*) in *Shinchō.*
April: *Seijō dayori II* (Tidings from Seijō II) published by Bungei shunjū.
September: "*Reite senki* ho'i" (Additions to *The Battle for Leyte Island*) in *Chūō kōron.*

1984.
July: *Ōoka Shōhei, Haniya Yūtaka: Futatsu no dōjidai shi* (Ōoka Shōhei, Haniya

Yūtaka: Two contemporaneous histories), an extensive dialogue published by Iwanami shoten.

September–Winter1988: *Sakaikō jōi shimatsu* (The real facts surrounding the effort to expel barbarians at Sakai Port) in *Chūō kōron bungei tokushū* [incomplete].

1986:

May: *Seijō dayori III* (Tidings from Seijō III) published by Bungei shunjū.

1988.

January: "*Reite senki* ho'i II" (Additions to *The Battle for Leyte Island II*) in *Chūō kōron.*

May: *Shōsetsuka Natsume Sōseki* (The novelist Natsume Sōseki) published by Chikuma shobō.

1989.

January: "Nikyoku tairitsu no jidai o ikitsuzuketa itawashisa" (The grievousness of living through an age of bipolarity) in *Asahi jaanaru.*

October: *Shōwamatsu* (The end of Shōwa) published by Iwanami shoten.

1994–1996.

Ōoka Shōhei zenshū (Complete works of Ōoka Shōhei) [23 vols.] published by Chikuma shobō.

Notes

Introduction

1. The third and fourth sentences of these opening lines intentionally echo Ikeda Jun'ichi's closing remarks in "Ōoka Shōhei to Hitō sensen" (249): "Presently, there are many people who have experienced war. If there are survivors who have forgotten their experience as distant nightmares from another world, there are also those who remain silent because they do not know how to talk about it. Only a small number [of veterans] can actually convey the truth of war. And while many can describe combat, those who can write about the dead are rare indeed. Ōoka will surely continue to write about the miseries of war."

2. Ōe Kenzaburō, "On Modern and Contemporary Japanese Literature," 44–47.

3. Ōoka Shōhei, "Hitomukashi shū," in *Shōwa matsu,* 460.

4. In the brief critical biography that follows, I have drawn heavily on the work of Higuchi Satoru. See his "Hyōden: Ōoka Shōhei," 2–96.

5. Paul Anderer, ed. and trans., *Literature of the Lost Home,* 6.

6. Ōoka Shōhei, *Sensō,* 270.

7. In 1936, Ōoka published two articles on Stendhal in the literary journal *Bungakkai:* "Stendhal" and "*The Red and the Black:* An Essay on Stendhal." Between 1939 and 1944, he translated and published the following works: Stendhal's *Life of Haydn,* Alain's *Stendhal,* Albert Thibaudet's *Stendhal,* and Honoré de Balzac's *Stendhal.*

8. Akiyama Shun, "Hyōdenteki kaisetsu," 417–448.

9. For Tominaga it took the form of lost love, and for Kobayashi and Nakahara, a traumatizing triangle relationship.

10. Akiyama, "Hyōdenteki kaisetsu," 436–437.

11. "Tsukamaru made" was originally published in *Bungakkai* in February 1948 under the

title "Furyoki" (A prisoner of war's account). When it appeared as the opening piece of a collection of prisoner-of-war memoirs in 1952, he renamed it "Tsukamaru made" and titled the collection *Furyoki.* To avoid confusion, I will consistently refer to the work as "Before Capture." "Before Capture" was awarded the Yokomitsu Ri'ichi Prize in January 1949.

12. In 1966, moreover, he adapted Stendhal's *The Red and the Black* for the stage.

13. The findings of two polls conducted by the literary magazine *Gunzō* make this clear. In the first, taken in 1955, readers polled concerning the "best ten postwar masterpieces" chose three of Ōoka's works—"Before Capture," *Lady Musashino,* and *Fires on the Plain.* In the same poll, moreover, Ōoka was voted the "best postwar writer." In the second poll of writers and literary critics conducted in 1960 on the "five best postwar works," *Lady Musashino* and *Fires on the Plain* were selected, the latter topping the list. See Ōoka Makoto et al., eds., *Gunzō Nihon no sakka,* vol. 19: *Ōoka Shōhei,* 326.

14. "Hyōden: Ōoka Shōhei," 48.

15. Two of the most important concerned what Ōoka considered to be unacceptable distortion of the historical record in Inoue Yasushi's *Aoki ōkami* and Mori Ōgai's *Sakai jiken.* Representative articles in this vein are "*Aoki ōkami* wa rekishi shōsetsu ka" and "Mori Ōgai ni okeru kirimori to netsuzō: *Sakai jiken* o megutte."

16. The first of these, "Yasunari Tōge," was published in *Bungei shunjū* in August 1953. It tells the story of Ōtori Keisuke's (1833–1911) unsuccessful effort to stage a coup d'etat. In January 1956, he published "Hibara," a sequel to "Yasunari Tōge." Between October and December 1963, he produced a series of works related to the *Tenchūgumi* (Gang of heavenly punishment): "Tenchū," "Kyohei," and "Yoshimura Toratarō." From November 1963 to September 1964 he serialized *Tenchūgumi* in the *Sankei shinbun.* Finally, between January 1965 and September 1967, he published a series of historical pieces on other prominent Restoration period figures: "Anekōji ansatsu," "Takasugi Kensaku," "Ryōma koroshi," and "Watanabe Kazan."

17. Nakano Kōji, *Ōoka Shōhei ten,* 55.

18. *Jiken* (1978) and the collection of short stories, *Saisho no mokugekisha* (1979), are representative works in this genre.

19. These studies were subsequently collected and published as a single volume, *Shōsetsuka: Natsume Sōseki* (1988).

20. *Sakaikō jōi shimatsu* (1989). In this incident, which occurred in 1868, loyalist samurai (*shishi*) from the Tosa clan killed a French national in the port city of Sakai (near Osaka). In the end, eleven of them were forced to commit seppuku in front of a number of French representatives.

21. Another important war-related work Ōoka wrote toward the end of his career was *The Long Journey* (Nagai tabi, 1981), a detailed study of Lieutenant General Okada Tasuku, the commander who was brought to trial as a Class B war criminal, found guilty, and given the death sentence for his involvement in the execution of thirty-eight American airmen captured after their plane went down during a bombing raid on Nagoya.

22. Ōe, "On Modern and Contemporary Japanese Literature," 45–46.

23. When Ōoka returned to the Philippines in 1967, he acquired a detailed map of Mindoro Island and discovered that the correct name of the town that Nishiya Company occupied was Central, and that San Jose was actually a smaller village closer to the coast.

24. Kali Tal, "Speaking the Language of Pain," 217.

25. In "Speaking the Language of Pain," Tal elaborates on these terms as follows: "National (collective) myth is propagated in such places as textbooks, official histories, popular-culture documents, and public schools. This myth belongs to no one individual, though individuals borrow from it and buy into it in varying degree. . . . Personal myth is the particular set of explanations and expectations generated by an individual to account for his or her circumstances and actions" (224–225).

26. Ibid., 230–231.

27. Ibid., 247.

28. Kali Tal and Philip Gabriel have both used this fresh, illuminating approach to interpreting the literary works of war-traumatized writers. See Tal's study of W. D. Ehrhart's poetry in *Worlds of Hurt,* 77–114; and Gabriel's analysis of Shimao Toshio's writings in *Mad Wives and Island Dreams.*

29. In this study, I draw upon the elements of Lifton's survivor psychology I have found to be most effective in interpreting and appreciating Ōoka's war writings. The application of a general interpretive approach to a particular case is a mutually informative endeavor. In approaching Ōoka's war literature in such terms, I seek not only to apply but also to test the paradigm. In the process, I contribute a detailed case study of a major postwar Japanese survivor-narrator that I hope can be fruitfully compared with other kinds of survival and trauma literature. As Kali Tal observes in "Speaking the Language of Pain," "The [social] structures that generate atrocities in each of these cases [e.g., war, rape, incest] are perceived as interconnected; each can serve as an analogy for the other. This is not because each situation is equivalent but because the result—trauma on a massive scale—is the same" (245).

30. Cathy Caruth, ed., "An Interview with Robert Jay Lifton," 128–129.

31. See Kanno Akimasa, "Kankyō to ko no geki," 71–121; Nakano Kōji, "Shi no riaritei ni oite," 93–180; and Ikeda Jun'ichi, "Sensō taiken o jiku toshite," 77–88, and "Ōoka Shōhei to Hitō sensen," 243–249.

32. Insights from these Japanese scholars will be introduced at appropriate points in the body of this study.

33. Lifton uses this term not just for visual, but for all forms of psychic representation.

34. Lifton, *Broken Connection,* 3.

35. Ibid., 6.

36. In *Broken Connection,* Lifton writes as follows about the three "parameters" of connection-separation, integration-disintegration, and movement-stasis:

> Images of death begin to form at birth and continue to exist throughout the life cycle. Much of that imagery consists of "death equivalents"—image-feelings of separation, disintegration, and stasis. These death equivalents evolve from the first moment of life, and serve as psychic precursors and models for later feelings about actual death. Images of

separation, disintegration, and stasis both anticipate actual death imagery and continue to blend and interact with that imagery after its appearance.

Each of these death equivalents has a counterpart associated with vitality and affirmation: connection is the counterpart of separation, integrity of disintegration, and movement of stasis. The predominance of a vital image (for instance, that of connection) or of a death equivalent (that of separation) is relative, a matter of degree, though there are some situations that dramatically evoke the one or the other. These three parameters relate to specific feelings and multiple observations already made by psychological observers. At the same time they are sufficiently general to apply to the various levels of human experience, from their primarily physiological character at birth to their increasingly elaborate psychic and ethical flowering over the course of life. (53)

37. Ibid., 169.

38. Lifton spoke at length about the significance of bearing witness in a 1990 interview:

> When one witnesses the death of people, that really is the process of becoming a survivor, and the witness is crucial to the entire survivor experience. The witness is crucial to start with because it's at the center of what one very quickly perceives to be one's responsibility as a survivor. And it's involved in the transformation from guilt to responsibility. . . . But carrying through the witness is a way of transmuting pain and guilt into responsibility, and carrying through that responsibility has enormous therapeutic value. It's both profoundly valuable to society and therapeutic for the individual survivor. And it's therapeutic in the sense of expressing the responsibility but also because that responsibility becomes a very central agent for reintegration of the self. One has had this experience, it has been overwhelming, the self has been shattered in some degree; the only way one can feel right or justified in reconstituting oneself and going on living with some vitality is to carry through one's responsibility to the dead. And it's carrying through that responsibility via one's witness, that survivor mission, that enables one to be an integrated human being once more." (Caruth, "Interview," 138)

39. Lifton, *Death in Life,* 480. Idem, *Broken Connection,* 169, 170.

40. Lifton, *Broken Connection,* 175, 170–171.

41. The corresponding Japanese terms used to describe such guilt are "*zaiakukan*" and "*ushirometasa.*" While I am well aware of the differing cultural nuances of "guilt" and "shame," I have decided to approach the matter primarily in terms of death guilt. In doing so, I follow Lifton's lead in *Broken Connection:*

> The image of debt to the dead conveys the idea of something one owes, a duty, and obligation, a matter in which there is some form of accountability. The etymological derivation of the word guilt is apparently uncertain but it is thought to have some relationship to the idea of "debt" and the associated ideas of obligation (from the old English *scyld* and German *schuld* or "should.") There are similar meanings in the different etymological derivations of the word responsibility (from the Latin *respondēre,* to respond), and the ideas of answering to something and accountability loom large in the history of the word's usage (*Oxford English Dictionary*).

> . . .Various cultures have parallel patterns of responsibility in human relations, which are considerably less extreme and of a more everyday variety, though they can include responsibility to the dead. Thus the Japanese speak of *giri,* which means "obligation" or "social obligation," and refers to feelings of accountability toward others in one's human web, especially those in authority such as parents, teacher, or employer. Should one, at least in traditional Japan, fail to live up to *giri,* he was not only severely criticized by others but felt badly [sic] and experienced self-condemnation as well. *The feeling has as much to do with guilt as with shame—the two are really part of the same basic constellation and constantly overlap, especially in extreme duress.* The Japanese evolved an elaborate set of principles around *giri,* but clearly there are related feelings of obligation in Western cultures as well, which are constructed around the anxiety of responsibility, and a ready sense of guilt should such obligations be violated. (144–145; emphasis added)

42. Lifton, *Death in Life,* 489, 56 (emphasis removed), 35, 55.

43. Lifton, *Broken Connection,* 171. Lifton continues as follows: "The image keeps recurring, in dreams and waking life, precisely because it has never been adequately enacted. And there is likely to be, in that repetition, an attempt to replay the situation, to rewrite the scenario retrospectively in a way that permits more acceptable enactment of the image—whether by preventing others from dying, taking bolder action of any kind, experiencing strong compassion and pity, or perhaps suffering or dying in place of the other or others. In that way the hope is to be relieved of the burden of self-blame."

44. Ibid., 139.

45. Lifton comments on this type of guilt in *Broken Connection* as follows: "Yet we can certainly use the term 'paradoxical guilt' for the psychological experience of victimized survivors, especially when the anxiety of responsibility, if not outright self-condemnation, is notably stronger than that of the victimizers" (145).

46. Ibid., 139.

47. Ibid., 170.

48. Ibid., 176–177.

49. Ōoka himself acknowledges this in a piece he published in the *Kyoto Newspaper* on August 13, 1969: "I was haunted by the battlefield experience I had in the Philippines, and it took me twenty-four years to determine its meaning." Quoted in *Bungaku no unmei,* 170.

Chapter 1: Memoirs of a Burdened Survivor

1. The primary source used in this study is *Ōoka Shōhei shū,* 18 vols. (Iwanami shoten, 1982–1984). (The complete works published by Chikuma shobō in 1994–1996, Ōoka *Shōhei zenshū,* 23 vols., was also consulted). Source references will appear in parentheses as follows: (vol. no.: page no.). Unless otherwise indicated, all translations from the Japanese are my own. Translations of "Before Capture," "The Rains of Tacloban" "Brothers-in-arms," "August Tenth," "Homecoming," *Fires on the Plain,* and *In the Shadow of Cherry*

Blossoms were made with the benefit of comparisons with those of Sakuko Matsui, Wayne Lammers, Ivan Morris, and Dennis Washburn, to whom I acknowledge my indebtedness and express my gratitude.

2. "Pleasant Company," in *Waga fukuin waga sengo,* 112.

3. Ibid., 118.

4. In "Ōoka Shōhei to Hitō sensen" (247), Ikeda Jun'ichi stresses the important point that Ōoka had two kinds of war experience in the Philippines: battlefield and prisoner-of-war. He goes on to observe that because of its intimate linkage with the war dead, his frontline experience was most relevant to war-related works such as *Lady Musashino, Fires on the Plain, The Battle for Leyte Island, Return to Mindoro Island,* etc. While I do from time to time refer to selected prisoner-of-war memoirs, the primary focus of this chapter is Ōoka's autobiographical writings on his precapture war experience.

5. Ōoka quit his job at the Imperial Oxygen Company and took a position at the Kobe Shipyard partly because the latter provided dependent allowances for conscripted employees.

6. Lifton, *Broken Connection,* 53.

7. "Thousand-stitch belts" were protective talismans given to soldiers by their mothers or wives at the time they set off for the front. In principle, a thousand women would each add one stitch to the belt using red thread.

8. Toward the beginning of *Broken Connection,* Lifton notes that there is a "compelling and universal inner quest for continuous symbolic relationship to what has gone before and what will continue after our finite individual selves" (17). When I write of symbolic immortality, I have this in mind. Lifton describes five basic "modes" of symbolic immortality: biological, theological, creative, natural, and experiential transcendence. For a detailed discussion of these modes, see pages 18–35 of his study.

9. Ōoka explains that he was exempt from these activities because his primary duty was to take care of the code books. He was responsible for keeping them safe at all times and was expected to destroy them before they fell into enemy hands. *Sensō,* 104.

10. Kamei Hideo, "Ōoka Shōhei no me," 153.

11. Ōoka, *Sensō,* 195–196.

12. Ōoka explains that after they joined forces with the Tanaka Platoon, which had its own communications man and wireless radio, he became a regular foot soldier. *Sensō,* 132.

13. While doing research for *The Battle of Leyte Island,* he learned from reading official American battle records that the invasion armada was larger than they had thought. In actuality, there were some 120 ships with twelve thousand troops on board (10:191, 201–202).

14. Ōoka details his experience from just before the second American attack until capture in "Before Capture."

15. Robert Lifton elaborates on this in *Death in Life:* "This sense of having virtually entered the realm of death . . . and yet returned from it, gives the memory its lasting power. The

indelible image of the 'death spell,' then, is the survivor's reminder that he has 'touched death.' It is therefore a reminder of survival itself. Such memories become repeat re-enactments of that survival" (483).

16. Kanno Akimasa argues that "Before Capture" and other war memoirs reveal the need Ōoka felt as a battlefield survivor to "cut off sympathy and empathy" for his fallen comrades in order to "force them into the land of the dead." He goes on to observe that Ōoka withdrew into a defensive "fortress" of callousness (*hijō*) both to sustain postwar psychological stability and as a means of directly confronting the brutal realities of war. "Kankyō to ko no geki," 72–77.

17. In "Memorandum Sent to an Old Friend" (Aru kyūyū e okuru shuki, 1927), Akutagawa Ryūnosuke writes as follows about the psychological effects of his decision to commit suicide: "In my present state, nature looks more beautiful than ever. You will doubtless laugh at the contradiction of loving nature and planning at the same time to kill myself. But the beauty of nature is apparent to me only because it is reflected in my eyes during my last hours" (translation by Donald Keene). The Nobel Prize laureate Kawabata Yasunari also wrote a famous essay, "Eyes of the Dying" (Matsugo no me, 1933), that Ōoka would surely have been aware of. Donald Keene, *Dawn to the West,* 587, 808ff.

18. Keiko McDonald, "Ōoka's Examination of the Self," 28.

19. Sigmund Freud, Ernest Becker, Terrence Des Pres, and others have all in their own ways stressed the fact that the self, or "ego" is necessarily composed of both symbolic ("spirit") and physical ("body") elements. Harold Bloom notes that to Freud, the "Ego was first and foremost a bodily Ego." Becker and Des Pres emphasize that there are two interrelated modes of being—symbolic and material. Trauma not only severely undermines the normally predominant symbolic mode of existence, but also brings into stark relief the fundamental significance of the physical mode. In extremity, both modes coexist and intermingle in substantial ways on the material plane of being. See Bloom, "Freud," 116; Becker, *Denial of Death,* 218; Des Pres, *The Survivor,* 65, 69, 174.

20. Kamei Hideo, *Koga no shūgōsei,* 131–132. Ikeda Jun'ichi, "Ōoka Shōhei no sekai," 212.

21. *Death in Life,* 489; *Broken Connection,* 170, 139.

22. In *Death in Life,* Robert Lifton writes as follows about survivors' conflicted emotions: "In a disaster . . . the extreme conditions drastically limit the possibilities of cooperation and mutual aid, and thereby greatly accentuate the awareness of ordinary urges toward self-preservation. The idea that an individual's first and strongest impulse is directed toward his own survival becomes vividly displayed and, in this death-saturated context, totally unacceptable. Even more unacceptable is the inner joy at having survived, whatever the fate of one's fellows" (47).

23. In "My Confessional"(Waga zangei, 1956), Ōoka commented on his autobiographical writings on the war as follows: "I have come to feel that since the memoirs I wrote on my war experience were accepted as fiction (*shōsetsu*), [writing about] my life itself has become my destiny. Consequently, I wrote a series of confessions (*kokuhaku*). Now that I have finished confessing, however, I am at a loss as to what I should write next." *Bungaku no unmei,* 293.

24. Quoted in Tal, *Worlds of Hurt,* 133.

25. Kawashima Itaru draws attention to the fact that Ōoka wrote very little about fear in "Before Capture." He takes this to be one of the important aspects of his traumatic encounter with the American soldier that Ōoka excluded from his memoir. Kawashima highlights Ōoka's inconsistency with regard to his treatment of his own frontline conduct by observing that in *The Battle for Leyte Island,* Ōoka interpreted the combat behavior of a variety of soldiers specifically in terms of fear (e.g., Vice Admiral Kurita) or the overcoming of fear (kamikaze pilots). "Hyūmanizumu to kyōda," 154–155.

26. Kawashima Itaru reaches a similar conclusion. In support, he draws attention to the fact that Ōoka repeatedly changed the distance initially separating himself from the American soldier before settling on the one that gave the greatest sense of danger. After detailing how Ōoka consistently acted in the interest of self-preservation during the encounter, he writes: "All the issues I have raised up to this point can be summed up as follows: Ōoka's conduct during this engagement is more accurately interpreted in terms of egoism (*egoizumu*) than in terms of humanism (*hyūmanizumu*)." Ibid., 143–144, 159.

27. Lifton, *Broken Connection,* 177 (emphasis added).

28. In *Death in Life,* Robert Lifton writes about scapegoating in the following terms: "The survivor's conflicts can readily lead him to a scapegoating formulation. By focussing blame upon a particular person, symbol or group of people, he seeks to relieve his own death guilt" (529). Lifton goes on to observe, however, that "a process at least bordering on scapegoating seems necessary to the formulation of any death immersion. It enters into the survivor's theory of causation, and his need to pass judgement on people and forces outside of himself to avoid drowning in his own death guilt and symbolic disorder. . . . What the survivor seeks from his scapegoating formulation is the reassuring unconscious message that 'You, and not I, are responsible for the others' deaths and my suffering, so that I have a right to be alive after all.' It is a message that he can neither fully believe nor entirely cease to assert" (531).

29. In "The Rains of Tacloban," Ōoka develops this point into a general theory on Japanese politics and the adverse effects it has on interpersonal relationships: "It goes without saying that the self-styled Japanese 'staff' [in the POW camp], as with those who distributed meals, inherited all the vices of the army—callousness, abusiveness, misappropriation, and so on. . . . Perhaps these vices are just the all-too-common manifestations of the weakness to privilege of a people accustomed to absolutism (those who have privilege can't help but abuse it fully, and those who don't can't help but curry favor with those who do)" (1:87–88).

30. Lifton, *Broken Connection,* 176–177.

31. Ōoka traces this chain of chance incidents back to his impulsive act of discarding his mess tin of water when the first shells began to explode around them:

> We stood up. Every face was expressionless. I said, "Looks like they're here. Why not try for the top?" Grunting in agreement, the others began to make their preparations.
>
> Once again, I tried to transfer the water from my mess tin to my canteen, but my hands were shaking so much that it spilled to one side. Muttering "Who needs water to die?" I flung the mess tin into the bushes.

> My friends often criticized me for giving up on things too readily. My being back home writing this account today, however, hinges on that single [impulsive] act of throwing the mess tin away at that time. (1:15–16)

Other crucial links include leaving the valley the Americans subsequently advanced through to search for water, having a dud grenade, and being discovered by the enemy while unconscious.

32. Ernest Becker comments on this important matter as follows: "accidents, as we know, are the things that make life most precarious and meaningless. Our knees grow weak when we think of a young girl of awesome beauty who gets crushed to death simply because her foot slips on a mountain path; if life can be so subject to chance, it mustn't have too much meaning." *Escape from Evil,* 7–8.

33. Ōoka himself eventually came to acknowledge that his early battlefield memoirs reflected his "twisted psychology" at the time:

> Kanno [Akimasa] kindly brought to my attention the fact that the keynote in *Records of a POW* was to sever all sympathy for the dead, and that, in reaction, or rather by a process of reversal, I came to feel like communing with them. It certainly is true that my insistence on "having no sympathy for those who died from the same cause that nearly ended my own life" reflected a kind of twisted psychology. Even though I actually did feel that way in the Philippines, I think I continued to insist on it afterward to compensate for the guilt I felt over survival. (*Waga bungaku seikatsu,* 193)

34. Lifton, *Broken Connection,* 178.

35. Robert Lifton writes about this survivor tendency in *Death in Life:*

> We have seen that the dropping of the atomic bomb in Hiroshima annihilated a general sense of life's coherence as much as it did human bodies. We have also seen that mastery of the experience depended upon re-establishing form within which not only the death immersion but the survivor's altered identity could be grasped and rendered significant. This quest for formulation turns both *hibakusha* and concentration camp survivors into what has been called "collectors of justice." Beyond medical and economic benefits as such, they seek a sense of world-order in which their suffering has been recognized, in which reparative actions by those responsible for it can be identified. (525)

36. Okehazama was the site of the famous civil war battle that occurred in 1560. In it, Nobunaga miraculously managed to rout a vastly superior army by means of an all-out surprise attack.

Chapter 2: *Fires on the Plain*

1. The first half of *Nobi* was serialized in *Buntai* between December 1948 and July 1949. Publication was suspended when the journal folded. A complete version of the novel subsequently appeared in *Tembō* between January and August 1951. The definitive book version was published in February of the following year. *Fires on the Plain* was awarded the Yomiuri Prize for Literature in May 1952. The renowned literary critic Etō Jun has written that *Fires on the Plain* is "perhaps the greatest postwar novel." Quoted in Akiyama Shun, *Sakka ron,* 38.

2. In this introductory paragraph, I echo and redirect the opening remarks Dennis Washburn makes in "Toward a View from Nowhere," 105.

3. The image of Private Tamura as a moving victim of war was taken up by Ichikawa Kon in his 1959 film version of *Fires on the Plain.* Ichikawa and screenplay writer Wada Natto not only ignored the second and third parts of the memoir (see pages 98–99 of this study for a description of the basic structure of Tamura's memoir), but also rewrote the story so that Tamura abstains from cannibalism and sacrifices himself on the battlefield.

4. Ikeda Jun'ichi has clearly established the intimate connection between *Fires on the Plain* and Ōoka's battlefield memoirs. His exhaustive work in this area can be found in "Ōoka Shōhei no kenkyū," 130–143, and "Ōoka Shōhei *Nobi* no kenkyū," 63–78. As will be shown in chapter 4 of this study, a good part of the story was also drawn from the testimony of Private Itō Waichi, a low-ranking medic in the Sixteenth Division. The novel, moreover, incorporates a good number of accounts Ōoka heard from other survivors in the prisoner-of-war camp. Here are three important examples: (1) Tamura's experience of falling ill and being rejected by both his company and the field hospital and being told to kill himself with a grenade closely follows the experience of a communications man Ōoka trained with. In real life, however, the man actually did use his grenade to commit suicide (*Sensō,* 100; 1:395); (2) The scene of Tamura and the insane officer was based on a story Ōoka heard of a man who actually offered himself to a starving comrade just before dying (15:426); and (3) Tamura's postcapture habit of bowing to his food tray before eating was based on Ōoka's own experience of seeing a psychically destabilized comrade act similarly in the POW hospital (1:145–146).

5. "Diary of a Madman" was the working title of the piece that eventually grew into *Fires on the Plain.* When the first half of the novel was serialized in *Buntai,* "Diary of a Madman" opened the work. When a full version of the novel was serialized in *Tembō,* however, Ōoka removed "Diary of a Madman" completely. In the definitive book version, Ōoka restored a rewritten and expanded "Diary of a Madman" and placed it toward the end of the novel.

6. See note 4 above.

7. Ikeda Jun'ichi is of the same opinion. In his view, *Fires on the Plain* is a work in which Ōoka "created a second self." "Ōoka Shōkei no kenkyū," 143.

8. In *Death in Life,* Robert Lifton comments on this psychological dynamic in the following terms:

> Survivors are also subject to acute episodes of *symbolic reactivation* of their entire constellation of death anxiety and loss. In Hiroshima we saw this reactivation produced by such classic stimuli as mass-media reports of people dying from A-bomb disease, and reports of nuclear weapons testing; as well as by the annual August 6th ceremony, the sight of the A-Bomb Dome, war or warlike behavior anywhere in the world, the onset of hot weather, or simply the sight of another's child when one's own has been killed by the bomb. (485)

9. Aharon Appelfeld, a Holocaust survivor and writer, makes a significant point in this regard: "While the survivor recounts and reveals, at the very same time he also conceals." Quoted in Tal, *Worlds of Hurt,* 133.

10. While Ivan Morris clearly had great respect for Ōoka's work and thought it to be one of the best novels to emerge from the Second World War, he apparently felt it to be a "flawed" masterpiece. He took particular issue with the last two sections of the memoir, feeling that the novel should have ended at the front. Consequently, it seems, he could not resist the temptation to "fix" it by excising sentences and passages he personally found to be undesirable or extraneous. See his comments in "*Nobi* ni tsuite," 105–117.

Morris' translation of the section in question reads as follows. Note the use of ellipses: "'It's very well written. It reads just like a novel, you know. . . . It's a shame that shock of yours blocked out the last part of your memories,' he adds after a while. 'We've got a good idea that this is just where we'd find the clue to your illness. . . .'" (236). The ellipsis following "illness" marks the deletion of another important exchange: "'I'm probably not even [mentally] ill.' 'Ha, ha. That's what all patients say. It is also common to harbor ill-will toward their doctors. How about you?' '. . .' 'Well, I'm sorry to have to say this, but you probably are ill. Your condition is called alienation. One of the secondary characteristics is distrust of others. In short, you distrust others because you can't trust yourself'" (3:405).

11. Emphasis added. Ōoka, too, "came up with" with this strategy as he was reworking and revising *Fires on the Plain.* As he notes in "My Intentions in *Fires on the Plain,* "There was no [mention of] 'God' in the 1946 draft of 'Diary of a Madman.' I came up with the notion of God as a being who could free one of guilt feelings (*zaiakukan kara no kaihōsha*) in 1948" (15:416).

12. "If there is a means of converting the chance that now dominates my life back into necessity, it will be by connecting my present existence with the life of chance forced on me by the military authorities. It is to this end that I am writing this memoir" (3:402).

13. Ōoka engages in a similar, if shorter, analysis of a fellow prisoner of war's story of capture in "Brothers-in-arms." The incident concerns Corporal Masuda, a seasoned veteran of the war in China. After the American attack on their highland encampment, Masuda and a group of others manage to slip through American lines and flee deeper into the mountains. After weeks of suffering, the men are detected and attacked as they rest by a remote river. While most flee upstream, and some escape across the river, Masuda heads downstream. Ōoka finds his elaborate account of how he was captured hard to believe: "I wonder whether the 'downstream' Corporal Masuda mentioned wasn't, like the 'highway' of the Leyte POW's account, the incriminating element of truth mixed in with his lies. As a seasoned military man, he surely knew that going downstream meant moving toward Americans and Filipinos. Soldiers with far less experience chose to go upstream" (1: 216). After concluding that Corporal Masuda was dissembling in an effort to avoid admitting surrender, Ōoka writes: "To the extent it has to do with human beings, the battlefield is a place only of action and reality. Everything else is strategy or fiction (*monogatari*). To the extent it had to do with the realities of the battlefield, Corporal Masuda was a complete liar" (2:217).

14. After this incident, Tamura repeatedly has the feeling of being watched, the clear sign of a deeply troubled conscience. Significantly, moreover, he has this sensation or recalls the woman when acting to save himself—while attempting to break through the American-held Ormoc Highway with his comrades, while preparing to surrender after the attempt fails, and when seriously considering cannibalism.

15. This incident, too, was based on a survivor story Ōoka heard in the prisoner-of-war camp. See "My Intentions in *Fires on the Plain*" (15:426).

16. The first memory loss Tamura mentions occurs when he initially considered cannibalism after failing to cross the Ormoc Highway. The second takes place after he returns to find the officer's spoiled corpse. He suffers the third just before shooting Nagamatsu. The fourth, and most protracted, begins after he wipes raindrops from his rifle at the end of the first part of his memoir. While Tamura's doctors speculate that his last and most extended period of memory loss is the product of concussion-induced retrograde amnesia, the first three are not explainable in such terms. Tamura's fourth memory loss, too, can be profitably viewed as the result of radical repression of unbearable experience.

17. This same dynamic was at work during Ōoka's traumatic encounter with the American soldier. Ōoka, too, blanked out as the enemy pressed in on him, and didn't recover consciousness until the danger momentarily abated as the American paused to listen to the distant gunfire. In "Jochū no ko," moreover, Ōoka describes how he completely repressed memory of the argument he had with Yasuda—and that Yasuda violently stabbed him in the side with a pencil—the day before the Americans attacked their mountain position. It wasn't until after he was captured and his wound began to fester that he was finally able to recover memories of this traumatic experience. See 2:260–279.

18. These ellipses appear in the original Japanese.

19. These ellipses, too, appear in the original Japanese.

20. Ōoka went through a similar process of inference to gain access to his repressed memories of being stabbed by Yasuda with a pencil after a heated exchange the day before the attack that killed most of his remaining comrades from Nishiya Company. See "Jochū no ko" (2:260–264).

21. Just before Sergeant Kurokawa and his companions were captured, they, too, heard warning drums being pounded (1:220).

22. As he struggles to regain control, the tense shifts back and forth between present and past in consecutive sentences.

23. The following series of ellipses appear in the original Japanese.

24. Lifton, *Broken Connection,* 177; emphasis added.

25. Ikeda, "Ōoka Shōhei *Nobi* no kenkyū," 69.

26. See note 4 above.

27. For the "foundation" experience, see 2:43–44.

28. Ikeda, "Ōoka Shōhei no kenkyū," 141.

29. Additional support for this can be found in *Lady Musashino,* a novel he wrote concurrently with *Fires on the Plain.* The protagonist of the novel, a young man recently repatriated from Burma, describes having a similar experience as he walks alone through a forest in the Musashino Plain. That Ōoka would include variations of this experience in two of his early works of fiction strongly suggests that it had special meaning to him.

30. Tamura subsequently writes, "I probably felt that it was strange that I would never pass along that forest path a second time because I had had a premonition of death at that moment" (3:239–240).

31. The observations Robert Lifton makes in this regard in *Death in Life* warrant repetition: "This sense of having virtually entered the realm of death . . . and yet returned from it, gives the memory its lasting power. The indelible image of the 'death spell,' then, is the survivor's reminder that he has 'touched death.' It is therefore a reminder of survival itself. Such memories become repeat re-enactments of that survival" (483).

32. This is particularly apparent in the descriptions of the extended animistic vision Tamura has after walking away from the officer's corpse, and in "Writings of the Dead," the last chapter of the work.

33. In his depiction of the land of the dead, Tamura describes a "black sun" shining like "obsidian" (3:411). Ikeda Jun'ichi notes that Carl Jung has written that imagery related to the "black sun" can be interpreted in both positive and negative ways, as a symbol of either death or rebirth. "Ōoka Shōhei no kenkyū," 142. The latter possibility points to the potential for Tamura/Ōoka to recover from death-immersion experiences.

34. The outline of the story is also closely based on Private Itō Waichi's testimony on his frontline experience. For details see page 259 of this study.

35. "*Nobi* ni tsuite," 106.

36. Lifton, *Death in Life,* 492.

37. Lifton, *Broken Connection,* 96.

38. Lifton, *Death in Life,* 493, emphasis removed.

39. Robert Lifton writes about this issue in *Broken Connection:* "The great problem for survivors in all cultures is to convert 'homeless souls,' particularly those of the recent dead, into comfortably enshrined or immortalizing souls. Funeral ceremonies are rites of passage precisely for this purpose. *What is involved is the symbolic transformation of a threatening, inert image (of the corpse) into a vital image of eternal continuity (the soul)—or of death as absolute severance to death as an aspect of continuous life*" (95; emphasis in original).

40. Tamura's anthropomorphism is given highest expression in the elaborate animistic vision he has after walking away from the officer's corpse.

41. Lifton, *Broken Connection,* 94.

42. Ibid., 93–94.

Chapter 3: *Lady Mushashino* and *In the Shadow of Cherry Blossoms*

1. *Lady Musashino* instantly became a runaway best-seller that was subsequently made into a popular film. *In the Shadow of Cherry Blossoms* earned Ōoka the Mainichi Publisher's Culture Prize and the Shinchōsha Prize for Literature.

2. During the course of the novel, Tomiko engages in extramarital sexual relations with several secret lovers, including Akiyama and Tsutomu; her husband does the same with other women. In the end, Michiko is the only important character who never commits adultery.

3. Alexander and Margarete Mitscherlich, *The Inability to Mourn,* 27. With the exception of Michiko, and to a lesser extent Tsutomu, all of the main characters in *Lady Musashino* are portrayed as calculating egoists incapable of sympathy or empathy.

4. Tsutomu was abandoned by his mother when he was a child, and his stepmother treated him coldly.

5. Michiko's explanation is effective because by this time Akiyama has already decided to have an affair with Tomiko himself.

6. Ōoka subsequently makes this clear in *Return to Mindoro Island* when he writes about his 1967 visit to Limon Pass, one of the most important battlegrounds of the Battle for Leyte Island:

> Some fought believing that by dying defending these small ridges they could save their homeland and families. They fought on literally intending to become guardian spirits of the nation, and they were progressively slaughtered by America's superior weaponry.
>
> . . . Some, however, truly believed they were dying for the emperor. There were also those who hated the Americans for interfering with the resolution of the Japan-China war and wanted to kill the enemy to the last man and eat his flesh. They felt that their deaths could prevent their wives from being raped and their children from being bludgeoned to death. . . . In this way, they sought to give meaning to their deaths. (2:452–453)

7. Ronald Spector writes about the fight for Iwo Jima as follows:

> By the time fighting finally ceased at the end of March, the marines had lost 6,821 men killed and close to 20,000 wounded. Nineteen of the twenty-four original battalion commanders who had landed with their men were killed or wounded. In one battalion of the 25th Marines, fewer than 150 of 900 men survived unhurt. The 21,000 Japanese defenders died almost to a man. Only a few hundred, mostly wounded, survived to become prisoners. They had conducted the stoutest defense of the Pacific War; for the first time in the island campaign, the Japanese had inflicted greater casualties on the invaders than they had suffered themselves.
>
> (*Eagle against the Sun,* 502)

8. Since the Japanese term "*ie*" is used to refer both to one's house and one's family, the destruction of the physical structure of the building simultaneously connotes destruction to the family unit itself.

9. Ōoka was clearly ambivalent about Michiko and Tsutomu's vow. After describing them make these vows, he has the narrator make the following comment: "To what was their vow directed? Michiko was wrong; vows should be made only before God" (3:156).

10. Buber, Martin. Quoted in Lifton, *Broken Connection,* 137–138.

11. In *Death in Life,* Robert Jay Lifton connects such wishes to "contagion anxiety": "For just as the individual survivor can become prone to retaliatory wishes that everyone else experience what he did, and the whole world be destroyed, so are others prone to see him as a 'world-destroyer,' as one capable of 'infecting the whole world'" (517).

12. It is clear, moreover, that news of Michiko's death will ruin Tsutomu's prospects for recovery and renewal. At the end of *Lady Musashino,* Ono goes to Tsutomu's apartment to reclaim his wife. Tomiko showed up at Tsutomu's door after getting drunk and having a fight with Akiyama, and the two ended up sleeping together. In the lines that bring the novel to an end, the narrator provides access to Ono's thoughts on the devastating effect the news of Michiko's death will have on Tsutomu: "Ono only knew that his informing

Tsutomu of Michiko's death would make him into a kind of monster (*kaibutsu*). He was filled with dread" (3:228).

13. Kobayashi Hideo writes that "the human spirit cannot believe in accidents (*jiko*)." He goes on to point out that those who are moved by tragedy don't affirm the external forces that bring it about, but always empathize with those whose lives are destroyed as a result. While people can use reason to understand the external circumstances that give rise to such tragedy, they cannot sympathize with them in their hearts. With these insightful comments, Kobayashi effectively highlights Ōoka's condition of what might be called impaired empathy. "*Musashino fujin,*" 94–95.

It is not my intention in writing about *Lady Musashino* to argue that Ōoka felt no sympathy or empathy for Michiko, but that open expression of such feelings for her was forestalled by defensive rationalizations concerning the impersonal dynamics of fate. Hiraoka Tokuyoshi suggests that even as Ōoka was concealing the pathos he actually felt for Michiko behind metaphysical meditations, he hoped that sensitive readers would be able to imagine how he really felt. "Chinkonka toshite no ninshiki: Ōoka Shōhei," 17. Akiyama Shun, too, notes that Ōoka treated Michiko coldly toward the end of the novel, but suggests that this was a function of Ōoka's own sense of existential isolation. *Sakka ron,* 36.

14. Mishima Yukio was one of the first to recognize the importance of this requiem: "I felt a chill go down my spine: this was language written by soldiers in the trenches at the moment of their deaths. But it is impossible to write a novel with this language. At the moment this poemlike thing welled up inside him, he probably didn't know exactly who or what he was. It is extremely rare for a literary man's diary to be so unadulterated (*muku*)." "Sakka no nikki: shohyō," 49. Hanazaki Ikuyo, too, has highlighted the importance of entries in "Writer's Diary" to full appreciation of *In the Shadow of Cherry Blossoms.* She argues, as I do, that this novella is intimately related to Ōoka's emotional turning-point experience concerning his fallen comrades and the effect of the news of Sakamoto Mutsuko's suicide. She points out, moreover, that Yōko's story is best viewed as a prose requiem written with the aim of putting the troubled spirits of the dead to rest. "Ōoka Shōhei *Kaei* 2."

15. In the following passage, Nakamura Shin'ichirō draws attention to this important aspect of the work, and Ōoka's additional intention of opposing social evil: "In all probability, the author felt that by vividly depicting how this pitiful woman was killed by her environment, he could console her dead spirit. It could also be viewed as his effort to call upon the power of lyricism to counter injustice. By beautifying her death, he sought to oppose the unfairness of her having been made into a pawn of fate. This being the case, the novel is both requiem and elegy." "*Kaei* no ichi," 180.

16. While there is no blood relationship between Tetsu's mother and Yōko, I will refer to her throughout as her grandmother both to avoid using awkward terms such as "step-grandmother" or "adoptive grandmother" and to convey the extent to which Yōko actually came to feel that she *was* her real grandmother.

17. Robert Lifton writes about this matter as follows in *Death in Life:* "As in the case of the Hiroshima survivor's identity of the dead, the life of suicide is a form of psychic numbing

in which the thought makes the act unnecessary. Hence the apparent infrequency, or at least lack of unusual frequency, of suicidal attempts among Hiroshima and concentration camp survivors. The suicidal attempt can, in fact, represent a desperate effort to emerge from psychic numbing, to overcome inactivation by the act of killing oneself" (507).

18. "*Kaei* oboegaki," 75.

19. For more detailed information on the epigraph, see "*Kaei* genteiban atogaki" (5:161–166).

20. "Chinkonka toshite no ninshiki," 14.

21. *War Without Mercy,* 212.

22. Ibid., 232.

23. Maurice Pinguet, *Voluntary Death in Japan,* 232.

Chapter 4: *The Battle for Leyte Island*

1. Quoted in Ikeda Jun'ichi, ed., *Gendai sakka nyūmon sōsho: Ōoka Shōhei,* 174.

2. Official American histories of the land, air, and sea battles fought in the Philippines began to appear in 1954. By 1959, they were more or less complete. Although the official Japanese history of the battle wasn't released until 1970, Ōoka felt that he could gather enough information to write his account by reading through American records and the memoirs of high-ranking Japanese commanders and strategists and by interviewing veterans.

3. *Sensō,* 212.

4. Commanding officers were required to keep field journals, and most battle accounts drew heavily on them.

5. In *Sensō* (215–216), Ōoka describes how men of the Leyte Brotherhood came into possession of these American records. After the Korean War, Colonel William J. Verbeck, commander of the Twenty-first Regiment, Twenty-fourth Division, visited Tokyo and arranged a meeting with Lieutenant General Kataoka Tadasu of the First Division. Verbeck's men had fought against Kataoka's at Limon Pass (Breakneck Ridge), site of some of the fiercest and costliest engagements in the Battle for Leyte Island. When the two men met, Verbeck praised Kataoka's men for their resolute fighting. He also gave him the battle account he wrote. *A Regiment in Action,* and Jan Valtin's book of reportage, *Children of Yesterday.* Since few could read English, these records were not fully incorporated into the First Division's battle account. They gathered dust until they were given to Ōoka, whose advanced knowledge of English enabled him to make full use of them.

6. Most bereaved families were sent a brief, five-line death notice, and they naturally hungered for more detailed information concerning the circumstances of their loved ones' deaths. One of the editors of *The Battle for Leyte Island,* Mamiya Haruo, wrote that his mother, who had bad eyesight, repeatedly asked him to read sections of *Fires on the Plains* so she could get a better idea of the circumstances under which her son had died.

7. In "The Conscious and Unconscious in My Literature" (Waga bungaku ni okeru ishiki to muishiki) Ōoka writes that while researching the Battle for Leyte Island, he realized how

he had misrepresented what had actually happened on Leyte Island in *Fires on the Plain.* He goes on to write that to "make up for [his] sin" of asserting his fiction at the expense of those who sacrificed their lives fighting bravely on Leyte Island, he would correct the record by writing *The Battle for Leyte Island* (16:27).

8. *Waga bungaku seikatsu,* 158.

9. "Survivor illumination" derives from Buber's idea that "man is . . . capable of becoming guilty and . . . of illuminating his guilt." Quoted in Lifton, *Broken Connection,* 139.

10. *Waga bungaku seikatsu,* 193.

11. Lifton, *Broken Connection,* 144–145.

12. Lifton, *Death in Life,* 369.

13. Ibid., 525.

14. *The Battle for Leyte Island* was first published serially in *Chūō kōron* between January 1967 and July 1969. In 1972, it was awarded the Mainichi Prize for Art. Although the primary focus of the work is the land battles, Ōoka also treats the Battle of Leyte Gulf and related air engagements because their outcomes had a profound effect on the experience of the men burdened with fighting American soldiers on the ground (9:160).

15. Ōoka continued to revise and expand the work as new records and studies became available. He finished his first version of *The Battle for Leyte Island* before the official Japanese battle history of the campaign had been released. It finally appeared toward the end of 1970. Ōoka incorporated information gleaned from this official, though distorted, record and from new scholarship related to the Battle for Leyte Island over the next fourteen years. The definitive edition, which takes up two of the eighteen volumes of his *Collected Works,* appeared in 1983.

16. The bibliography for *The Battle for Leyte Island* contains more than 350 entries.

17. Masuda Kazutoshi, "Ōoka Shōhei ron," 128–129.

18. As Ōoka continued his research into the *Battle for Leyte Island,* he increasingly realized the extent to which he owed his life to his comrades who fought so resolutely on Leyte Island. In *Return to Mindoro Island,* he writes that because of their fierce resistance, General MacArthur had to postpone the invasion of Mindoro Island from December 5 to December 15. Ōoka was convinced that this delay enabled him to survive: "Viewed in this way, I owe my life to my compatriots who fought so well on Leyte Island. While my survival and ability to write this kind of memoir twenty-five years after the war was the end result of innumerable chance occurrences, I was moved to learn that I was connected by an invisible thread to the men who died on Leyte Island" (2:437).

19. Ōoka not only draws upon English-language sources to reproduce the American soldiers' battle experience, but also praises the way they fought in several places. He was particularly impressed by the accomplishments of two mobile attack units (Twenty-fourth Division, Nineteenth Regiment) that succeeded in outflanking the Japanese forces defending Limon Pass and cutting off their supply line from Ormoc. As is made clear in the following passage, however, thoughts of his fallen comrades placed certain constraints on him in this regard: "Were I an American, I could write an epic battle account about the actions

of these two mobile units. I cannot, however, out of consideration for my compatriots who had to die so miserably as a result" (9:408). See also 9:532 and 9:537.

20. While the Americans lost about thirty-five hundred men during the Battle for Leyte Island, the Japanese lost close to ninety thousand (10:500, 504).

21. Lifton, *Death in Life,* 493 (both quotations).

22. Wilfred Owen, *Wilfred Owen: The Complete Poems and Fragments,* 1:99.

23. At the beginning of chapter 7, "The Thirty-fifth Army," Ōoka describes how shocked and exasperated soldiers from the Sixteenth Division were to see that virtually no attacks were made on the many ships continually unloading troops and supplies in Leyte Bay. After recounting the experience of several men who thought that the single Japanese fighter plane they finally saw was "fleeing" from the five Grummans chasing it, he comments as follows about how the overall performance of Japanese soldiers came to be so grossly misrepresented: "This account is based on the stories survivors told after the war. These testimonies were made after Japan had already been defeated and the hundred million people of the nation had surrendered, after it was commonly thought that the Japanese army fought poorly throughout the Pacific. Behind these stories was the desire to justify the fact that they had been taken prisoner without having been able to display their competence as soldiers" (9:85). In addition, he has the following to say about Major General Tomochika Yoshiharu's memoir:

> Major General Tomochika was so out of touch with the actual situation [on Leyte] that he only crossed over from Cebu to Leyte to direct the Carigara plains battle just two days before the First Division was landed at Ormoc. Even though it would have been reasonable to have imagined that the situation had deteriorated upon learning that several units [of the Sixteenth Division] were unaccounted for, he was so taken up with his dream of triumphantly retaking Tacloban that he refused to consider anything that didn't accord with it. He directed the bitterness he felt over losing his dream at the troops [fighting near Limon Pass]. It is true that only the Forty-first Regiment was composed of active-duty soldiers, and the rest of the reinforcements, lacking as they were in training and equipment, were not fit to stand up against the attacking American forces. As has been shown, however, this was not due, as Major Tomochika would have it, to sloppy, ignoble fighting. (9:329)

For comments on the role played by correspondents who reached Leyte toward the final stage of the campaign, see 10:225–226.

24. Ōoka writes in *Return to Mindoro Island* (1969) that when he visited Limon Pass in March 1967, he felt the spirits of the dead rise and begin to approach him: "Most of the men who died in battle are buried in this area near the highway. It is believed, however, that where the mountains are high and deep to the southeast, the bones of the dead still lie exposed to the elements. . . . This battlefield was wholly different from those on Mindoro Island. I felt a clutch at the heart. As we read sutras and wept, I had the illusion that the dead were rising up here and there from the grass-covered slopes" (2:452–453).

25. Kamei Hideo, *Koga no shūgōsei,* 13, 15.

26. Ibid., 29–31.

27. Shokatsu Ryō (Zhuge Liang) was a renowned Chinese general of the San-Kuo (Three Kingdoms) period (toward the end of the Han dynasty). Sanada Yukimura was a famous general (1567–1615) of the Muromachi period.

28. Ōoka writes about this in greater detail in "Brothers-in-arms" when he observes that "the battlefield is a place only of action and reality. Everything else is strategy or fiction" (2:217).

29. Ōoka details their surprise attack on the airfields, how many Americans they killed and the number of planes destroyed in the second volume of *The Battle for Leyte Island.* See 10:98–102.

30. Both the navy and army organized and employed Special Attack Forces in the Philippines. The kamikaze was, perhaps, the best known example. Ōoka argues convincingly that despite the claims of surviving staff officers that commanders in the field came up with this inhumane tactic, existing evidence clearly indicates that it was actually dreamed up, researched, and implemented by Imperial Headquarters (10:519–520).

31. Ōoka traces the origin of the concept of using fighter planes to make body blows (*taiatari*) to the tactics used by American pilots during the Battle of Midway. During the heat of battle, American airmen who had used all their torpedoes came up with the idea of skipping bombs off the water into the sides of Japanese warships. This required a high level of skill; pilots had to fly in fast and low, come in extremely close before releasing the bombs, and then pull up sharply to avoid hitting the ships with their planes. Inevitably, some were unable to pull out in time, and inadvertently crashed into the ships. Japanese strategists subsequently modified this American tactic, and ordered their pilots to intentionally steer their planes into enemy warships. The development of the Zero fighter facilitated the emergence of Special Attack Forces in the Philippines. The Zero, which was designed for long-range attack, was equipped with spare fuel tanks that could be jettisoned when emptied. The planes were converted for use in suicide attacks by removing these tanks and replacing them with 250-kilogram bombs.

32. *Sensō,* 225.

33. In "My Intentions in *The Battle for Leyte Island,*" Ōoka describes the experience of a young pilot who longed so intensely for his wife and children that he flew back to his home in Japan rather than toward his assigned target. Knowing that he would be court-martialed and executed if he returned to the airfield, he simply circled his house until just before his fuel ran out and then killed himself by crashing his wing into the high-voltage electrical lines nearby (15:499–500).

34. Ōoka identifies most closely with the Special Attack Forces pilots in *Return to Mindoro Island.* As he approaches Leyte Island in a commercial jet, he imagines what it must have been like for his comrades as they flew toward certain death and engages in one of three distinct dialogues with the spirits of the dead (the full significance of these dialogues will be turned to in the conclusion of this study):

> The young men who flew Special Attack Forces planes moved through this landscape as I do. They, however, had no time to look at islands or beaches. The work that lay ahead of them required their undivided attention. They had to locate the warships hidden like so many black specks amidst the sparkling waves. They constantly had to be on guard for

enemy planes, which could dive down at them at any moment from any direction in the blue sky above them.

By the time you were aware of the dark spots approaching from the direction of the sun, it was too late. The American pilots were more cunning and skilled than you were, and they maneuvered unpredictably before your eyes. They approached with incredible speed and riddled your planes and bodies with bullets.

They dropped down like bolts of lightning from the invisible heights above you to interrupt your course. They fired round after round and then slipped away through the airspace below. Or before you realized it, your body was pierced with bullets, and you sank into the darkness of death without ever knowing whether it was your plane or consciousness that was slipping away.

If fortune smiled on you, and you were able to proceed unimpeded by any harrying, encumbering enemy, you made for your target, barely visible in the distance amidst the shimmering waves, and began to dive sharply. When long-range antiaircraft fire began to explode around you, you had to grasp the joystick firmly to stabilize your wildly pitching aircraft and stay your course.

In order to crash your planes into the enemy ships, you had to hold on even when your wings sheared off and you were hit by bullets. These things occurred in a world known to you, and to you alone. (2:444)

35. In chapter 9, "Battle at Sea," Ōoka writes as follows after describing how fear and other factors kept Admiral Kurita's fleet from entering Leyte Bay: "We are the survivors or descendants of these soldiers who lost their fighting spirit. We can probably be proud, however, that the *tokkō,* a particularly Japanese mutation, emerged from amidst this spiritual decay. While extremely small in number, the extraordinary example of courage and self-sacrifice they set is worthy of inclusion in the modern mythology of our people" (9:247).

36. In *Return to Mindoro Island,* Ōoka elaborates on what his comrades were thinking at this time:

Although the soldiers came to Leyte with faith in certain victory drummed into them, they simultaneously harbored the rational fear that they might be the next to die. Once they received their orders and were sent to the front, however, they had to overcome this fear. Some fought believing that by dying defending these small ridges they could save their homeland and families. They fought on literally intending to become guardian spirits of the nation, and they were progressively slaughtered by America's superior weaponry.

. . . Some, however, truly believed they were dying for the emperor. There were also those who hated the Americans for interfering with the resolution of the China Incident and wanted to kill the enemy to the man and eat his flesh. They felt that their deaths could prevent their wives from being raped and their children from being bludgeoned to death. . . . In this way, they sought to give meaning to their deaths.

At the instant of death, they could have been thinking of nothing but slaughtering the American devils. They died consumed with animus, and their bones are now exposed to the elements on a foreign land thousands of miles from home. (2:452–453)

37. *Koga no shūgōsei,* 27. Kamei actually writes about "hell scrolls." I have taken the liberty to translate this as "hell screens" since it sounds more natural in English.

38. In chapter 25, "The Sixty-eighth Brigade," Ōoka praises the tenacious fighting and endurance of the First Division soldiers who fought in and around Limon Pass as follows:

> I have already described (in chapter 18) how the First Division had reached the "point of collapse" at Limon Pass by December 5, how Intelligence Staff Office Doi proceeded to army headquarters, and how the Imabori Detachment was put at this disposal. Because of the American counterlanding at Ormoc, however, the division never did receive these reinforcements. Nevertheless, the men held on for eighteen days on the brink of collapse. They were partially able to do this because the American army had limited fighting strength at the time and because the Thirty-second Division and First Cavalry Division in the area didn't go on the offensive until resupplied by units that landed at Ormoc. In light of the subsequent course of battle, however, it was phenomenal that the men managed to hold on to the heights above the main highway south of Limon Pass amid such overwhelming adversity. Resolved to die to the man, they held their position until the withdrawal order was issued on December 20. (10: 234)

39. Verbeck, *A Regiment in Action,* 32, 34.

40. Ōoka, of course, incorporates the testimony of scores of individual survivors in *The Battle for Leyte Island.* I chose to focus on Private Itō not only because he served as model for Private Tamura, but also because there can be little doubt that Ōoka treats him in such detail and at such length because he felt that Itō's experience was somehow representative of the experience of defeat.

41. *Koga no shūgōsei,* 31.

42. Since Ōoka wrote this, there have been direct confessions of cannibalism in the Philippines and elsewhere. See, for instance, Hara Kazuo's 1987 documentary film *The Emperor's Naked Army Marches On.*

43. Ōoka notes that the local inhabitants called both the southern ridge of this mountain and the village beneath it Bukabuka. The Japanese, however, preferred to use Canguipot, the name for the main peak, since it transliterated as Kankipō, or Jubilation Peak.

44. Ōoka points out that Kankipō, the Japanese name for the peak, had also been applied to a mountain in New Guinea. The name was clearly ironic; it was used to designate the site of a last stand (10:357).

45. *Embracing Defeat,* 486.

46. In his discussion of Ibuse Masuji's *Black Rain* in the appendix of *Death in Life,* Robert Lifton writes about the challenges the main protagonist-survivor Shigematsu Shizuma faces in terms of the "formulation of responsibility":

> Shigematsu's immediate "burden" (or pressing responsibility) is arranging a marriage for his niece [Yasuko], but it is part of the larger—indeed limitless—burden imposed upon both by the atomic bomb. This "limitless burden" is elaborated through an interweaving of present-day occurrences in a village far from Hiroshima with survivors' diaries describing the time of the bomb—mostly Shigematsu's, but also those of Yasuko, of Shigematsu's wife, Shigeko, and of a doctor who had miraculously recovered from early bomb effects. As a family head and a *hibakusha,* Shigematsu is faced with several levels of responsibility: to Yasuko; to himself and his community; to the dead and their other survivors; and

> to history. These layers of formulative struggle . . . comprise what can be viewed as the novel's central psychological theme. (543–544)

In this study, I apply the basic concept of survivors' formulation of responsibility to the matter of defeat in war. Rephrasing Lifton, I note that Ōoka, too, was faced with several levels of responsibility; in his case they involved his responsibility to his dead comrades on Mindoro in particular and on Leyte Island in general, to fellow survivors from the Philippines, to bereaved family members, and to posterity.

47. *Sensō,* 222.

48. In *The Battle for Leyte Island,* Ōoka argues that Imperial Headquarters decided to go forward with this extremely risky plan partially because of the confidence they placed in the "secret weapon"—the Special Attack Forces—they had developed. Even after overwhelming defeat in the Philippines, their irrational reliance on these suicide attack forces led them to go forward with the Decisive Battle for the Homeland (10:519–520).

49. Because the Japanese pilots who took part in the aerial attacks were undertrained and inexperienced, they were unable to make accurate damage reports. They mistook the planes exploding all around American ships and the downed aircraft burning on the surface of the ocean near them as damage they had brought about to the ships themselves. On October 15, Imperial Headquarters announced to the emperor and the nation that eleven enemy aircraft carriers, four battleships, and three cruisers had been sunk; eight carriers, two battleships, and four cruisers heavily damaged; and 112 planes destroyed.

50. The Battle of Tennōzan, or "Emperor Mountain," which took place in 1582, is said to have been decisive in Tokugawa Ieyasu's rise to the pinnacle of power in Japan. By calling Leyte Tennōzan, Prime Minister Koiso was saying that victory at Leyte would mean victory in the Greater East Asia War. After the Battle for Leyte Island failed, Okinawa and then the homeland became the next Tennōzans.

51. Maruyama's thesis can be found in English translation in *Thought and Behavior in Modern Japanese Politics.* See "Thought and Behavior Patterns of Wartime Leaders," 84–134. Ian Buruma summarizes Maruyama's argument as follows:

> The political theorist Maruyama Masao called the prewar Japanese government a "system of irresponsibilities." He identified three types of political personalities: the portable Shrine, the Official, and the Outlaw. The Shrine ranks highest. It is the supreme symbol of authority, shouldered (like a shrine on festival days) by the Officials. The Shrine is the icon, but those who carry it, the Officials, are the ones with actual power. But the Officials—bureaucrats, politicians, admirals, and generals—are often manipulated by the lowest-ranking Outlaws, the military mavericks, the hotheaded officers in the field, the mad nationalists, and other agents of violence. One result of this system of irresponsibilities is that political cause and effect disappear from view. History will seem like an endless string of faits accomplis, periods of oppressive stillness interrupted by violent storms whose source is always mysterious: foreign demons, nature, or, in the words of Hayashi Fusao, the father of Japanese revisionism, "the coldheartedness of history." (*Wages of Guilt,* 170)

52. Underestimation of the enemy also had serious consequences to the south of Limon

Pass when the Americans, guided by local guerrillas, succeeded in crossing from east to west coast over the Abuyog-Baybay road. The Sixteenth Division had judged the road to be impassible. As Ōoka observes, however, the Imperial Army should have known better what the Americans were capable of:

> With the help of guerrillas, however, the American army was able to repair the road within a week. On November 2, a vanguard company of the Seventh Division advanced to Baybay. This development, one wholly unanticipated by the Thirty-fifth Army, provided more grounds for criticizing the Sixteenth Division. Ever since Guadalcanal, however, the army had had ample proof of the Americans' superior engineering ability. It would probably be more correct to say that the problem arose because of the deficient imaginative powers of army staff officers who failed to consider the possibility that the Americans might immediately be able to make the road passable. (9:493)

53. Technically, the Wa Operation referred only to the ground-based portion of the overall attack plan.

54. *Embracing Defeat,* 22.

55. Since the Combined Fleet had lost many of its carriers and much of its air power, the Shō Operation was designed to draw upon the navy's remaining strength—the power of its massive battleships. Air support would be provided by the army. The naval part of the Shō Operation called for the division of the Combined Fleet into three task forces: Vice Admiral Ozawa Jizaburō's group of aircraft carriers and destroyers; Vice Admiral Nishimura Shōji's smaller attack force of battleships; and Vice Admiral Kurita Takeo's main attack force. While Ozawa used his force as a decoy to lure Halsey's Third Fleet to the north away from Leyte, Nishimura and Kurita would lead their attack forces through the Surigao and San Bernardino Straits respectively, join forces off the east coast of Leyte Island, force their way into Leyte Gulf, and destroy the American transports and beachhead.

As it turned out, Ozawa succeeded beautifully in drawing Halsey's fleet off to the north. And, while Nishimura's task force was virtually destroyed before it could exit the Surigao Strait, Kurita's main attack force managed to punch through the San Bernardino Strait according to plan with much of his fleet intact. Because of miscommunication between Admiral Halsey and other tasks forces guarding Leyte, there was no substantial American force waiting for Kurita when he emerged through the strait. Instead of heading directly for Leyte Gulf according to plan, however, Kurita chased a convoy of insignificant escort carriers and destroyers he mistook for the main American mobile force. After giving chase and wasting precious time, he turned back toward Leyte. Instead of entering the gulf, however, he shaped a course back to the San Bernardino Strait thereby effectively sabotaging the entire Shō Operation.

56. The pivotal naval battle fought during the Russo-Japanese War of 1904–1905.

57. Ōoka subsequently describes how the navy's focus on building big battleships resulted in a debilitating lack of transports: "As is commonly observed, the Imperial Navy was so inordinately concerned with building battleships and training crew that they weren't attentive to the transport and escort ships need for carrying out modern war. This was one of

the primary reasons they were unable to [successfully] wage war throughout the vast area of the southwestern Pacific" (9:480).

58. Ōoka notes that even this new defense-in-depth tactic had its limitations. As he explains in the following passage, it seemed to be effective only on smaller islands:

> The month before the Battle for Leyte Island began, Colonel Nakagawa Kunio and the men of the Fourteenth Division's Second Regiment defending Peleliu resisted the Americans for two months using the same tactic. These islands, however, were not comparable in size to Leyte. Because Leyte was the largest island in the Pacific on which battles were fought, both the Japanese and Americans made numerous mistakes. None, however, invited pointless casualties and miserable annihilation like the tactic of using a part of the defensive force to put up resistance at the shoreline. (9:98)

59. *Chi* was the code name of the operation to evacuate the remnants of the First Division to Cebu after Reite kessen had been formally abandoned.

60. Throughout *The Battle for Leyte Island,* Ōoka subtly argues that this kind of egoism was at work at each important level of the military: Imperial Headquarters, Southern Army, Fourteenth Area Army, and Thirty-fifth Army. In his battlefield memoirs and *Fires on the Plain,* moreover, he clearly demonstrated how survival egoism was frequently manifest at the platoon, squad, and individual level as well.

61. Ienaga Saburō, *The Pacific War, 1931–1945,* 255, 252.

62. It is surely no coincidence that Ibuse Masuji's *Black Rain,* Ienaga Saburō's *Pacific War, 1931–1945,* and Ōoka Shōhei's *Battle for Leyte Island* all appeared in the mid to late 1960s.

63. Indeed, Komori Yōichi observes that to fully understand the Pacific War, critical works like *The Battle for Leyte Island* will have to be written about every battle. "Shisha to seisha no aida de," 260.

64. Ienaga, *Pacific War,* 245.

65. It is important to note here that Ōoka is primarily concerned with identifying *what* his government and countrymen needed to do in this regard. He leaves the matter of *how* to present to future generations.

66. *Sensō,* 230.

67. Ienaga, *Pacific War,* 137–138.

68. Ibid., 151.

69. Ibid., 137.

70. *Sensō,* 260.

71. Ienaga, *Pacific War,* 53.

72. *Embracing Defeat,* 504.

73. Ibid., 553.

74. Ibid., 552–553.

75. Ibid., 23.

Conclusion: Lingering Obligations

1. Lifton, *Death in Life*, 495–496; Des Pres, *The Survivor*, 47.

2. *Sensō*, 270.

3. I intentionally echo and modify Michael Molasky here. The original passage reads as follows: "How does Japan's response to the American occupation relate to the structures of domination within Japanese society itself? To what extent are these structures inherited from prewar days? Finally, whose responsibility is it to rectify those injustices that remain? In a nation that has often viewed its militarist past as an aberration, these questions retain their urgency today and demand that the reader consider the present through the past—and seek the occupier within." *The American Occupation of Japan and Okinawa*, 177.

4. Mitscherlich, *The Inability to Mourn*, 50, 24.

5. Ibid., 16–17.

6. *Bungaku no unmei*, 177. Leading up to this statement, Ōoka describes how President Nixon was forced out of office by the pressures brought to bear on him by the American media, people, and judiciary.

Selected Bibliography

Japanese sources were published in Tokyo unless noted otherwise.

Akiyama Shun. "Hyōdenteki kaisetsu." In *Gendai nihon no bungaku vol. 36: Ōoka Shōhei shū,* 417–448. Gakushū kenkyūsha, 1970.

———. *Sakka ron.* Daisan bunmeisha, 1973.

Anderer, Paul, ed. and trans. *Literature of the Lost Home: Kobayashi Hideo—Literary Criticism, 1924–1939.* Stanford, Calif.: Stanford University Press, 1995.

Becker, Ernest. *Denial of Death.* New York: Free Press, 1973.

———. *Escape from Evil.* New York: Free Press, 1975.

Bloom, Harold. "Freud: Frontier Concepts, Jewishness, and Interpretation." In *Trauma: Explorations in Memory,* ed. Cathy Caruth, 113–127. Baltimore: Johns Hopkins University Press, 1995.

Buruma, Ian. *The Wages of Guilt.* New York: Farrar, Straus, and Giroux, 1994.

Caruth Cathy, ed. "An Interview with Robert Jay Lifton." In *Trauma: Explorations in Memory,* 128–147. Baltimore: Johns Hopkins University Press, 1995.

Craven, Wesley Frank, and James Lea Cate. *The Army Air Forces in World War II.* Vol. 5: *The Pacific: Matterhorn to Nagasaki, June 1944 to August 1945.* Washington: Office of Air Force History, 1983.

Des Pres, Terrence. *The Survivor: An Anatomy of Life in the Death Camps.* New York: Oxford University Press, 1976.

Dower, John W. *Embracing Defeat: Japan in the Wake of World War II.* New York: The New Press, 1999.

———. *War Without Mercy: Race and Power in the Pacific War.* New York: Pantheon, 1986.

Duus, Peter, ed. *The Cambridge History of Japan.* Vol. 6: *The Twentieth Century.* Cambridge: Cambridge University Press, 1988.

Field, James A., Jr. *The Japanese at Leyte Gulf: The Shō Operation.* Princeton, N.J.: Princeton University Press, 1947.

Gabriel, Philip. *Mad Wives and Island Dreams: Shimao Toshio and the Margins of Japanese Literature.* Hawai'i: University of Hawai'i Press, 1999.

Hamlin, Cannon. *United States Army in World War II.* Vol. 2, pt. 5: *Leyte: The Return to the Philippines.* Washington: Office of Chief of Military History, Department of the Army, 1954.

Hanazaki Ikuyo. "Ōoka Shōhei *Kaei* 2: mitsu no 'genzai no' 'shi'—'Sakka nikki' yori." *Kokubun mejiro* 28 (1988): 189–196.

Higuchi Satoru. "Hyōden: Ōoka Shōhei." In *Shinchō Nihon bungaku arubamu: Ōoka Shōhei,* ed. Higuchi Satoru, 2–96. Shinchōsha, 1995.

Hiraoka Tokuyoshi. "Chinkonka toshite no ninshiki: Ōoka Shōhei." In *Gunzō Nihon no sakka.* Vol. 19: *Ōoka Shōhei,* ed. Ōoka Makoto, 13–21. Shōgakukan, 1992.

Ienaga, Saburō. *The Pacific War, 1931–1945.* Translated by Frank Baldwin. New York: Random House, 1978.

Iguchi Tokio. *Akubun no shoshi.* Kōdansha, 1993.

Ikeda Jun'ichi, ed. *Gendai sakka nyūmon sōsho: Ōoka Shōhei.* Tōjusha, 1979.

———. "Ōoka Shōhei no kenkyū: *Nobi* to shoki sakuhin." In *Nihon bungaku kenkyū shiryō sōsho: Ōoka Shōhei/Fukunaga Takehiko,* ed. Nihon bungaku kenkyū shiryō kankōkai, 130–143. Yūseidō, 1978.

———. "Ōoka Shōhei no sekai: 'Furyoki' no hōhō to shudai." In *Nihon gendai shōsetsu no sekai,* ed. Sanekata Kiyoshi, 192–243. Kōmyōsha, 1969.

———. "Ōoka Shōhei *Nobi* no kenkyū: kaikō o chūshin toshite." In *Gendai sakka nyūmon sōsho: Ōoka Shōhei,* ed. Ikeda Jun'ichi, 63–78. Tōjusha, 1979.

———. "Ōoka Shōhei to Hitō sensen." In *Gunzō Nihon no sakka.* Vol. 19: *Ōoka Shōhei,* ed. Ōoka Makoto, 243–249. Shōgakukan, 1992.

———. "Sensō taiken o jiku toshite." In *Kokubungaku kaishaku to kanshō,* 77–88. Tokushū, 1979.

Isoda Kō'ichi. "Ōoka Shōhei ron: tōshi no bigaku." In *Nihon bungaku kenkyū shiryō sōsho: Ōoka Shōhei/Fukunaga Takehiko,* ed. Nihon bungaku kenkyū shiryō kankōkai, 76–80. Yūseidō, 1978.

Kamei Hideo. *Koga no shūgōsei: Ōoka Shōhei ron.* Kōdansha, 1977.

———. "Ōoka Shōhei no me: Ryunkoisu no fukō." In *Nihon bungaku kenkyū shiryō sōsho: Ōoka Shōhei/Fukunaga Takehiko,* ed. Nihon bungaku kenkyū shiryō kankōkai, 144–159. Yūseidō, 1978.

Kanno Akimasa. "Kankyō to ko no geki: Ōoka Shōhei *Reite Senki.*" In *Shōsetsu no genzai,* 71–121. Chūō kōronsha, 1974.

Kawashima Itaru. "Hyumanizumu to kyōda: Ōoka Shōhei 'Furyoki.'" In *Bungaku no kyojitsu: jijutsu wa fukushū suru,* 122–162. Ronsōsha, 1987.

Keene, Donald. *Dawn to the West: Japanese Literature of the Modern Era.* Vol. 1. New York: Holt, Rinehart and Winston, 1984.

Kobayashi Hideo. "*Musashino fujiin.*" In *Gunzō Nihon no sakka.* Vol. 19: *Ōoka Shōhei,* ed. Ōoka Makoto, 92–96. Shōgakukan, 1992.

Komori Yōichi. "Shisha to seisha no aida de: Ōoka Shōhei no sengo." In *"Yuragi" no Nihon bungaku,* 254–281. Nihon hōsō shuppan kyōkai, 1998.

Lifton, Robert Jay. *The Broken Connection: On Death and the Continuity of Life.* Washington, D.C.: American Psychiatric Press, 1979.

———. *Death in Life: Survivors of Hiroshima.* Chapel Hill: University of North Carolina Press, 1968.

Maruyama, Masao. *Thought and Behavior in Modern Japanese Politics.* Edited by Ivan Morris. New York: Oxford University Press, 1963.

Masuda Kazutoshi. "Ōoka Shōhei ron: sensō no 'onnen' to 'hōhō.'" In *Nihon bungaku kenkyū shiryō sōsho: Ōoka Shōhei/Fukunaga Takehiko,* ed. Nihon bungaku kenkyū shiryō kankōkai, 118–129. Yūseidō, 1978.

McDonald, Keiko. "Ōoka's Examination of the Self in *A POW's Memoirs.*" *Journal of the Association of Teachers of Japanese* 21 (1987): 15–36.

Mishima Yukio. "Sakka no nikki: shohyō." In *Nihon bungaku kenkyū shiryō sōsho: Ōoka Shōhei/Fukunaga Takehiko,* ed. Nihon bungaku kenkyū shiryō kankōkai, 48–49. Yūseidō, 1978.

Mitscherlich, Alexander and Margarete. *The Inability to Mourn.* New York: Grove Press, 1975.

Molasky, Michael S. *The American Occupation of Japan and Okinawa: Literature and Memory.* New York: Routledge, 1999.

Morison, Samuel Eliot. *History of United States Naval Operations in World War II.* Vol. 12: *Leyte, June 1944–January 1945.* Boston: Little, Brown, 1958.

———. *History of United States Naval Operations in World War II.* Vol. 13: *The Liberation of the Philippines: Luzon, Mindanao, the Visayas, 1944–5.* Boston: Little, Brown, 1959.

Morris, Ivan. "*Nobi* ni tsuite." In *Nihon bungaku kenkyū shiryō sōsho: Ōoka Shōhei/Fukunaga Takehiko,* ed. Nihon bungaku kenkyū shiryō kankōkai, 105–117. Yūseidō, 1978.

Nakamura Shinichirō. "*Kaei* no ichi." In *Gunzō Nihon no sakka.* Vol. 19: *Ōoka Shōhei,* ed. Ōoka Makoto, 180–188. Shōgakukan, 1992.

Nakano Kōji et al. *Ōoka Shōhei ten,* ed. Kanagawa bungaku shinkōkai. Kanagawa kindai bungakukan, 1996.

———. "Shi no riaritei ni oite." In *Zettai reido no bungaku: Ōoka Shōhei ron,* 98–180. Shūeisha, 1976.

Nihon bungaku kenkyū shiryō kankōkai, ed. *Nihon bungaku kenkyū shiryō sōsho: Ōoka Shōhei/Fukunaga Takehiko.* Yūseidō, 1978.

Ōe, Kenzaburō. "On Modern and Contemporary Japanese Literature." In *Japan, the Ambiguous, and Myself: The Nobel Prize Speech and Other Lectures,* 39–55. Kōdansha International, 1995.

Ōoka Makoto et al., eds. *Gunzō Nihon no sakka.* Vol. 19: *Ōoka Shōhei.* Shōgakukan, 1992.

Ōoka Shōhei. *Bungaku no unmei.* Kōdansha bungei bunko, 1990.

———. *Fires on the Plain.* Translated by Ivan Morris. New York: Alfred A. Knopf, 1957.

———. *Ōoka Shōhei shū.* 18 vols. Iwanami shoten, 1982–1984.

———. "Prisoner of War: The Prelude to Capture." Translated by Sakuko Matsui. *Solidarity* 7 (1967): 54–84.

———. *Seijō dayori.* 3 vols. Bungei shunjū, 1981–1986.

———. *Sensō.* Daikōsha, 1970.

———. *The Shade of Blossoms.* Translated by Dennis Washburn. Ann Arbor: University of Michigan Press, 1998.

———. *Shōwa matsu.* Iwanami shoten, 1989.

———. *Taken Captive: A Japanese POW's Story.* Translated by Wayne P. Lammers. New York: John Wiley & Sons, 1996.

———. *Waga bungaku seikatsu.* Chūō kōronsha, 1975.

———. *Waga fukuin waga sengo.* Tokuma shoten, 1978.

Owen, Wilfred. *The Complete Poems and Fragments.* Edited by Jon Stallworthy. New York: W. W. Norton, 1983.

Pinguet, Maurice. *Voluntary Death in Japan.* Translated by Rosemary Morris. Cambridge: Polity Press, 1993.

Scarry, Elaine. *The Body in Pain: The Making and Unmaking of the World.* New York: Oxford University Press, 1985.

Shay, Jonathan. *Achilles in Vietnam: Combat Trauma and the Undoing of Character.* New York: Simon & Schuster, 1995.

Shinchōsha Nihon bungaku arubamu: Ōoka Shōhei. Shinchōsha, 1995.

Spector, Ronald H. *Eagle Against the Sun: The American War with Japan.* New York: Virstage Books, 1985.

Tal, Kali. "Speaking the Language of Pain: Vietnam War Literature in the Context of a Literature of Trauma." In *Fourteen Landing Zones: Approaches to Vietnam War Literature,* ed. Philip Jason, 217–248. Iowa City: University of Iowa Press, 1991.

———. *Worlds of Hurt: Reading the Literatures of Trauma.* New York: Cambridge University Press, 1996.

Tachihara Masa'aki. "Kaei oboegaki." In *Nihon bungaku kenkyū shiryō sōsho: Ōoka Shōhei/ Fukunaga Takehiko,* ed. Nihon bungaku kenkyū shiryō kankōkai, 68–75. Yūseidō, 1978.

Verbeck, Col. William. *A Regiment in Action.* N.p.: N.p., 1946 (self-published?).

Washburn, Dennis. "Toward a View from Nowhere: Perspective and Ethical Judgment in *Fires on the Plain.*" *Journal of Japanese Studies* 23 (1997): 105–131.

Yoshida Hiroo et al., eds. *Kanshō Nihon gendai bungaku.* Vol. 26: *Ōoka Shōhei/Takeda Taijun.* Kadokawa shoten, 1990.

Index

The subentry "brothers-in-arms" refers to Japanese soldiers who fought on Mindoro Island; the subentry "comrades" denotes those who fought on or around Leyte Island and elsewhere.